SUCH IS LIFE

True Tales,
Ruminations
and Poems

Virginia Rea

isbn 978-17310127-9-1

Photos of Croatia by Virginia Rea.

For my mother and her sisters,

who taught me how to laugh,

and for my beloved children,

who lived through it all

and still laugh with me.

CONTENTS

True Stories
&
Ruminations

Motherhood

MOTHERHOOD IS A great equalizer. No matter how clever a market analyst you may have been in your previous life B.C. (Before Children), it will not adequately prepare you for the sight of a 2-year old playing happily with the dozen eggs he has just scrambled in the middle of the kitchen floor, or a one-year old spreading poop over the freshly painted living room walls. Those who have dressed for success will find it a slightly more complicated proposition when faced with an infant's proclivity for spitting up on you five minutes before you were due to walk out the door. You may have been, in your previous life, an attorney with the argumentative skills of F. Lee Bailey; try talking a 4 year-old out of wearing her favorite dirty, tattered cartoon character dress to her auntie's wedding.

Child-rearing theory is a wonderful invention until you are faced with the reality of a freshly changed, bathed, fed, and completely hysterical, red-faced three - month old at 2 a.m. No amount of psychological training can prepare a mother for hundreds of days of mindless repetition of the same instructions: put the cat down, leave your brother alone, eat your dinner, lunch, breakfast, because I said so, go back to bed, don't climb on the furniture, how many times have I told you not to... Sometimes I think I could easily be replaced by a tape. Every time I hear a non-parent with a fond, faraway look in his or her eye speak longingly of children, I want to slap them and shout, "Get a grip!" I have no doubt their idealized version of parenthood - children squeaky clean, relaxing in front of a cozy fire reading stories together before they toddle off obediently to bed - bears absolutely no relation to the reality of screaming, hair-pulling, frenzied escapes and endless excuses before the children are tackled and tossed, protesting, somewhere in the vicinity of the bed. I have no interest in any advice about parenting I may be offered by anyone unless they have spent most of every day with at least one child from birth to age three.

Some days I can't remember my own name, but I can clearly recall every single line of every Disney movie ever made, along with every thing I swore I would never do or say to my child, all of which I have at some time done or said. I remember, before I had children, looking at the toys scattered around my best friend's house, thinking with a mental sniff that I would certainly never spoil my child with so many things. It didn't take long after my first child was born to realize that toys are not a matter of indulgence, they are a matter of pure survival. I learned early on to haunt garage sales in search of the ultimate toy - one that was cheap, inedible, and good for hours of enter-tainment.

Children are God's way of humbling the proudest spirit. I now view a mother of six with the awe and respect I used to accord the ruler of a nation; anyone, after all, can make decisions affecting the lives of millions of people, but how many can simultaneously carry on a conversation with a whining 6-year-old, calm a bouncing 3-year-old who has a firm grip on a howling dog's tail in one hand and a dripping ice cream cone in the other, argue on the phone with a credit card company computer over late charges, and direct the gas man to the meter he needs to read while chopping vegetables for the evening meal?

Do we have a crisis in the Middle East? Forget career diplomats - send a mother of three or more children under the age of 6 - you will never find a more skilled architect of lasting peace. There is not a mess in the world an experienced mother cannot clean up. She is afraid of nothing: lurking strang-ers, frogs in pockets, twenty 5-year-olds at a birthday party clamoring for more ice cream when you've just run out.

Mothers form a sisterhood as powerful as the mafia, as generous and be-nevolent as Mother Theresa's Little Sisters, with as many shared bizarre expe-riences as a reunion of Woodstock attendees twenty years on.

A mother is generally an excellent interior designer, a talented packer and organizer, a passable repairman and untangler of knots, an expert furniture cleaner, chewing gum remover, barber, pharmacist, mid-wife, and nurse practitioner. She can entertain any number of children in a broken-down bus in the middle of nowhere for hours with endless repetitions and various renditions of "99 Bottles of Beer on the Wall" "The Twelve Days of Christmas", "The Eensy Beensy Spider", and any other mind-numbing children's song known to humanity, without batting an eyelid. She is cook, cleaner, home entertainment center, fountain and source of all knowledge, and comforter of the broken-hearted 4-year old, all in a day's work - and all she wants in this world is five minutes alone in the bathroom. And, of course, world peace.

A Christmas Tail

ONE CHRISTMAS SEASON I went out to my car and noticed that a packet of hot chocolate mix left in there for emergencies – you never know - had been opened. Naturally I suspected one of my teenagers of desperate consumption in a moment of weakness for chocolate, a family trait, but they adamantly denied it. Casually tossing the incident into the "one of life's little mysteries" category, of which I have many, I went on with my life.

A few days later I discovered a box of chocolate mints I had in the trunk (no idea why) had been chewed open, and the light dawned. A rodent with a taste for chocolate had taken up residence in my car. I'm not generally afraid of mice; I had become used to rodents when my son adopted a rat we named Basil. He (the rat) was fond of cleaning the teeth of anyone who would let him and peed everywhere he went. In a moment of rare freedom, he also chewed through a comforter and its cover, but we loved him anyway.

You would think I would be more careful, but I'm a forgetful kind of person, so when I was given a box of See's candy (my favorite) a week or so later and had to leave it in the car while I went to an appointment, I thought nothing of it. When I came back, no more than an hour later, my furry friend had chewed his way through heavy cardboard in order to get to my chocolate.

This was too much. We are veritable chocolate fiends in my family.

It is not wise to come between us and our chocolate. I resolved to keep all chocolate out of the car. This worked fine for a while, until one of the kids left a granola bar in the back seat. Our friend worked his way through the wrapper and demolished half the bar before expressing his opinion of health food (and potentially religion) by peeing on a Bible also left there. Such sacrilege could not be ignored; he had to go.

My teenage son was drafted to devise a humane trap. He did a lovely job; it was scientifically sound and baited with peanut butter, but it didn't catch the wily beast. I combed the car for food items, removed every crumb I could find, and slept in peace; if there was nothing left to eat, surely he would de-camp. The next day I discovered he had eaten a hole in my favorite woolly hat and chewed through the plastic wrap on a new blanket; he must be getting cold. Well, it was the Christmas season.

Christmas – I began to have a change of heart. It was cold outside; maybe he had a family to support. To my husband's horror, I began to leave granola bar offerings in the footwell. My uninvited visitor ate them, so he must have been desperate.

Soon after, I opened my glove compartment to get the ice scraper out and found he – she? - had torn apart all of the napkins and other paper products I keep there for emergencies and made a cozy nest. As I reached in to remove the mess (while driving, of course), I had, to my shock, a mouse encounter and nearly drove off the road. I shrieked, he shrieked (or the mouse equiva-lent of a shriek), he ran, and I drove faster (when in doubt, I always drive fast-er. My theory is, if you're lost, drive faster; it won't necessarily get you where you're trying to go, but it will make you feel as if you're making progress).

It must have frightened him/her even more than it did me, because after that brief crisis, I heard no more from him. No more holes in hats, no nests, no missing chocolates, granola bars left uneaten. Now I began to worry about him/her, cold and alone in the city, wandering from door to door, car to car, looking for a bit of kindness, chocolate, or even a granola bar, perhaps trail-ing several babies and grandmice, or worse yet, looking for crumbs to bring back to the little ones waiting anxiously at home, seeing their sad small faces, doomed to yet another disappointment when s/he came back empty-pawed.

I never saw or heard from him again. But I think maybe this Christmas, I'll leave a tiny cookie and a little milk out in the car for him, just in case. And if I can do that for my mouse, maybe, just maybe, we could all think about the humans in dire need in our towns and our world, and extend some Christmas kindness to them, in the true spirit of the season.

Merry Christmas!

A Matter of Life and Death

THERE IS A HUGE hairy spider in my bathroom sink, and he is causing an internal moral battle of epic proportion - for me, that is. He's been there for days, although at times he disappears, and I assume he's gone down the drain for reasons of his own. Unless he's finding sustenance down the pipes somehow, he will eventually starve to death, and this bothers me. I like my lunch as well as the next person, and I find the thought of anything starving to death to be unappetizing, to say the least. Especially in my bathroom. On the other hand, I am not a big spider fan. I know they eat bugs that I find even more objectionable than themselves, but the thought of all those hairy little legs jumping out at me or whisking across my face while I am peacefully asleep gives me the shivers. Some of them bite, too; I know too many people who have had chunks of skin and muscle removed, or who have swelled up like basketballs because some angry arachnid took offense at them. It appears to be entirely too easy to rile the little critters accidentally, and boom - you're toast.

Most spiders, like most snakes, they tell me, are harmless. While logic assures me this is true, instinct urges me to whomp them first and ask their intentions later. However, I am a child of the 70's; I know that all living creatures have their special niche in the ecosystem which I ought not disturb. Therefore, we normally live in some sort of harmony with our housemates, both invited and uninvited. It comes down to a modified "Don't ask, don't tell" policy; if they will agree to stay out of sight in the daytime, I will pretend that they all live outside. This policy was unwittingly violated one night when I was living in San Francisco in an insalubrious studio apartment. Although I had my suspicions that I was sharing my quarters, I lived in blissful ignorance until I broke the rules by getting up late one night to get a drink of water. Turning on the light was met with such a mad dash for safety by both myself and the hordes of cockroaches I had disturbed that it would be a very long time before I made the same mistake.

But back to the spider in my sink. He seems healthy enough, so maybe there is nourishment down the drainpipe. But if he's only hiding down there, not dining, then he may well die in my bathroom, and I don't want his eight legs on my conscience. Should I end his misery quickly, Dr. Kevorkian style, by dropping a dictionary on him? This guy is so big I'm afraid he'd throw it back at me. I'd try to pick him up with something and drop him outside, but he's a quick little devil, and I have no doubt about the outcome of a footrace to the front door, with him scampering up 25 sheets of toilet paper toward my arm at warp speed (why do they DO that??). Then, of course, he's loose in the house, searching for the love of his short little spider life so that they can reproduce in the millions. Not a pretty thought. Flash flood and down the drain? Quick or slow, he's still a dead spider on my conscience. I could advance the arguments of survival of the fittest and natural selection (after all, he was dumb enough to get into the sink in the first place), but they are cold comfort. If all of us were condemned to die every time we made a stupid mistake, the earth would be uninhabited (except, perhaps, for spiders). But perhaps we ought not to go there.

And why, I wonder, do I continually refer to this spider in the masculine gender? I certainly can't claim to have gotten close enough to check for secondary sex characteristics (whatever they might entail in a spider). What if it's a she? All sorts of further moral ramifications arise. What if it's a she, and she's pregnant, or there's a nest of baby spiders anxiously awaiting her return? Then I would be responsible, not just for this one spider's demise, but potentially hundreds, if not thousands, if "Charlotte's Web" is anything to go by.

Meanwhile, I can't use my bathroom sink. I can't bring myself to add insult to injury by spitting on him or her, so I'm trekking all the way to the kitchen to brush my teeth, and it's beginning to be annoying. But perhaps there is a solution - one used by every generation. We have trained our children to be better people than ourselves; let them solve our moral dilemmas. My husband has insisted that I not pass on my "irrational" fear of creepy-crawlies to our son or daughter, so I shall simply enlist one of them to gently remove the creature from the sink and put him/her outside. Let the next generation deal with it; I have no doubt they'll do a better job of it.

DENTAL DILEMMAS AND
MEDICAL MAYHEM

I WAS OUT ON a rare date one night when I was twenty-one when I noticed an odd phenomenon: I couldn't open my mouth. I immediately decided I had lock-jaw, not realizing that was caused by rabies and I hadn't been bitten by anything foaming at the mouth lately – even my date.

As unusual as it was frightening for me to not be able to open my mouth, having spent my entire life with it open, it seemed, I went home and alerted my mother, who immediately drove me the forty-five minutes into town to the hospital, where the attending physician ordered me to open my mouth so he could look inside. With some hostility, I responded, "I can't" through clenched teeth, but no matter; he pried open my jaws with a tongue depressor, ignoring my howls of pain, and announced that it appeared to him I had four impacted wisdom teeth and would have to arrange for surgery. Did I mention it was a Friday night? And the best I could hope for was sometime the following week?

He then prepared to send me home, but my mother, in true mother-bear style, insisted I be given some pain medication to tide me over the weekend. She needn't have bothered, really; the pain was so intense I just cried for two days until the renowned Dr. Slaughter knocked me out the following Monday. When I regained consciousness, I discovered I was weeping as if my heart were broken; when my mother, in some alarm, asked what was wrong, all I could do was explain, between sobs, that absolutely nothing was wrong, but I couldn't seem to stop crying. The nurse finally intervened to explain that some people, especially women, had that reaction to the drug used to put them out. Frankly, I was so relieved to be out of the intense pain, I didn't care if I cried for the next week, but I eventually regained control over my emotions, slapped a couple of tea bags over the holes in my mouth, and went home.

Unfortunately, it was soon afterwards I discovered a violent reaction to the painkiller Vicodin; vomiting uncontrollably, I spent the next several days developing an intimate relationship with the toilet, wrapping myself around it and sleeping on the bathroom floor to save time. The teeth were beginning to feel like the least of my problems.

Milestone birthdays seem to be my medical Waterloo; when I was eighteen, I came home from babysitting, decided I had the stomach flu, and went to bed. Have you ever noticed that you seem to develop a violent aversion to whatever you ate just before becoming ill? Well, I do – I wasn't able to eat sour cream and onion potato chips for years after one bout with the flu. I was convinced that my last act before becoming ill, ironing, had been responsible for making me sick; I've rarely touched an iron since, just to be on the safe side. In any case, I then turned my face to the wall and prepared to meet my maker, as I always do when I feel sick, as I am always convinced whatever I have is terminal and I will surely die this time.

Much to my surprise, my mother came into my room, examined my face, declared she didn't like the way I looked (which, of course, I had suspected for years but never had confirmed until that moment), and commanded my father to take me to the hospital. As I hadn't been in a hospital, or even a doctor's office, since the day I was born, I was now seriously terrified. My father, always a rock of Gibralter in times of emergency, carted me down to the hospital where we waited for several hours to be seen. At last they examined me, but couldn't figure out what was wrong, so I was sent (on foot, mind you) to another building for more tests.

I was beginning to feel really sick by this time, but my father dutifully led me outside, where I promptly threw up in the bushes, and on we went, my father, bless his heart, assuring me no one would notice the mess I'd left behind. Maybe that's why they now give you a wheelchair. They eventually determined I had appendicitis, and removed the offending organ, but refused to give it to me in a jar as I'd requested. Bureaucracies.

I discovered upon coming out of the anesthesia my father was not so good at recovery as he was at emergencies; when I murmured "It hurts" in my delirium, he had to leave the room. I don't blame him; I've never liked hospitals.

When I had my daughter, I cried until they let me go home early after a cesarean section. By the time I had my son, I was slightly less enthusiastic about leaving – I had a two-year old at home by now, after all. Besides, I got an inkling of things to come when I woke up after his delivery in a linen closet. I asked, calmly, if I were indeed in a linen closet, seeing linens all around me and thinking I might be hallucinating from the drugs; they apologetically assured me I was, indeed, in the linen closet as they had temporarily run out of space, and I, satisfied, immediately went back to sleep. It didn't help that the doctor who delivered my son was later accused of using his surgical instruments on his herd of ostriches.

At least the second time I didn't immediately throw up when they handed me the baby; so much for mother and child bonding. It was the darned ice chips; I was so thirsty after the surgery that I practically threatened my husband with bodily harm until he gave me way more ice chips than you're allowed, and I discovered sometimes there's a reason for rules.

Meanwhile, I await my next milestone birthday and medical emergency.

CAR TREK: THE NEXT GENERATION

HOW IS IT THAT BOTH our children are sleeping in closets? How do these things happen?

And no, we're not child abusers; they are both at college, trying to save money, a concept with which we are in complete, if not fervent, agreement, having a vested interest in the subject.

Our daughter got a great deal on a place from a friend of mine. It has lovely views of the Bay Area, though it unfortunately lacks an oven – but hey, who has time to cook, anyway, when you're in school? It's a kind of a studio with a hall space she uses as a closet, and where she also puts her mattress.

Our son, desperate to find a place to live only a few days before school started in Santa Cruz, was rescued by a friend who said he and his girlfriend had managed to secure a one-bedroom apartment our son could share. Great, I thought; he can sleep in the living room, which is probably bigger than his sister's closet. Then the friend elaborated: what was available was, actually, the closet. The closet? Are you kidding me? No, no; it's a nice, big closet, the friend insisted.

When my son and I took the trip down to inspect the premises, the friend was not available, so we took the tour with the maintenance man. It revealed a tiny closet in the bedroom not big enough for a ferret, much less our almost six-foot son. When I enquired of our tour guide how this could possibly work, he said "No, no, the closet is through the bathroom!" and proceeded to show us that the door in the bathroom that I had assumed was a linen closet instead revealed – a closet, big enough to sleep in, with a window even!

Our son insists it's larger than his former dorm room, that he can fit not only a mattress, but a small dresser inside, and that other than the tiny inconvenience of not being able to emerge from his closet until everyone has vacated the bathroom, he is perfectly happy. We raised them to be flexible.

We were finally convinced by our son that a car was necessary for his survival at school, this being his third year there, and his first year living off-campus, commuting from his pitiful closet. But we are not the kind of parents who indulge our offspring with expensive vehicles, especially since we don't even buy them for ourselves, so off went my beloved with our son in order to instruct him in the fine art of "finding a bargain vehicle" the day before our son was leaving to return to school. We tend not to plan too far in advance.

My beloved having located several promising (to him, anyway) potential modes of transport, they soon settled on a likely looking prospect and made a deal (after the seller, a young man, came down several thousand dollars, my beloved, always one with an eye for the main chance, asked if he'd come down a thousand more. This was politely declined). Our son was now the proud owner of a $1,500, 2001 Chevy Malibu.

Off he went the next day in his "new" car, only to call us from somewhere near Williams in a panic. "My bumper fell off!" were the first words out of his mouth. "What?!" "My bumper fell off" he repeated. After some discussion, his father instructed him to go back and find it, but it was apparently lost forever. How it disappeared from the freeway, we never discovered. Unfortunately, it took the license plate and light with it, but my beloved decided this was a minor issue, as it had Colorado plates that expired in a few days anyway. Or did have. A few hours later, we got another emergency call: "The check engine light just came on!" My beloved: "What color is it?" "Yellow." "Well, that's all right; you only need to worry if it turns red." Not exactly reassuring, but at least he could continue his journey.

Since then, our son has discovered that the ABS braking system has quit, the turn signals come to life only briefly after the car has warmed up, then gets cranky and refuses to stay on unless he pounds the dashboard in just the right place – and the tape deck only works when you hold the tapes in place manually. And no, it does not have a CD player.

On a recent trip home with his sister, they were pulled over because the car's back lights weren't working (this was news to all of us). After getting his fix-it ticket and having the Highway Patrol officer tell him to use his hazard lights in place of the rear lights, he had to drive past the officer while holding the hazard light button on – it wouldn't work otherwise – and steering while his sister held the overhead light on, so they could see how fast they were going (did I mention that none of the dashboard lights were working, either?) and banged on the dashboard to make the turn signals operate, however briefly.

Thank heavens it was an automatic, or they would have needed more passengers just to drive the thing. It's somehow comforting to know the family's bad luck with cars (well, my bad luck, truthfully) has been passed on to the next generation.

SEW WHAT?

I'VE NEVER EXACTLY BEEN a dab hand with a sewing machine, I'm afraid. I can embroider all day, as long as I'm allowed to use the only stitch I ever learned and my eyesight doesn't give out, but sewing on an actual machine appears to be beyond my limited capabilities.

It started with the patterns. When I was a teenager, I bought the simplest pattern I could find in the vain hope I could figure it out, but no luck. Their instructions didn't seem to make any sense, and I appear to be lacking the ability to comprehend any two - or is it three? - dimensional models. It must be genetic, because as good at sewing as my mother was, she spent her entire sewing life asking my father to interpret patterns for her.

I remember when I was very young, taking what I believe was an IQ test, which I found fun and challenging until we got to the part where they show you diagrams with lines on them and ask you to picture them folded along the lines, and tell them what shape they would be. I struggled and struggled with those little buggers until I gave up in frustration and despair. They really shouldn't do such things to little kids; I'm sure it stunted my intellectual growth for decades. Although, truth to tell, I put the current date instead of the year of my birth on the form, so they never could figure out my IQ. Kind of tells me all I need to know about my intelligence, really.

Come to think of it, I took another one of those tests as an adult, and when they asked whether the sun rose in the east or the west, I was completely stumped. I mean, it comes up every morning, and it goes down every night; what else do you need to know? The only way I could figure it out, which I did, was to remember that quote from "Romeo and Juliet": "What light through yonder window breaks? It is the east, and Juliet is the sun!" or something like that. At least that made some sense to me.

I tried making shorts for my son once from a pattern, and they ended up upside down; no one I know can figure that one out. In any case, patterns really were not my cup of tea, so I gave up on them. At some point I just started whacking away at fabric in a rather random manner, which worked okay for the children's Christmas pageants at church, as long as they were playing shepherds, who are expected to look pretty raggedy, and not the three kings, who had, I suspect, some rather higher standards of sartorial splendor to uphold. It may be all right for a shepherd to have one sleeve longer than the other, but not, for heaven's sake, a magi. I'll bet HE could follow a pattern; if they could navigate using a star, I'm sure they had that whole spatial relationship thing down, even if they didn't ask for directions. And I'm guessing they knew where the sun rose, too, the show-offs. But I'm willing to bet they'd struggle with sewing machines.

I told my mother my whole life that sewing machines see me coming and immediately wind their bobbins into knots. Invariably, I'll be sewing, if not happily, at least calmly along, when suddenly the entire operation comes to a grinding halt because the needle is stuck in position due to the bobbin thread having gone berserk and winding itself up so tightly it takes major surgery to release it. Maybe it needs therapy to learn to relax. Or maybe I do.

My daughter, who sews like a professional (without patterns, I might add, and on the exact same model sewing machine I use), insists it's because I don't speak nicely to my machine before beginning; she thinks it senses my presence and my innate hostility and becomes recalcitrant, if not downright uncooperative. Perhaps it's unhappy at its name (Beelzebub). Perhaps I should approach it the way I'm told I should approach my computer: stealthily, at a low angle, so it can't see me coming.

Once I decided, in an excess of holiday zeal, to make a stuffed turkey (out of cloth) from one of those yardage kits – how hard could it be? The instructions were printed right on the fabric, along with the lines to cut along. I was zipping along quite happily when I realized I needed to make a whole lot of long lines of stitches in his tail, which was rather tedious, but never mind – I was almost finished! How exciting! I was going to have my own homemade cloth stuffed turkey for my table centerpiece, at a fraction of what it would cost to buy it already made! Suddenly I noticed my turkey's tail was stiffer than I thought perhaps it ought to be; when I turned it over, I realized, with sinking heart, that I had sewn a large manila envelope to the back of the turkey tail.

That turkey, so to speak, was my last sewing project for a very long time.

BUGGY

As a self-described vegetarian half-pacifist, I try to avoid killing things, but I must admit I do have my limits (hence the "half"); anything that bites me, might bite me, or carries diseases is pretty much a goner if it gets within range, and it you're an ant and you're on my kitchen counter, you're going to die. I have certain rules about what belongs in the house and what belongs outside, and if you cross that line, you're dead meat, so to speak. I keep a knife under my pillow (reassuring if occasionally painful) and a gun under the bed, just for peace of mind. And the neighbor's dog, which tends to bark ceaselessly in the middle of the night, is definitely living on borrowed time if I ever wake sufficiently to load my gun. I've never claimed to be consistent, just conflicted.

It doesn't help my moral dilemma that we live in a log home, which practically invites fauna to move in, or that the head of our bed rests against said logs, making a natural bridge for the hungry and curious spiders who inhabit them (the logs, not the bed, although it's getting nippy-tucky). Some nights I swear I am awakened by the sound of certain small creatures gnashing their teeth (if they have teeth) and licking their chops (do bugs have chops? These are the questions that keep me lying awake at night) in anticipation of a late dinner at our expense. My beloved, normally a kind, non-violent man in the arachnid sense - the type who will normally remove a spider out of doors should he come across one in the house – has had no hesitation in going on a murderous spree these days when he sights anything with more than four legs, ever since he swelled up like a big toad and developed breathing issues that landed him in emergency after being bitten by, we think, a spider (I am certainly denying any responsibility in the matter –this time anyway). At least perhaps now I can remove the spider webs decorating the house like Halloween all year long, which he insisted, in the whole "Lion King" circle of life thing, were good to have because they were catching the flies. So much for ecological harmony.

And then there are the pets. The dog appears to have slowed down with age to the point that the ground squirrels are finally safe from him, and he has learned that deer kick, which has dampened his enthusiasm for hunting. Three of our four cats are card-carrying members of the Society for Lazy Felines, but the fourth, creatively named Girl Kitty, is a massacre on four legs. The arrival of spring apparently inspired her not with the sap of love, but with an ardor for revenge-killing unrivalled by any in recent history; I can only wonder what the local vermin have done to so offend her. I have lately discovered outside our front door the remains of such a wide variety of animals that I am considering loaning her out to the CIA as a mercenary: a snake, a squirrel, and a huge packrat have all been lovingly deposited on our front door within just a few days – or perhaps I should say, parts of all of the above – sometimes only a tail remains by which to identify the body, and since I am no expert on internal organs, it's hard to say what else may be out there. Even belling her has made no impact on the rising death toll outside my door; it's getting to the point where I'm afraid to go out in the morning. She appears to have no qualms about attacking animals larger than herself, and I fully expect to find a bear carcass any time now – or part of one. Clearly SHE has no pacifist issues.

WHAT'S THAT SMELL?

SO, I NOTICED A PECULIAR smell emanating from my car a few weeks ago. It got worse, rather than better, to the point where I thought something had crawled in and died, like maybe a squirrel or a rat or something equally unpleasant. I actually began to think I smelled the odor all the time, as if I carried it with me, and I was showering on a pretty regular basis, so either I was getting paranoid or I had become one of the Walking Dead.

I tried to investigate, but there's so much stuff in both my trunk and my glove box that it would take a major excavation to ascertain exactly what was going on, which I didn't feel I really had time to do, so I took the obvious solution of just opening the windows really wide and driving fast. Of course, it was very smoky from forest fires about then, so although the smell of smoke was WAY better than whatever had passed on in my trunk – or my glove box – it was still hard to breathe.

After a few weeks, even the dog didn't want to get into the car, so I figured it was time to do something about it. I started with the trunk, as the odor seemed marginally worse in there, and after a fairly short time I found out what had died – a quart of milk. As our beloved editor David pointed out to me later, there is probably nothing that smells worse than really, REALLY sour milk that has been marinating in an enclosed space in the heat – trust us on this one.

How one can lose a quart of milk in the trunk of one's car is a conundrum I cannot explain; it takes the concept of addle-brained further than I like to think about. What really bothers me is why I didn't miss it. I suppose I missed it at the time, but as I constantly remind myself, matter does not disappear; it may change form, but it does not disappear. So where, exactly, did I think the milk had gone? Did I just dismiss its disappearance as one of life's little mysteries, never to be solved, of which my life is so full? Or did I convince myself that I did not, in fact, buy the milk I thought I had purchased, or that I had in fact bought it for my father and delivered it to him without remembering doing so? In my world, all of the above are very real possibilities.

In any case, having now solved that particular mystery and discovered the source of the smell, I disposed of the milk immediately, but of course, the odor remained - the spilled milk, so to speak, having doused the trunk carpet in a rather overpowering fashion.

So I did what I usually do in such cases: I researched. Not on the internet; no, I asked several friends, and got different answers. Tonya (what a woman) recommended baking soda, while Kelly suggested vinegar; I myself thought Pine-Sol might do the trick. So I decided to save time and be super-effective by combining the three.

I started with the vinegar, which I reasoned might be best diluted in water, having dyed enough Easter eggs in my day with the children to know how very strong that odor can be. Feeling clever, I then added the baking soda – whoa!! I almost dropped the plastic container I was mixing them in as it fizzed almost out over the edge of the bowl. I then decided perhaps adding the Pine-Sol would be a bridge too far, and abandoned that idea. When I told Tonya about the reaction, she stared at me in disbelief. I don't know why; she's known me a very long time, and shouldn't have been surprised.

She asked, "Are you telling me you didn't know that adding baking soda to vinegar would make it fizz?" I nodded. "Didn't you do that experiment in school, making volcanoes?" I said what I always say when any gaps in my educational history are exposed, even though I'm certain it's quite unfair: "Religious school!"

"Well, you do know, of course, that adding ammonia to bleach can kill you?" At least I think that's what she said. I looked at her blankly. "It will??" I said in the utmost shock. Tonya was aghast. "How could you not know that?" "I try not to do too much housework that involves those substances?" I thought for a moment as she sort of tore at her hair. "Well, that's OK; I don't have any ammonia in the house anyway. At least I don't think I do."

In any case, the car is smelling much better, and I had it cleaned, too, so I'm sure all will be well, as long as I stay away from the ammonia. I can always open the windows again; fall is coming and the smoke appears to be clearing.

NOT SO SMOOTH

IT'S OBVIOUS TO ANYONE who's known me for more than a minute that I'm a klutz. I blame this primarily on my feet; they're pretty short for someone my size, and to add insult to injury, they're double jointed, which means when I start to lose my balance (which is often and for no discernable reason), the toes go up, giving me even less surface area on the ground, and over I go. It's a physics thing, I suspect.

I'm sure you're wondering where all this is going – I often wonder the same thing myself. Where are we going? What does it all mean? Oops, sorry; I got lost in philosophical reflection for a minute there. The point is that generally speaking, if something can go wrong in my life due to physical incapacity, it's likely to. The other day, for instance, I decided to paint my deck furniture blue. There I was, happily painting away, when a bug came after me. I waved at it several times, and not in a friendly manner, when I suddenly realized I was still holding the paintbrush in my hand. Covered in blue paint, I now resembled Mel Gibson in "Braveheart", ready to do battle with the English. Or the bugs. Or both.

But the case in point has to do with smoothies. Being a cheap kind of person (hence the idea to paint ancient deck furniture rather than buy a new set), I make my own smoothies for breakfast. Some frozen fruit, bananas, yogurt, juice, and greenery, and I'm good to go. Because I'm usually late, I take my smoothie with me to the car, and drink it on the way to work, and usually at work, too (I'm a slow drinker). Fine so far, but then the klutz part kicks in. Because I take it in an open container, so to speak, in a very short period of time, I spilled my smoothie three times: in the parking lot, all over me, and on the last occasion, over the car, my purse, my paperwork, AND the parking lot.

The last event was particularly classic for me; everything was fine, I was out of the car, realized I had left my sandwich on the floor of the car, and reached in to pick it up, completely forgetting that I had tucked the smoothie under my arm. The ensuing mess ensured the local car cleaning company got my business. When a concerned co-worker enquired why I didn't use a cup with a secure lid, I was stunned; I had never thought of that. Still, I was too cheap to buy one, so she kindly gifted me with one (thanks, Diana!).

So, the next day or so, I proudly carried my smoothie to work in my new container, and voila! No more spills! The miracles of modern science! One day, however, as I got to the end of my smoothie at work, I noticed a lump in the bottom. That was odd; why would my smoothie have a lump? I peered into the darkness of my new container quizzically, but couldn't tell what it was. Had the bananas not been blended, and massed together in the bottom of the container? Shrugging, I put it to my mouth and smartly (in more ways than one, in an ironic sense) smacked the container to dislodge the lump. It worked; I now had smoothie all over my face, my desk, the floor… somehow I had miraculously avoided my clothes, but that was about the only thing in the vicinity not colored purple and dripping. It's a wonder I get any work done, as much cleaning up as I do.

After restoring myself and my office to some semblance of order, in the spirit of scientific enquiry, I took the container to the kitchen to discover the story behind the lump. Eventually, as I examined it like a CSI lab worker, it came to me: the day before, I had cleaned the cup out and dried it with a paper towel, and in an excess of concern that I not grow vegetable matter in it, left the paper towel in to absorb any leftover liquid. The next morning, in a hurry as usual, I completely forgot about the paper towel, and happily and blindly poured my smoothie on top of it.

But I come by these tendencies honestly and genetically. Family legend tells the story of my sister, in my brother's car, on which he had expended many hours of labor, ready to go somewhere and applying a perfume called "Ambushed". When my brother asked her what time it was, my sister efficiently flipped her wrist to read her watch, forgetting she had the open perfume bottle in that hand. My brother never could stand the smell of that particular brand of perfume again, although he had the opportunity to enjoy it every time he got into his car for many years, and darkly took to calling it "Bushwhacked". This same sister, running away from someone throwing a snowball at her, and looking back at them rather than where she was going, once accidentally leapt off the edge of a snow cliff and into the road, which didn't do her back much good. But hey, the snowball missed her.

My parents, who used to own a small store downriver, had their moments, too. My mother was sitting on a stool at the counter next to the register, prepared to ring up someone's groceries, when my father reached under the cash register to get something. He was leaning on my mother's stool, which he forgot rotated, so he accidentally gave her a little twirl. Throwing her hands up in alarm as she twirled, my mother accidentally hit a cash register key. This key happened to be the one that opened the cash drawer, which came out in time to whack my father on the head – are you seeing a pattern? The customer waiting to be rung up shook his head slowly and remarked, "If I hadn't seen it for myself, I never would have believed it." We're like that in my family: always up for entertaining each other and the public with smooth maneuvers.

HEALTH CARE

WE LIVE IN A SMALL rural town in (the real) northern California. Rarely does a week go by that we don't read about another fundraiser for a family whose child, or father or mother or brother or sister, is suffering from a life-threatening illness. Our community is amazingly generous, but that isn't the point. The point is that the United States is the only developed country in the world that requires a large proportion of its citizens to beg for financial help from their neighbors through bake sales or spaghetti feeds to pay for life-saving medical care.

I have lived under a number of health care systems; when I was a student, I couldn't afford health care. As a result, when I contracted strep throat, I didn't go to a doctor. Later that year, when I had access to health care at my college health center, I discovered I had had mononucleosis. The doctor was furious with me; she told me that it could have resulted in serious complications, including permanent disability. Guess who pays for the long-term effects of untreated illnesses when someone can't afford a doctor visit? Those who are insured, and those who pay their own medical expenses. Every time someone without insurance can't afford to go for a check-up and ends up in emergency, the most expensive form of health care, the same people pay those costs. If people are too destitute to pay for doctor visits during pregnancy, resulting in premature births, poor nutrition, and birth defects, who pays for that child's care for the rest of its life? Same answer.

I hear a lot of disparagement of Britain's National Health System (NHS). Here is my question for the critics: how many opponents of the system have actually experienced it? Because I have, and I have not one single complaint. I lived in Scotland for a year. When we moved into a little village outside Glasgow, I found my local general practitioner (GP) down the block and was added to his register. If I hadn't liked him, I could have gone to any GP of my choice. If I needed a specialist, he referred me to one. Prescriptions cost the equivalent of one U.S. dollar (this was a while ago – now it's up to about $12). My husband worked for a company that paid extra for private insurance (yes, it does exist in Britain); if I had needed surgery, I could have recovered in a private room. Some Americans say they're afraid they may have to wait a few months for, say, a hip replacement, as they sometimes do in Canada. But if you don't have insurance or a lot of money in America, you will never get a new hip.

Years ago, when I worked for the State of California, I had Kaiser Health Care; it was the closest thing I've seen to Britain's health care system, except I didn't get to choose my doctor. Still, I never saw a bill and rarely filled out forms, and all my health issues were taken care of without any payment on my part except one dollar for prescriptions. But why should this privilege be reserved for government workers, those with employer-supplied healthcare, politicians, and/or those with money?

Since then, the cost of healthcare has risen so much that even the insured are being asked to pay prohibitive amounts in premiums, deductibles and co-pays for their health care. Here are some statistics: In 2008, the United States spent 15.3% of its Gross Domestic Product (GDP) on health care, and millions are uninsured; Britain spent 8.3% of their GDP, and every single person has access to health care. Afraid of higher taxes? The average British income tax is similar to the average American's, 20-40%, but that isn't what pays for their healthcare. That comes from a combination of employee and employer deductions close to 24% of every person's gross salary, and it covers not only health insurance, but pensions, unemployment insurance, and disability. Compare that, if you will, to the 30% my employer and I currently pay for social security, medicare, and health insurance.

Ask any senior you know with MediCare how they like it. MediCare is a public option for seniors, a government-run program that works and is liked by most who use it. Why are the politicians working so hard to piece together a patchwork quilt of options, including experimental models like cooperatives no one knows anything about, that will be expensive, inefficient, and probably fail, when we have a good working model right now in MediCare? Could it be the profit-motivated insurance and pharmaceutical companies and their very well-funded lobbying organizations which fear a drop in their profits?

It's a matter of priorities. Many years ago, this country chose to subsidize public education because we believed it to be a vital part of democracy – to have a well-educated public make its own decisions about how to govern. Oddly, I never hear anyone talk about "socialized education". Isn't having a healthy public a priority too? Here's another statistic: the life expectancy in Britain is 79; in America, it's 78.1. I guess the "death panels" over there aren't very efficient.

A recent survey conducted by researchers at Mt. Sinai School of medicine in New York published by the New England Journal of Medicine found that 73% of 2,130 doctors favor either a single-payer system or a combination of public and private options (as in England). Only 50-70% of patients favor a public option. What are we afraid of that our doctors are not? When will we Americans, liberal and conservative alike, stand up for what every industrialized nation except our own has? If public education has been accepted as the right thing to do, why can't we do the same for health care for every man, woman and child in this nation? When will we stop being afraid, and stop letting others do our thinking for us?

There is so much misinformation in this country about health care, and where does it come from? Who has a vested interest in making sure we are frightened of health care for everyone? The insurance companies, who spend billions of dollars every year to ensure that they can continue making their profits. People say they are afraid of the government making decisions about who gets needed health care. Who makes those decisions now? Companies whose sole purpose is to make a profit for their executives and shareholders. I do not find the prospect of every man, woman and child in the United States receiving adequate health care frightening. What I do find frightening, and appalling, is the idea of people in America not going to doctors, and not taking their children to doctors, because they cannot afford it. In this great, wealthy nation of ours, I find that a disgrace; as a parent and a citizen, I find it heartbreaking.

FIRE

I'VE BEEN SLEEPING outside. I hate being inside, caged like a wild animal; I can't breathe. Most nights, once he's asleep, I creep out and sleep under the stars. That's where I feel safest, under the arms of the trees and the endless sky where no one can find me. I lie on my back and stare up at another world, and dream my own dreams.

I never know when he might have been drinking, and when he drinks, the bad things happen. I can hear my mother cry, and there is nothing I can do to stop it. He's so much bigger and stronger than I am. Sometimes, if I'm not fast enough, he grabs me, too, so I've learned to be quick, to run like the wind, back outside into the woods. Not my mother, though; she's somehow always too slow. When he catches her, he leaves me alone, but I hate to hear her cry. So I spend as much time as I can outside, where I can hear the birds singing in the morning. When I get older, bigger, stronger, I'll kill him.

Early this morning, I'm still dreaming, dreaming it's summer; I feel the heat of the sun, odd on this cold winter morning, and then I smell the sharp smoke, and the strange sounds wake me. I hear the crackle and then the roar of flames, and suddenly I am wide awake and running towards the house as fast as I can, but it's too late, I can tell as soon as I see it; the fire is unbelievably, unbearably hot, and it's eating the wooden structure like a starving animal.

I stand and watch, breathing hard as the house burns, until suddenly, my mother appears in the doorway. She looks right at me, as if she knows exactly where I stand hidden, and I am weak with relief. I wait for her to walk out of the house to safety, to come to me, to escape the hungry flames, but she doesn't. Instead, she looks straight at me, into my eyes. She reaches her hand out to me, and smiles slightly; I can see the love in her eyes. And then she turns and steps back into the inferno.

Scientific Mysteries

SCIENCE HAS ALWAYS baffled me, especially subjects like chemistry and physics. How is it, for instance, that a 16 ounce bag of something as light and airy as potato chips somehow transforms itself into an extra five pounds on my hips and thighs? Is that some mystery of chemistry? Or physics, for that matter?

I actually, in some misguided attempt to improve my store of scientific knowledge, took both chemistry and physics in college – and I wasn't even forced to do so. Silly me; it was, of course, an utter disaster. Even though it was called "Physics for Non-Science Majors", I wasn't fooled, and neither were they; all of us liberal arts majors, and the professor, knew there was not a hope we were going to understand what they were talking about. Amongst ourselves, we called it "Physics for Dummies".

But we all muddled through, and somehow I managed not only to pass the class, I got a pretty good grade; I think they confused me with some other student, someone who understood why they were winding copper wire around a magnet, or why that somehow makes it into a motor. I still don't know, and I don't want to know, so don't bother trying to explain it to me. You definitely wouldn't want to share a desert island with me; I'd be of no use whatsoever.

The teaching assistant was pretty cute, though I'm not sure whether that was an advantage or a disadvantage; while I may have paid more attention because he was nice to look at, I'm pretty sure I absorbed not a word of what he said. Which reminds me of a story a friend told me: She took some sort of science class, where the T.A., a young man named Rob, was also quite good looking (is there some sort of rule that says the T.A. in classes you know nothing about must be handsome?). At the end of the semester, a snotty girl remarked to my friend, "I got an A; what did you get?" To which my friend replied, "I got Rob"; they were married when I met them.

And why, pray tell, do you divide fractions by flipping them upside down and multiplying them? Where is the logic in that? I actually had a friend explain it to me once (he was a math teacher), and for one brief shining moment, I understood, but that was a long time ago.

But I digress. Chemistry was also a challenge, to put it mildly. It was just a little two-unit course, also intended for non-science majors, but it may as well have been in Swahili as far as I was concerned. In fact, I was doing all right, despite a tendency on my part to get distracted by things like the attraction of sodium to chlorine, which I saw as a tragic love story ("No, Sodium, they can't keep us apart! We were meant to be together!"), until mid-semester, when I managed to contract mono without, I might add, having any fun doing so, and that was it. Chemistry is the one class I managed to fail in my long educational history, although I came pretty close in Economics; I believe my evaluation in that class read, in its entirety, "Virginia flunked the mid-term and barely passed the final." You wouldn't want to ask me any questions about the economy, either.

I decided pretty early on in life that science was magic, and that was all I needed to know about it. You flip a switch, and lights come on; if they don't, you need to call someone, and that someone, fortunately, would be my husband, who understands all the mysteries of science and works for free - for me, anyway. Him, you would want to share a desert island with, believe me; he'd have a five-star resort built in a matter of weeks. When we were dating, we had a very romantic discussion about toilet siphons, so I should have known.

Our son appears to be made in the same mold; he called me from college, in his third year I believe it was, to report, "Mom, I just finished my first structural geology class, and I'm practically vibrating with excitement!" He wasn't joking, either; I made appreciative noises and handed the phone to my (geologist) husband, and they proceeded to have a very animated, if completely incomprehensible (to me, anyway) conversation. This same son, when we delivered him to his dorm room on his first day of college, took out his pocket knife and immediately began repairing the wall socket so that he could plug in even more electronic devices, none of which I understand, nor do I want to. Even our daughter, the traitor, who is an artist and actress, understands science; she's also a whiz with a table saw and a drill, and is a welder who can have animated discussions with my father about metallurgy. I can spell the word, but that's about it.

I've decided I'm happier just believing it's all magic.

Under Construction

FOR A PERSON with absolutely no talent, experience, or inclination to do so, I have spent an inordinate amount of time in the building industry. I suppose it's because I became unemployed at one point and felt guilty enough about not pulling my financial weight that I actually volunteered to help my husband in his construction business. After some careful consideration (he knows me pretty well, after all), he agreed to train me. Fearing for my safety, and fully aware of my propensity for accidental self-harm, he kept me far away from sharp objects and anything else that might result in expensive hospital visits. Mind you, he has no room to talk; he managed at one point to nail himself to a roof he was working on, with a ring-shanked nail, no less, which necessitated removal by his partner with a hacksaw (of the nail from the beam, not my beloved) and a quick trip to emergency to remove said nail from his finger. His partner related that in his usual calm, collected manner, my beloved had informed him of the situation by announcing quietly, "I appear to have nailed myself to the roof." As he had called me on the way to the hospital, I was able to watch the entire fascinating procedure of nail removal; he declined to observe, but I gave him a blow-by-blow description in case he was interested.

We started with painting. It seemed simple enough: just wear old clothes, put paint on the brush, and slap it (the paint, that is) on the wall. I hadn't reckoned on ceilings. Note to self: close mouth when painting ceilings. Soon I found it necessary to wear a neck brace to avoid frequent visits to the chiropractor. Wearing a neck brace, I've noticed, also tends to cause concern when visiting salesmen come to the door, and also get personal injury lawyers overexcited.

Walls weren't much better than ceilings. Rollers are helpful (until you have to clean them), but when some lunatic (that would be my beloved sister) insisted on "accent walls", we came to a parting of the ways. Even with various implements specifically designed to create straight lines of paint, the wrong color would invariably bleed on to the other wall, causing much gnashing of teeth (mine) and anguish (my sister's). Besides, I suffered great trauma when I was spray-painting away and didn't notice that a baby squirrel had somehow crawled out from who knows where onto the wall I was painting. He made a frantic-squirrel kind of noise, I shrieked "Rodent!" at the top of my voice, and my beloved had to come take the poor skunk-striped mammal out into the bushes, where he was no doubt shunned for life by the rest of the rodent community.

Next I was sent on to the roof to paint eaves. Of course, I am afraid of heights, but work is work, so I decided to grit my teeth, square my shoulders, and be manly. Up I went. It was summer, and the metal roof was very hot, but this did not dissuade me from crawling across it with as much of my body making contact as possible so as to avoid sliding off and falling twenty or so feet. Naturally, at some point I knocked the paint can over and spilled blue paint all over the roof, but as the roof, too, was blue, I didn't see what all the fuss was about.

Still, my painting career was cut short, and I was dispatched to carry dry-wall sheets, which are unbelievably heavy, until I got a full-time job just to preserve our marriage and my aching muscles.

BEAR NECESSITIES

WHEN WE WERE IN ALASKA recently, everyone was very keen to see a bear; they paid big money to take special tours to try to spot one. What's the big deal, I thought; just go on down to the Happy Camp dump and you'll see all the bears you want, for free. Well, there is the dump fee, I suppose.

I was out walking a while ago and saw a bear. He was a long way off (although not nearly far enough for my taste) and not very big, but I had just read a story about a woman in Alaska who had been chased and attacked by a young, very hungry bear, so I did what any normal person would do when faced with a bear – clutched my throat and gasped. Fortunately, he saw me and, deciding discretion was the better part of valor, fled in the opposite direction. At least one of us had some sense.

I was not wearing my "bear bells", as they have been lost in one of our many moves. The theory is that if you wear bells around your neck, the bear will hear them and be frightened away. Great theory. A friend of ours, when he saw my "bear bells", referred to them as "dinner bells". The woman in Alaska blew an air horn at her bear with no appreciable effect. Also hit him in the head with a branch, poked him in the eye, and played ring around the rosy round a tree for about fifteen minutes, none of which seemed to deter him. I figure an elephant gun might have some effect, but other than that, you'd better be REALLY quick. I take my dog along as an appetizer, but he has an annoying habit of stopping stock still and staring fixedly at some point just beyond my view, which makes me nervous.

The other day as I was hiking near the house with the dogs, I heard a commotion and saw a bear cub racing up a tree; I knew what that meant, and sure enough, I heard a loud, strange noise in the bushes beside me – Mama was letting me know it was time to leave. By then, I was tearing down the hill, leaving the dogs to fend for themselves; they're faster than I am anyway.

The closest I've come to a bear (that I know of) was when we lived in Carson City, Nevada. I was in the habit of hiking up the hill in the mornings, and one day as I came around a corner, I found myself almost nose to nose with the biggest bear I had ever seen. He was at least six hundred pounds, and obviously hard of hearing, since my gasp could have been heard in the next county, at least. He had just come up over the hill, which explained why he hadn't seen or smelled me, but I'm fairly certain he saw my throat-clutching and heard my fervent prayers, because he did finally turn around and lumber back down the hill.

A few days prior to that, I had been on the same trail and saw an opened package of spaghetti noodles. Odd, I thought, some backpacker must have dropped them on their way up the hill. Later I found out a bear had broken through a neighbor's screen door and ransacked their kitchen while they slept. Apparently he didn't care too much for pasta, even though he had taken it to go. Honestly, I thought, some people can sleep through anything.

Just before we moved out of our house there, we had a little going-away party with some friends. I woke up at about 6:00 the next morning and wandered out to the kitchen for a glass of water. That's odd, I thought, I could have sworn we cleaned up last night, but the kitchen was certainly messy.

Then I noticed that the flowers I'd had in a vase the night before had fallen over on the counter. My goodness, I thought, we must have had quite a wind last night (I've never claimed to be particularly quick on the uptake). Then I noticed the fruit bowl. The day before, I had purchased about twelve pounds of fresh fruit – I was just in the mood for fruit, I guess – and there was very little left of it other than a few rinds. Hmm. Finally, I saw the remains of the cheesecake I'd worked so hard on – apparently someone had taken a bite, spit it out, and to add insult to injury, hurled the dish on the floor and broke it. I guess when you don't like cheesecake and you're a bear, you make that fact plain. Sort of a "Goldilocks" in reverse. I had thought it was a pretty good cheesecake, too.

Anyway, we figured out that he had climbed up a chair outside the window, which we had left open, came through the screen, helped himself, and left the same way. He thoughtfully tore the screen out in the corner, which was easily fixed and not even noticeable at first, and left us to sleep in peace down the hall. Some people can sleep through anything.

After consultation with our real estate agent, we decided we had nothing to disclose to the new buyers.

Dead Reckoning

I REALLY WANT TO BE present at my own autopsy. Well, I suppose I probably will be, but more as a participant than an observer, which is not what I have in mind. I mean, there are things I'd really like to know.

For instance, why is it that my physical therapist tells me, when I complain that my shoulder hurts, that I appear to have the shoulder damage seen in a major league baseball pitcher, when I've never thrown anything, much less a baseball, in my life? Treatment involves an electrical device that, when attached to my shoulder, feels as if I have tiny mice nibbling on me. Then it seems larger, heavier mice are running across my shoulder and down my arm, and then they get serious about chewing. Maybe by then they have been replaced by gerbils; it's hard to tell, really. At last all vermin are removed, ice is applied, and I fall peacefully asleep.

And why do my toes turn up at a ninety-degree angle (I've always claimed this helps restore my balance, but that theory is as yet untested)? This results in holes in the tops of my shoes, which is hard to explain. A friend once suggested I just get myself some elf shoes, but this is more difficult to accomplish than you might think.

I have issues with my Achilles tendons, too, probably caused by my deformed feet, but that isn't all: the bottoms of my feet are wearing out. I am getting so tired of hearing the phrase that seems to begin every sentence having to do with a physical ailment these days: "As we get older…" It seems that as we age, the soles of our feet lose their padding – who knew? Couldn't we just transfer the padding from the many other areas of the body where it seems to have accumulated to the areas that need it? A sort of "padding graft"? Apparently not.

And why do I have double-jointed fingers as well which, as far as I can tell, serve no useful purpose at all, and result in me never being able to snap my fingers in time to the music?

A while ago, I discovered a brown spot on my leg; terrified that I might have cancer, I went to the doctor, who looked at the spot, then looked at me, and stated calmly, "That, Virginia, is what we call an age spot." It's mortifying, really.

The older I get, the more peculiarities I discover about myself, and I would like to have some answers. Is that too much to ask? Although I suspect I won't be asking too many questions from my resting place on the slab. Why, for instance, did I start throwing up in certain movies a few years ago? It's not all movies - no, that would be too simple. For instance, relationship movies appear to have no effect on me, but give me an odd camera angle (and until recently, I'd never noticed a camera angle in my life), or "swoopy" movements, or anything that takes place on water, and I'm on my way to the bathroom.

With my luck, I'll die of entirely predictable, "natural" causes, there will be no autopsy, and I'll be cremated to save space and money, although I was deeply disappointed to learn the gold in my teeth cannot be extracted by my grieving family while the doctor's back is turned, as I have often instructed relatives to do. And I've also sworn to come back and haunt the children if they spend any money on funeral services, other than a party. I researched the matter and decided not to buy a pre-paid burial plan, because what if I die in a plane crash, am cremated in the wreckage, and the funeral home refuses to give my family a refund?

In any case, if there is no autopsy, no one will ever explain these numerous oddities about me, and at least one person will be disappointed – me. Still, I'd like to be there.

VETERAN'S DAY

THE BACK OF my sister's car has a decal bearing two stars, one for each of her two sons serving in the military. They're both good country boys, raised in Butte Valley; I say boys, but of course they're grown men with children of their own. One joined the Marines and participated in the initial invasion of Iraq; the other, seventeen months younger and always ready to outdo his brother, is a Navy Seal. We never really know where he is, but we do know he has a bronze star for bravery in action on a rooftop somewhere in Ramadi, rescuing fellow soldiers. I could not be more proud of them.

We have a picture of my father's father in uniform during World War I; he served in France and had something to do with horses in the infantry, apparently because he was a ranch boy from New Mexico. My father is the youngest of four brothers. I remember as a child seeing a photograph of his mother's front door, and asking him why there were four stars on it. He explained that each star stood for one of her sons, all of whom served in the military during World War II. They were all pilots: the eldest, Casper, taught flying to pilots in the U. S.; the next eldest, Grant, flew a B-24, called the Liberator, in the South Pacific. Then came John, who flew B-17's on missions over France and Germany, where the plane was shot up many times but made it home every time by some miracle. My father, the baby, was a cadet in flight school when the war ended. In my parents' wedding picture, all four men are wearing uniforms, and my mother is in a borrowed dress worn by seven different women.

The boys grew up in Pasadena, California, back when it was very rural, and because it was a small town, a newsman began following the story of my Uncle Grant and his crew. He called them The Nine Old Men, because of the way they aged over the course of the war, young as they were; you can see it in their faces in earlier and later photographs – what they had seen and experienced. My uncle was shot down near a place called Koror Harbor near the island of Palau. Crews on nearby planes said they saw parachutes and thought at least some of the crew escaped the plane and may have been picked up, but they were never heard from again. It was believed my uncle, as pilot, stayed with the plane to the end to keep it steady enough to allow his crew to get clear; then observers saw the plane blow up. It was their 75th mission, and was meant to be their last; one of the crew members had written home the night before that he was coming home the next day. It was highly unusual for anyone to make that many missions and survive. We have since learned that it is very probable that Grant was captured, held prisoner, and later executed. A Japanese military man was quoted as saying that "the lieutenant was a very honorable man". My uncle was 23 years old. My son is named for him.

I think of myself as a quiet patriot: I don't generally wave flags, and I've never said, "My country right or wrong", but I love my country deeply. I appreciate it even more after spending time in countries without the gift of democracy and a constitution or the right to free and fair elections, where voting is not taken for granted, but is a precious and hard-won right. I can't help thinking of my uncles, my father and my grandfather, and all the men and women who have died in the service of this country, every Veteran's Day. I have to admit that every year at the rodeo, when a rider carries the flag around the ring, I can't help crying. My son is away at school, hopefully learning how to be smart enough to keep our country out of wars, but if I felt America were directly threatened, I would encourage him to defend this country with his life. But as I am a mother I don't want to see any parent's precious son or daughter die in war. I pray for peace, and I honor and am grateful to every one of our veterans for their sacrifice.

"I hate war as only a soldier who has lived it can, only as one who has seen its brutality, its futility, its stupidity." General Dwight D. Eisenhower

"I abhor war and view it as the greatest scourge of mankind." Thomas Jefferson.

The Frozen Chosen

I MUST CONFESS that the title is a stolen reference to Episcopalians; if you're confused about what it means, ask one.

I really love it when it snows, don't you? I especially like it when it melts quickly, and/or I am observing it from a cozy indoor location and don't have to go anywhere or do anything.

I was very happy to see the snow this year – at first. It was, as always, beautiful, and my dog loved it. But I did rapidly tire of sweeping snow off my car every morning (I don't own a snow shovel and have no intention of buying one any time soon; I'll just hibernate until spring) and off my extensive front steps (there are 53 of them).

When it got icy, I got a little bit nervous, I must admit, but I decided to take the dog on a little outing to get the mail after having been house bound with cabin fever for a few days; I figured it would be really great exercise for both of us and wouldn't involve any post-holing in the snow since the road was relatively clear.

Suddenly I found myself flat on my back, although it happened so quickly I have no memory of slipping or even falling, my head having hit the pavement so hard I felt it bounce, sporting an aching backside, with the dog solicitously sniffing my face, apparently puzzled by my choosing this particular time to take a nap in the middle of the road when I had a perfectly comfortable couch in the house for the purpose, not to mention a bed. I lay there a few moments, as one is wont to do under such circumstances, taking a mental and physical inventory: Am I alive? Is anything broken? Am I still breathing? Can I get up anytime soon? Do I want to? Eventually I decided my hard German head had survived without even a lump to show for it, none the worse for the wear, so I peeled myself off the pavement and checked the mail, of which there was none. Sigh.

Unfortunately, the weather was just beginning its entertainment. When it dropped into single digits, I smugly congratulated myself on remembering to leave my taps dripping overnight – until I forgot one night. My house was icy cold, me being too cheap to turn on the baseboard electric heaters, and – no running water. No problem, I thought; it's bound to get warmer soon, and the pipes will all thaw out. It didn't, and they didn't, and I began to get a little nervous about the possibility of the haz-mat team showing up with the health department to evict me any moment as dishes piled up and the bathroom – but let's not go there, even figuratively. Do you have any idea how much melted snow it takes to fill a toilet tank?

Fortunately, my intrepid friend Tonya, property manager and real estate agent extraordinaire who knows about such things, brought over a heater, crawled under my house, placed the heater near my frozen pipes, and crawled back out while I stood by wringing my hands helpfully. What a woman. Unfortunately, the pipes didn't thaw right away, and I spent two days gathering snow water to melt for the dog and I to drink.

Now, your average person would probably have realized that the quickest way to melt snow would be on the stove, which was, fortunately, working, but that would be too easy for me. No, I felt I was very clever to think of putting the bowl full of snow next to the heater to melt. Do you have any idea how long it takes a bowlful of snow to melt in a cold house? When Tonya suggested melting it in a pot on the stove (after commenting in exasperation, "You're killing me, Virginia!"), I decided she was brilliant. That certainly speeded up the snow-melting process, and I was going great guns, outside gathering buckets of snow, when the pipes thawed and every tap in the house, which I had left open so I'd know when the pipes had unfrozen (or, as a friend of mine once said, unthawed), began to run full blast.

I raced back in to turn them off, just in time, which is when I realized that during the entire time my pipes had been frozen and I had no running water, the leak under my bathroom sink had continued to drip steadily. Tonya asked if I had put a bowl under it, but I proudly announced that I had used the bowl to gather up all the sodden items under the sink, and put a towel under the pipe. Patiently, she explained (after another muttered "You're killing me" under her breath) that if I put the items elsewhere and placed the bowl under the sink, it would catch all the drips, keep the cupboard dry, and eliminate the necessity of having to wring out the towel every few hours. What a woman.

I am now the happy possessor of running water, including under the sink, appropriate snow-melting technology, and crampons for my shoes. I'm ready for the next big freeze, which guarantees balmy weather until next year.

NOT A HAPPY CAMPER

I'VE NEVER HAD MUCH luck with camping. For one thing, I hate bugs, and wherever we choose to camp, about a gazillion various breeds of carnivorous biting insects converge upon us, smacking their proverbial lips (or jaws, or teeth, or whatever it is they have) with glee at the site of our bared flesh. Once in Trinidad we went to a beach called the Beach of the Thousand Steps; a lovely, romantic name, but one we quickly modified to "The Beach of the Billion Biting Bugs" after about thirty seconds on said beach. I had so many bites I couldn't shave my legs for a week without needing a blood transfusion.

Anyway, another reason I hate camping is that as I get older, I really can't sleep on the ground. I even have trouble sleeping in bed, but that's another story. In fact, the other day I approached my beloved and inquired as to his thoughts regarding a new bed. He looked at me, mildly puzzled. "But we just bought a new bed." "Sweetheart, that was two years ago, and it was a used motel bed. Very used (and I don't want to think about that in any more detail, thank you). We got it for $20.00." He smiled reminiscently. "Great deal, huh?" I gave up. The point is, I have bad hips (I mean, as in sleeping, among other things), so after sleeping for an hour or so, I have to turn over onto my back. Then my bad tailbone kicks in (so to speak - another story altogether), and I have to turn over onto the other side, where my bad shoulder acts up, until I feel like a rotisserie chicken on a bad day. As little actual peaceful sleep as I get, it's a wonder I'm not a homicidal maniac, although a few people might dispute that. So, sleeping on the hard ground is not my idea of a good time.

Then there's the cooking. I'm not an enthusiastic cook in a lovely kitchen with all the modern conveniences, much less in a campsite, or even better, what is euphemistically referred to as "dry camping" - somewhere out in the wilds with no running water or power other than that supplied by the car battery, looking nervously over my shoulder for various threatening beasts, cooking on a camp stove I'm convinced will blow up any minute (I cannot bring myself to trust propane). I always discover I've forgotten something crucial, like matches, or a can opener, or food. My husband took over the packing long ago in the interests of self-preservation. The cooking, too, on occasion.

Setting up the tent is always an adventure. In my youth, my family used an old army tent that was fiendishly complicated to erect. On one occasion I remember several aunts and uncles getting tangled up inside the thing as they tried to assemble it until it slowly, gracefully collapsed on top of them, necessitating an intricate and convoluted rescue mission by the remainder of the family. We, of course, have the latest in technological design in tents. All right, it's a quarter of a century old, but it keeps most of the bugs out, it's relatively easy to set up, and it has a fly sheet. I just wish it came with a feather bed and a maid.

Once we went to something in Wyoming called The Cirque of the Towers, which I prefer to call The Cirque de Soleil. My husband and his friends wanted to climb, and I was more adventurous back then, so I decided to go along. This involved a forced march up several thousand feet with my young daughter on my back, over switchbacks to a sheer rock wall sloping down to a lake with Arctic temperatures. I looked at my husband, who had already navigated the ninety-degree cliff as if he were crossing the street. After I became tired of arguing this was a feat beyond my capabilities, he took the baby, I removed my shoes and socks, and, clinging to the rock face as if it were my last hope, I slowly traversed the distance to the other side, spider-like.

It was hardly worth it; when we finally arrived at the campsite, it rained for three solid days. Our three friends had neglected to bring a tent, so five adults and a baby ate, slept, and played cards (well, the baby didn't play cards much) the entire time in a three-man tent until we gave up and had to repeat the tortuous route back down.

For some reason (I think it was because I had insisted, actually), one of our friends was carrying a bottle of maple syrup in his backpack, which naturally broke, dousing him in maple syrup for the entire trip back, and causing me to keep a nervous watch for bears. He still can't stand the smell of maple syrup. Somewhere along the way I tripped over a tree root and went down like a sack of wet cement; I discovered later I had chipped bits of bone off my shoulder, causing excruciating pain. As I say, I've never had much luck camping.

SILK PURSES

I HATE PURSES. The trouble is, most of them suffer from what I think of as the La Brea Tar Pit Syndrome. For those of you who are unaware, the La Brea Tar Pits, in or near Los Angeles, are places where a long time ago, unsuspecting animals (probably males who refused to ask for directions) wandered into what looked like solid ground, only to find they were rapidly sinking into sticky goo and died before they could extricate themselves. It's sad, I know, but the point is that every once in a while something, or its bones, oozes slowly to the surface and everybody gets excited, yanks it out and studies it. What, I hear you asking, has this got to do with purses? Everything; what you are trying to find in your purse has inevitably sunk to the bottom, never to be retrieved in this lifetime, while things like yucky hankies surface unexpectedly, and always when you least want them to.

I'm told you can't make a silk purse out of a sow's ear, but that doesn't stop the fashion industry from trying, or us women from buying them. I have so many shoes in my closet my husband calls me Imelda, but somehow I never seem to have the right purse to go with them. In fact, I only have about three: one black, one white, and one sort of tan one my beloved bought because he was puzzled that I only had two to go with all those shoes, and figured he'd help out. Of course, as all of us women know and no man ever seems to be able to figure out, black goes with everything, white is for spring and summer, and tan doesn't seem to go with anything in anybody's closet.

It took me years to get used to carrying a purse, which I only did under duress, so for a long time I forgot them everywhere I went, and then spent days replacing everything in the one I'd lost. I mean, what was the point? Men, the lucky dogs, have pants with pockets and therefore have no need for purses. Mind you, I just heard there's an actual syndrome that men get from sitting on their wallets that throws their backs out, so maybe there is justice. Is this a chauvinist plot, ladies, like high heels so we can't run, and the old Victorian hoop skirts that almost completely immobilized women for years?

Corsets that kept us short of breath and fainting constantly? And let's not even discuss nylons, those mid-century instruments of torture. I do get some satisfaction when I see a woman in nylons accompanied by a man wearing a tie, however.

I have to admit a purse was handy once I had kids, though, and got through the diaper bag stage. Every child needs a Kleenex or a handkerchief at least once in every church service, and woe betide the mother who hasn't got one – she is viewed as inadequate in her parenting skills, if not actually unnatural. If he has one, Dad's hanky is always so disgusting you wouldn't use it to wrap the dead pet hamster before burial, much less ask your child to blow his or her nose in it. Besides, the furor that erupts when said child is presented with Dad's hanky is enough to get you thrown out of church altogether; come to think of it, maybe that was the point.

Anyway, my purse, when I can find it, is still full of weird and wonderful things, as is almost any woman's – just ask to see the contents sometime. My husband absolutely refuses to look inside mine for anything. I'm not sure what he thinks is lurking there, even though I assure him there's nothing live or harmful. At least, I don't think there is. There are usually food items, though – you never know when you might need a packet of peanuts, or cheese and crackers. Until recently, I carried an extra pacifier for my daughter, who's nineteen. OK, she hasn't used one for about fifteen years, but if you had ever been present on the rare occasions she needed one and we didn't have one, you would understand; we've been known to search the street outside the house with flashlights at midnight in desperation while she howled inside as if we were torturing her.

We women always need pens, for those of you men who never carry them, and checkbooks, makeup, because heaven forbid we should get caught on a desert island without it and you might actually see what we look like, breath mints, safety pins so we can feel superior when some other woman's elastic gives out at a crucial moment and she hasn't got one, a wallet for the all-important credit cards so we can buy more shoes and purses, various coupons, address books, cell phones, reading glasses, extra vitamins, aspirin, band aids, first-aid kit (it's a BIG purse), flashlight, fire extinguisher – ok, I'm just joking about the fire extinguisher. I think. I haven't looked lately.

I suppose purses are a necessary evil for most of us. But why can't we have pockets?

Bowling Greens

A WHILE AGO, we were invited to a garden party where bocce ball was played. Having, to my knowledge, and much to my regret, not a drop of Italian blood, and being the least athletically inclined person I know, not to mention never having played the game before, I fully expected to be immediately eliminated from the competition, and so paid little attention when the rules were explained.

For any of you unfamiliar with the game, bocce ball involves throwing out a small wooden ball, called the jack, onto a lawn, and then trying to get your large, colored balls as close to the jack as possible; a simple game, really, and not one involving much athletic prowess, I thought, although I suppose it's really a challenge if one is actually trying to play well, as the lawn is uneven, and the balls can hit a lump or a hole and bounce in entirely the wrong direction. You play in teams of three or four people, but I use the term "team" loosely, because the point of the game is really to eliminate your teammates from the game as quickly and ruthlessly as possible by knocking your teammates' balls away from the jack with yours, and substituting your ball for theirs next to the jack. Well, I suppose it's actually a lot more complicated, really, and involves much strategy and skill, but as I said, I wasn't paying a lot of attention.

Now, I am not really a competitive person; I come into any game prepared to lose, as this is invariably what happens, especially if physical or mental activity of any kind is required. In fact, the last time I bowled, I was in my teens and was talked into going to an actual bowling alley by my best friend; I'm not sure why, as neither of us had ever tried it. She distinguished herself by forgetting to let go, and flinging herself down the alley, still attached to the ball, while I became overbalanced on my backswing and fell over backwards; we were asked not to return any time soon.

On this particular day, it was about 104 degrees in the shade, and as I am not fond of heat, the thought of standing around in the sun throwing things across the grass was not my idea of a good time. I determined to lose as quickly as possible so that I could return to the shade and drink iced tea, or pour it over my head, whichever felt better – maybe both. I therefore simply followed instructions and stood where they pointed, tossed the ball heedlessly in the general direction of the jack, when I could see it, and went back to stand in the shade.

The first round was a real nail-biter: everyone in my group won once, which meant we all had to play again until someone won again in a sort of sudden-death arrangement; I can tell you, there was going to be a sudden death from heat stroke if it didn't end soon. To my shock, I was informed that I had won the first, appropriately named, heat. This meant I had to advance to the next round, a thought that did not fill me with joy as it further delayed my retreat into the shade. I determined to concentrate on aiming away from the jack and so lose quickly. Unfortunately, it appeared that the more I aimed away from the jack, the closer I got to it. I decided to just toss the ball without thinking about it at all or aiming for anything, and to my dismay, advanced to the third round.

Now it was really getting hot, and I had run out of strategies of any sort; I tried aiming for my opponent's ball and not only missed it entirely, but again got closest to the jack, much to my chagrin. I was telling my husband I would be joining him shortly when a small crowd gathered around me to announce that I had won that round, too. Good Lord, I thought, gnashing my teeth; would the torture never end? And how the devil did one lose this game, anyway? No, I was told; I had actually won the entire game! I retired to the shade in bemused triumph, clutching my prize: an artistic toaster.

The very next day, I came upon a fat, sluggish gopher snake in the road while hiking, and while all snakes are, as far as I am concerned, potentially poisonous, even when I know they're not, and as I recognize that they have their place in that whole circle of life deal, I decided it would be better for him (and for my nervous condition, as I had nearly stepped on him and was still trying to get my breath back) if he were to move off the road and back into the grass from which he had sprung, I decided to toss rocks at him – well, small pebbles, really – in an attempt to get him to comply with my grand life-saving design. Not one of the pebbles I threw in his direction came even close.

Some days, you can't lose for winning…

Dog Daze

WE RECENTLY ACQUIRED a rescue dog – a pit bull cross – and while I've had bigger dogs, I have to say I've never had a stronger one. Trying to take him anywhere he doesn't want to go is like dragging a 200-pound anvil behind me (even though he only weighs 60 pounds), and my arm strength was clearly not up to the task. After a month and a half of mutual misery, however, I learned you can teach an old dog (that would be me) a few new tricks, and now he's the best-trained dog I've ever had.

He's also a total sweetie pie, unlike the reputation pit bulls have acquired; he loves to cuddle, and anytime we make a move to sit on the couch, he's there before us, taking up most of the space and trying his best to convince us he is a sixty-pound lapdog, where he definitely does not fit, despite his best efforts. As the acquisition of our couch involved a sidewalk pick-up in the dark of night, we're not too worried about any damage to it from his nails, so it's kind of cute. I have, however had to sew up the holes in my leggings three times now due to his enthusiasm.

The day I picked him up, I drove carefully home, talking to him reassuringly – that is, until I had to step rather forcefully on the brakes for a stop sign I didn't see until it was almost too late. The poor baby slammed into the dashboard, his nose firmly implanted in it, where he made not a sound – no whimper, not even a whine – and, not removing his head from where it had come to rest, simply rolled his eyes at me reproachfully, as if asking "Really? Is this how it's going to be from now on?" But he had his revenge; he threw up in the car just as we pulled into the garage.

He does have a number of peculiar habits. For instance, he loves shoes, especially mine, and takes every opportunity to declare his love by carting them off and having a little chew on them. I'm told he chews my shoes when I leave due to separation anxiety; he must have been really feeling traumatized the other day, because he destroyed two pair and dragged my back rest over to his bed, and I was only gone about an hour. I'm getting much more vigilant about putting the shoes away lately. My husband, who is constantly falling over them, is quite pleased with this development; I've told him if it bothered him that much, he should have just chewed on them once in a while to get the same result, but he seems reluctant to do so. The dog eschews chew toys altogether, although he did viciously attack an empty egg carton the other day. When I gave him a pink rubber squeaky pig, he hid from it, and has since studiously ignored it. Lately he's taken to dragging his food dish and various assorted other heavy plastic dishes full of water across the deck; I'm not sure what message this is meant to convey, but I suspect he'll let me know eventually.

And I don't want to say it's quiet around our house, but the other day when I turned on the radio, he barked at it. He also barks at the vacuum cleaner, but as he sees and hears it so rarely, he's to be excused for being frightened of it; I am, too. He takes to his bed and clings to his stuffed hedgehog on the unique occasions that it appears. The hedgehog is the third one so far; his affection for it, like my shoes, appears to be demonstrated by chewing it to bits. In the interests of economy, I've sewn this version up several times, and it currently sits next to his bed, stuffing spread liberally around the room.

It appears that he's an intellectual dog, too; one day recently I discovered he had dragged a magazine from the rack over to his bed and appeared to be perusing it in an interested manner. I'm not sure which article he was reading, but perhaps I should start previewing them for him. It was National Geographic, so I'm sure he was edified.

He also seems to be a yoga enthusiast; when he first wakes up in the morning, he stretches himself into a lovely "downward dog" pose, followed by the opposite, "upward dog" motion, then finishes with a general head-shake that has caused my beloved to christen him "The Flap-Eared Dog".

He rarely barks at visitors, as he loves company and the attention he gets; the only time I've heard him growl is in his sleep, and once recently he made a most peculiar howling noise in his dreams, a long sort of "Oooh woo woo" that sounded like the Hound of the Baskervilles. If he tries that on intruders, they'll never come back. And they'd better keep a tight hold on their shoes.

LEAKAGES

OVER THE COURSE OF our marriage, my beloved has often had to be away for long periods of time for various reasons, all of them plausible. I've decided if I were married to me, I'd have to be gone a lot, too, but that's another story. It seems that every time he leaves, I have a leakage issue, and I don't mean just the tears in my eyes.

The first time he left was soon after we were married. We happened to be living in Scotland in a rented flat, as they call them, and he had to go live on a drilling rig in the North Sea for a couple of weeks. So, the first night he was gone, in my loneliness at his absence, I decided to take a nice, hot, comforting bath. Imagine my surprise when I turned on the hot water and found myself staring stupidly at the tap, which had come off in my hand, and the geyser of hot water shooting all over the bathroom. That's panic, let me tell you. Here I am in a foreign country where they don't really even speak English (have you ever tried to decipher a Glaswegian brogue?), in a rented apartment, and I don't even understand American plumbing, much less an undoubtedly ancient Scottish system; they probably had it all on the wrong side, anyway, like their steering wheels. Fortunately, I found the master handle, or what-ever you call it, and called the landlord for the rest. I would have ample op-portunity over the next thirty years to learn the intricacies of plumbing the world over.

A short four years later I was eight months pregnant with our daughter and living in Placerville, California, where, the real estate agent assured us, we would be "above the fog line and below the snow line". My beloved had found an urgent reason to work in the Mojave Desert, and I woke up to two feet of snow (so much for the promises of real estate agents) and an odd sound coming from the garage. Curious, I went outside, trudged through the snow, and located the source of the noise: there was water spouting from the wall in two places. Unnerved by the apparent miracle (if Moses could get water from a rock, who was I to doubt water from a wall? Although I didn't remember an urgent need for water from this particular area of our establishment), I quickly located the main water supply and shut it off. I was getting better at this. When hubby returned a week or so later, he explained the copper pipes had frozen and burst, and cheerfully set about repairing them while I seriously considered taking a plumbing course.

Fast-forward a few more years, and we are taking a vacation in Colorado; I am, coincidentally enough, now eight months pregnant with our son, and having learned that vacations with my beloved usually involve camping in places where there is no running water (which ought to have been a relief, but makes life tricky when you have a toddler) and life is generally uncomfortable and makes me crabby, I insisted that while he and his buddies went off to climb some cactus-infested mountain, I would remain behind in a motel, with a pool, thank you very much. He agreed to the plan, and dropped us off at a likely-looking spot.

It was hot, and the pool sounded lovely, so my daughter and I changed into our suits and stepped in. That's when I noticed two things: First, the pool appeared to be filled with glacial melt-water, and second, it seemed to be covered with green algae and various other floating things that did not look at all appetizing, or even like anything I thought we would survive for more than two minutes. Granted, nothing was leaking or spouting out of a wall, but this was water I didn't want to be anywhere near. We beat a hasty retreat and I sulked in the hotel room for a while before getting violently ill and taking a bus ride for what I thought would be two blocks but ending up in another city altogether, but that's another story.

The next event occurred while my beloved was working in Africa (is there a trend here? Is it my imagination, or is he getting further and further away?) and I was living in Winnemucca, Nevada. The children were quite small, and all I remember is kneeling over a picnic bench in the garden, in the dark, trying to find the hose attachment while he shouted instructions over the phone at $10 a minute and water shot out over the lawn. Then there was the sprinkler system malfunction in Carson City, and … Perhaps my memory is mercifully fading. All I know is, there's snow on the ground, he's gone again, and I think I hear water dripping…

WELL MET

I MET MY HUSBAND in high school, which is not so unusual; what's a little different is that I met him because of John Lennon.

I had quite the crush on John Lennon, but it was a long-distance relationship; so long-distance, in fact, that he knew nothing of my existence. Still, when I heard an English accent across the classroom, I responded like a good hunting dog, nose (and ears) up, until I tracked down the source of the accent. Unfortunately, it wasn't John Lennon, but he was still English – an exchange student - and I fell for him.

Also unfortunately, at least from my perspective anyway, was the unlucky circumstance that, in the short time he had been in the country, he had already managed to secure a girlfriend. It was a pattern that would emerge more than once, but I'm getting ahead of my story.

I contented myself with sharing my yogurts with him (in point of fact, I hated yogurt and only brought them for him, but my attempt at luring him astray with curdled milk products was unsuccessful). I was so shy, and he so faithful, that we ended up with a friendship of sorts; the closest we got to a romantic encounter took place at a mental asylum, but that's another story. A short one, with a disappointing end; all I got to do was make him a daisy chain.

Much to my chagrin, he returned to England without me. We wrote each other for a couple of years, and then I decided to hitchhike all over Europe with my best friend – in winter. I looked up my English friend at Leeds, where he was attending university, but he had another American girlfriend. Interestingly, at a party I attended at his house, a guy neither of us knew came up to us as we stood talking and asked if we were married. The glares he got from both of us, for different reasons, sent him scurrying from the room. My girlfriend and I stayed there for two weeks while I pined for the fjords with no success and my girlfriend railed against Leeds, which she dubbed "The Armpit of the World" (it's really not that bad – she was just cranky and interested in seeing more of England than a depressed industrial town), until I finally had to admit defeat and tearfully board a bus for home – and a plane, eventually, of course; it's hard to find a bus line that goes from England to America.

Fast forward several years – ten, in fact. I decided to attend a summer session of law school in Cambridge, England, as it was actually cheaper than my law school, even including the plane fare. Go figure. By now, my beloved (at least, my future beloved) and I had completely lost touch, but as I had a couple of weeks to kill before classes started, I decided to look for my John Lennon substitute. There's not enough space to go into my clever sleuthing methods (basically, I asked at the post office and then got a lucky break from a former neighbor, then had to get past his mother, who thought I was the first "American floozy" he had dated in the States - okay, I did have space); suffice to say, I hunted him down once again, only to find he had yet another girlfriend - an English one this time.

Nevertheless, we talked until 2:00 in the morning, saw each other quite a bit for romantic walks along the river Cam, and had 24 hours in Paris before he left for Mozambique. A month later, he had ditched his girlfriend, I had dumped my boyfriend (oh – did I forget to mention I'd finally found a boy-friend?), and he asked me to marry him on a trip over to the States.

After all this, you'd think I would have gratefully fallen to my knees and blessed him for finally coming to his senses (or for not giving up in exhaus-tion, at least), but no; he had to ask three times and go back to England before I made up my mind, at which point I (being careful with money) sent him a telegram stating succinctly "The answer is yes", and he had to sell everything he owned, including his precious saxophone and sailboard, which was proof positive he loved me, to make the trip back here to marry me and take me immediately back to Britain, where we began our adventurous married life.

After about ten years and two children of hearing me remark that he only married me for a green card, and it must be a marriage of convenience (by this time he had his citizenship), one day he calmly remarked in response that if he spent his life searching, he could not possibly have found a less convenient marriage, and I began to think it was the real thing.

And he may not be a Beatle, but he's still got the accent.

I Had It All Thought Out

IT ALL STARTED WHEN I went to get some superglue. Well, I suppose it actually started a little before that, when I went on a major cockroach massacre, and in my frenzy, broke a small tile. Then I needed the superglue, so off I went.

I really had no intention of buying a mattress, but there it was. Although the mattress was squished into a box about 18" by 48", it was very heavy, and even though it had wheels and a handle, I had to have someone get it down for me and into my car. I then suddenly realized that it might not fit into my car, but had the brilliant idea of putting the front passenger seat down, which worked a treat. Not having planned on buying a mattress, I had of course not measured my bed, but then, even if I had been planning on buying a mattress, I probably would not have measured. Such things do not occur to me, and even if they did, I would pay them no attention, being of the "Somehow I'll make it work" mindset.

I was on my way home when I looked more closely at the box and decided I had the wrong mattress. Rats! I would have to take it back and get the right one. Muttering under my breath, I went up to bed, exhausted by my efforts and determined to attack the issue the following day.

When my friend Tonya called the following afternoon to inquire what I was up to, I recounted my sad saga and admitted that I had as yet done nothing about returning the cursed thing, feeling overcome by it all. She generously offered to help, and I said I would pick her up so that she could assist me in getting it out of the car and back into the store. As I was leaving, it occurred to me that the bed being in the front passenger seat, my car being a two-door, and Tonya having recently undergone knee surgery, cramming her into the back seat might not be a good idea, so we agreed to meet at the store.

Upon arrival, while waiting for Tonya, I idly glanced at the box and discovered there was a good chance that this was, in fact, the correct bed, even though, as I explained to the infinitely patient Tonya when she showed up, it looked a lot more square than the one I had chosen. Demonstrating the aforesaid patience, she pointed out that most mattresses were squarish, but just in case, we went into the store to verify the matter, and confirmed that, yes indeed, I had the correct mattress.

We returned to the house with it once again, and here is where I felt particularly clever; I had really thought this bit out carefully. Rather than drag the very heavy mattress up all 53 stairs, which might well result in the mattress and I tumbling back down said stairs with injury to us both, I had another plan: I would instead drag it gradually up the side of the hill. On the record, I feel compelled to point out that Tonya had repeatedly offered to help me carry the mattress either up the stairs or up the hillside, whichever I preferred, but being mindful of her knee surgery I gallantly and stubbornly refused her help.

This would explain why I was dragging a mattress that probably weighed 75 pounds up a grassy slope in 90-degree heat while wearing a skirt, while Tonya filmed me doing so, having for some reason found the whole episode funny. I was nearly to the top when the handle suddenly broke free from the cardboard box, and the thing rolled down the hill, bounced over the curb, and came to rest in the road as I desperately attempted to throw myself bodily onto it in an effort to stop its progress but failed miserably. Tonya asked if I had intended to ride the thing down, but with my dignity intact, I ignored her.

Just at this juncture, my wonderful neighbor James showed up like a knight in shining armor, and seeing my predicament, heroically shouldered the mattress in one arm, and carried it up all 53 stairs for me. What a man!

The next day I managed to wrestle the thing onto my bed and slice open the 40 layers of plastic, whereupon the mattress began to emit alarming hissing noises; after checking carefully for snakes, I watched in some apprehension as it inflated itself and spread over my bed all by itself. I have retained and posted in my house the sign that came with the mattress, reading "Please allow 48 hours for full recovery"; I'm sure it will come in handy very soon, my life being what it is. And I now have a lovely mattress that's so high I need a footstool to get into bed, but hey, it's all part of the plan…

On Aging, or Men: O, Pause!

WHY IS IT THAT the older I get, the more everyone mumbles? When I try to watch a DVD at home, I spend most of the movie demanding querulously of my husband, "WHAT did he say? Why does everyone have to mumble? Doesn't anyone know how to enunciate anymore?" which of course means that while I'm complaining, we both miss the next few paragraphs of dialogue, and now neither one of us knows what's going on. The other night I went to a choir concert and had to wonder what the world was coming to when they announced the next song was "Rachel the Trumpet Blower"; the fact that it was actually, as the program announced, "Bridge Over Troubled Water" reassured me somewhat, but I still can't understand why people don't speak up. I spend a lot of time these days very puzzled, trying to sort out things people say that make absolutely no sense, until I realize I've misheard what they've actually said.

Of course, it has nothing to do with my advancing age or the fact that I can't see anything without glasses or very long arms, or both; they just print everything in the tiniest type possible now to save space, I'm sure. I can't read the backs of aspirin bottles even with my glasses on. There's probably nothing there I need to know, anyway, just like directions in general, which I rarely read until I'm either finished doing whatever I'm doing (just out of curiosity), or I get stuck or something goes wrong because I haven't read the directions. When I needed to read off the number on my router to someone the other day, I had to wear not one but two pairs of glasses to make it out.

A while ago my husband had to dye his hair for a play; because he's not the kind of guy who's ever dyed his hair for any reason and also doesn't like to read directions, he asked me for advice. As a person with extensive (past) experience with cheap hair dye who also doesn't like to read directions, I responded nonchalantly, "Oh, I just leave it on about 30 minutes and then rinse it out." Unconvinced for some reason, he persisted in reading the directions, then announced, "It says here to rinse it out after 10 minutes." Really? That explains a lot. Maybe that's why my daughter keeps urging me to have my hair dyed professionally, and why it's three different colors.

I remember my sainted grandmother commenting that as she got older, she couldn't remember words, and in a spirit of scientific observation, remarked that "the nouns go first". Her eyesight wasn't too good by then, either; she used a huge magnifying glass to read. My parents use it now, and I'm reserving my place next in the line for it. She told us that one morning she thought she saw a spider in the corner and just about beat what turned out to be a dustball to death with the broom. My grandmother was a remarkable woman in many ways, but my favorite story about her involved her desire to help out when my father owned the Horse Creek Store. She sat, slowly and laboriously stamping prices on boxes of canned goods in a corner, while a friend of ours watched. After a while, he observed, "Good help must be hard to find. By the time she gets them marked, the prices will have gone up!"

And then there are the issues peculiar to women. Some call it a power surge; the more delicate among us, a "glow", I only know that upon occasion, usually when it's most inconvenient, and for no apparent reason, I suddenly experience a mini-fever that results in the irresistible need to strip off all my clothes and stand outside in a howling gale, which is generally a bad idea on a number of counts, not least of which would be the numbing shock my co-workers would experience, not to mention the general public or the congregation when I happen to be in church when it strikes. So far I have managed to resist the urge, but I make no guarantees. My long-suffering beloved is convinced a roomful of similarly situated women as myself could solve the energy crisis; he swears he can feel the heat radiating off my body in nuclear meltdown quantities. And they wonder why we're cranky at times!

Cherry Picking

I CANNOT HELP BUT wonder: why do so many who call themselves Christians spend so much time carefully calculating, down to the minute, when they believe the "Rapture", or the second coming of Christ, will occur, and so little time focusing on his first coming? Especially when Jesus himself said that end times would come like a thief in the night; when he told stories of people being unprepared for it; when he himself said no one, not even the Son of Man (Jesus himself) knew the day or the hour? Why is this an important topic, other than for the general admonition that none of us know the time of our death, and therefore ought to be busy doing God's work for as long as we are able to do so?

Why is it that so many sermons, especially those preached on religious radio stations, focus on the Old Testament, the Epistles (letters written presumably by later followers of Jesus, given the timing of their authorship), the book of Revelation, or even on the speaker's opinions on any of the above, rather than on the actual words attributed to Jesus himself? When was the last time we actually read the Gospels for ourselves? What are we afraid of?

We appear to have regressed to the Middle Ages, when people had to listen to others' interpretations of the Bible, or learn the stories from the stained-glass windows in church, either because they were illiterate, or the Bible was written in a language they could not understand, such as Latin, or because they were forbidden by law to read or possess their own copies of the Bible. Why is it that a nation of such educated, independent free-thinkers, who have the privilege of being able to read and decide for ourselves, instead rely on others, such as pastors, popes, or St. Augustine, no matter how fine a person they may be, to tell us what the Bible says and means?

I believe that, if we read the Gospels for ourselves, we will find a man whose harshest criticisms are reserved for the religious leaders of his day; the holiest, most revered, most learned, and least humble men of the time. What does this tell us?

Jesus sometimes said shocking, inconsistent things; he was fully human, and finding his way. He was not afraid to do so; why should we be? Rather than parsing every reference to "end times", why not spend some time discussing what he may have meant by some of these statements and how they apply to our lives today, what the historical context might have been? Why spend so much effort attempting to make everything "fit" and be consistent, if it appears not to be so? There is much to be learned, if one is so inclined and keeps an open mind. Why can we not listen and learn from each other, without judgment even when we disagree, rather than fight, condemn others as heretics, and distance ourselves from those who hold different opinions from our own?

If we read the Gospels, we note a man of compassion and love, urging us over and over again to not be afraid, to love one another, not to judge each other, to care for widows and orphans, to find freedom in trusting God as a loving parent; to trade riches on earth and others' good opinion of us for joy in God and each other. I would suggest that these very lessons are the reason so little is said about the Gospels, the stories of Jesus' life: what he told us to do, what he demonstrated with his own life and death about how to live, is such a difficult message to even comprehend, much less to live, is so radical in its simplicity and counter-cultural message, that we find it much easier to calculate how long it is to the Last Days – how many angels can dance on the head of a pin – than to endeavor to act on his instructions. He told us that following him would be difficult, that it would involve sacrifice of all we hold most dear – our lives, our lifestyle, our riches, others' good opinions of us – and it is so much easier to quibble over the finer points of the Old Testament, much as the religious leaders of his day did, than to cease judging each other and begin to practice loving one another.

Yet, if one advocates focusing on Jesus' message of love and care for our brothers and sisters, which he demonstrates in the story of the Good Samaritan is everyone, especially the most marginalized people in society, which I suggest in our day, much like his, would be the elderly, the homeless, the mentally ill, the developmentally disabled, the imprisoned, alcoholics, drug addicts, prostitutes – the list is nearly endless – in short, the people Jesus spent the majority of his time with and was constantly criticized for doing so – one is accused of "cherry-picking" verses to suit one's own agenda. I must ask: which of us does not cherry-pick? Do any of us sit down, for instance, with the book of Leviticus and decide to begin focusing on verses that advocate the stoning to death of disobedient or disrespectful children? Do we enforce, unless we are observant Jews, the strict dietary laws advocated in the Old Testament? Is it "cherry-picking" to decide to put such verses into historical context, and concentrate instead on instructions for living a life of compassion and caring for others? Did Jesus own a nice house in a desirable neighborhood, a BMW, and an extensive wardrobe? How much do our lives resemble his? Did he not urge us to observe the lilies of the field, that they neither toil nor spin, yet are clothed more beautifully than Solomon in all his splendor?

How did Jesus spend his time on earth? Healing the sick, feeding the hungry, teaching us to love and serve each other by word and by example, to observe the spirit of the law rather than the letter of the law, which condemns us all. He knowingly broke the religious rules of his day, and taught us guidelines to use to figure things out for ourselves rather than slavishly following the dictates of someone else's ideas about what is right. But instead, so many Christians go to the Old Testament, which is full of God's love if you look for it, and choose passages of judgment, death and destruction, representative of the values and vicissitudes of that time, to use as a model for their lives. The reasons for this, I believe, have more to do with psychology and sociology than theology, but how are such choices not "cherry picking" as well? If we are going to choose passages from the Bible to live by, I would so much rather use examples of Jesus' life; otherwise, why call ourselves Christians? Would not the world be a better place if we modeled our lives after his acts of love and compassion than the "eye-for-an-eye" vengeance often exacted by Old Testament laws?

It's a hard life to live, Jesus', and he told us that it would be, in no uncertain terms. He never promised us riches or comfort or popularity among our peers for following his example – quite the opposite. He said, "Blessed are the peacemakers", but have we ever gently, humbly, and lovingly told a friend or a group of co-workers we could not, in good conscience, gossip or say unkind things about another, unpopular and unpleasant co-worker? Do we ever defend someone we find truly obnoxious? He told us we would be persecuted, not for shunning people unlike ourselves and judging them as inferior and unworthy of our time and attention, or even, God help us, condemning them as "unchristian", but, I believe, for loving them, feeding and housing them, defending them, and sharing their lives. Do I do this? Not enough, but I aspire to it, as I think Jesus meant us to.

I choose to "cherry pick" the hard verses that lovingly demand that I give of my time, my wealth, my talents, my heart, to serve God by serving my fellow human beings rather than spend too much of my time in philosophical debates about if, when, and in what manner the end times will come. I know my own personal end time is guaranteed to come, at a time I will not, in all likelihood, know in advance, and that's enough for me. I do know a lifetime isn't long enough to do everything I'm meant to be doing.

I believe Jesus is with us now, as he said he would be, every time we help someone in need, every time we smile at a stranger, visit someone who is sick or in prison, every time we recognize each others' humanity as being exactly the same as our own, and refuse to judge them, despite a lifetime of being taught to do so. It's a work in progress for me, and will be, with varying degrees of success and failure, until I die, as long as I try my best to follow Jesus' example and read his words. If that's cherry picking, so be it.

FRISKY

WE FINALLY CONVINCED my elderly parents to take a cruise to Alaska. Once we got over the panic of the fact that their passports had expired, and spent enormous amounts of time and money getting certified copies of their birth certificates expedited to them in time for the trip (my sister remaking along the way that she felt sure their births had been recorded on parchment, and that was why it was taking so long), we breathed a sigh of relief and got them on the plane, although I have to say that at their age, even though they do pretty well, I wanted to pin their names and destinations to their coats and ask for them to be accompanied through the airport.

We agreed to take care of their dog while they were away, even though my sister and I share a definite case of sibling rivalry with said dog; she's really pretty sweet (I mean the dog, although my sister is pretty sweet, too), but they spoil her (the dog) like they never spoiled us – or even the grandkids, for that matter. In fact, I believe we have just cause for envy; my mother recently remarked, "Today is her birthday – the day we brought her home – the happiest day of our lives." I felt compelled to remark, "Really? Beats out the births of all of your children and your wedding day, huh?" at which she looked a bit sheepish, it's true.

So, once we got my parents on the plane, we took the dog back to the hotel with us, where my husband watched her while I went for a swim. I came back, refreshed, and took a shower. After a while I idly inquired of my beloved where the dog was (she likes to hide under chairs), and we suddenly realized she was missing; needless to say, panic ensued. All I could think was that we would be struck off the child list completely if ANYTHING happened to that dog. So I threw on a towel and ran down the hotel halls, frantically calling her name. It wasn't until someone later kindly explained it to me that I realized why a somewhat scantily clad woman running down a hotel corridor exclaiming "Frisky!!" (the dog's name) might raise a few eyebrows.

Thoughts of dog-napping (and I don't mean sleeping) crossed my mind; then I worried about her getting outside and being hit by a car, or of me roaming the halls on both floors, endlessly looking for her as she crossed to another hall feet away from me, but I was spared fears of her immediate death, kidnapping, and permanent loss when I spotted signs of her and was able to track her – by following the poop scattered like bread crumbs down the hall, heading straight to the breakfast area. I should have known; the dog does love to eat. She wasn't having breakfast, fortunately; someone had taken her to the front desk, where I found her happily wagging her tail. I retraced my steps, picking up poop in a Kleenex for later disposal and muttering under my breath, but all was right with her world – food, an indoor bathroom, attention from strangers, and all the comforts of home – what else could a dog ask for?

My beloved later received a text message from a friend who had heard the story, inquiring how "Frisky" was doing, and I have reason to believe he was NOT referring to the dog; my beloved replied succinctly that "her tail was up". Clearly I won't live this one down for a while, and it's all that dog's fault.

Bits and Pieces

SOME OF YOU may know that I am not the most handy home-repair person on the planet. However, having had some success with said home repairs, which I must truthfully admit consisted of supergluing the fish to the shower-curtain-thingy - that is, the plaster of Paris fish attached to the metal thing that holds up the curtain, not a real fish, naturally - I was feeling pretty confident, so I decided to finally install the little solar lights that have been rolling around in my trunk for the past, oh, let's see, about three months. They were accompanied in the trunk by the heavy metal stakes my friend Tonya insisted I buy, as they would be more substantial than the rather pathetic plastic ones the lights came with. I was a bit worried, truthfully, that the combination of heavy iron stakes and glass lights in the trunk might yield less than optimum results.

But recently the weather dropped below 110 degrees, so I decided to give it a whirl. And I must say, they looked lovely by the time I finished installing them. Unfortunately, they didn't light up. Tonya suggested there might be some sort of tab to be removed, but a cursory look on my part did not reveal anything. I know it was a cursory look, because when I happened to mention the issue to my neighbor James, he found the tab at a glance and proceeded to remove all of them, and now they actually light my path in a quite useful way, besides just being decorative. Thank you, James.

Encouraged by this success, I enlisted Tonya's aid in my next project: putting up a small curtain rod and valance over the kitchen sink. As a side note, it's amazing how useless a valance is; it neither blocks the light nor ensures any kind of privacy, but hey, it's decorative, right? I had to borrow Tonya's electric drill, and Tonya for instructional purposes.

The first lesson was How to Be Sure the Drill Is Set on Safety So That We Do Not Accidentally Drill Ourselves Into the Hospital, which was quite useful. Next, we moved on to How To Measure Distances So Many Times You Want To Give Up the Project Entirely. And even after it appeared that I had measured and re-measured from every possible angle, it was a little bit off. Who knew there would be so much measuring involved?! I am not the most patient of souls in this area – I'm much more the "eyeball it and whack it up there" sort of person, I'm afraid, than the "measure twice, cut once" type – which is not, I may add, a good trait when it comes to home improvements, and it shows.

Up and down the footstool I traipsed, while Tonya gave the occasional instruction, such as "It's a really good idea to put the drill on safety while you're hauling it up and down like that." At one point, I became panic-stricken, searching madly for a missing screw; I counted them over and over and was almost reduced to cleaning the floor to look for it, when Tonya intervened, calmly remarking, "Now, let's think about it. Where might that screw be, logically speaking?" But I hate riddles, and subtle hints are lost on me; she had to not only bring this horse to water, but shove her nose into it, metaphorically speaking: I had already screwed the screw into place in the curtain rod holder-upper thing (technical terms are not my strong suit). After a few minor adjustments, and several re-drills of holes, the curtain and its rod look just dandy, although there is a slight lean to the right.

I next moved on to the bathroom in my office, which had no toilet paper roll holder thingy. How hard could it be?

Really hard, as it turns out. Having by now succumbed to my drill envy and bought one of my very own at Ace Hardware, I proudly toted my brand spanking new drill, and all its accessories, down to the office. I proceeded to drill a hole in the wall – so far, so good – but the second hole did not go smoothly. It felt as if I were trying to drill through concrete, and when I tried to put the little plastic thingy in, it stoutly refused to be inserted. Consumed by rage at my failure to even drill holes, I left everything in the sink, where it remained for several days, and went back to work in a huff. And it stayed that way until the day I came in and noticed that it had magically been installed in my absence by my workmate's wife. Thank you, Susan. Some people have all the talent, while others of us – like to surround ourselves with talented people.

Mr. Congeniality

I'M TRYING TO FIGURE out where we went wrong with our son. Don't get me wrong – he's a wonderful, intelligent young man, in spite of his up-bringing with us – but he doesn't seem to be able to get the hang of human interaction. Come to think of it, the fact that we raised him might have a lot to do with it.

This wasn't clear to us for some reason until he went away to college. We were a bit surprised that he didn't party every night like most freshmen, but then, he had been the designated driver in high school, so we weren't too terribly shocked at his lack of a social life.

It's true he was busy studying chemistry and physics, but surely he had some time to socialize? I will admit I was a bit disturbed when he called me on a Friday night (he is occasionally given to phone calls home wherein he will ask random questions that occur to him, such as "Mom, is it really possible for someone to be paying $50,000 a month in child support?" Yes, dear, especially if you make $50 million a year, and even likely; or "Hey mom, what's another word for a crypt? I think it has a lot of silent ph's in it." Sarcophagus? "No, I don't think so." It turned out to be sepulcher, but really, what 19 year old asks these things, especially on a Friday night? Besides mine, I mean) to enquire indignantly, "Mom, do you have any idea how much lint collects in dryers? How come nobody ever cleans out the lint trap in a laundromat dryer?" Probably because, like him until that year, they've never even heard of a lint trap, much less been able to locate one on a dryer.

Slowly, the tales of his possibly genetic inability to communicate effectively with the opposite sex began to emerge, mostly through his sister. The first story we heard was "Toaster Girl". This was an interaction that took place in the cafeteria; apparently, a nice girl came up to our son and remarked that the toaster was really hot. He related that he looked at her, amazed at the inanity of her remark, and replied, "Yeah, they tend to do that," and walked away. He told us he realized ten seconds after the words had come out of his mouth that it had sounded a lot harsher than he meant it to, but by then she was gone and he was too embarrassed to find her and apologize.

Next was "Breakfast Girl" (he never gets a chance to know them well enough to learn their names, for obvious reasons). Being antisocial, he always got to breakfast early enough to find the one table that seats only two people so he didn't have to talk to anyone, but one time, a girl dared to sit down opposite him and actually engage him in conversation.

She was a lovely girl (we knew this because when we went down to visit him, he pointed her out in the cafeteria, hissing, "Don't look at her! No eye contact!"), but it never seems to have occurred to him to further the acquaintance by asking her name, even after she lingered in the hallway with him after breakfast; he was apparently struck by the idea after a friend of his pointed out that she might have been waiting for him to ask her out, but by then she was long gone.

He told me later that he met her at the cafeteria entrance by chance one day, and she "sort of forced" him to take her phone number. What would he do if he didn't like her, I wonder?

Then came the "Vampire Incident". He explained that he liked to get to class early, before anyone else had arrived, and sit up in a far corner by himself, listening to music on his I-Pod. One day a girl came in, noticed him in his aerie, and asked helpfully if he would like her to turn on the light, to which he replied forcefully, "No! I prefer the darkness!" She apparently immediately vacated the area, never to be seen again. Will I ever have grandchildren?

The last event was when a girl from his dorm, a very nice girl, he says, knocked on his door and asked if he wanted to go to lunch with her. In the middle of an exciting part of his book, and anxious to finish the chapter, he replied "No." and shut the door in her face, realizing immediately thereafter that his response might not have been calculated to make him voted "Mr. Congeniality" on campus.

Perhaps I should create a dating service for nice young men with no social skills, and sign up my son as my first customer. Since he gets his difficulties from me, however, that might not be such a great idea.

O HOLY NIGHT

USUALLY IT'S MY father's duty to be sick over the holidays, but a few years ago we broke with tradition and I got sick instead.

Fortunately, possibly through some intuitive sense, I got things done early and was more or less ready for Christmas, and since it wouldn't be Christmas for me without attending midnight mass, we dragged ourselves out in the cold and went.

We were a bit late, which meant there were no seats left; we resigned ourselves to standing throughout, but a kindly usher took pity on my sniveling and trotted us up to the very front of the church to some apparently empty seats. Just as I was about to sit down, the sweet elderly lady nearest to me whacked me smartly on the knee with her hymnal and snapped, "That seat is taken!"

Broken but unbowed, we retreated to the back of the church where the ever-intrepid usher sallied forth once again with us in tow, elbowed two rows of communicants to one side, and wedged us into the ends of the pews.

Thus happily ensconced, I was singing (or more accurately, croaking) along with the choir to my favorite carols when I was overcome by a particularly lovely version of "O Holy Night", which in conjunction with my cold, forced me to reach behind and beneath me for the hankie in my purse. Unfortunately, by then we were holding lit candles, and I nearly set first myself and then my seatmate afire as I groped around on the floor.

After profuse apologies and a little judicious sprinkling of holy water, the crisis was averted and we all got back to the service. I once knew a female pastor who actually did set her hair on fire during a baptism; a memorable event for all concerned.

My teenage son, who is not much of a churchgoer (he has had since infancy a tendency to fall asleep and snore – loudly – in church) and had until now been happily playing solitaire on his cell phone, suddenly raised it aloft as if in offering or supplication. "What are you DOING?" I hiss in his ear.

"Looking for reception!" he hisses back, as if it ought to be obvious. "You're in CHURCH!" I hiss in response. "I know," he says gloomily, "No reception."

This is actually an improvement on former days, when he was renowned for running up the aisle and trying to rip the altar cloth off in one fell swoop like a magic trick – and failing, I might add - knocking the paschal candle flying as two grown men make a leap for it, and finishing up by lodging himself in the bishop's chair as if he belonged there.

His sister, however, gets the prize: When she was about two years old, she managed, all in one service, to fall into the organ, hitting most of the keys, toss her baggie of toast from the back pew where I had hoped (in vain), to contain her, while all the parishioners watched it sail to the front of the church, probably placing bets on whom it would land, and then, deciding it was too hot to remain clothed, try to pull her dress off over her head, get it stuck behind her head, and proceeded to howl like the hounds of hell, which was not really appropriate given the setting. It certainly did make for a stressful morning in church.

I would come home, bedraggled and fuming, and my heathen husband would inquire sweetly, "Have a spiritually uplifting morning, dear?" while I thrust the children at him and stalked off like a demented escapee searching desperately for the asylum.

Alleluia!

Mixed Semaphores, So to Speak

I'VE ALWAYS CONFUSED certain expressions (as opposed to wearing confused expressions, another specialty of mine). My personal favorite "oopsy" appears to be spoonerisms: I once referred to a meal as "flan-tried pout" with a "crimp and shrab" salad, and remarked that a guy in a robbery had a "shawed-off sotgun"; you really have to watch out for THOSE guys. But my little slips are as nothing compared to my mother's talents, whose mixed quips are legendary, at least in our family.

My mother is wonderfully intelligent, and has a gift for grammar, but for some reason, she mixes her metaphors. Usually, people who are not native English speakers do this, and as she grew up speaking English (unlike, say, Sam Goldwyn), we've never been able to figure out why she does it, but it can certainly be entertaining.

She's creative, too; it's not just the usual "Take the bull by the tail". No, my mother goes for the really confusing mix-ups, like "There's a flaw in the ointment." An artist friend was so impressed with that one she illustrated it for me. When mom tried to console me after a boyfriend broke up with me, she said bracingly, "Don't worry dear, there are plenty of other fish on the beach." I'm still trying to figure out what I was supposed to do with dead fish. Although they might well have been an improvement, come to think of it.

The other day she remarked to someone that her grandson had just "bought another one of those fancy IHOP things". We stood for a while, contemplating this modern generation of teenagers that can afford to purchase entire food franchises, when I realized she was talking about my seventeen-year old and meant "I-POD", and we straightened that one out.

Then there was the dream she described: "Well, all I remember is there were underclothes police beating people with their nightclubs."

Or, "He had a mind like a clam." "What, mom, do you mean he was close-minded?" No, she said, holding her hands together at the wrists and opening and closing them like a, well, a clam. We finally ascertained she meant "A mind like a steel trap". Of course – same unhinged principle, after all.

If she was confused and couldn't make up her mind, she was "sitting in the middle of the fence"; if you're being hard on yourself, she might tell you to "stop castrating yourself". If you're in a bad mood, you've "got a burr in your bonnet", and if it's crowded, you might be "crammed in there like oysters" - or some other kind of dead mollusk, perhaps.

If it's difficult, it's "like pulling hen's teeth". If you don't like something, don't be rude and "curl up your nose at it", and doing something the hard way would be "taking the mountain to the molehill". And my all-time favorite, the Oscar award-winner for bringing up mental pictures and showing absolute confusion, "Running around like a chicken with his legs cut off". Sometimes I know exactly what she means, which is a little concerning.

Occasionally after my mother makes a remark, there's a little silence while we all ponder the deeper, more obscure inner meaning. Then we figure it out, there's a collective sigh of relief, and we all move on. Except, possibly, my mother, who occasionally knows there's something wrong, but can't quite work out what it might be.

My husband started doing it after we'd been married a while; I think it's infectious. One day after some strenuous exercise he remarked the blood was "cursing through" his veins; that brought up some pictures, I can tell you. Another night as he fell asleep, he confessed he was having trouble concentrating, and his words were "wandering out of their sentences". Trying to calm a person down became "smoothing their wrinkled feathers".

Even my daughter got into the act; it's obviously genetic. She tried to comfort us one night by beginning, "If it's any constellation to you..." Speaking of which, she once excitedly pointed out "O'Brien's Belt" in the night sky. Sometimes I think I am living in an alternate universe.

I began to notice other people doing it, too. Recently a friend remarked that a person in town "Knew where all the sacred cows were buried." Ew. Someone else related that a person doing something risky was "skating on very thin cheesecake". Another friend came up with the very accidentally creative "He's cutting off his feet to spite his face", and she and I once argued for a while whether the correct expression was "Like a boat out of water" or "a duck out of water" before someone had to intervene with "a fish out of water". My sister recently contributed "That ship has left the building". To this day I don't know if, when I'm unwanted, I'm a third wheel or a fifth wheel; isn't that a trailer?

Thanks, mom, for all the love and entertainment over the years – you're the best ever, and that ain't whistlin' down the wind. In the dark? Or whatever.

MY LITTLE TOWN

I LOVE my town.

How can you not love living in a town where the local park has signs warning you to "Beware of Mountain Lions"; below it is "Beware of Rattlesnakes", and the deer roam free down the city streets? When I hike on my lunch hour, I see the same people most days. We don't know each other, but we notice if somebody misses a day or two, and we're relieved when we see each other again. There's an older gentleman in a wheelchair who fishes; I don't fish, but we exchange comments on the weather and he keeps me informed as to whether he'll be having bass for dinner that night. I worry if I don't see him for a while.

This is a place where you rarely need to wait in line at the Post Office, and even if you do have to wait a minute or two, it's all right, because you know everyone in line with you and it's a good time to catch up on the news. There's always parking for everything, with no meters, and even the two-hour limit is negotiable if the parking enforcement guy has a day off.

And of course you'll know what his day off is, because in a small town, everyone knows what you do before you even think about doing it. It tends to put most people on their best behavior. Those who aren't, well, everyone knows who they are, and there's a surprising amount of tolerance for them, too; after all, without them, what would there be for everyone else to talk about? My mother once said the same things happen here as in the big city; it's just that here, you know everyone.

A lot of us rent videos from the same locally owned place we've always rented them from; they know when you live downriver and give you an extra day or two to send the movies up with the mailman, or a neighbor who happens to be going into town. Try that at Blockbuster.

It stirred up a major controversy a few years ago when we got our third traffic light; most folks said two was more than enough, and if somebody didn't stop this out-of control growth, why, we were all just gonna have to move out as a protest and find someplace less crowded - like maybe Alaska. But most people calmed down after a while, and accepted with resignation that third light, although if we have to wait more than thirty seconds for it to change, mutterings can be heard about traffic lights being a Communist plot. Some of us remember when we used to have cattle drives down Main Street; now that was a traffic jam!

Getting directions becomes an adventure in small-town history. "Well, you go out past the old Johnson place (there hasn't been a Johnson near it for at least fifty years, but by gum, they used to own it, so it will always be the old Johnson place), turn left where they used to have that general store before it burned down..." If you have two or more old-timers together, heaven help you, because there will inevitably be some heated argument. "That ain't where the old general store used to be; it was downriver four miles or more." "I'm not talkin' about the old Smith store, I'm talkin' about the Jones store." "Well, you couldn't hardly call that a store, that was just a little café." "They sold dry goods." You get the drift. But not the directions. "Oh, that's easy. You turn left over the Walker Bridge, but make sure it's the FIRST Walker Bridge, not the second one." "That second bridge ain't the Walker Bridge." "Well, what is it, then?" "Come to think on it, I don't rightly believe it has a name." "Well, it's over Walker Crick." "No, it ain't; they're both over the river, not the crick. Walker Crick is five miles downriver of the second bridge." "Is that the one near the old Jones store site?"

When I lived downriver, I had a flatlander friend come visit. She got lost (an interesting feat, since there's only one road. Well, only one MAIN road), and stopped at someone's house to call and ask me for directions. Me: "Where are you?" Brief consultation. "The Smith's." "Which Smiths?" Another consultation. "Ron Smith." "Ron Jr., or Senior?" "Neither. He says he's from the valley." "Huh. Don't know the valley Smiths. What house is it?" Consultation. "He says it used to be the Taylor place." "Well, is it the place the Taylors lived in before or after they bought the old Johnson place?" My friend became slightly hysterical about this time and I had to come get her, after discussing the house history with the current owner and establishing that they were, indeed, distant cousins of the Ron Smiths. Senior.

Txting 123

WE JUST GOT BACK from vacation, but as we actually made hotel reservations in advance and rented a car when we weren't staying with relatives, I have no adventures to report other than the fact that the airline "randomly" held back five pieces of luggage both on the way over to Kodiak Island and on the way back, for reasons unknown to me, and guess whose luggage was chosen and retained BOTH times? Never mind, I'll get over it, and someday I might even remember to pack my toothbrush and an extra pair of underwear in my hand luggage. In fact, from now on maybe I'll only take hand luggage with me, just in case.

I imagine that those of you who actually read this column and are my age or older (which narrows the field to one or two people) also, like me, don't text. The rest of you needn't read any further. Of course, if you don't read the column, you aren't reading this anyway, but that gets me into some twisted metaphysical thinking I can't manage after a vacation, so I won't go there. Back to the point (and I promise you there is one, or will be any time now): I have stubbornly resisted texting so far, and I suspect I will pass on to my somewhat dubious reward without having mastered the technique. Occasionally I receive wrong number text messages (is that grammatical? Does it even make sense?), but once I figured out what it was, I simply handed the phone to my son, who rolled his eyes again (he does this fairly often with me), read it and deleted it, or whatever it is these young people do with such things (he announced the other day that as old as my eggs were when I had him, it's a wonder he has any brain cells at all, but it appears he is smart enough all the same).

Anyway, I recently received a text message to which I needed to respond, and my son is away at college, so I had to enlist the help of my husband, who has at least got that far in this newfangled technology. He showed me how to hit the phone version of reply (I've already forgotten how to do it), and I started to reply, but then realized that I couldn't see the keyboard on the tiny flip phones we use, so I had to go find one of the many pairs of glasses I keep all over the house in the vain hope that I'll be able to find a pair when I need one, which is more and more often now that I'm this old – just ask my son.

Once I had located the glasses, it took me an age to work out that you have to hit the same button several times to get, say, from an "a" to a "c" – who knew? And if you're slow, as I am, it just prints the first letter, and then what do I do? I couldn't find an "erase" button, or even "delete". Once again my husband came to my rescue (I forget how), and I was able to move on to the next issue: Where was the spacebar on this phone? It's bad enough that I never took typing in school (in a vain attempt to keep from doing office work all my life; my somewhat bizarre logic was that if I didn't type, I couldn't get stuck doing it. As a result, I had to pay people to type my papers for me in college while I flipped burgers to pay them and my tuition, and I hate cooking. I am now a very slow, bad typist, apparently too old to learn to do it properly, and I spend most of my working days typing reports – go figure. But I can still flip a mean burger); now I had to type on a telephone using letters and buttons so small only Santa's elves could manage it, and do so at warp speed.

My husband patiently pointed out the # key, which also said "space"; how was I to know they weren't referring to hyperspace, or some other concept I know nothing about, of which there are legion? I had never noticed it, and if I had I would have been afraid to push it; who knows what might have happened? Besides, I work on the theory that it's not safe to cram too many pieces of information into my already crowded brain – something important might fall out.

My next problem was, how do you capitalize letters? Where are the punctuation marks? I am a person to whom the concept of "free writing" is completely foreign; I will start to twitch if anyone insists I not use punctuation, correct grammar and capital letters to the best of my abilities even if I am writing in my sleep, or under hypnosis, which I suspect wouldn't work on me anyway, and I struggle to think of an occasion on which anyone should wish to hypnotize me in order to get me to stop using punctuation, or an occasion in which I would be writing in my sleep, for that matter, but hypothetically speaking…Thank you, religious school.

In any case, I never solved any of those grammatical puzzles, and I suspect the recipient of my efforts fell asleep waiting for me to finish my three-word response, so I'm guessing they won't be texting me again any time soon. I didn't really want to join the 20th century anyway.

Exercises In Futility

THE OTHER DAY I happened to look over my shoulder and caught sight of somebody else's hip; then I realized they were mine. Whoa!! Where did THAT come from?! Guess I'd better get thee to an exercise class. I am, to put it mildly, not the world's most graceful person, so it was with some trepidation that I noted the only one available in my time slot was a "step" class. I had taken such a class many years ago, when I was quite a bit more spry (although no more coordinated), and the result had not been a happy one. I was older now, and more mature and determined, I told myself; surely things would be better.

The sight that met me when I walked in was not encouraging. Every member of the class was at least twenty years my junior, dressed in coordinated outfits; bouncing on the balls of their feet, they greeted me with perky smiles. I tried to smile back.

I had no idea there could be so many combinations of routines, on or off a step. I'm lucky if I can go up or down any step without hurting myself. Then just when I began to think I was getting it, the instructor would switch from the right foot to the left, and we were off again - or they were; I stood in total bewilderment, sweat running off the end of my nose into a puddle on the floor.

Dressed in my old sweats and a baggy t-shirt, my cheap shoes shedding caked-on mud, I looked like a bag lady who had accidentally wandered in to this bevy of beauties, the ugly duckling amongst the swans of exercise.

Suddenly, the instructor decided to change tactics; when she announced we were going to put the steps away, I breathed a sigh of relief - until she told us to get out the jump ropes. Dear heaven, not the jump ropes! I hadn't even looked at one since I was ten - and for good reason. But everyone else was cheerfully getting them out, so I thought, maybe they're going to do something different with them, something even I could do, something easy. Maybe they'll use them to do arm exercises. Right. Within the first few jumps, I had hopelessly entangled both feet in the rope; the instructor, looking nervously in my direction, suggested helpfully that we not stand too close to our neighbors and moved on to the balls, probably looking for an activity that wouldn't result in a fatality for anyone in my immediate vicinity.

I discovered at this point just how dangerous a large ball can be - if not to my neighbors, certainly to me. We were meant to clasp the ball securely between our legs and raise it over our heads while lying on the floor. The first time I tried this, I dropped the ball squarely (if such a thing is possible with a round object) onto my head. From here it escaped and rolled across the room over several other participants like a runaway train, wreaking minor havoc, with me chasing after it, apologizing profusely. No doubt hoping she could hit on something I could manage, she then had us lie on top of the ball and roll over it. No luck – the ball shot out from under me and retraced its path into hapless exercisers.

Probably in desperation by now, the instructor moved on to weights. They weren't large weights, she probably reasoned; how much harm could I do? The answer is: None - at least to anyone else. It is possible, however, to blacken both one's eyes and cover oneself in weight-shaped bruises with small three-pound weights. And don't even ask about the bars; suffice to say it is possible to knock yourself out cold with a nine-pound bar while trying to raise it to your forehead.

With a somewhat grim smile affixed to her face, the instructor moved on to mat exercises. We were told to put our mats on our steps and sit on them, in preparation for a more complicated task, no doubt. Simple enough, except that I didn't account for the overhang of the mat over the step, sat down on the unsupported side, and fell noisily onto the floor. When I tried to get up, I found I had pinned my t-shirt to the mat with a weight and fell over again. Let us draw a veil over the "bosu", another bouncy instrument of torture that threatened to launch me into the stratosphere.

When we moved on to simple stretches, I discovered my cheap shoes had no traction whatsoever, and found my feet sliding apart until I looked like Bambi on the ice. And let's not even discuss balance. When she asked us to stand on one foot and do leg lifts, I looked around hopefully for the bar I could hold on to, but I was doomed to disappointment. I guess I'll take up exercise classes when they develop the one with handrails.

Rising Reptile

IT SEEMS THE MARLAHAN mustard eradication campaign I've been conducting has left me with more than feelings of deep satisfaction and vindication; my overly enthusiastic approach to uprooting said dastardly weed has resulted in back injuries. As this accompanied a tooth that's been a pain, so to speak, for several weeks, I was finally convinced that neither was going to go away without outside intervention, and off I went to seek help.

I guess I'm the only person I know who is actually relieved to get a diagnosis of a serious medical problem; then at least I can believe I'm not just a crazy, hypochondriacal wuss. So I was actually somewhat pleased to hear that I had a "bulging disc", whatever that is (I wanted to tell the physical therapist who diagnosed it that, at my age, that's not all that's bulging, but I refrained, figuring that would be an overshare) and that I needed a root canal – on the tooth, that is. We want to keep those straight, I'm sure. It seems my nerve had gone bad (so to speak), the dentist had explained sadly, and it (the nerve) would have to be removed. Just shoot it, I wanted to say, zap it, kill it dead in any and every possible way, as long as it stops hurting; you'll not get any grief from me. The dentist delivered his news about my root, in fact, in much the same tone of abject personal failure that my doctor announced, 22 years before, that our first child would have to be delivered via Caesarian section. After 24 hours of labor with no drugs, I explained through clenched teeth that he could take the baby out my nose for all I cared, as long as they delivered her post haste. And just for fun, when our son was born two years later, they let me wait 30 hours, also with no drugs, before they gave up and delivered him C-section. Personally, I would have been happy to give up on natural childbirth a lot sooner, but the doctor seemed determined. Next time, let HIM go through 30 hours of labor and see how he feels about it, but I'm not bitter. Really.

So, what's a little tooth and back pain, I reasoned? Besides, I reminded myself, I am the daughter of a man so tough that, at age 86, we took him to the hospital for back pain (an event unheard of, as we have a family policy of never going to the hospital if we can help it. The very fact that he said he might need to go was enough to terrify us). When the doctor came back with the test results and asked my father to rate his pain level on a scale of one to ten, after some thought, he decided it might be a five. He was passing a kidney stone. They don't call them the Greatest Generation for nothing.

But I digress. I practically skipped to the dentist's chair and enthusiastically threw myself into it in anticipation of an end to pain – or I would have, if my back hadn't hurt so much. I think I was the most cheerful root canal patient they had seen in months, if not years, or ever. After numbing what felt like (or more accurately, didn't feel like) the tops of my eyeballs to my knees, the dental assistant approached me with a tube the size of my garden hose, and I decided it was time to close my eyes. Of course, being me, I got the jitters from the novocaine, which always seems to contain enough epinephrine to fell an ox, but at least nothing hurt for the first time in what seemed like months – even my back. I contemplated requesting that they shoot a little in there, too, just for good measure, but I was afraid they would decide I was a drug addict.

Next came the rubber "dam", spread like a tarp in a heavy rain in my mouth, presumably to isolate the tooth in question and keep it dry, which immediately and invariably causes me to produce enough saliva to solve the water shortage crisis, and then begin to choke on said saliva, just as the dentist – excuse me, the odontist – is approaching a particularly sensitive phase of the operation. And why is it that this is the exact moment most dentists choose to ask you to expound on some particularly profound philosophical concept, or to give them your life story? Possibly because they know that with your mouth full of instruments and dams, you won't be able to speak, and they won't have to listen to it, but they get points for asking? The old rubber dam technique is certainly an effective bar to conversation, although difficult to work into your average discussion, I find.

In any case, I felt much better, and can highly recommend a root canal for back pain, although it's not, unfortunately, a permanent fix in that department. So, it was on to the physical therapist, where I am learning to move properly for the first time in my life in order to avoid such issues in the future, and where they've already taught me two yoga-like poses, which I refer to as the "rising reptile" (or, if you prefer, as I do, to keep snakes out of it, the "lifting lizard") and the "bust thrust". They have recently added the "angry cat", to which I can often relate, and the "old cow", at which I try not to take offense, as I no doubt resemble one at times. And they seem to work, so I'm not complaining.

My summer words of sage advice: Beware the marlahan mustard scourge! Constant vigilance! And bend carefully when you pick it – but do pick it!

VEGETABLE MATTER

HAVING BEEN A HAPPY omnivore my entire life, no one could have been more stunned than I when I decided to become a vegetarian. It was actually almost a whim, close to New Year's, although I never make New Year's resolutions – no point setting myself up for failure – but it's now lasted several years, which is longer than I've ever kept any resolution regarding food. I've often tried to diet, with no luck, and I know plenty of pudgy vegetarians, so weight loss wasn't really a factor, although it would have been nice (no luck so far; might have something to do with all the sugar I consume on a regular basis).

Growing up, with at least six people in the house at any given time, we were just grateful to get food of any type, and never were fussy about anything other than getting enough. We were not allowed to be picky eaters, nor were we allowed to waste food, which meant, of course, that we always cleaned our plates, and developed food issues. I always rolled my eyes at vegetarians, and even if I wanted to do it for health reasons, it seemed more complicated than I could manage. In fact, it's actually been surprisingly easy, other than the whole major lifestyle change thing.

The truth is, I hate killing things, and I always believed that if you're going to eat meat, you ought to have the courage of your convictions and kill it yourself, but those sanitized, shrink-wrapped, unrecognizable packages of meat in the grocery store were so comforting that I never lived up to my own principles. I have great respect for people who hunt and eat or use every part of the animal; I just can't do it. Well, I suppose I could if I were starving, but

I'm not, fortunately, and there are lots of other options for me; my fondness for animals does not extend to vegetables, in the killing sense, and besides, I have to eat something, even if they do scream when I wrench them out of the ground (I don't garden, either). Also, I'm pretty convinced I'm higher on the evolutionary scale than carrots, whereas I'm not so sure about cows. I'm just not ready to be a fruitarian or a vegan; I'd starve to death, I'm sure. And if I'm lost in the woods and starving, and it's me or the bunny, the bunny is going to die. I guess I really don't have the courage of my convictions; it's a complicated world.

But whole new vistas have opened up to me! Sections of the grocery store I never even knew existed have suddenly become my regular haunt, and foods I'd never heard of a few years ago have suddenly been added to my vocabulary, words like quinoa, which I pronounced, phonetically, as kwin-o-ah, until a kind store clerk corrected me (it's kin-wa; I thought they were two different kinds of grain). Until that time quinoa had been what we refer to as a "reading word" – words you've read but never heard said out loud until you use it, feeling erudite, and someone has to correct you once they've stopped laughing. Mine was cacophony, which I pronounced "kak-a-foney". Then there was pseudo, which I once pronounced "peswedo" and puzzled over for a while as a new word in a moment of brain fade.

For the first time in my life, I wandered down the natural foods aisle – my goodness! I've been formally introduced to more different types of beans than I ever knew existed, like anasazi beans – weren't they a Native American tribe in the southwest that died out centuries ago? I hope it was nothing to do with the beans… I'm amazed at the variety of food available outside of meat.

Creativity in the kitchen has never been my strong suit, but with the help of vegetarian friends and a simple "starter" cookbook, I'm not only surviving, but enjoying the new foods. Nuts, beans, grains, and, of course, vegetables, come in an amazing variety, I've discovered, and are remarkably filling. Of course, some recipes are more successful than others; "Veggie Pie" (pie crust with cinnamon, flour and veggies) was notable for its weirdness, prompting my beloved to comment for probably only the second time in 25 years of eating my cooking that I needn't bother making that again on his account. The recipe for "roasted roots" was notable for the fact that a chainsaw was needed to slice them in their natural, i.e., raw, state.

One advantage of the new regime is that I almost never go to fast food restaurants anymore; most of it isn't vegetarian, of course, but even a bean burrito is pretty easy to cook for myself, and I can get no-fat, "zesty" beans in the store that taste better than theirs, anyway.

But some things never change. My daughter has remarked, truthfully, that I'm the most unhealthy vegetarian she's ever known; she makes "green smoothies" that sort of taste like you're drinking pulverized lawn clippings, but I'm sure they're healthy.

And of course, anything cooked by someone else is still my favorite.

*I was a vegetarian for eight years. I began eating meat again in 2018, although I am conflicted about it....

SOUNDS AND FURY

AS I MAY HAVE mentioned once or twice, I am not the most technologically savvy person around, and I recently had a small disagreement with the CD player in my car which unfortunately combined with my impatience with technology. And yes, I still have a CD player, because I still play CDs, and because my car is old, but they both work. Or they did until recently.

The CD player has, it is true, been a bit recalcitrant about releasing the CDs when I ask it to, in a manner reminiscent of my toaster, which either firmly grasps my toast until it is carbonized and sets off the smoke alarm, or tosses it out onto the counter untoasted. It (that is, the CD player, not the toaster) usually tells me to "Check CD", until I rudely remind it that I have done so, and want it out, at which point the player digitally announces that there is no CD inside it. As this is a patent lie, as I, and it, well know, since I have just put a CD in there, it sometimes gives up and spits out the hostage CD, but occasionally it decides it wants to have some fun with me, and refuses to return the CD altogether, at which point I start stabbing it viciously with a plastic toothpick I keep in the car for just such an occasion, and which normally does the trick. Sometimes I have to jab it with the toothpick and simultaneously keep pushing the "Eject" button, while it alternates the two messages, but eventually it gives up the battle and the CD.

The other day, however, we were clearly not going to come to an agreement; détente had failed, as had violence. I wish I could tell you that there was some logic in what I did next, but alas, to do so would not be truthful. The stuck CD was one of a set of two, neither of which I liked, having discovered after playing the first one that although they were Oldies, they were not by the original artists. I am a stickler about such things (there's always a reason things are cheap). So, in a move I cannot now comprehend and could not have explained at the time, I shoved the second CD in after the first.

Perhaps the original idea was to try to unstick the first CD with the second, as in the toothpick maneuver. Perhaps I thought, as my friend Tonya suggested, that if I gave it two, it would become overstuffed and throw up both of them. I think she was just being kind, trying to find reason where none existed. It did not, of course, do the trick, so now, in a rage, I got out my pocket knife and started digging around in the player, perhaps hoping to skewer both like a shish kebab and retrieve them; I cannot say there was much, if any, logic involved there, either. Temper, yes; logic, no.

After a few minutes of vigorous action, a small strip of cloth flopped out, but no CDs. I think it might be some sort of belt crucial to the operation of the CD player, or maybe the car itself – who knows? But by now in a rage with all things electronic, I cut it off as extraneous to my purposes. As my mother would say, hindsight is 50-50.

The CD player remains silent and rebellious, and the CDs have not been seen since, although the car itself continues to run. When I described the event to Heidi Coppi, she informed me, after she stopped laughing, that Rob does not work on CD players, so I, like the CDs in their ultimate revenge, am stuck. I drive with the radio on and glare malevolently at the CD player, with no visible effect.

Then something odd began to occur. When I first got the car, back when the electric locks I was so excited about still worked, the CD player would obligingly digitally display the name of the CD I was playing, and even, on special occasions, the name of the track that was on. The radio generally told me at least which station I was listening to. Ever since the whole two CDs stuck in the player incident, however, it stopped displaying anything other than "Check CD". This I put down to its general cantankerousness, until a few days ago, when the name "Rupert" suddenly appeared in the digital display. Rupert? I can think of no musical group by that name, no artist at all other than Rupert Grint, the young actor who played Harry Potter's sidekick in the movies. I know no one named Rupert, so, whence this mysterious name? Then I began to get other random words, perhaps messages being sent from some alien planet?

In any case, I am beginning to enjoy the silence…

TOILETRIES: OR FLUSHING, AND IT AIN'T IN NEW YORK

THE OLDER I GET, the more issues I have with public toilets. To begin with, the stalls are so narrow you'd have to be Olive Oyl to move comfortably in them. I mean, I'm not looking to move in furniture and call it home, but it would be nice if I could turn around to flush without damaging internal organs – mine, that is, not the toilet's.

I know nothing of men's toilets, of course, and so cannot address their shortcomings, never having been in them except by accident, or out of complete desperation when the line at the women's toilets is so long it's clear it will be three or four days before I can get in – which is every time I need to use one. Clearly, some woman-hating man designed women's toilets.

Anyway, just to make life more difficult, they manage to install toilet roll holders (locked, of course – you never know when someone will decide to steal the entire roll) on BOTH sides of the stall, or throw in a sanitary disposal device on the opposite wall, so you can bruise not one but BOTH hips as you turn to hang your purse on the hook. Of course, usually there is no hook, so one is forced to hold the purse strap in one's teeth, along with any paperwork one might be holding, such as the grocery list.

Then they like to install the toilet itself so close to the ground that you have to be a yoga master to sit on it and require the assistance of a crane to get back up. And you'd better be careful once you've settled down, because if you move a millimeter, even a twitch, and you've got one of those automatic flushers, it will seize this opportunity to flush madly, whether you're finished or not, frightening the life out of me and invariably causing me to leap from the seat and do harm to myself on the stall door, which will, just this once, have a hook on it, the better to impale me.

One of these diabolical machines lurks in Greenhorn Park, where I take almost daily hikes; I've tried sneaking up on it, but invariably it senses my presence and begins flushing before I've even come close to it, thereby soaking the seat before I can even sit down. And this is supposed to save water? Alternatively, if I can turn around in the confined space available, I find myself staring suspiciously at the flushing device, waiting, until I finally realize it's not an automatic flusher and I'll have to do it myself. It's kind of like doors these days; I can't remember how many times I've stood expectantly in front of a door, waiting patiently for it to open, until I finally realize it's not going to – it's a "manual".

I have become a bit of a toilet connoisseur, a dilettante of the flushing world, one might say, as I have experienced toilets the world over in my travels. French toilets, for instance, come in a wide variety of styles, from the "standers", which are really disgusting and which I refuse to dignify by discussing them, to the one I recently encountered in a cheap hotel I stayed in there. I used the facility and searched in vain for a flushing device, finally giving in despair and attempting to slink out unnoticed; when I opened the door, the toilet flushed! What will they think of next? Some toilets there have a plunger device you have to pull up; I worked this out in another hotel room, but then had to shut off the water valve altogether to keep it from running all night. In England, the older toilets have a chain you pull to flush, and the toilet tank is above your head; they're powerful little devils, and likely to make you think you've just unleashed Hoover Dam, except, of course, that you're in Britain.

I was once in the airport in San Francisco and decided to use the facilities. I was in a hurry, as usual, and thought it odd that as I walked in, I saw a gentleman looking at me in some bemusement. I was wondering what he was doing in the ladies room until I saw the urinals and realized I had walked into the men's room by mistake. I made a quick U-turn and hastened out the door. Then I realized I should have stayed; there was, as usual, a line outside the ladies.

Small Miracles

A WHILE AGO, I was invited by a neighbor to join a Bible study group. Reluctantly, I agreed to come. I was hesitant for several reasons: I didn't know the participants very well, but I did know we were very different from one another, not only in our religious beliefs, but in our political and world views. I had been going to church since I was a child – a different church from theirs – and had attended religious school, so I didn't think I had much to learn from them. I also hated to commit to a study that would involve giving up every Wednesday night for a very long time, and I didn't want to spend that time arguing with people with whom I disagreed.

Some of my friends discouraged me from going; no good could come, they said, of spending so much time with people of such different belief systems. Still, I decided to give it a try – the first small miracle.

Sometimes, I must admit, I went grudgingly, feeling I had so many other important things to do, obligations to attend to, more enjoyable events to attend. But I always had a good time, and I was always glad I had gone – another small miracle.

We shared a meal, to which we all contributed a dish. Not being an enthusiastic cook, I was assigned salads. Everyone raved about the salads, which I suspect was a kindness on their part – how can one ruin a salad, anyway? The meals were delicious, and we actually traded recipes – a small miracle for someone as undomesticated as I.

We listened as the leader of the group, my neighbor, gave us the benefit of his research. Although he had a very demanding job, he always found the time to consult commentaries – a miracle in itself. As far as I know, none of us changed our minds about our politics or our religious beliefs, but I think we all learned something – a small miracle for people as familiar with the Bible as most of us were.

Surprisingly for me, as passionate as I am about such things, when we disagreed, I discovered that I didn't always feel the need to change anyone's mind, or even necessarily express my opinion on every topic – a major miracle. I learned that I could listen, and disagree, and be silent, and not feel superior, but instead respect someone else's belief, even though it was different to mine – sometimes very different. This was new to me, and a not-so-small miracle. Once or twice, discussions became heated, but we always left as friends – another small miracle.

In fact, I can't think of a night when we didn't laugh, heartily and in companionship. We especially liked to tease our leader, who was quiet and unassuming and had a dry wit you had to listen for, but which was well worth waiting to hear. I found myself enjoying my time with these folk more and more. They became good friends to me, despite our differences. In fact, over time they became family. I learned to trust them; they mattered to me as family does. We shared each other's joys and sorrows, births and deaths, marriages, family issues. I couldn't quite understand how people who held such very different views could have so much fun together, respect each other, learn from one another, listen to each other, and love each other. Certainly American political life had not prepared me for such civil discourse, especially about the two things I had promised myself I would not discuss with people I disagreed with – politics and religion – having experienced the discord and anger such discussions usually produced. That we could do so on a weekly basis and remain friends was nothing less than a miracle to me.

Then, on December 14, 2014, our group was forever changed. The leader of our Bible study, my friend and neighbor, Dr. Urs Bryner, died suddenly and unexpectedly of a brain aneurism. His wife Darlene, whom he clearly adored, his family, his co-workers, the medical community, and from the attendance at his funeral service, half the county, were all devasted. Dr. Byrner's compassion, his integrity, his skills, and his dedication to his calling were all small miracles in this age when doctors seem to have little opportunity to take the kind of time and care Urs took with his patients. Many people in this community owe their lives to him – a miracle for them.

But for me, the small miracles will continue. The lessons I learned at Urs and Darlene's dining room table will stay with me. Hopefully, the friendships we established there will continue to be nurtured, and will lead to other relationships, other lessons, other small miracles, for the rest of our lives. Vaya con Dios, Urs, and thank you for all the miracles, large and small.

TRAFFIC STOPS

MY DAUGHTER RECENTLY received her first speeding ticket; she was very remorseful and it will no doubt slow her down for a while, which is always a good thing. I must admit that I have always exceeded the speed limit (not now, of course; in my old age I have reformed – honest, officer!). I blame it on my parents and the church. We were always late for church, and we raced there every Sunday, so I grew up believing that if it was okay to exceed the speed limit going to church, it must be okay with God to exceed the speed limit at other times, too. My theory, in fact, is that if you come upon those lights timed for, say, thirty miles an hour, and go sixty, you ought to get through them just dandy, and in half the time. I hasten to add, it's only a theory.

Naturally, my predilection for speed has resulted in an inordinate number of traffic tickets. I have, in fact, spent so much time in traffic school I know all their jokes; I could probably teach the class. Except for the speeding part.

I got my first ticket when I was eighteen. I had only been driving about six months and was coming back from Los Angeles with a friend late at night when I decided to see how fast her Volvo could go. Who knew? When I was stopped, the officer, slightly incredulous, asked that classic question, "Do you know how fast you were going?" What is the proper response to that question, anyhow? Yes, I just wanted to see if you could catch me? No, I wasn't paying the slightest attention; how fast was I going, anyway? My sister says she wants to ask someday, "Why, is there a prize if I guess correctly?"

The officer appeared to be so shocked that such a young girl would be driving that fast (as I recall, it was over 100 mph) that he just about had us spread-eagled over the hood. As it was, when he looked at the registration I handed him after nervously grabbing the first random piece of paper I found in the glove compartment, he remarked it was from 1970 (several years prior); I brightly responded, "Yes, it's a 1970 Volvo." By the time we had straightened that out, he must have decided we were too stupid to do any harm and let us go. The fine, I might add, was so huge it effectively curbed my impulse to speed for quite some time.

But the quintessential traffic stop occurred when I was in college, coming home to Siskiyou County for Christmas break. I was speeding (just a little) and was, of course, pulled over. I sighed heavily and prepared to sign up for traffic school for the umpteenth time. Suddenly I remembered that in the rush to get packed and on the road in time for Christmas, I had neglected to renew my license. I waited, terrified. The officer, an older, fatherly type, smiled at me kindly. "Now, miss, you really ought to slow down," he remarked. I agreed humbly. "I'll let it go this time," he finished, and turned to go. I was almost weeping with relief when he turned back to me and asked, almost as an afterthought, "May I see your license, please?" Dejected, I handed it to him. Smiling broadly, he said, "Well, it looks like somebody's had a birthday!" I sighed that yes, I had, actually, only a few days prior, and tried to explain why I was driving on an expired license. He shook his head and told me to have a merry Christmas as he turned to go.

Weak with gratitude at my reprieve, I was about to start the car when some wicked impulse prompted him to ask for my registration and insurance. Fortunately, they were up to date. Unfortunately, I couldn't seem to locate them. As I searched madly through my glove compartment, he leaned into the car slightly and asked, "Exactly what would that white powdery substance in your glove compartment be, ma'am?"

With sinking heart, I regarded it. "Chalk dust. I'm a teacher and I keep an extra piece of chalk in my car just in case I run out, and it must have got caught in the door and…" It was quite true, but by now I was jibbering. He contemplated me. "So, we have speeding, driving on an expired license, no proof of insurance or registration, and a suspicious white powder in your glove compartment. I ought to take you straight to jail, young lady. Where do you teach?" Succumbing to despair, I answered truthfully. "San Quentin." Regarding me with the interest he might show a zoo specimen, he shook his head slowly, said, "Merry Christmas", and walked back to his car.

In that one incident, I used up more ticket karma than I can ever expect for the rest of my life, so I now drive slowly. Well, more slowly.

CHRISTMAS CHEER

THE NIGHTS ARE GETTING longer, the days shorter; there's a festive feeling of good cheer and a chill in the air, and we all know what that means: it means my driver's side door lock has frozen shut and I have to crawl across the center console five times a day - every time I want to exit my vehicle, in fact. It means poor Rob Coppi, my mechanic, also has to crawl over the console, from the passenger side, and remove the driver's side seat in order to get to the driver's side door to fix the problem. But he is so familiar with all my vehicles by now that I have him on speed-dial, and I have great confidence in him; it is, after all, the season of hope.

It means gifts of lovely soft hand-crocheted socks that cause me to unexpectedly skate across the wood floor and land face-first in the rock fireplace.

It means a light dusting of snow, covering everything and making it beautiful, and resulting in more trips outside to the frozen woodpile to retrieve wood for the fire in sap-covered PJ's, not to mention more awkward sliding, this time across the deck, stacks of wood in my arms.

It means the cat gets sick and throws up who knows what on the carpet, rather than the linoleum, which would of course be easier to clean, thereafter retiring to the newly-cleaned bathtub, where he proceeds to upchuck some more until he feels better, eats whatever he can find on the counter (usually butter), and curls up on our bed, content that his job here is done.

It means yet again setting up the fake Christmas tree, already dropping its fake needles, and having my beloved set the angel, which he insists on calling the "Christmas Fairy", atop the decorated tree.

It means getting busy and forgetting to send out Christmas cards until the day before, and also forgetting to buy groceries for Christmas dinner for 13 until the snowstorm of the century has blown in and it would take a team of sled dogs, of which I happen to be a few dogs short, to get me to Raley's.

It means a futile search for decorations the children have stolen for their own households when I wasn't looking, or have alternatively convinced me

I no longer need and have therefore donated (that would be the decorations, not the children) to the Hospice thrift store, where I have to go buy them back.

It means in desperation for a quick meal during the busy holiday season serving my long-suffering beloved the turkey soup left over from Thanksgiving, which, although in all fairness I had frozen and defrosted, had unfortunately been left out on the counter to defrost perhaps a little too long. Come to think of it, maybe the cat…? Nah. "That's the third time you've tried to poison me," my husband croaks during yet another trip to the bathroom during the night, but honestly, in 30 years, that's not a bad average, right?

It means another anxious search through the closet for all those perfect gifts I know I cleverly bought throughout the year and hid away, feeling very smug until I remember them in the middle of the night and cannot seem to find, no doubt because they are buried under piles of items I should have given to the thrift store but could never bear to part with until now, as I fling them to one side and mutter to myself. I do, however, find candy canes from several years ago which I can put in the children's Christmas stockings, apparently not having learned any lessons from the turkey soup episode. Serves them right for stealing my decorations.

It means carefully setting out the stockings by the fire on Christmas Eve, only to find the next morning that the dog has discovered them and decided he, too, was in need of some Christmas cheer, and since we neglected to give him his own stocking, he has taken matters into his own paws and jaws. As he is a pit bull, I decline to argue with him.

It means another year of setting up the manger scene inherited from my beloved grandmother, with the strange animals she somehow decided had been to visit the baby Jesus: the usual camels and sheep, of course, although at least one camel suffered a broken leg on the journey that never seems to heal despite repeated gluing, accompanied by a large bear, a goose, three tiny kangaroos and a lion. I try to keep the lion and the bear a safe distance away, because they are, after all, unpredictable animals.

Most of all, it means my favorite time of year, when we can be with family and friends and celebrate this season of love and cheer, caring for one another, counting our blessings, which are many, and practicing kindness and generosity with all those we meet.

May the next year be a good one for you, and a Merry Christmas to all!

DOUBTING THOMAS

I WAS BORN ON the Feast Day of St. Thomas. That would be "Doubting Thomas", Didymus, meaning a twin or a double, the literalist who in the Gospel of John declares to the other disciples after Jesus' death and resurrection that he will not believe his Lord is risen unless and until he puts his fingers in the wounds created by Jesus' crucifixion: the holes in his hands and feet, the slit in his side made by a soldier's spear to ensure Jesus was dead.

When Jesus does appear to Thomas and invites him to do that very thing, to put his hands in Jesus' wounds, Thomas falls at his feet, announcing to himself and others, "My Lord and my God." Faced with the evidence, he is finally convinced. Jesus gently rebukes him, saying, "You have believed because you have seen; blessed are those who have not seen and yet believe."

It is interpreted as a commendation on the power of faith, of belief in things unseen. But I have a different idea about doubt.

What, after all, is doubt? It is the willingness to question, to ask the hard things, to not blindly accept all we are told without careful examination. Are we to follow the charismatic leader without thought? To drink the Kool-Aid because someone tells us we should, without inquiring further? I believe Thomas was a disciple for a reason, and that this story is told for another purpose; not necessarily as an example of the folly of doubt, but perhaps as a lesson about its value. Perhaps there is a deeper message under the simple one: to look beyond the obvious.

Without doubt, there is no growth. If I accept without question the beliefs I was taught as a child, I continue to think like a child: in rigid black and white terms, with no gray areas, no nuance or subtlety. I never mature. But life is full of subtlety, of shades of coloration and complication; to ignore that is to think in simple ways about an intricate world. And sometimes that is helpful, and sometimes it is not. "When I was a child, I spoke as a child, I thought as a child, I reasoned as a child; but when I became an adult, I put away childish things. Now we see a blurred image in a mirror. Then we will see very clearly.

94

Now my knowledge is incomplete. Then I will have complete knowledge as God has complete knowledge of me. So these three things remain: faith, hope and love. But the best of these is love." 1 Corinthians 13, 11 and 12.

There is a time to think and reason as children do – when we are immature children - and there is a time to grow up, to face the world as it is, not its blurred image. There is a time in adulthood to give up the fantasy that there exists a Prince or Princess Charming who will solve all our problems and take us away to the ideal world; that the "magical other" will be perfect, exactly what we want, with no faults. There is, one hopes, a time when we stop believing in the Tooth Fairy, Santa Claus, and the Easter Bunny, and understand that while the world is not perfect, it certainly is interesting as it is. Life is about growth and understanding that continues to evolve, and that is the joy of experience as well as its heartbreak at times.

Interestingly, of the three things discussed at the end of the passage, faith is not the one held in the highest regard, but love. Not the sticky, sentimental kind, either, but the roll-up-your-sleeves, do something about injustice, love your neighbor as well as you love yourself, even when they stink because they haven't had a bath, or are your boring relative, or the other political party member, love-the-unlovable kind of love.

Some of the best laws we have came about because someone doubted. Someone said wait, that's not fair. Just because it's always been so doesn't make it right. And slavery was abolished in this country, civil rights were born, women were allowed to vote, people without money were given the right to a lawyer to defend them against crimes they might not have committed.

The visionaries, those who are dissatisfied with things as they are, with "business as usual", the one who is ahead of his or her time – crucified, assassinated for having a dream, and yes, sometimes the doubter – these are the people who bring about change for the better, who find a new wisdom, new discoveries, new worlds.

Scientific theories are an evolving thing; the scientist who does not wonder is no scientist, but a mere defender of what is true now, but will be proven false in time, by thinkers who do question, without fear, or maybe with some fear and trembling, but the courage to move ahead anyway. We do our children a grave injustice if we do not teach them to question, to think for themselves, to analyze and work it through on their own. Otherwise, the world would still be considered flat. To question the status quo is to make changes, to seek justice, to innovate, to create.

Perhaps with faith comes doubt; perhaps faith without doubt is dead. We need to keep asking questions, to continue wondering, to keep looking for things that need change, in the world and in ourselves, without judgment and with an open mind. We need to be clear-eyed, not just starry-eyed, to be "wise as serpents and as innocent as doves" (Matthew 10:16): to practice that difficult balancing act of kindness and love and, perhaps, some skepticism about the way things are, and that what we are told is right. I think perhaps God expects us to use the brains we have been given as well as our hearts, to see for ourselves, to allow a dose of healthy doubt along with our belief.

How many times in the gospels does Jesus calm us with "Fear not!" Why should we be afraid to follow his example of questioning the conventional wisdom of the day? Jesus died because he questioned the status quo, because he threatened the institutional power structure with a radical new idea: not that we topple the political entity that ruled the day with violence, but that we love one another. That was the message that rocked the world, that tilted it on its axis and sent everything tumbling. Jesus doubted the authorities of his day, questioned their message and devised a belief system that changed everything.

Do we have that same faith and courage – the courage to doubt?

DETAILS

I AM KNOWN FOR not noticing details, but I'm afraid I must admit it has actually become so bad it has led me into a life of unintended crime. I once had to have it pointed out to me that the largest building in town had burned down; I had driven past the spot where it used to stand several times without noticing it was gone. In my defense, I did notice the nice plot of green grass in the front yard, however.

I'm not sure why I don't notice things. I like to believe it's because I have so much on my mind, so many serious thoughts to think, that I don't see unimportant things, like buildings, but sometimes I have to wonder. There was that time I got half way to my destination – a housewares party I didn't want to go to in the first place – when I startled my mother, who was next to me in the car, by shouting out in panic, "The baby!" I had completely forgotten him. Fortunately, I had also forgotten that I had arranged for my father to watch him while I was gone. I once forgot the children when they were in summer school – I had a lot on my mind – and I was surprised when I got back to my office in the afternoon to find the children sitting there coloring. "What are you guys doing here?" I enquired, reasonably, I thought. My long-suffering children patiently explained that summer school had finished at lunch, the teacher didn't know what to do with them, and they had to call my secretary to come pick them up. Resourceful kids.

I don't always pay attention when I'm in the car, either. I mean, I pay attention to my driving, sometimes to the extent I miss things other people think are obvious, like other people. I warn friends not to take offense if I don't wave back; I'm not sure exactly what I'm always looking at, but faces don't seem to register. Once I was driving down the street with my kids in the back seat, windows open because it was really hot, deep in thought, as usual. Suddenly a rabid rodent leaped in through the window and into my lap. I screamed, frightening the children, and juggled it, trying to get it away from me, until I managed to toss it into the back seat with the children, thereby sending them into hysterics, until we all realized my furry steering wheel cover had sprung loose.

Another time, I realized I was going to be sick while driving home. In a panic, I rolled down the window and vomited all over the car, down into the window slot, everywhere – all while driving down the street towards our house. When I got home, my husband, drafted to help clean up the mess, asked reasonably, "Why didn't you pull over?" I looked at him, stricken; I hadn't thought of that.

A while ago my daughter and I went shopping at a clothing store, where we tried on dresses, skirts, and blouses. I was interested in a particular blouse, and got a skirt to try it on with. I didn't care for the skirt, you understand, I only needed it to see how the blouse looked, which is logic probably only a woman would understand. I decided not to get the blouse, and off we went to the grocery store, where, some time later, I needed to use the bathroom. Coming out of the ladies' room, I was pulling down the slip under my dress when I suddenly remembered I hadn't worn a slip that day, and the slow realization began to dawn that I had just accidentally shoplifted a skirt. I'm not sure who was more horrified, me or my daughter, who of course immediately announced in a carrying voice, "Mom, I can't believe you just stole that skirt! And right after church, too!" I hasten to add that I did return it, although the poor clerk was pretty confused by my explanation. And every time we walk past that particular store, my daughter feels obliged to announce, "Look, mom; there's the store where you stole that skirt! Want to go shoplift in there again?"

I became truly alarmed recently when I realized I had on two separate occasions walked out of the grocery store without paying for my mushrooms, simply because I hadn't noticed them sitting in the cart next to my purse, even when I reached into the purse to get my money. I finally couldn't take the guilt and had to go in a third time, buy mushrooms I didn't need, and instruct the bemused clerk to please ring them up three times, just so I could sleep at night.

Details…

Avian Attack

WE RECENTLY WENT down to the Bay Area to visit our daughter. She and I were driving down a back road in the Oakland hills when we were suddenly confronted with what I believe was a pair of very large wild turkeys. I slowed down, the better to have a closer look and exclaim over them, when they turned around and began to walk towards us in what I can only describe as a threatening manner. I backed the car up, so as not to hit them and to demonstrate that we came in peace, but they kept coming, and soon they were aggressively pecking at my tires, not to mention my paint job, but that's not much of an issue, really.

Now, I don't know about you, but the turkeys in my neighborhood are rather shy, timid creatures who run off gobbling at the approach of humans, no doubt expecting to be shot at any moment – we live in the country, after all. But these were clearly tough, hostile, big-city turkeys, intimidated by no one and out to show me I was on their turf. I half expected to see bandanas and tattoos on them, but all I noticed was a sort of neck-tie on the male – not quite gang paraphernalia. Still, I came back with a whole new appreciation for rural wildlife as opposed to city wildlife.

But the weirdest thing that's ever happened to me in the way of feathered fowl – and that's going a ways – occurred a while ago. I was driving home when suddenly, out of nowhere, something splattered on my windshield. In fact, it was all over my car, and it was red. Then the smell hit me: I can't even begin to describe it, except to state categorically that it was not a pleasant odor. In fact, it was foul. What the heck had hit my poor car? I looked around but saw absolutely nothing, and there was no way on earth that I was going to get out of my car to investigate further. No overhanging trees, no wildlife, no bodies, no wild man with a gun lurking nearby. So I headed home, where I immediately leaped out of my car and yelled for my beloved, which is always my fallback position in times of crisis.

He and my son came out and examined the car, concurring that yes, whatever was on the car was red, and yes, it smelled awful, and yes, it was all over the car. We even took pictures; I'm not exactly sure why, except that I wanted some sort of proof that something bizarre had yet again occurred in my life for which there was no reasonable explanation.

After documenting the evidence, we washed off the car, which needed scrub brushes to remove the gunk that had by now hardened to cement-like consistency, and then trotted down the road to do a crime-scene investigation. Although there were splotches of red stuff on the road about as far apart as the width of my car, there were no feathers, bone fragments, fur, teeth, or anything larger than what was on my car, which was very small pieces of something that none of us recognized. My beloved theorized that some poor bird had gotten sucked into an airplane jet high above the earth and somehow the remains had rained down on my car. Lucky me.

The mystery remained a mystery for weeks, until I got to chatting with a neighbor about my odd experience. He related that years earlier, he had been driving down a long, straight stretch of road when he suddenly spied a flock, or coven, or whatever they come in – of vultures happily munching on a breakfast of carrion (I just checked Wikipedia out of curiosity and, depending on what they're doing – i.e., flying or just sitting around – they can be a wake, kettle, committee, volt, venue, cast, meal, or vortex of vultures. The last is my personal favorite. I mean, who knew how complicated vultures could be?). He (my neighbor) slowed down, afraid they wouldn't get off the ground in time before he hit them, but they all managed to lumber off – except one, which was a bit slower than the rest and probably too engrossed in his tasty meal to pay attention (I can relate). So our neighbor watched as, almost in slow motion, the bird made an heroic effort to take off, managing, as I recall, to get nicked just a bit by the car and showing his intense displeasure with the entire proceedings by vomiting his meal all over our neighbor's car. Red stuff. Hard to scrub off. Yuck.

He then commented that he'd seen a lot of vultures in the neighborhood the day of my bizarre occurrence. So I, or rather my car, had been the target of yet another angry, or at least queasy, avian attack – yep, a vortex of vulture vomit. I guess that's just how my life goes.

CULINARY ADVENTURES

THANKSGIVING IS rapidly approaching, which means I will once again venture into that most dangerous of places – the kitchen. I've never been an enthusiastic cook; this probably explains why my family sniffs suspiciously at meals I produce, and friends check the expiration date on everything in my cupboard before consenting to eat with us. My intense scrutiny of their faces to ensure it looks as if they will survive for a half hour before I eat it myself probably doesn't help. My theory is, if it's in the fridge, it must be ok, and if it isn't there's nothing a little zap in the microwave won't cure. And anything in the freezer has to be good forever, right?

I once convinced a friend (and myself) the green stuff on the sour cream was actually guacamole from the week before. Hey, nobody got sick; who knows, maybe it was guacamole. In fact, I firmly believe that's why my children have always been so healthy: early exposure to many disease-causing agents builds immunities. We don't think about the other alternatives; they've survived almost to adulthood, so it must be ok. Don't they get antibiotics from mold? If in doubt, we employ the age-old family tradition: "Hey dad, taste this, will you? It smells bad." The really peculiar thing is, he always does taste it, although I'm not sure his seal of approval is to be relied upon; he was raised during the Depression, after all, and ate carrot sandwiches.

We actually ate part of our wedding cake on our tenth anniversary; it was in an airtight case, and it was covered in marzipan, so how bad could it be? Mind you, my husband had to slice it with a rock hammer and chisel, but boy, was it romantic! Even I admit to being nervous about the canned haggis in the pantry, though; it was a wedding present twenty-four years ago. So far, it's only serving a decorative purpose, but if we get hungry and desperate enough, I'm sure we'll be glad we have it. In fact, I operate on the theory of mass natural disaster and keep so much stuff in my pantry it looks like a grocery store. When I come back from shopping and we start unpacking the bags, my husband raises one eyebrow and inquires sweetly what inside information I possess about the coming cooking oil shortage? Or was I perhaps planning to run our car on the excess? And we needed four jars of mayonnaise because...? You never know – there might just be a shortage, and then I'll be ready. Besides, it was on sale.

Also, I'm not patient, and cooks need to be patient. If I'm supposed to be "constantly stirring" something, I start out with the best of intentions, but then I get distracted, usually by something interesting to read, and the next thing I know, I'm dancing around the kitchen with a towel, trying to deactivate the smoke alarm while aiming the baking soda at the conflagration on the stove.

I come by it honestly; my mother once melted an aluminum pot and welded it to the stove top when she got sidetracked. We used to say that dinner was ready when the vegetables were burned; in our house, it's generally when the smoke alarm goes off. Occasionally mother forgot some courses altogether and we had the rolls for dessert, or better yet, discovered them in the oven three days later when we wanted to cook something else.

I have continued this fine family tradition; my children no longer yelp when I shriek and leap for the oven or the stove in the middle of the meal. When my husband wanted to surprise me with flowers one day (once, and only once; he objects to giving me "dead things"), he knew to hide them in the oven; they could have been there for years without being discovered. Some months it only gets opened to clear out the cobwebs.

But my real problem with the kitchen has to do with its inherent dangers.

In fact, I am generally not allowed to have anything in my hand more lethal than a potato peeler, and I've been known to inflict some damage with that. My husband gets very nervous, almost to the point of twitching, if I'm involved with knives. I have a habit of cutting towards myself, and although I assure him hara kiri is not high on my list of suicide methods, he still watches me carefully and inquires as to the status of my life insurance policy if I'm carving the chicken. I have so many burn scars on my hands I look like a glass blower. I've been attacked by the oven element, the stove burners, plates, pans, pots, oil in the skillet …If there's a way to hurt yourself in the kitchen, I've perfected it.

THE DARK SIDE

I'M VERY MUCH afraid my beloved and I have gone over to the Dark Side; in the last few months, we've purchased a double recliner, a new used car, a wide-screen television, a Rubic's Cube – no, wait – a cubio? Rubio? Roku – that's it!, a C-Threepio (actually, I'm told it's an MP3 player, but I get confused – they all have letters and 3's in them), a Ping Pong table, and, worst of all – smart phones.

All right, the Ping Pong table doesn't really bother me; I became addicted to the game on our last vacation, and it's good exercise – for me, anyway, as I spend all my time chasing after the ball because I can't hit it to save my life. And the recliner is good for us, our kids tell us, as we're now approaching senility. But the other items… Frankly, I'm worried about us.

Our old television was so ancient it's analog, or digital, or whatever it is that's out of fashion, but it never mattered because we never watched it other than to view the occasional DVD. It was never hooked up to anything like a satellite or cable or whatever, because there's very little on television we care to watch, although we have also succumbed to Netflix. I blame it all on my husband (as he would be the first to say, it's always all his fault), as he suggested the wide-screen television. Now we are busy catching up on past episodes of shows everyone else watched years ago, like "Lost", although my beloved can't watch it for more than 30 seconds without shouting, "They're all too stupid to survive! That's right, run back into the jungle like idiots! Natural selection!"

I actually wanted the MP3 player, so that I can listen to my music anywhere, just as soon as I figure out how to get my records on it – yes, I am that old that I still have all my LPs – and the CDs. Then I have to work out how to play it in the new car. Modern conveniences are wonderful, I'm sure, but I am quite technologically challenged, and lacking the patience required to learn how to operate things. This means I ignore the Roku completely and let my beloved deal with it; if he were to ever leave me, I don't believe I would ever see another program on the new television.

The car is less technological than many, but it still baffles me. I now have to use a touch-screen to change the temperature or turn up the radio, and it's a wonder I haven't wrecked the car trying to do either. It's really better if I just pull over to adjust anything. It took my beloved and I working together about 15 minutes to figure out how to take off the parking brake, and he's much better at these things than I am. I'm still a little afraid of the car, but fortunately, I don't drive it much

But the most dreadful, to me, is the smart phone. I have never wanted a device that talks to me, much less tells me what to do, and it does both – or would, if I could figure out how to program it. As a friend says, she doesn't need a smart-phone - a dull-normal phone would be just fine. But our son talked us into it - so it's all his fault. He keeps trying to give us in-service trainings on the thing, and explain all the wonderful tricks it can do for us – my beloved, in fact, has just informed me he can now operate the Roku through his cell-phone. I just sit and stare numbly at him; it's all Greek to me. In fact, I took two semesters of Greek in college, so I can honestly say I have a better – if tenuous – grasp of Greek. And it was ancient Greek, at that. When we gave the salesman our old flip-phones, he just stared at them in shock, as if he had never seen anything like them before, and then gave them back to us, shaking his head.

After weeks of practice, I can just about answer it when it rings, and on a good day, I can find the number I need to call and call it, but that may be the permanent extent of my skills. The only real advantage I have found to it is that I can now waste away hours playing solitaire on it, and am fast becoming as addicted to that as to Ping Pong. I am told that I can use it to find my way around should I become lost, which happens on a regular basis, but I'm pretty certain I'll have to pull over to do that, too. And I still shake it to try to make it light up.

WEATHER – OR NOT

I LIKE TO HIKE on my lunch hour. Well, perhaps "like" is too strong a word; I pretty much have to hike to get away from work and people, in order to preserve some small portion of my already suspect and rapidly declining sanity. In any case, I go out in all weathers except the heat of summer, because the state of California, for which I work, hasn't seen fit to spring for showers in the building, and you really wouldn't want to be near me after a hike in the hot sun without a shower. Come to think of it, maybe that's a tactic I should employ... No, probably not.

So, out I go, rain, shine, or snow, my head hidden in a scarf in the winter. It's not that I crave anonymity; I never, ever use an umbrella, because I used to live in San Francisco. If you've spent any time in San Francisco, that statement needs no further explanation, but if you aren't familiar with The City, let me explain: every umbrella I ever unfurled in San Francisco promptly turned itself inside out in the wind and broke every major rib (the umbrella's, not mine), thereby rendering itself completely useless. And that was in the summertime. If I by any chance managed to get it to wherever I was going, I would, of course, forget it there, also rendering it useless, and I got tired of buying new umbrellas. Full skirts are also dicey propositions in The City; I've found myself hurling my body against random walls, grabbing as much skirt as I can get my hands on, trying to keep myself from doing an unintended and bad Marilyn Monroe-on-the-grate job when the wind comes up suddenly.

I find the best way of keeping the rain off my head while hiking is to wrap my hooded scarf around it, and then cover it with my bright yellow fisherman's slicker, but the slicker is so noisy and sweaty, I often just use the scarf, which is black and reminds me of "She Walks These Hills in a Long Black Veil", but hey, it keeps my head warm. Of course, as I move, the ends, which I have securely tucked into my shirt, often come loose, even though I'm walking, not running. My theory is that running is bad for all sorts of things, like knees, and those parts of me that move in uncomfortable ways when I run (which would be all my parts, from my cramping toes to my bouncing eyeballs), so I tend to run only if something with really big teeth is behind me, which happens rarely, fortunately.

In any case, as the ends come loose, I have to grab them and rewind, so to speak, which distracts me from whatever deep thought I happen to be meditating upon, but it's a small price to pay for remaining dry, although if it's raining really hard, I can't seem to avoid getting at least my hair wet, which is why I keep a blow dryer in my office. And just what is the past tense of "to blow dry one's hair", anyway? Blew dry? Blow dried? Blowed dry? Even spellcheck doesn't like that one! Well, it doesn't appear to like "spellcheck", either – so there you are - one of life's little mysteries. Usually I just avoid the issue (as I avoid many grammatical conundrums) by saying I dried my hair and skipping how I accomplished the feat; no one cares, anyway, right? But, to return to my point, I once became so engrossed in the scarf rewinding process that I tripped over the edge of the path and fell flat on my face – excepting my nose, of course, which broke my fall if not itself, miraculously – and filling my mouth with dirt.

I really don't particularly mind the snow, as long as I'm not sliding headfirst through it, which has been known to happen, or even the rain, providing I don't return to work soaking wet, which would probably be frowned upon. Or looking as if I'd taken up mud wrestling on my lunch hour, which would also probably not meet with my supervisor's approval. But post-holing through the snow tends to exhaust me pretty quickly, and I worry about becoming lost, as everything looks so different in the snow, and my already wobbly sense of direction is completely lost when everything is covered in white.

So, if you're out in the park at lunchtime and you see a piece of black scarf sticking up out of the snow, please come over and say hello after you've dug me out, and perhaps point me in the right direction back to work…

POSSESSIONS

I THINK OUR HOUSE is possessed. Well, not the house itself, just every appliance in it.

It started slowly, soon after we moved in. We had an automatic garage door opener, a luxury entirely new to us. The trouble was, the door would start to open, then reverse itself. I replaced the batteries in the opening device, and made sure there was nothing in the way of the door. It persisted. Some days, it's just fine, then all of a sudden it will go half way down, catching me off guard, then start back up again. Sometimes it will do this several times in a row. Sometimes it will go almost all the way to the bottom just to get my hopes up, then start back up. I have to sit and watch, punching the button madly, to make it work. It would be quicker to do it manually.

Then there's the microwave oven. It will heat one item quite nicely for seven minutes, or two items for three and a half minutes each, but then it has had its limit, and it returns to union rules and refuses to work anymore for the evening. If I try to force it, it will pretend it's going to work, then quit half way through heating the item. Alternatively, its little digital numbers will count down and I begin to think we will have lift-off, but when I get closer, I realize that the lights are on but no one is home; i.e., the motor is not running and nothing is heating. Apparently, it is exhausted and overheating, so I am forced to placate it with offerings of frozen vegetables in an attempt (mostly unsuccessful) to appease the microwave gods. I have even been known to add ice cubes and wave a towel at it, get on my knees and pray to the microwave gods, but it refuses to adhere to any schedule but its own.

The heater has quit twice so far. Both times the repairman replaced a part; the last time he assured me there were no parts left to replace, and commiserated with me at my bad luck. "It's unusual for both these parts to wear out so close together." Not if it's my house, and I didn't bother with homeowner's appliance insurance.

Then the garbage disposal stopped working. No sound, no movement, nothing. A friend came over, removed a chicken bone, and pronounced it cured. I explained to him that we hadn't had anything even approaching a real chicken in the house for three months. He shrugged and left. It even worked for a while after that. Then it quit again. My father came over and attacked it with a broom handle, and apparently successfully beat it into submission for another few months. It quit again, apparently on the same union schedule as the microwave, and I am prepared to rip it out altogether rather than live in the vain belief that I have a working garbage disposal.

I burned a cake and two batches of muffins before it became clear to me that the timer on the oven does not now, has never, and probably will not, work in my lifetime.

The toaster has begun to either hold the toast hostage firmly in its grip, until it is burnt to a crisp, or to fling it out with abandon at least two feet over the counter and onto the floor, completely untoasted.

My sewing machine has always, I claim, seen me coming and gleefully tied the bobbin into knots. My daughter asserts this is because I'm mean to it, but I firmly believe it is due to the evil impulses of machinery everywhere. I would read poetry to it if it would just do what I ask it to do, which is no more or less than what I bought it for – to sew.

Even the computer conspires against me. I can't get on-line; I try everything I can think of, even talking nicely to it. When I attempted to sign up my daughter for an on-line SAT test, I was reduced to jibbering hysteria and had to be talked down by the friendly support person they hire specifically for people like me. She seemed to think it was all in a day's work. Thank heavens when I took the SAT test, they still used stone tablets, or I never would have made it into college.

A friend suggested that I attempt ducking out of sight of the screen so that it can't see me, and trying again. I haven't sunk that low yet (literally or figuratively), but I'm getting closer. When the power goes out, I am blissfully happy; I no longer have to pretend that technology is my friend and can go peacefully back to the old days of simplicity. I can feel my blood pressure dropping just thinking of it. At least then if I see something in the dark, I'll know it's a ghost and not some possessed appliance coming to get me.

HOPPING MAD

MY HUSBAND IS British, and despite the newspaper's best efforts to print articles describing good beers to be had, my beloved has trouble finding beer that he likes as well as the stuff they brew back home. As a result, he has made his own for many years now, which means I, who loathe both the taste of brewed beer and the smell of brewing beer (although I'm perfectly OK with root beer), am forced to abandon the homestead when he gets a batch going, but it's a small price to pay for a happy hubby. He insists that British beer is drunk at room temperature, not "warm", as most folk here would call it, but then, I have to remind him that "room temperature" in Britain as I have experienced it, even in the height of summer, if one can call it that, is generally pretty Arctic.

Brewing appears to be a complicated process, if all the paraphernalia I find in my kitchen when hubby gets going is any indication. I discover plastic tubing draped from my cupboards, pots the size of Texas on my stove, odd ingredients spread over the counters, and net bags hanging from the clothes-line when he's finished.

Then there are the many containers the beer has to be moved into and out of as it brews, or ages, or whatever you call it: the aforementioned huge pot, which takes up my entire stove, thereby delaying dinner significantly; an enormous plastic container which bubbles alarmingly; a glass container so big I'm having trouble finding synonyms for it; and finally, some sort of keg system that takes up most of the basement. Half the time I feel as if I've moved to Transylvania and we're creating Shelley's monster – or am I mixing up my stories?

In his efforts to be thrifty about the project, he located friends in the valley (who shall remain nameless, lest both of you reading this stampede over to their home) who actually have hops growing more or less wild in their back-yard. If you are unfamiliar with hops in their natural habitat, I can describe them as resembling a lightweight green blossomy kind of thing that grows on vines and probably makes our friends' cows very happy. They should be picked carefully, lest too many leaves and stems go into the bag, which will require many hours of sorting later. My beloved and I differ in our approach to the task; he is more of a "Git 'er done" kind of person, who picks at random and flings everything into the bag, whilst I, hoping to save time later by taking more time now, carefully sort out undesirable objects like bugs as I pick.

So, of course I was drafted into going over and picking said hops like the field hand I never aspired to be, amid much grumbling on my part ("That's why I'm an office worker!" I wailed, to no avail). With the aid of a promised picnic in the back yard in order to lure me into physical labor, we managed to gather sufficient hops, take them home, and lay them out in bags on our back deck to dry. Unfortunately, a rather brisk wind came up while hubby was gone, which necessitated my chasing bags of hops around the deck, but eventually they were mostly corralled and brought inside to rest awhile, along with me.

My friend Tonya came over to visit not long afterwards and noted the fine green film covering the coffee table on which the bags of hops rested. Oh yes, we replied languidly, we noticed that; we think it's some kind of pollen from the hops. Tonya, younger and with better eyesight than us, peered more closely at the film and remarked grimly, "I've got news for you – your hops are hopping! Those are aphids!" Alarmed, we leapt to our feet to examine the dust more closely, and sure enough, it was on the move. In a panic, we dragged out the vacuum cleaner, dusted it off (if it ran on a battery we would have to have jumped it), and began frantically cleaning every available surface: coffee table, carpets, couch, lamps, and window sills were thoroughly and vigorously attacked until no trace of green remained.

The hops were removed to the nether regions of the house, where I assume they have divested themselves of their unwelcome passengers. Very soon, I expect I will be leaving the house while my beloved brews his potion, and he will happily keg and bottle his latest creation, which I am sure will be a very hoppy beer. Because after all, the last thing you want is an unhoppy beer.

PICTURES

LIFE TENDS TO BE confusing for me, because when people speak, I get pictures, and not the kind you get with a digital camera, either.

It started in grade school. I still remember the look in teachers' eyes when they would ask a question, and I would excitedly raise my hand and blurt out my answer, only to have them get that look, and say, "Well, that's an interesting answer, Virginia; not the right one, but interesting," and move quickly along. When I took geometry in high school, I was in trouble. They would start talking about tangents and irrational numbers, and I was off; I saw teachers going off subject and numbers on the floor having tantrums. In chemistry, when they discussed the attraction of sodium for chloride, I was writing love stories: "Oh Sodium, how can they keep us apart when they know we're meant for each other?" It's tough to pay attention properly when you get pictures, which makes passing the class challenging.

I read a lot, which results in what we refer to as "reading words": words you recognize and know the meaning of from the context, but have never heard pronounced. This often causes embarrassing slips, as when I pronounced "cacophony" "kak-a–fony", emphasis on the first syllable, or when my son confessed he thought façade, pronounced "fasad", and "faykade" were two different words with a very similar meaning.

At our house, we tend to have interesting discussions (to me, anyway) about random subjects, like grammatical constructions, geology, and sponges. The other night, for instance, my husband suggested he ought to be a forensic geologist, which brought pictures of a sort of CSI episode: "Yes, I sink zese rocks haf been dead for, oh, I should say, two or three billion years, give or take a few million – but hand me ze thermometer to be sure!"

Then we got into a discussion about sponges (I forget how). Someone was unaware that in the old days, sponges came from animals living in the ocean that look a lot like the ones in the kitchen sink. Someone else said they thought sponges were endangered, so we had to clarify we meant the ones in the ocean, not the ones in the sink, which are mostly synthetic now, and suddenly I had a picture of a kitchen sponge with the green scratchy stuff on the other side, cowering in the sink, in danger and fearful. My son (apparently afflicted with the same disease), who had been unenthusiastically reading Hemingway, added Hemingway aiming a rifle at the sponge, with a beer in the other hand, and we were off. Well, some of us were, anyway.

Added to this is the fact that I don't hear very well, which keeps life interesting. I hear all kinds of weird things, but everyone around me looks completely unfazed, which tells me the bizarre thing I think I have just heard wasn't heard by anyone else, and I have to spend some time trying to unravel and make sense of what I thought I just heard. Sometimes I work it out, sometimes people just say bizarre things, and I nod and smile a lot.

As a child, I didn't always hear song lyrics correctly, either. For years, when someone played or sang "Home on the Range", I heard "Where Selda misheard a discouraging word", which, while complicated, made perfect sense to me, whoever Selda was; I never did figure out why or how she was out there roaming with the buffalo, though. Occasionally, I'll hear an old song lyric and suddenly, everything becomes clear after years of confusion.

Just the other day it was the old Roger Miller song, "England Swings Like A Pendulum Do". I heard him sing, "bobbies (English policemen) on bicycles two by two" and the light dawned; for my entire life, I thought he was singing about some guy named Bobby, riding a bicycle, totally ungrammatically, as in "Bobby's on bicycles two by two". I never could understand why he needed two bicycles, or how he could be on both of them simultaneously, like some kind of circus act, and since the rest of the song was so grammatically incorrect, I just eventually gave up the fight in despair.

But then I'm a person who, even as a teenager, had to mentally correct pronoun cases in my favorite rock and roll songs every time I heard them, or I would have developed a severe twitch. No wonder I never fit in with my peers; they apparently never got pictures, either.

Kid Stuff

YEARS AGO, WHEN our daughter was younger and smaller, she decided she wanted to sleep in our clawfoot tub. We couldn't think of any good reasons to say no, so we let her. She filled the tub with her favorite blankets and pillows, and we all settled down to sleep. The bathroom is "en suite", a fancy way of saying there's no door between it and our bedroom, but she doesn't snore, so we weren't too worried, and everything went fine.

The next night her brother, not to be outdone, decided he, too, wanted to sleep in the tub, and as we wanted to give them an equal opportunity to experience the wonders of bathtub sleeping (after all, they never got to Disneyland), we agreed. However, during the night, he somehow managed to turn the cold water tap on with his foot. He and I slept peacefully through this development, but his father suddenly sat bolt upright and leapt out of bed in the general direction of the bath. This woke me up, and we both proceeded to remove soggy bedding from the bath while our son slept serenely on, completely unaware of any problem. As we couldn't seem to wake him sufficiently to move him, we left him there the rest of the night. The next morning, he remembered nothing of the night's events

It wasn't the first time my beloved had been roused from a deep sleep by unexpected developments involving the children. Once I was sound asleep when he again leapt from the bed, crouched on the floor, and stared fixedly underneath said bed. Alarmed, I squeaked "What is it?" and he replied tersely, "Lizard." I thought I was still asleep until he explained that our son's pet lizard had somehow escaped its cage and was hiding under our bed. How a man who managed to sleep through crying children and other loud noises for years managed to hear a lizard enter our carpeted room and crawl under the bed still eludes me.

At times, the dog will bark endlessly at nothing, as dogs sometimes do, never managing to disturb my beloved's slumber; he tends to levitate and wake up in hurry when I shout "Woof! (the dog's name – long story) Shut up!" over his head in the general direction of the window, though. I imagine the neighbors are a little puzzled, too, to hear me echoing the dog, but I try not to worry about that.

I came in for my share of terror caused by the children, too. I am deathly afraid of snakes, but my son insisted on having a series of them as pets. This was all right, as we occasionally got to watch it eat lizards, goldfish, and other creatures; since we don't watch television, we all lined up on his bed and had our own "Wild Kingdom" on a Friday night, which was a little gruesome in retrospect, but educational.

Anyway, one day my husband took me gently by the arm and told me he had something to show me downstairs, but not to be alarmed, which of course immediately struck fear into my heart. Somehow the snake had escaped (you would think at some point we would have caught on and bought a new cage, but no), slithered down a flight of stairs, up the couch, over a cabinet, and was comfortably ensconced in a plastic plant, regarding us calmly and testing the atmosphere with its tongue while I ran screaming hysterically from the room. I'm just grateful Basil the rat never escaped.

Years later I was walking in the park with my daughter when a small garter snake made a hasty dash across our path (probably some form of snake "chicken" if that's not too confusing; come to think of it, I'm not certain snakes can dash, but never mind). I made a credible effort to climb up her as if she were a tree, shrieking incoherently the entire time, before she could get me calmed down. She hadn't even seen it, but I'm sure if she had, it wouldn't have alarmed her; my beloved insisted I not pass on my "irrational" fear of snakes and spiders to the children, and it seems to have worked.

O Tannenbaum

SO, IT BEING THE Christmas season and all, my daughter was dispatched to her grandparents' house to get their Christmas ornaments and the (fake) tree down from the garage attic. Normally, this task is delegated to our son, but as he's away at college and she's the only other one in the family thin enough, young enough and athletic enough to get up and through the hole in the garage ceiling and back down without doing serious damage to herself, it was her lucky day. Well, I wasn't completely useless; I held the ladder and fended off the spider who lowered himself down on his silky thread to check out what was going on. Pity I couldn't get HIM to go back up and throw down a few boxes. Fortunately, our daughter does not, as my beloved puts it, share my "irrational fear of spiders". Hah! I'm not the one who swelled up like a big toad and had to be taken to emergency when one (spider, not toad) crawled out of the logs and into our bed in the middle of the night and bit him. He can blame it on the hand sanitizer all he wants (we thought he was allergic to it), but I know better. And I noticed he vacuumed all the logs shortly thereafter (not out in the forest or the woodpile, you understand – we live in a log home; even my beloved isn't THAT picky about cleanliness).

But I digress; I was, as I recall, waxing lyrical about this beloved season, or at least the lead-up to it, and I seem to have left our daughter hanging by a thread, so to speak, from the attic crawlspace. So, she begins, indeed, crawling about (it was, after all, a crawlspace), handing down random boxes, none of which are what they say they are on the labels, but eventually emptying the attic and managing to locate the ornaments, decorations, and fake tree.

I have always been scornful of fake trees; I think it goes back to my childhood when we always went to my grandmother's house in Los Angeles for Christmas, and she had an aluminum tree. Somehow the aluminum tree - which, much as I loved my grandmother, I have to say was the tackiest tree I have ever seen - got tied in with Los Angeles and the lack of weather of any type and the fact that, although I was born there, I hope never to have to spend time there again, and I treated the idea of a fake tree with disdain for most of my life.

In any case, I didn't like fake trees because they looked fake (even the green ones) and didn't smell like Christmas. However, the last time we had a family outing and cut down our tree in the woods, when my son was young, he and I both cried, and I haven't had a real tree since. I can always gather up fallen boughs if I want the smell.

In fact, fate intervened; I was with a friend at Costco (being too cheap to have our own membership), and the fake Christmas tree floor model was on sale; I couldn't resist, especially when the salesman told me it came with all the ornaments free. I mean, how cool is that? I almost didn't even have to decorate it; that's MY kind of tree. Mind you, stuffing it into the back of my friend's car along with our kids was a challenge, but life is full of challenges, including the fact that I have the only fake tree in existence, as far as I know, that sheds needles every year. I thought one of the advantages of a fake tree was no needles to vacuum, but what do I know?

I also remember, when I was very young and my parents were pretty pressed for cash, the family tradition regarding the Christmas tree. We didn't have a tree for most of the lead-up to Christmas, because our practice was to go to midnight Christmas Eve services and then go to the by-now deserted Christmas tree lots and pick one up for free. I am convinced there could have been no moral, ethical, or religious dilemma here, as the trees had been abandoned, after all, and besides, who comes out of church and steals Christmas trees?? Of course, there was that skirt incident with me, but that was an accident, so it doesn't count; besides, I brought it back.

And believe me, these were definitely Snoopy trees. In fact, as my father was in charge of picking out the tree, it was ALWAYS a Snoopy tree, even when we paid for them. I remember my mother raising her eyes to heaven and calmly pointing out the flaws in every tree he brought home, while he protested there was nothing wrong that a little work couldn't cure, like cutting off this branch and drilling a hole and inserting it over there, as he got out the drill and the saw and my mother, shaking her head, went back into the kitchen. Honestly, I think his criteria for picking a tree was how sorry he felt for it and how neglected and lonely it looked.

In any case, although my parents now have their tree and ornaments, my house still has none, except for one half strand of outside lights still up from last year for unknown reasons. Since I have less than zero interest in crawling 40 feet off the ground onto the roof to install said lights, I'm afraid our house will not glow with Christmas cheer anytime soon. I'll be happy if I can get baby Jesus and the crèche scene into the house before history repeats itself and he's born into the modern-day equivalent of the stable – my garage.

May we all have a blessed and peaceful time on this day Christ was born and may the spirit and memory of that day be with us throughout the year.

PET PEEVES

I WAS TALKING TO some friends awhile back, and we got to discussing pets we had as children. I confessed that one of my siblings had captured a snake and put it in a jar, as kids do. Now, I don't like snakes – I hate them in fact – but I got to feeling sorry for this one, because it was a really hot day, and I could not imagine that it was very comfy in that hot little jar. So, I dumped it out into a deep pan of water to cool off. Apparently it was not a water snake. When last seen, it was headed down a heater vent in the house, never to be heard from again. Needless to say, it was one of those little stories we never did feel compelled to tell our mother, whose fear and hatred of snakes is, if anything, even worse than mine. I will never forget the sight of my mother, fearless protector of her children, hacking a harmless garter snake into pieces with a shovel, screaming in terror the entire time, because it (the snake) had dared to venture into our garage when we were trying to disembark from the car.

But this was a story about pets, not wild animals. My confession seemed to open the floodgates of guilt, so to speak; all of us were adult women – mothers even, as I recall - but the burdens we had been carrying over the accidental, premature deaths of long-ago innocent pets was enormous. One friend related that when her children were small, they had a pet hamster. Now, she had never been particularly fond of the thing, as she found it boring, but she had no violent feelings towards it, either. So when she came into her daughter's room one day, found it dead, and buried it in the back yard, she believed she was simply protecting her child from excessive grief. She claims that it was a complete misunderstanding on her part of the hibernation habits of rodents that caused this one's untimely demise.

Then another woman confessed that when she was young, she was given the task of vacuuming the house. Being an efficient person, even at that age, she decided it would be a waste of time and energy not to vacuum the bird's cage as well. It really was NOT her fault, she insisted, that she was momentarily distracted and managed to suck up the bird while her back was turned. Besides, she maintained, the bird did survive the trip; she removed it alive from the bag. It just didn't last very long after that. We attributed its death to shock.

My favorite story was from the woman who related that as a child, she had a goldfish. One day in the winter, she began to worry that her goldfish might be too cold, so she thoughtfully decided to give it warm water to swim in. When she watched the fish begin to swim rapidly and frantically in manic circles around the bowl, it began to dawn on her that hot tap water might not be this, or any fish's, cup of tea, so to speak; she quickly replaced the hot water with cold water again, and watched her little fish anxiously. The fish appeared tired, but unhurt. In the morning, however, she realized the entire traumatic event must have been too much for its tender piscine psyche; the fish appeared to have snapped under the strain of an uncertain world and leaped out of his bowl onto the dry, but temperature-constant, tile floor, and expired.

My sister's pet story is family legend. A somewhat feral cat came to live with them, much to my brother-in-law's displeasure, and she (the cat) was pretty timid around people. One day, my brother-in-law called my sister at work to remark tersely that she needed to come home immediately. It seemed the cat had crawled under the bed; at some point my brother-in-law became aware of howling coming from that direction, and went in to investigate. Somehow, the cat had managed to get her tail caught in a bedspring and couldn't get loose. She was pretty frantic and definitely dangerous at that point, so my brother-in-law enlisted my sister's aid to get the cat loose, but even with heavy gloves and determination, they couldn't get her tail untangled from the bedspring. They picked the bed up and set it on end to make it easier, to no avail; the cat remained hostile and the tail firmly attached to the spring. Finally, my brother-in-law left the room in exasperation; as my sister worried he had gone to get his gun and shoot the cat, which she suspected he'd always wanted to do anyway, she heard the sound of a chainsaw revving. She and the cat looked at each other in equal measures of alarm and terror, the cat worked harder to get loose, and in came my brother-in-law with the chainsaw.

Fortunately for the cat, his intention was not to reenact the chainsaw massacre, but to cut the board attached to the spring, which he did. Suddenly free and definitely spooked by now, but before her tail could be freed, the cat took off, spring and board still attached, pinballing down the hall with the board slamming against the walls on either side, howling as if the hounds of hell were after her.

She was not heard from again for a very long time, but I understand she did survive the experience and now lives comfortably in the garden shed, as far away from beds as she can get.

ICE ESCAPADES

MY GOAL IN LIFE IS to remain upright. Not in the moral, ethical, sense, although that is also a lofty aim, but physically erect. And not all the time, of course; horizontal is very convenient for sleeping. My roommate in college used to muse that it must be my great height (she was barely five feet tall to my 5'9") that caused me to remain prone so much of the time – there wasn't much I couldn't do from my bed, but that's really just because I was lazy – and the altitude must have tired me. No, I simply want to keep from falling, which happens with alarming frequency and tends to hurt when I land – probably because it's so far to fall when you're tall.

This fear of falling has kept me as far away from any form of ice or snow as I can manage, but when I was younger, smaller, and less careful, someone, probably my mother in yet another desperate attempt to have a moment to herself away from her four children, took us ice skating (don't get me wrong – she's a fantastic mother – but who wouldn't need a break from four kids roughly two years apart? Besides, she reads my stories).

Why anyone would want to cross ice on anything, much less on blades you could use to mince celery, escapes me, but there we were, strapping the things on and having a go. The first thing I noticed was that the blades were very thin, which made my movements very wobbly, as balance is not my strong suit, and the second piece of information to catch my attention was that I had double-jointed ankles, as I was now skating on them rather than the narrow blades on the ice skates. It was a lot more stable, I must admit, but kind of an attention-getter.

After this unfortunate incident, I avoided ice rinks, but there was nothing I could do when it snowed and iced over at home. So there have been "incidents". Like the time I was coming down my fairly steep, icy drive in Carson City to take the dog for a walk and fell backwards so quickly I landed on my elbows, which didn't stop my head from banging smartly down onto the icy cement; not a soft landing at all. I lay there for a while, waiting to see if anything felt broken, moaning quietly as little electric shocks ran up and down my arms from my hands to my shoulders and literally seeing stars (my fingers were numb for days). Eventually I realized no one was home, and if I didn't get up the children would come home from school to find their mother frozen to the drive, which would undoubtedly traumatize them for life. I finally cautiously moved one limb at a time, loathe to experience a repeat performance and reenacting the scene of Bambi on the ice, and slowly made my way on hands and knees to the side of the drive, where I rested briefly before making my way painfully up the hill, into the house, and onto the couch, where I remained until spring thaw.

When we moved here to Siskiyou County, of course, winter followed. Just the other day I managed to load myself up with three or four bags of groceries and four or five other bulky items, not willing to make more than one trip from the garage up the outside stairs in the ice and cold, got them balanced just right, holding several items in my teeth for good measure, and made my way cautiously out the garage door, where I promptly went down like a sack of wet cement, ripping open most of the bags and scattering groceries to the four winds. Of course, making several trips would have saved a lot of time and aggravation in the long run, but where's the challenge in that?

The previous year, my husband and I were about to leave for the store, having already packed ourselves into the truck, when I realized I had forgotten something in the house and scampered around the back to go back inside. I slipped on the ice and went down yet again, and lay there whimpering, waiting for my beloved to come rescue me. I waited a very long time. Finally realizing my white knight must have fallen asleep on his steed, I picked myself up and dragged myself back to the truck, only to be greeted by his laconic inquiry: "What took you so long?" Nothing, dear, I wanted to reply; I was just ice-skating.

LUDDITE'S LAMENT

LAST FALL WE TOOK our youngest off to his college dorm room. For my more sensitive readers, I draw a veil over the copious weeping and fond farewells suffered by his mother, and move on to my point: technology. That boy had more wires, cords, lines, and cables than the average television station or major power plant crammed into a room the size of a broom closet, and it still wasn't enough. I think he's STILL frantically ordering more cables for who knows what, but it all seems to be essential for the average student these days. When he complained about only having two outlets in his room, I tried to tell him that when I attended this same school, we didn't even have computers, much less all the rest of these gadgets, but he just looked at me briefly, the way you would an alien being, and continued connecting wires, some of which he apparently had to yank out of a wall socket by their throats. These country boys are very handy with a tool kit.

I'll be the first to admit I am not a technological wizard. All right, I can barely operate my stove, but still, it's all getting to be a bit much. We used to have a microwave oven I could handle: you put in the food to be heated, set the timer for your best guess, watched it, and took it out when it either dinged or exploded. When we got a new one, I felt as if I were programming a jet; pick your temperature, your time, what type of food you're cooking – and do you want fries with that? I was pleased about the popcorn function, though; cool, I thought, I can just toss it in there, push the button for popcorn, and let 'er rip. Unfortunately, my microwave doesn't seem to understand popcorn, at least not the way I do; it manages to either cremate it or pop a few kernels and leave the rest to break my teeth.

Watching a movie at home has become an epic struggle with technology. In an effort to get surround sound, my husband has somehow wired the stereo to the television set; this is a wonderful idea, but it has added yet another remote to the collection – we had five at last count - when I can hunt them down from wherever they have disappeared to. Once I have located them, I can't see any of the buttons without my glasses, so we have another search. Then I don't know which remote goes to which piece of machinery, and I can spend hours pointing the VCR remote (yes, we still have one of those; I just got it figured out when they changed to DVDs) at the stereo, with no luck. We don't even watch television; we're not hooked up to a satellite system or even cable because we only use the TV to watch DVDs. Or videos. I think if I had to figure that stuff out, I'd be ready for NASA.

I'm not ashamed to admit we still have a record player, which I do know how to work, and lots of records; I hear vinyl is making a comeback, and it's a lot simpler than the I-Pod my son has to deal with. I will always call them albums.

I finally came around to computers; it's embarrassing to realize I remember when they were called "mainframes" and took up a whole room, but then I remember the advent, not just of color television, but of television itself. Computers are awfully useful, but if Microsoft comes up with one more version of Windows, I'm going to blow mine up. I don't know why I'd bother; it's so old it belongs in a museum and takes an hour to warm up; my beloved refers to it affectionately as being "steam driven". None of the current programs work on it, but I hang on to it because I know I'm not going to be able to figure out how the new ones work.

I still shake my cell phone (or, when I get frustrated, smack its little face) in an effort to make the screen light up; my son just rolls his eyes and goes back to his I-Pod and videogames. The other day I had a major triumph when, for the first time, I managed to put a new telephone number into its little electronic address book – and I've had the phone for several years.

Is anybody else old enough to remember transistor radios? I saw a sign in a grocery store recently that said, "If you've never listened to an eight-track tape, we won't sell you alcohol"; boy, did that make me feel old.

When people around me start talking modern technology (or current TV shows, for that matter), I just nod and smile vacantly. And now I'll never be able to watch another DVD (or video) at home, because my son is the only one who knows how to work it, and he's in his dorm room. That, and just missing him, are enough to make anybody cry.

MORE MIXED METAPHORS

AFTER I PUBLISHED A story on mixed metaphors, several people gave me their own (and others') slip-ups, which, along with a few other quotes and observations, I duly pass on. First, some slips, thanks to Annie Kramer and her friend:

"She was making Gestapo soup" (much more scary than gazpacho, I imagine). "Let's all go out to the placebo" (versus the gazebo). "It was six of one, two dozen of another" (clearly another math-impaired person like myself). "It was bigger than her eyes"; I believe they were aiming for "Her eyes were bigger than her stomach", although perhaps not for long. "He had too many guns in the fire (as opposed to irons)"; "Israeli soldiers were using Isuzus" (as opposed to Uzis; perhaps they ought to drive them instead). And I've left my favorite for last: "They were serving steak and squid with testicles" (assuming they meant tentacles, but who knows?).

My mother added "I've been dragging my brain" (she meant she was trying to remember something, and I think she meant "racking her brain", but it's hard to say); "It's time to hit the bucket", a creative combination of kicking the bucket and hitting the hay, when she meant to say sleep; and one of my favorites: "You know, hindsight is always 50-50". She also remarked (about an issue that was in the past):" That's all under the rug now". Maybe we should vacuum.

My daughter: "That doesn't cut the cake." After some cogitation, I came up with what she actually meant (cut the mustard), to which she replied in protest, "Well, cake is easy to cut, too!" She also recently contributed "I'm drawing a hard line in the sand", "He's a sheep in grandmother's clothing", "I was swamped under" and "I don't have a dog in that race", but I'm now so confused, that one may be right. I thought it was supposed to be "hunt", but who knows? Clearly the issue is genetic.

My beloved further contributed "You know, they lift and celebrate" (bras);

and "We'll burn that bridge when we get to it".

I have not escaped the malady, either: the other day I couldn't think of the word "rebound" to describe a relationship; all that came to me was "bounce back". My daughter then added that she thought there was no bounce left, period. I also came up with "You know, the pepper jack!" one time when I couldn't think of "zip drive"; the scary part was that the friend I was talking to immediately knew what I meant. And when I couldn't remember the phrase "beat the bushes" as in looking for something, all I could come up with was "rattle the bushes" or "shake the bushes". I once said something about a room's "Sheng fui", but I never understood the concept anyway.

Another friend, a former English teacher, recounted a few of her principal's errors: "He left of his own violation"; on eating uncooked food: "the dangers of bottle-ism"; an old tradition was "not a scared cow anymore"; someone with unrealistic expectations, or possibly desperate – hard to say - was "grasping at stars", and someone had a "pour-pot of ideas" (or, perhaps, a potpourri?). This inspired a memory of my former boss, who referred constantly to having "fruit compost" for dessert.

And there's the anonymous contribution (because I can't remember its origin): "He was making money hand over foot!" and about something that wasn't their favorite thing: "It's not my cup of fish".

I used to know a guy from Oklahoma who had his own repertoire of colorful expressions: if you were happy; you were "smilin' like a dead pig in the sunshine". If you were making a lot of noise, you were "squealin' like a pig stuck under a gate". And my favorite: "That room was so small, you couldn't cuss a cat without gettin' fur in your teeth."

A cowboy in Winnemucca, Nevada, where I used to live, once colorfully described trying to get a recalcitrant relative to do something as "Like tryin' to stand a snake up on its tail".

When I worked in the prison, we made tapes of the teachers and used something called a character generator in the process, which I found ironic.

I loved the sign I saw in England: "Heavy plant crossing", but I must be the only one who saw mental pictures of overweight rutabagas, roots trailing, in special crosswalks. Even better was "Pavement Rehabilitation", which was not found in the prison next to the character generator, unfortunately.

And when we lived in Ghana, we discovered the interesting custom of naming shops and affixing slogans to taxis that occasionally gave us pause:

there was the "God Is First Chainsaws" shop, the "Blood of the Lamb Butcher", "Jesus Saves Electrical Contractor", and the "God Is In Charge" taxi, which definitely made us nervous, as we would really rather the driver be in charge, or at least awake. But my favorite was a roadside sign: "Safe Journey! Donated by Weapons of God Prayer Group". Definitely inspirational, one way or another.

VEHICULAR MATTERS

A WHILE AGO A friend commented to me that he was certain there would be two sights visible from space - the Great Wall of China, and my car. Although I am certain he was exaggerating just a bit, I must admit my vehicles are somewhat distinctive - and that's just from the outside.

My car was rather old - 1984, in fact - but that wasn't what made it stand out to the average driver and pedestrian. I imagine that what caught the eye of the casual observer might have been the peculiar color scheme. It began life as a yellowish Toyota Tercel, but after one too many encounters with suicidal deer, something had to be done. After twenty years of driving in this county with no loss of life (unlike my sister, who has done to death every conceivable form of wild and domestic fauna, including cows, deer, skunks, possum, a bat, and a goose, although she firmly declares the latter was suicidal), in one year I did to death three deer and a skunk. After the first deer hit me, my husband energetically removed the hood and pounded it back into roughly the same shape, but when the second depressed hoofed, four-legged, antlered animal decided to end it all somewhere in the vicinity of my hood, even my husband gave up and went to the nearest scrap yard to replace it (the hood, that is, not the deer. There are more than enough deer to go around, apparently, since he hit another one not too much later). Unfortunately for those with any esthetic sensibilities, the hood he proudly brought home was - RED. The car now resembled an overlarge ladybug; all we needed were some big black dots and a set of wings. Actually, the wings might have increased the speed.

I ought to be grateful. One day, before the color changes, I had a quick errand to run, so I dashed into the store and out in record time, hopped back into my car, and found the key didn't work in the ignition. I suddenly realized that while I was almost certain I had locked the car, since as a matter of habit I always do so, it had not, in fact, been locked when I got in. I next noticed that someone had cleaned the car while I was gone. Eventually I realized that although it was an exact duplicate of my car, my car was parked several spaces down. I slunk furtively off to my mobile trash heap, or as a friend of mine dubbed it, "The Tenement on Wheels". And that was BEFORE I had children.

There's no doubt the inside is messy. A boss who (reluctantly) rode with me once, having finished a cup of coffee and set it down on the floor, wryly asked me to return it to him "if you ever find it again". In the years B.C. (Before Children), I kept changes of clothes, extra food, important papers, and garbage (I do hate to litter) handy in the vehicle. Since having children, the general milieu has attained a distinct flavor, if not character. Now the extra clothing includes smaller sizes and more variety: dirty socks, old McDonald's toys, sweaty T-shirts, grungy baseball mitts, and moldy shoes. Added to these are stale french fries, shriveled apple cores, homework papers, toiletries, and animal as well as human hair. Like an archeological dig, as the deeper layers are excavated, they tell a tale of family life stretching back years, if not generations. And, like the famous La Brea Tar Pits, occasionally some forgotten bit of ancient history bubbles to the surface, amidst cries of "So that's where my jock strap went!" The frustrating rule of nature appears to be that the item you are frantically searching for never appears, while things you are decidedly NOT looking for suddenly materialize. The children hate to litter, too - except in the car, of course - but this, I point out to my husband, has its advantages; should we ever become stranded in a howling blizzard, we'll never starve to death. Although resorting to cannibalism may seem the more desirable option compared to eating what lurks in the dark recesses of the passenger side foot well. The dead (in fact, mummified) wasps and flies in the back window would at least provide instant protein. When my son was little, I looked in the rear-view mirror one day to see him munching on a French fry. As I knew we hadn't had fast food in quite some time, immediate removal was necessary, although he did not take it well; heaven only knows where he found it or how old it was. I was able to point out to hubby in some triumph that we also have enough of those little packets of catsup and salt and pepper to survive at least as long as that guy they found over a snowbank a while back, providing they don't kill us, of course. That is, the catsup packets.

While I am normally fairly sanguine at the idea of anyone stealing my car, I am careful to lock it. There is rarely anything of value in it, and even if there were, if I can't find it, I don't imagine anyone else can, either. My vague hope is that the police, seeing that the car is locked, might be less likely to tow it away as an abandoned vehicle after seeing the mess inside. Perhaps if I cleaned out some of the junk in the back, we might go up hills faster than 45 miles an hour. As it is, on a good day, going downhill with a following wind, we might manage a whopping 55 mph. And when passengers point out with some alarm that the oil light is on, I hasten to reassure them that it's always on - has been for years, in fact - some sort of intermittent electrical failure, no doubt - and that we're only to worry if it goes out, according to my husband. Rattles don't bother him, either; he claims the time to be concerned is when the noise stops, signaling that the rattling bit has now fallen off and no doubt lies 300 miles back on the freeway for someone to run over. It's always an essential bit, too.

I've learned a little about mechanics the hard way; as things go wrong with the car, I learn of their existence, their vital importance, and how excessively expensive parts are. For a while I had a car with the annoying habit of going completely dead at 70 mph on the freeway. I learned, eventually, to pull over and restart it in record time until the "logic module" could be replaced. Another car decided to gradually lose its lights as I drove a completely deserted stretch of highway in the middle of the night, and I learned about alternators. My current car occasionally refuses to start, but so far has been considerate enough to do it in crowded parking lots with pay phones, so that I can call my beloved and wail at him to come get me. He invariably arrives, calm and rational, and does something simple like scrape corrosion off a battery terminal, whereupon the car obediently starts up. I have discovered that, unlike a friend of mine, beating the engine with a hairbrush does not provoke it into starting. Maybe she had a more expensive hairbrush and had some idea what to hit, while I pound energetically but ineffectively on anything that presents itself.

There is also a rather complicated arrangement with the clutch that I don't fully understand. I only know that my instructions are as follows: should the clutch start to slip (that is to say, badly; it always slips occasionally), I am to reach down to the clutch pedal, pull on a ring, and thereby remove a piece of metal which will somehow make everything fine. I have a technicolor picture of myself performing this procedure on the freeway or in a busy intersection, but there's no point in worrying about that now.

Using drive-throughs is always entertaining, too - it takes two hands to roll down the window, so I usually just open the door and walk over to the bemused employee to pick up the meal. So much for fast food. I've been meaning to give it up anyway.

We've had several other vehicles to contend with - all fully paid for, mind you. One was a truck we actually purchased for cash, which tells you about what it was worth. It, of course, had its own idiosyncrasies; it was impossible to open the passenger side door, for instance, unless the vehicle was in the mood, which wasn't often, and only when one was least expecting it. It also tended to slip out of third gear at will, and the turn signal had to be held in place when turning left. Also, every once in a while the power steering would quit, usually when making a sharp turn, of course, against oncoming traffic. This led to an interesting experience one day when I was attempting to turn left onto an onramp; I was holding the gear shift in third and the turn signal up, steering with my elbows, when the power steering gave out.

One day I drove the truck over to the neighbor's house to feed their chickens, ducks, and horses. I parked up the hill from their pond and set the parking brake, leapt out to feed the livestock - and watched the truck roll slowly toward the pond, picking up speed as it went. It was up for grabs whether I'd lose it in the pond or get to watch it take out a small tree. Thus we discovered that the parking brake was, as we used to say in Ghana, faulty. Naturally, I did exactly the wrong thing, leaping back into the truck and slamming on the brakes. At least I avoided murdering the ducks and the tree.

In addition, for the princely sum of $600, we acquired a Volkswagen Quantum diesel, with the distinct advantage of being all one color. Unfortunately, it was so nondescript that I once again got into another car by mistake. I really have no excuse; the car I got into, while the same basic shape, was a totally different model, and even a different color. At least my red hood was distinctive. There were, of course, one or two drawbacks to this car, too. The front defroster didn't work, although the back one did. I suppose in an emergency I could always have driven in reverse. The back left passenger door opened neither from the inside nor the outside of the car, and if one became insistent, the handle fell off. The speedo cable didn't work, but this was a minor handicap, as I never paid attention to my rate of travel anyway. At least when the police stopped me for speeding and inevitably asked, in shocked wonder, "Do you know how fast you were going?" I could honestly say I had no idea.

One night when I was driving us all to dinner, the clutch broke off under my foot. I don't mean it went all the way to the floor, as it has in other vehicles, I mean it literally broke off and fell onto the floor. My beloved was impressed; he said he'd never seen anyone break through a half inch of solid steel while driving.

The other morning on the way to work the dashboard started smoking, which my hubby says I'm not to worry about. I was really annoyed, however, when I tried to fill the tank and half the gas cap came off in my hand. It still isn't fixed.

Perhaps it's time for another not new car…

CAT THINGS, ETC.

SO, THE OTHER NIGHT I threw three of our four cats outside before retiring but, even after searching in all the usual hiding places, could not for the life of me find the fourth one – cat, that is.

I finally gave up and went to bed, hoping she would decide I'd gone to sleep and come out so that I could pounce on her (life in our house involves a great deal of strategic planning). As predicted, before I fell asleep I heard a thunk, and after creeping stealthily downstairs I managed to find her in the pantry, headfirst in a bag of cat food. We don't call her Fatty-Catty for nothing, but that was novel, even for her.

I had been missing one of "the boys" (the other three cats are male) the day before, which surprised me; these cats know better than to miss the breakfast train, because if they do, they don't eat again until I come home after work. He missed dinner, too, so I assumed he'd been eaten by something bigger and higher in the food chain and had almost begun to mourn when I discovered he had holed up in the garage, and then proceeded to run under a car where I couldn't get at him to throw him out. Like any reasonable person, I went in two seconds flat from worry, mourning and missing him, thinking of all his good qualities (a short list, in his case, but I am unreasonably fond of him), to cursing him six ways to Sunday since I did not have time to cajole him into coming out before I left for work, and therefore had to leave the garage door open all day.

This is the same cat who was involved in one of the funniest things I had ever witnessed, so he was close to my heart. One day I heard a ruckus out on the front deck, and hearing hissing, knew it was the cats fighting. This made me angry (no fighting is allowed in our house, or even outside it – at least, for the cats), so I whipped open the door and started yelling, as I am wont to do when angered by animals. This cat, Buster by name, was sitting innocently on the railing, completely uninvolved in the cat fighting match, but my shouting apparently frightened him so much that he leapt straight up in the air like a cartoon cat, and when he came down, he entirely missed the railing he had started on. Did I mention that the deck is about 20 feet from the ground? When he came down, he went straight to ground level. I ran over to the edge, worried that he had hurt himself, only to see him land and take off running as if the hounds of hell were after him. He's a survivor, that one.

But I digress. I was about to launch into another story regarding cats: when our daughter was small, I didn't allow her to drink colas, explaining that they weren't good for her because they contained caffeine. One day I heard her refuse a cola at a friend's house, sniffing disdainfully, "I don't drink those; they have cat things in them." You really want to avoid those cat things – they'll keep you up all night.

It's been quite a week altogether: one day, very tired after the days that had preceded it, I decided to go for my usual lunch-time hike, even though every bone in my body begged me to just take a nap. When I arrived at the park, feeling virtuous, I discovered that the lid to a jug of water that I keep in the car (don't ask) had somehow loosened and the jug had poured its contents into one of my hiking shoes, soaking both it and the sock residing in it. So much for the hike.

Our daughter, who is currently residing in the Bay Area going to college and has been riding her bicycle everywhere due to a few too many speeding tickets, got a flat tire she was unable to fix. The car we left there for emergencies was in the shop, so she's been walking to school and back, which takes her an hour and a half each way. She has not once complained about this, which I take as a mark of great character; we build 'em tough in this county. She did, however, call one day to tell me her feet were aching, so I suggested she soak them in a basin, since she doesn't have a bathtub. This advice was greeted by a brief silence. She then responded that she was, sort of. Upon further enquiry, it transpired that she was soaking them in her crockpot. While I was impressed with her ingenuity, I requested that she remind me not to eat stew at her house any time soon.

Meanwhile, our son, in college in Santa Cruz, has wisdom teeth coming in - painfully. I've made innumerable calls to dentists and oral surgeons from here to Santa Cruz to Oregon and back trying to organize their removal (the teeth, not the surgeons or dentists – them we're going to need). He updates me with regular bulletins to let me know whether I'll need to drive down there (a seven-hour trip) at a moment's notice to accompany him to the oral surgeon to have them yanked out (again, the teeth, not the surgeon), but so far he's hanging tough with Ibuprofen.

Which reminds me: when our daughter had her wisdom teeth removed, she came up with a brilliant solution to the chipmunk-like swelling that ensued afterwards: she simply took a bra, filled the cups with ice, and wrapped it around her head so that the cups of ice rested on her swollen cheeks. It looked a little odd, but then, she wasn't going anywhere, and it worked a treat.

I have decided that while I thought my children's issues were difficult when they were young, the issues just get more complicated – and more expensive – as they get older.

While my husband has been away at work in Mali and missed all of this, I hope to join him soon on an adventure involving floating down the Niger River (hopefully in a boat, because you never know with him) to Timbuktu - really. It should be restful compared to home, even though I've been told that camels may be involved. I'll keep you posted.

WHAT'S COOKING?

"WHAT ARE YOU DOING?" my husband inquired mildly, one eyebrow raised, as he entered the kitchen. My beloved is generally careful, in such situations, to approach me gingerly, as one would a coiled rattlesnake; I was pounding energetically on a bag on the counter with a ballpeen hammer. "Cooking" I replied grimly through gritted teeth. He nodded sagely and strolled away as rapidly as he could manage without appearing as if he were in any kind of a hurry.

I was cooking, after a fashion, and there was, as always, a reasonable explanation: I had brought home one of those bags of frozen fruit, but forgot to put it in the freezer right away, which as anyone knows who has dealt with such things, is always a major error; they melt. But that's not the real issue; the real issue is that when you put them, eventually, into the freezer, they freeze, which is, of course, the point in putting them into the freezer, and the juice somehow contrives to transform itself into a substance harder than concrete, which explains why I was doing my best imitation of a chain-gang member with a pick-axe on my kitchen counter.

I can often be found hammering on various items in my kitchen, but usually it involves my little wooden Ecuadorian mallet, created, I suppose, for tenderizing meat, although I've never personally used it for that purpose. My theory is that if meat needs that much work, I'm just going to toss it in the crockpot for a few days and let it fend for itself or walk away, whichever comes first. No, I use my wooden mallet for creating breadcrumbs. No one in my family particularly likes the heel of the bread, and rather than waste them, I place them carefully in a plate holder for a few weeks, where it looks quite decorative, if a bit odd, but dries them out nicely. Then I attack them with the mallet, which is quite effective and also cathartic. Nothing like cooking to get out your aggressions.

My beloved is also very helpful about announcing "Black smoke" in a serene voice when I have wandered away from the stove, having left a pan covered in oil on high heat, or "Fire in the oven" on the not-so-rare occasions that occurs. He really is a calm sort of individual, which is a very good trait in a husband, I've decided.

One day years ago I answered the door to find my friend on the doorstep. "What are you doing?" she asked, clearly mystified by the fact that my chin was immersed in a mug of cold water. "Making jam" I replied tersely, returning to the kitchen. I then explained to her that I had actually been sterilizing canning jars in a pot of boiling water prior to filling them with jam. I had accidentally let one slip, and it fell (of course) into the pot of boiling water, which caused the hot water to leap up into the air, where it made contact with my chin. Feeling the immediate need to cool the lower part of my face, and unable to think of any other way to do it without immersing my entire head in the sink, I grabbed a mug, filled it with cold water, and sank my chin into it, which is about when the doorbell rang. Fortunately, I don't often get unexpected visitors, especially when cooking; the explanations take so long that I am usually compelled to employ the fire extinguisher.

GROWING OLD GRACEFULLY – OR NOT

THIS WHOLE CONCEPT of "growing old gracefully" eludes me. The skin on my elbows, for heavens' sake, wrinkles no matter how much lotion I apply. All my joints ache at various times, sometimes all of them at once, and getting up from the couch is a major production which, ideally, should involve a crane. I have developed "chicken wings", that extra upper arm flab that jiggles of its own accord when you move and is responsible for some of us neglecting to wave good-bye even to our closest friends for fear of creating a wind tunnel.

My children are grown up and don't need me anymore to kiss their boo-boos better (although I can still be useful in times of crisis). Young men now call me "Ma'am", and I look around to see to whom they are referring. I no longer am aware of the latest high school gossip. People who are reported in the obituaries (which I now read religiously) to have died at age 85 seem to have passed on awfully young. Vacuuming gives me back spasms. I'm no longer so anxious to take adventurous vacations involving unpredictable situations and sleeping on the hard ground in the cold rain; these days, I prefer cruises with pre-booked land tours where everything is taken care of and there are no surprises.

No one asks for my I.D. to do anything at all, and they automatically give me the "senior discount". I cry over minor things, and yell for no reason at all, always at completely inappropriate times. I bulge in places I never used to, and even when I lose weight, what remains appears to have migrated south. No amount of diet or exercise is able to remove those stubborn pockets of fat. My clothes no longer fit the way they used to, and the lady at the maternity shop thinks I have the longest-lasting, most mature pregnancy she's ever seen, although she's too polite to say anything; maybe she thinks I'm trying on and buying clothes for my granddaughter. If she ever does ask how far along my baby is, I'll have to say "28 years".

On the up side, I can use being old as an excuse for a lot of things: forgetting everything, not going places I don't want to go because I need my sleep, getting out of doing any sort of physical labor, and flirting shamelessly without any danger of anyone taking me seriously.

GRAMMATICAL CORRECTNESS

IN THE COURSE OF my life and work, I have had the dubious pleasure of reading a great deal of writing, and have noticed a few issues common to most, which I now take the liberty of addressing, in all humility, as a former English teacher and permanent member, according to my children, of the Grammar Police. As with all rules of English grammar, these are general rules only, and, as always, subject to the multitude of exceptions equal only to those of the rules of evidence, especially the Hearsay Rule, which is one of the primary reasons I no longer practice law.

Rule # 1: No commas between the subject and the verb. First, of course, one must be able to locate the subject, and then the verb (whatever the subject happens to be doing, thinking, feeling, plotting, etc.). Once one has ferreted these important issues out, it is important NOT to bring the subject to a screeching halt, or even a long pause, by inserting the equivalent of a "Yield" sign between the subject and what the poor subject is trying to accomplish. Let us have some sympathy for the poor subject; there he, she, or it is, eager and ready to begin his/her /its journey into the great unknown of action (or, perhaps, the less energetic but equally important "state of being"), when suddenly a comma is inserted and all must pause for unknown and always completely unnecessary reasons while the writer cogitates on what to do next. Imagine the frustration of our poor subject as he/she/it anxiously awaits developments, only to discover that there was no earthly reason for he/she/it to wait; he/she/it could have been acting, thinking, or being long ago, could have got on with its intended life, yea verily, even unto the end of the sentence, if only the writer had followed this simple rule.

Rule #2: Whenever possible, do try to keep modifiers/describing words somewhere in the vicinity of the word they are modifying. Imagine our poor beleaguered readers, plowing through whatever incredibly paragraph-long sentence we have managed to fiendishly construct, replete with random phrases, independent and dependent clauses, dangling participles, split infinitives, et cetera, happening upon a word ending in -ly, which, because they are conversant with grammar, immediately signals to them that we have here an adverb; they begin searching for the word it modifies, as one is wont to do in such cases, but do they find it next to the word it modifies, as expected? No! In vain do they search the surrounding words, denied the simple satisfaction of logic, only to discover, when they finally find said modified word half way down the paragraph, that they have completely lost the thread of the sentence, not to mention the modified word and its modifier, and are now happily asleep in the corner or in the nearest teapot, dreaming of conjugations to come (or, as we all surmise, the future tense). Of course, some of us are equally bemused by the lack of the –ly ending, as in the recently aired radio ad: "…makes your wedding day go smooth and flawless"; not without those –ly endings, it doesn't. Having a twisted mind, which comes with free visuals, when I hear, as I too often do: "Drive safe!", I am immediately distracted by visions of folk piloting large locked burglar-proof devices down city streets.

Rule # 3: About apostrophes… I go after misplaced apostrophes the way some people go after bathtub ring, or organized crime. I see one too many "it's" when they obviously mean "its", and I start to twitch.

Speaking of which, let us explore the mysteries of these two short, but diabolical words. Understandably, people become confused because they expect, when they see an apostrophe, that it is a flag in the wind warning them that what they are seeing is the possessive form of a noun (or in this case, a pronoun).

However, this particular warning sign is, to say the least, misleading. It is not, in this case, a possessive form - however much it may try to pretend to be, with the apostrophe right there in plain sight - it is only masquerading as one, the apostrophe acting as camouflage in one of those dastardly English language traps set for the unwary. What we actually have here is a different category of apostrophe usage: that of the contraction. So, in actual fact, "it's" is the contracted form of "it is", and if we remember our grammar, the apostrophe substitutes for the letter "i" in "is", and serves to draw the two words together, which is not at all what occurs in the kinds of contractions any mother is used to, but never mind.

The other day I walked past a sign that read "Remember to break down box's" and I thought, break down box's what? Its spirit? Its will? And why? Because resistance is useless? Is this some sort of new torture for innocent boxes? Did the writer not realize that putting an apostrophe there rather than adding an -es made the poor unsuspecting box the owner, the possessor in fact, of it knows not what?? Clearly not. And so the long-suffering box must be the possessor of nothing, rather than share its misery with other boxes that need, apparently, to be broken down, for reasons we know not, and the mystery will never be solved.

And other punctuational issues...How can we mean what we say if we don't say what we mean? You can end up saying some pretty scary things by putting in a comma when you don't need to, or especially by leaving one out.

Take, for instance, the ever-popular "Let's eat, Grandma" as opposed to "Let's eat Grandma", an entirely different proposition and one to which grandma, I am assured, would object vociferously, along with law enforcement.

And then there's the differently punctuated "A woman without her man is nothing" as compared to "A woman: without her, man is nothing."

Punctuation makes all the difference.

And finally, Verb Tension: I admit I cannot, in good conscience, fault a normally obedient domestic animal that refuses to "lay down"; perhaps if we improved our grammar to their obviously superior level and requested said pet to "lie down", we would get a better response. While I am the first to admit that English is a diabolical language to learn, and that the conjugations of the verbs "lie" (as in both to tell an untruth and to recline) and "lay" (as in to set something down) alone would drive a saint to drink, it can, mostly, be mastered with about twenty years' effort, so take heart, my friends; buck up, hit the books, and steam onward into the (relatively) calm waters of grammatical correctness!

FOWL FRIENDS

THE OTHER DAY I was on the phone with my daughter, telling her about our recent activities, which involved sorting our recent vacation pictures on the computer: "Your father and I have been working on our Turkey slides." "Your what?" "Our Turkey slides," I repeated, puzzled by her apparent sudden loss of hearing. A long silence ensued. "Mom, what kind of weird new exercises are you and dad doing now?" I hastened to explain that I meant the photographs we took on our trip to the country of Turkey, although her idea seemed kind of intriguing, and certainly brought up some interesting mental images. Just goes to show how difficult long-distance communication can be in this modern world.

Fowl have been on my mind lately anyway. Not so very long ago, I was startled awake at the uncivilized hour of 4:30 a.m. by a very loud cockadoodle-doodling right outside my bedroom window, or so it seemed; it would actually be rather difficult for anything to be going on right outside my bedroom window, as it is, thankfully, about 20 feet above the ground, but it sure did sound like it was. I leaped out of bed several hours later to investigate, and discovered a large, rather beautiful, and very loud rooster on the back deck. How he got there, why he was there, and how long he planned to stay were all mysteries to me, but he seemed right at home, strutting around as if he paid the mortgage and knew how gorgeous he was – at least to hens, of which we have exactly zero. As some of our neighbors actually own hens, and one has a rooster with, I might add, a really pitiful call, or whatever you call it that doesn't necessitate typing cockadoodledoo more than once; he starts out enthusiastically, with a loud and confident "Er-ah-er-ah" and then suddenly ceases, as if someone has choked him mid-doodle, which would certainly be understandable, at least to anyone who's been awakened by him at 4:00 a.m. In my thankfully limited experience, roosters don't appear to be very accurate timekeepers. Another neighbor did have ducks as well as hens and a rooster, but something "got them", as we euphemistically say out here in the country, one by one; our neighbor said when it got down to the last duck, she (the duck) would swim nervously around their small pond, looking over her shoulder every few paddles, until she, too, was carried off by some four-footed fiend of the night. At least I assume that's what happened.

But as I was saying, I began calling neighbors to see if, hopefully, one of them was missing a rooster. Eventually I found one (neighbor missing a rooster), or at least one willing to admit to it, and began to plan how to return it. This presented me with a problem, or rather, several problems: how does one capture a rooster? My husband suggested throwing a blanket over it, but I worried about asphyxiation – the rooster's, that is – and besides, he (the rooster) didn't seem all that keen to let us get very close to him, and I felt dis-inclined to chase a rooster for miles around the back yard. And what would we do with him, assuming we caught him? How do you transport a rooster on a road trip? A box? I've tried that with hens, and it was a less than suc-cessful enterprise. Put him in the cat carrier? It's hard enough to stuff the cats into the cat carrier (although they are somewhat obese, it's true), much less a rooster; he seems a bit tall for it, and carrying it sideways would be awkward, I'm willing to bet. Besides, the neighbor doesn't seem especially keen to get him back, for obvious reasons.

While we pondered these difficult and weighty issues, the rooster, hav-ing established his dominance over the demesne, moved down to the "lower forty" as we call it, and made the acquaintance of my sister's horse. They soon became fast friends, and my sister started feeding the rooster, now affection-ately and creatively named "Roostie", as he has moved far enough away to cease waking me at all hours. He roosts comfortably on a beam above the horse's head at night and accompanies the horse on his rounds, both of them no doubt searching for female companionship, which both are unlikely to find. I think we may be living with him for a while.

DIRECTIONS

I DON'T LIKE MANUALS; they're really boring, and they make no sense to me unless there are pictures, and even then, if there's a wrong way to do it, I'll find it and do it that way. Why can't they make the directions more interesting, more exciting, like a good crime novel? "And then, just before you put that screw in that hole, you're going to discover …" Now that would be a real page-turner, something I might actually read.

I have to admit I find the pictures in directions confusing anyway; I appear to be missing the gene that controls what I refer to as "that whole spatial-relationship thing" which enables my beloved and both our children to pack everything from a suitcase to an entire storage facility within a hair's breadth of accuracy and to assemble everything they care to with no problem.

Leave me alone with a kit or something to build and directions with or without pictures, and you're likely to come back to parts scattered everywhere and me, weeping copiously on a chair. Ask me to pack, or even unpack for that matter, and you'll find items randomly strewn about the suitcase or the house, with several of one unimportant item packed and missing everything crucial, or pictures hung randomly on available hooks if I'm unpacking. I pack to move by opening boxes and throwing in whatever comes to hand; I wrap glassware in boxer shorts and toss in whatever happens to be within reach to fill up the rest. The organization gene also appears to be lacking, which explains why I married my husband: I like to surround myself with people who supply what I lack, including sanity and a rational thought process – or so he tells me.

The other alarming occurrence I experience when trying to build or repair things is the "leftover bits" phenomenon. I once took apart my vacuum cleaner (I have a long and unhappy history with vacuum cleaners, as does my mother; we have no idea why, but clearly that, too, is genetic), bought the replacement for the broken bit, installed it, and proudly put the whole thing back together, only to find several extra screws on the carpet that I'm pretty sure used to belong to the vacuum cleaner – although who knows, in my house? Besides, it ran just dandy, so who cares about a few extra screws, right? Clearly, they weren't crucial to the operation.

Besides, the English in most directions uses the most obscure, bizarre grammar I've ever seen. It is obvious that those who write the booklets often do not have a firm grasp on the language. As exhibit A, I here quote verbatim from the instructions accompanying a pedometer: "The paces are detected via the movement of waist…False mounting or walking away will possibly arouse inaccurate…After stopping its counting, the LCD will display paces… Press Set Key to Change the adjust modes…At stride "Mode", Press "Mode" Key to up, the stride number add 5 cm. If letters display unwell or no letter display. Note: Precise instrument is and be sure operated and maintained properly. Ensure your walking method is right. Replacing new battery is necessary. Don't disassemble the instrument except replacing battery. Or will cause damage to it or influence on its measuring accuracy."

And as Exhibit B, from our bread machine "in structions", cheerfully entitled "Let's Bakes Bread!": "If the top cave in, it is probably too much moisture inside the bread…You are better to drain well and blow them dry first or to reduce your water by 1 tablespoon…Cratered bread also happen with cheese bread because of each cheese has its own moisture content. A soggy sides and silly shapes could be happened from leaving a loaf in the bucket after the baking is completed… There is too much yeast, so that it's blown its top. Another possibility is too much of water used. If a recipe still explodes to the top…You can see that climate can change the results of you bread due to different temperature, and humidity of different locations in the world." If a cake is sticking "at the bottom of bucket": "This is happened due to the amount of liquids is too much." A balance of ingredients will make a good loaf of bread "…according to your desired fluffiness (personally, I can't think of any "desired fluffiness" that I could possibly want), weight, and browning." "Please not to believe a recipe that can work until you have already made it."

No wonder I'm confused. Who needs directions, anyway?

ACCENTS

MY HUSBAND IS FROM England, and therefore has an accent; in fact, that's how I met him, but that's another story. It has caused some confusion; I never quite know, for instance, whether he is going to the "pawn shop" or the "porn shop", which can make a person nervous. When we used to live downriver and locals asked him where he was from, he would reply "Horse Creek" without thinking; they would look at me, puzzled, and I'd elaborate: "Southern Horse Creek".

He tends to forget he has an accent, and can't figure out how everyone knows it's him on the phone before he's said three words or identified himself. One day he almost got into a shouting match with the girl at the Burger King drive-thru when she handed him a "Whopper" and he insisted he had ordered "water"; I finally translated for them and when the dust settled, he had his water and I ate the burger, just to make peace.

When we went to a Chinese restaurant in San Francisco with a friend, also British, we discovered the waiter understood nothing they said, and they understood nothing he said, but for some strange reason they all understood me, and I found myself translating English to English.

My husband is really bad at any other kind of accent, though; hearing him trying to do southern is a riot, although he thinks he's pretty good, so don't tell him I said so.

A while ago we bought one of those dictation programs (since neither of us can type – but that's another story) where you talk into a machine and it types it out for you. After hours of practicing to get it used to his voice, when he tried to make it work it came out as complete nonsense; I am convinced it threw up its (figurative) hands in despair over the peculiar pronunciation and quit in a huff.

Some of my friends and family members and I, on the other hand, have a bit of a gift for mimicry, and enjoy putting on accents just to entertain ourselves. Once my good friend Tonya and I went shopping in Medford and were conversing in a vaguely Eastern European accent when the sales clerk asked us how long we had been there. "Oh, about fifteen minutes" we replied, puzzled. "No, I mean, how long have you been in this country? Are you just visiting?" Loath to burst her bubble, we whispered that we were heading for the embassy immediately to ask for asylum and begged her not to blow our cover.

Whenever I travel, I conscientiously bring along a phrase book in whatever language the natives speak and string together completely ungrammatical words and phrases in hopes of sounding like a native, which gets me some strange looks and, occasionally, maniacal laughter. I'm sure my accent is pretty good, though. I remember asking for some salami in France; a reasonable enough request, I thought, but not only did I not get my lunchmeat, the woman gave me a look only the French can give, indicating her complete and permanent disgust with me and all my forebears (some of whom, I might add, are French. Or were). When my friend who spoke some French (why SHE wasn't asking the questions escapes me, but it was probably for entertainment value) finally stopped laughing and we were a long way down the street, she explained to me that through some error in syntax, pronunciation, or grammar, I had asked the lady, not if she had a salami, but if she were a salami; a minor, forgivable mistake, I thought – but then, I wasn't the salami in question.

One time, trying to obtain a cold remedy, the phrase book failed me altogether and I was reduced to charades; I began sneezing and blowing my nose in pantomime. Suddenly, I saw the light begin to dawn in the clerk's face and he disappeared into the back room; I sat back in relief and exhaustion until he came back with – snuff. Good luck finding that word in a phrase book. I didn't even think they still sold the stuff.

In Italy, a friend was having trouble making herself understood by the waiter, so I helpfully repeated exactly what she had said, in English with an Italian accent, which seemed to work. Trying to buy stamps for postcards was also a challenge; I paged frantically through the phrase book, trying to ascertain the difference between a greeting card and a post card, wondering if "post" meant a hitching post or "to mail", and whether the clerk would understand I meant the noun, not the verb, while he waited patiently until I managed to work it all out, and then asked me in perfect English whether I wanted it to go out in today's mail, or tomorrow's?

Our group also had an involved discussion about the difference, in Italian, between a fish and a swimming pool, but we were reluctant to put that one to the test and actively avoided both in conversation whenever possible.

We lived in Glasgow, Scotland, the first year we were married, and although I'm pretty good at accents, Glaswegian is a challenge. I worked in an area called The Gorbals, an inner-city working man's slum, and I don't think I understood anything anyone said for a good six months. When they discovered I was American, they all wanted to try their best John Wayne imitation, and if there's anything harder to comprehend than a Scot, it's a drunken Glaswegian doing John Wayne – I needed subtitles. I got pretty good at nodding and smiling, though.

BUG BITES AND ENGINE TROUBLE

IT WAS A LONG WEEK. I awoke Monday morning scratching, and discovered a strange bug bite on my chest – so strange I decided to show it to my husband. "Look at this," I said, pointing. "It's red and swollen, with a black spot in the middle. It must have taken quite a chunk out of me." He inspected the bite, shrugged, and we went on with our lives.

A few days later our daughter came home for a visit, and I showed her the bite, too – at this point I was showing anyone who would look, which was admittedly a little awkward with complete strangers: "Here, look at this bite" , but never mind. She also looked closely, then remarked calmly, "Mom, it's got legs. It's a tick. You guys are old; you need to wear your glasses when you look at things!" Minor surgery ensued, involving a pair of tweezers, then rapidly escalating to a needle and progressing to a razor blade. We don't like spending money on doctors if we can avoid it. Besides, I was raised that way; I remember my father digging a tick out of the back of my neck with a pocket knife when I was about four years old and too little to defend myself.

Of course, then I was up at 4:00 a.m., Googling Lyme's disease and discovering just how many awful illnesses you can get from tick bites, but it appears to be healing nicely.

Friday night I came down with a wicked sore throat; it looked like a major battle had been waged on my tonsils, and they had lost. Never mind; I needed to organize a cake and dinner for my parents' 70th wedding anniversary on Sunday.

I had forgotten it was All Saints Day that Sunday and they would be reading the names of the deceased, which would take a while; we're an elderly church. But I still had plenty of time to get the cake, buy other necessary supplies and organize the party, so I went on with my planned day of shopping in Medford. My beloved being away climbing something for the weekend, I was alone and could, for once, do as much damage as I liked.

Because it was winter and I feared getting stuck on the summit, I was driving my parents' little Kia, which is at the best of times a gutless wonder but has four-wheel drive, and I was almost to my exit when I noticed I wasn't getting much power. With a sinking heart I heard a knocking sound I have heard too many times in too many different cars, and within moments smoke was billowing from under the hood. I pulled over and called Triple A. My friend Tonya later asked me, aghast, "Didn't you call 911? What if the car was on fire?"

"Why would I do that?" I replied reasonably. "I called AAA because I knew there was, yet again, a tow truck in my future, and the sooner they arrived, the sooner I could get on with the process of getting home. If the car was on fire, I'd get out, but in the meantime it was cold outside, but warm inside, especially with the heat emanating from the engine bay, and there was no point in opening the hood and adding fuel to the fire, so to speak."

But apparently someone else had the same thought process as my friend, because suddenly a huge fire truck pulled up behind the car and spilled out several handsome firefighters. There's something about a man in uniform, especially when he's coming to your rescue. I got out and explained about the smoke, which had subsided by now; we raised the hood and stood, lined up in front of the engine like birds on a wire, contemplating the situation and offering our opinions. One of the firefighters and I were voting for a thrown rod, as I had experienced that particular disaster before, while the other two offered competing theories; one thought perhaps it was a loose hose, while another ventured a guess that it was the water pump. Having experienced that particular phenomenon, among many others, I begged to differ. Eventually they got in their truck and drove away, having exhausted the subject, and the tow truck driver arrived.

It all ended well for me, although not so well for my parents' vehicle – sorry, mom and dad! – as my friend showed up and we went to lunch; then she drove me home before I could do any damage shopping. She must be in league with my beloved.

The car, I discovered, was not terminal, which was a relief. Now all I had to do was organize my parents' anniversary surprise, which did not originally involve destroying their car, of course, but rather a cake in a large pink box that I had to somehow disguise as something else and get past them and into the building without them seeing it. Piece of cake, as they say.

CABLE ISSUES

MY BELOVED HAD BARELY stepped out the door to embark on his epic journey up Denali; the tears of farewell hardly had time to dry, when things began to go wrong.

First I tried to print something, only to find that, while a green light was on, apparently nobody was home inside the printer. I checked all the cables, pushed the button and held it, several times, as I knew my beloved would instruct me to do, to no avail.

My suspicion is that we had both tripped over the printer cord one too many times and done permanent, fatal damage to some essential part of the infernal machine, which costs us more in printer cartridges in one year than four years of college tuition for both our children combined. We trip over the cord because the printer normally resides on the dining room table, which serves as our impromptu office desk because we are both too lazy to go down to the basement, which is where our actual office is located. However, we both forget the location of the printer on a regular basis, even though the printer itself is hard to miss; it becomes a part of the scenery, unlike the cord, which hides on the floor where we can trip over it.

I called my beloved in a panic before he scaled the heights of the mountain, where, he had assured me, there would be no cell reception, probably in an attempt to forestall any such phone calls and keep me at bay. He had made it all the way to McCloud by the time I reached him. He repeated all the same advice that I knew he would (there's something about having been married for 30 years), and when he learned I had already tried all of the above, advised me to buy a new printer. "I can't!" I wailed. When he asked why not, I responded by sobbing, "Because then I'll have to hook it up to my computer and read the manual! You know I can't read manuals!" The truth is, I can read them, of course; I just can't make any sense out of them. I resigned myself to being unable to print anything for a month.

Even nature is conspiring against me. Several times lately, I have come out onto the back deck to enjoy the sunshine, only to find a garter snake sunning itself –or, as I think of it, lying in wait for me - in various places. I really, really hate snakes. I realize that it's nonsensical, but I can't help it; it's just a gut reaction over which I have no control. I suspect it's that whole Garden of Eden thing.

One day I went down to the garage, only to find the same snake (at least I assume it's the same one – I've never gotten close enough to it to note any identifying marks) stretched out across the threshold, apparently luxuriating in a spring sunbath. Because he was in plain sight, meaning I did not come upon him unawares, I did not scream like a banshee, which is my usual response. Instead, I tossed a few pebbles at him to encourage him to vacate the premises, and went about my business.

Several hours later, I came back to the garage again. I approached cautiously, as if the place were booby-trapped – which as far as I was concerned, it was - but seeing no snake, confidently opened the door, only to have the thing leap out of the doorway at me, causing me, of course, to shriek as if the hounds of hell were after me. In fact, my own personal hound of hell – our beloved rescue dog - took care to stand about thirty feet behind me, obviously alarmed at whatever I was screeching at, or maybe just alarmed at my shrieking. Grabbing a nearby umbrella (don't ask), I once again encouraged said snake to decamp to greener pastures, outside the garage, as he (for some reason I don't care to explore, snakes are always male in my world) had somehow managed to fall inside the garage.

Next, the dog decided to demonstrate his displeasure with my beloved's absence by chewing up his bed – that is, the dog's bed. I'm sure there's some logic to this response, but I refuse to explore it or dwell on it.

And finally, I discovered a pile of large, dead ants and wood product in my bathtub. I assume this means they have taken up permanent residence in the logs that comprise our home, and fully expect that the house will be a pile of sawdust by the time my beloved returns from scaling the heights of Denali.

Still, if this is the sum total of disasters that befall me in my beloved's absence, given my past track record, I shall count myself lucky.

By Any Other Name

IT SEEMS I HAVE SPENT my life spelling my name. I don't mind spelling my last name at all, because it really does break all the rules of spelling – and pronunciation, just for good measure. If it's spelled correctly, people almost always mispronounce it, and if they pronounce it properly, they generally misspell it. It's a losing battle, and it's no one else's fault that my ancestors either couldn't spell, or more likely, were on the run from the law and misspelled the name on purpose when they got into the country in order to avoid, shall we say, repercussions.

It's very handy, though, when telemarketers call; if you mispronounce my name, I generally hang up. I do find it a bit odd, however, that I have to spell my first name so often. I'll say, "You know, like the state", only to be met, entirely too often, with a blank stare. I suppose learning to spell the names of states has gone the way of instruction in making change and cursive handwriting in schools these days, not that I was ever a fan of the latter; I spent too many recesses inside trying to make letters look the way they did in the books, only to fail miserably. I mostly print these days.

When my husband and I married, I didn't change my name. You would think, given the inconveniences of spelling my name, that I would have taken the opportunity to take my husband's perfectly lovely, spellable name as my own, and lose the difficulties associated with mine, as so many of my friends did (that is, took their husband's name, not my husband's name), but that would be too logical. Besides, when people ask my husband how to spell his last name, which is really quite simple, he looks at them in astonishment and elucidates, "You know, like the street", but the fact that he is British and

146

referring to a street very famous in Britain, not America, is apparently lost on him.

I had many reasons for not changing my name, but one of them was that I used to work in a prison. We were listed in the phone book under my husband's name, on the theory that if you didn't know me well enough to know my husband's last name, I didn't need to hear from you. Especially if you were calling collect. Of course, he didn't change his name, either, so we were both fine with the situation, but it has caused some confusion at times; I find myself insisting, vehemently and almost guiltily at times, that we really are married – really!

When the children were born, I struggled with what to do; my beloved remarked calmly one day that as the mother carries the child for nine months, maybe the children should take the mother's name, but this was a bit radical even for me. Of course, he now denies he ever said this; I should have taped it. In the end, we decided to hyphenate the children's names, which is not an ideal situation if taken to its logical conclusion: what if two hyphenated people decide to get married? Do you end up with Jennifer Smith-Brown-Jones-Garcia? And what about their children? And what if they get married, take each other's names, then get divorced, but keep their hyphenated names, then marry again, someone else with – yes – a hyphenated name? These are the things that keep me awake at night.

But it wasn't my problem, I decided blithely, not realizing that, like her father, our daughter would be dyslexic, and saddled with not only a hyphenated, hard to spell last name, but a long and complicated first name. I've been apologizing to her ever since.

Having made my point by hyphenating their last names on their birth certificates, I thought I was through; the children could call themselves whatever they wanted after that. Our daughter used both names, but our son used his father's, easier to spell last name. However, he had another major problem, as it turned out: for some reason, my sister began calling him by a variation of his middle name even before he was born – before the rest of us even knew he was a boy – and it stuck. Every time I called to make an appointment for him at the doctor or the dentist's, the same scene would play out: "What's his name?" "Well, it might be listed under (his father's name)." A search would ensue, which was sometimes successful, sometimes not. If not, I would ask them to try under my name, or the hyphenated version.

Whereupon the poor receptionist, frustrated, would sometimes ask for his first name. "Well, it might be under (his legal first name), but don't call him that, because he won't know you're talking to him. Or, he might be under (his middle, nickname – not even his proper middle name)" at which point most receptionists threw up their hands in despair and handed me the appointment book, unless of course they were using a computer, in which case we all sank into a deep decline.

What's in a name, anyway?

UNCOORDINATED

I REALLY HAVE LED A deprived life, unable to participate in the simplest of activities. I accept the fact that I've always been uncoordinated; I couldn't even square dance as a kid because I was always going in the wrong direction, grabbing the wrong person, and kicking when I shouldn't have been in other dances, injuring innocent bystanders.

In high school I took a fencing class – the kind with swords, or more properly, foils, heaven help us. There's a move I think they called a "fleisch", which I believe is German for "flesh" - for good reason; it involves running a few steps and then basically skewering your opponent. I managed to take about two steps, tripped over my foil, and landed at the feet of my instructor, in what I tried to convince him was a clever ploy on my part to demoralize him, but he wasn't going for it.

PE was required in high school, much to my distress, and I was forced to participate in all sorts of physical activities that nearly killed me. I remember "gymnastics": I would run full tilt up to that diabolical "horse", bounce off the springboard, determined to get over the dratted thing this time, and splatter myself over the front of it, even with "spotters" on either side trying desperately to heave me over it. I never did make it, despite their best efforts. The balance beam completely unnerved me, for obvious reasons, and the trampoline was downright dangerous for someone like me; I had visions of propelling myself right out through the ceiling, or bouncing off onto the floor and breaking every bone in my body. Dance wasn't any better. This was the early seventies, and the teacher must have been on drugs; her instructions were to move as if we were making our way through a jar of peanut butter, or sometimes Jello. I felt as if I did that all the time, but not while dancing, which I couldn't do anyway.

I met my best friend in high school playing tennis. Well, she was playing; I was mostly chasing tennis balls. She couldn't understand how I could miss every serve sent my way, and eventually came over to examine my racket, convinced there was a hole in it.

In college I took karate out of desperation; PE was required to graduate. My instructor was very excited to see my double-jointed, straight-up-in-the-air toes, as I could kick without breaking them or even getting them involved. Or I could have if I had been able to stand on one leg long enough to kick, which was, unfortunately, not the case. He was deeply disappointed in me, I fear. When I took jazz dance, also in a bid to graduate, they just put me at the end of the line and hoped no one would notice. Ballet was equally painful – the dancing hippos in Fantasia looked better.

Even everyday, ordinary activities become dangerous if you're me. For instance, as I was leaving the house for work recently (late as usual), my sweater caught on the edge of an easel that's sitting there, waiting to be disposed of. Now, this would have been no big deal, having happened several times before (you would think I would have got a clue by now, but no, I hadn't gotten around to moving it yet), except that this morning I had in my hand, among many other things, my breakfast smoothie, which in my alarm at having my sweater jerk me backwards and seeing the easel start to fall, making an attempt to grab it, I proceeded to fling all over everything else that was on the deck: a box of videos, a snow shovel (it was summer, but never mind), the dog, stuff I was going to put in a yard sale, deck furniture, the deck itself, and, oh yes, the letter in my hand I was going to mail to the college my son would be attending in the fall; I'm sure that made a good impression.

I can't begin to recount all the bruises I've acquired in various run-ins with inanimate objects; they are so common I rarely even notice them, and can never recount where I got them when they are brought to my attention.

I'm sometimes okay as long as no one asks me to do more than one thing at once, such as talk and walk. In my brief acting career, the director gave up asking me to speak my lines and move simultaneously; one of them had to be sacrificed, which does not make for good theater. I continue to piteously request small, but pivotal non-speaking roles, where I can sit in one place and act the heck out of the scene, but they appear to be in short supply. Broadway will have to survive without me. In the meantime, I'm just trying to master walking without hurting myself.

SICKENING

I'VE BEEN THINKING ABOUT getting a vaccine for the flu this year. I never have before, but my beloved has contracted something awful, and sleeping with Typhoid Mary the last few nights has made me seriously reconsider.

I don't get sick often, but when I do, it's a doozy, and it usually comes with very little warning. I feel a tightness in my forehead, decide my waistband is too tight, and boom, my head's in the toilet – if I'm lucky. I've always been prone to seasickness, and I tend to stay away from carnival rides just out of self-preservation and good sense, but lately, I've discovered I get sick in theaters. Go figure. The first time it happened I was watching The Incredibles with the kids and thought it was something I ate, which would be very unusual, as I have a cast-iron stomach (unless, of course, I'm sick).

The next time, I remember remarking to my husband that the camera angles in the movie were really peculiar – and I've never noticed a camera angle in my life – just before I made a rapid exit to the ladies' room. I've tried sitting in the back, breathing deeply, closing my eyes – even taking Dramamine - but nothing works, and it's kind of pointless to pay the admission fee if you're going to spend the entire movie either with your eyes closed or in the bathroom developing an intimate relationship with the toilet. It doesn't happen with every movie, but just to be on the safe side, I usually rent a video. Relationship movies tend to be OK, as no one tends to move much, but anything "swoopy", like action films, which I love, and I'm gone.

I always think I'm on death's door when I'm sick anyway. I've found people fall into two categories when they're sick: there's the "I'm sick and I'm going to die so just leave me alone to turn my face to the wall and go in peace" types, mostly, if I may be sexist just for a moment, women. Then there are the "I don't feel well so I need someone to wait on me hand and foot for the next week at least, no matter what other crises might be occurring in other parts of the house, not to mention the world" types, who are generally, I'm sorry to say, men. And the second kind is completely unsympathetic to the first, I might add, when the first category finally break down from the stress of caring for their spouses of the second variety and collapse into a bed of pain and fever. There is no justice in this world, ladies – we might as well get used to it, if we aren't already.

When my children were small I discovered I could deal with smells and sights that would cause an emergency room doctor to pass out, but thankfully, they weren't ill often. The children, that is. I remember objecting when my three-year old daughter threw up in her bed so many times I ran out of clean sheets, but she hasn't been sick since (sixteen years later), so I guess it all averaged out. My son, on the other hand, gets the sniffles and passes out in a heap on the bathroom floor, so we tend to keep an eye on him. It's the gender thing again.

When we lived in Ghana, I contracted something called shigella, which always sounds to me like a cross between a dance move and an Irish drinking party, but is actually bacterial dysentery, and believe me, it's no party. I threw up until I burst blood vessels in both my eyes and used every fixture in the bathroom. Lost ten pounds in twenty-four hours, though – best quick weight-loss plan I ever tried. And to think I'd been hoping for a tapeworm. I was so sick I didn't eat anything for a week, and when I did, it was macaroni and cheese, which I normally hate, but hey, it didn't come back up, and it tasted fantastic. In fact, I've since developed a fondness for it.

My husband developed malaria (and as we later learned, giardia at the same time). I told him the good news was he had the non-recurring type of malaria (there are four kinds); the bad news was, it was the fatal type (if you don't take the cure). He sensibly took the cure, came home to Siskiyou County for Christmas, and promptly came down with it again.

Question: How many doctors in how many counties in the western United States does it take to find the blood tests you have to do to determine you have malaria? I could almost see them, getting the books down from the top shelves, dusting off the cobwebs, cracking open the aged pages… It took seven hours and apparently countless doctors to get a diagnosis, but we finally got there, and he took the cure again. I've never actually seen him that color before or since. On that occasion, he deserved every bit of sympathy we could muster, I must admit; it made shigella look like a party after all.

He's not looking so hot right now, either. Maybe I'd better get that flu shot; somebody has to take care of him.

THRIFTY

I WOULD HAVE TO SAY we're pretty thrifty people, and were long before it became fashionable. This is due primarily to my husband, for whom it appears to be a genetic component, but over the years it's worn off on me as well.

For one thing, we've never purchased a new car, and not just because we can't afford one. My beloved proudly informed me a few years ago that he had never owned a vehicle that cost him more than $500 before he married me, and he fixed them all himself, too, which was handy because they broke down a lot. In fact, when we were dating he was driving an obscure car called a Reliant Scimitar; on one of our first dates, we drove a while, then stopped to get something in a store, got back in, drove about a hundred yards, and it stopped dead. No problem, he said cheerfully; he hopped out, retrieved a bottle of water from the trunk, opened the hood, poured water on what turned out to be the (glass) fuel pump, jumped back in, started it up, and off we went. He called it his anti-theft device. We actually imported the car to the States with us, but I won't go into that particular epic at the moment. In any case, his argument is that a new car loses value the minute you drive it off the lot, which is, of course, true – and besides, I wouldn't have nearly as much material for my columns.

Most of my favorite work clothes were purchased in thrift stores, but my beloved is the one known for his sartorial splendor; he wears shorts (also bought in thrift stores; he gave up on department stores when he discovered he could no longer find $5 shorts in them after about 1990) with sandals and socks pretty much year-round, with a hat added in the winter. One night at a party, someone made a comment about the age of his coat. In some indignation, he responded that it was a perfectly useable coat, and it was a very good deal when he bought it. In 1973. Used.

We then embarked on a discussion of "the house suit". When he was at university, in the interests of economy, he lived with ten roommates, five of whom were male, in a house he described as having cold running water – down the walls. The toilet also leaked; finally one day the water that had pooled under it collapsed the floor, and the toilet ended up on the stove on the floor below, but that's probably another story. In the further interests of thrift, all five young men, being about the same size and shape, shared a single bell-bottomed, wide-lapelled, paisley-lined, pin-striped polyester suit in which they took turns interviewing for jobs. Somehow my beloved ended up with the suit. He still had it when we married about ten years later, but some time after that I managed to sneak it into the Goodwill bag. When he realized it was gone, he protested mightily that it was still a perfectly good suit, and he was right, as usual; it wasn't long before they came into fashion again – as Halloween costumes.

STUFF

SEVERAL YEARS AGO, our son was talking to a classmate from Los Angeles who was stunned when my son revealed we heated our house with a wood-stove; she wanted to know if we cooked on it. She was disappointed when he told her only when the power went out, although she found that concept almost equally intriguing. She regained interest when he mentioned we never locked our front door, however; he said her jaw actually dropped.

The truth is, for a long time we couldn't lock the doors because we had removed the locks to have them re-keyed, and it took a very long time – roughly several years. We had to have them re-keyed because somewhere along the way we apparently lost all the keys, and never bothered about it because – you guessed it – we never locked our doors. Then when we got the locks back, it took a while to get them reinstalled, my beloved having many other priorities. The original keys were probably in one of our junk drawers, and good luck with that; we have so many junk drawers we've had to divide them into sub-categories: there's the "paper junk drawer", the "kitchen utensils junk drawer", the "miscellaneous junk drawer", etc. We keep extra car keys in one of them, but we don't worry much about that, either, because: 1. No one would ever want to steal one of our cars, and 2. Even if they did suffer from temporary insanity and/or desperation and decide to steal one, they would never be able to find the keys in the appropriate junk drawer – we certainly can't. In any case, anyone wanting to steal from us would have to find the house first, and they're only likely to accomplish that if they've gone on a long hunting trip and gotten lost; our best friends have trouble finding our house, even after they've visited.

We came by this non-locking habit honestly; my parents never locked our doors when I was growing up in Oakland, either. While my parents were big on location, they were short on belongings; I still remember the damaged, used stereo which took up most of one wall, the enormous, ancient, second-hand black and white television on which I watched history unfold, sitting on the plastic re-upholstered couch donated by our more well-heeled aunt. We drove used cars and wore hand-me-down clothes we were happy to have, and as the youngest of three girls, they had been handed down plenty by the time they got to me. Then there were the kitchen implements, which my mother later lamented having thrown away, as we kept seeing them in antique shops, but back then, they were just old junk she was anxious to replace with more modern items; besides, she was a bit chagrined to realize they were antiques, as this made her feel aged. She used to say that if a thief entered the house (hardly necessary to break into an unlocked house – another advantage to not locking the doors), he'd leave a donation.

Anyone wanting to steal from us ought to have their heads examined anyway; the only thing we have of any value, and that's sentimental, is my grandmother's dining room table, and it would take a dozen strong men to disassemble and carry it and the extra leaves, not to mention a large moving van. While they were in the process of accomplishing the aforesaid process, our rescue dog would be happily disassembling any intruders; he's very big, and very loyal, and does not take kindly to interlopers, as friends of ours could attest.

Besides, what else would they take? While we have plenty of stuff, I'm pretty certain none of it is anything anyone else would find useful or valuable. Would they want the very old, small television in the far corner that we never watch (it's not hooked up to cable or satellite), and probably wouldn't notice was missing for weeks? Our photo albums (yes, we're old enough to still have those)? Yard-sale buys we now regret but haven't the energy to re-sell? The used coffee table encasing the stuffed, slightly mangy raccoon that seemed so charming at the time? My geologist-husband's huge collection of obscure rocks decorating the back deck, one of which (the rocks, that is, not the deck, as far as I know) I'm pretty certain is radioactive? The beat-up, stained leather couch our daughter dragged in from the street? We have no video games, no expensive computers, and basically, nothing anyone but us would want, which is rather liberating, in a way; when you own nothing of value to the outside world, you don't spend any time worrying about getting it stolen. Mind you, I carefully lock my car every time I leave it, even though my daughter rolls her eyes and insists no one is interested in stealing any of the used books I keep with me at all times, in the strong belief that someday I will be stuck somewhere and actually have the spare time to read them.

And if all else fails and some poor idiot does manage to find the house, bypass the dog and break in, there's always the gun under the bed or the knife under my pillow; while I'm generally a non-violent kind of person, I resent being awakened in the night, and tend towards crankiness at being awakened. Stuff may not be important, but my sleep is precious, so enter at your own risk at night.

SNAKES IN THE GRASS

WELL, SUMMER IS definitely here. Not because the summer solstice has just passed, although that, too, is true. No, I know it's summer because: 1. The temperatures are going up into the 100's soon, 2. Ringe Pool is open, 3. The fair is coming, and 4. The snakes are out.

Now, I know snakes are part of that whole circle of life thing; the rational part of my brain tells me this, and we do not kill them or interfere with them in any way, other than to occasionally involve recalcitrant rattlers in an involuntary relocation program – anywhere but the basement of the house - although my husband did once take one to the children's school for show and tell until he was informed it was illegal. He transported it there in a large mayonnaise jar in a backpack, riding his bike, but that's another story.

Unfortunately, the dominant, irrational part of my brain sees every stick in the path as a snake, and not just a snake, but a poisonous snake. Normally, as soon as summer arrives, I stop hiking, as it's too hot and the snakes are out, and go to the pool instead. This summer, however, circumstances dictate that I do both – circumstances being a nasty weight gain.

So a while ago, as I huffed and puffed my way up the hill, I came across my first summer snake – dead as a doornail in the middle of the road, having been flattened by a passing car. It was upside down and very flat, and therefore of indeterminate origin, but I spared a moment to mourn its passing - only a moment, mind; it was a snake, after all. Next, the dogs and I nearly stepped on a (live) garter snake; it's hard, even for me, to mistake the colorfully striped garter snake for anything other than what it is. The dogs were not at all alarmed, apparently not even having seen it, while I suffered a minor heart attack before moving on, undeterred from hiking.

The other day as I took the shortcut between my house and my parents' house, I again came across a snake, and moved backwards so rapidly I fell over. Scrabbling backwards on hands and knees, trying to get a purchase so I could get up again – not an easy task at my age – I had time to observe the

156

creature. I was able to ascertain that it had its tail towards me and its head pointed away, and was stretched out flat as opposed to coiled – always a good sign – and was only about 18 inches long, although my imagination stretched it out to at least three feet. It was at about this time I noticed the rattles.

Screaming hysterically at the dog, who had of course gone over to investigate it, I managed to regain my feet in record time, and when I turned around, the snake was coiled and rattling, and my beloved, stupid dog had moved even closer to it, much more curious about this thing that made noise than he had been about the harmless garter snake a few days before. He must have heard the panic in my voice, because he came over to me at last, and we beat a hasty retreat back the way we had come. Needless to say, I took the long way home.

My beloved, ever helpful, suggested I take a ski pole with me the next time I hiked (whatever made him think there would be a next time??). I enquired what the pole was for – perhaps to shish kebab any potentially harmful snakes? To which he replied I could rattle the bushes with it (rattle not being my favorite word at the moment), and/or fake out the snake by waving it at any I came across. Dubious but determined, I took it with me a few days later when I got my courage up. At first I held it out in front of me like a divining rod or a Geiger counter, talking in a loud voice to warn anything threatening out there that I myself was armed and dangerous. Then I whacked the bushes with it. So far, so good.

My beloved, who likes to ride his bike along some of the same trails I do, and ever the gentleman, volunteered to ride before me and, like St. Patrick, no doubt drive all the snakes out of the area, if not the country - probably right into my path. Then I had a horrible vision of a rattler striking at the bike and getting caught up in the spokes of his tires...It didn't bear thinking about. Fortunately, he was a long way ahead of me and I was spared any such sights.

But summer is definitely here, and I am going to Iceland, where, as far as I know, it's cool, and while there may not be many trees, they are definitely short on snakes.

STAPLES

A WHILE AGO AS I was removing the staples from my tights (no, of course I wasn't using a staple remover – that would be silly), I got to thinking about – why did I have staples in my tights, you ask? Because I was at work, and the tape didn't do the job, of course. What job? Well, I had holes in the toes of my tights, and not only was it cold in the office, I was wearing toeless shoes, or whatever you call that. I had one set of black toes (covered by tights) and one set of pink toes (holes in the tights), and it looked weird, even to me, and I'm not known for my sartorial splendor. Or my fashion sense, for that matter. Besides, I was beginning to lose the sensation in my toes due to the constriction caused by my toes extruding from the holes in the tights.

So I tried taping them (the holes in my tights, not my toes. That would have looked very strange indeed), but it didn't stick, so in a burst of inspiration I grabbed the stapler, and with only three little staples, voila! Problem solved.

However, I knew said staples might wreak further havoc on the tights, so I removed them that night and stitched up the holes (I had by then discovered another hole in the heel, but as my shoe covered that one, who cared?). Really, there's absolutely no reason to waste a perfectly good (and rather expensive) pair of tights just because there are a few holes in them, especially when the holes are only in one foot and can be stitched up.

Waste not, want not, as we are fond of saying in our family as we eat leftovers from the same meal seven days in a row. Mind you, as the holes get more extensive, and I keep sewing further and further up the toes, that leg of the tights gets shorter and shorter, which can cause some imbalance and discomfort in the whole tights situation, but hey, it saves money on new tights. If you should see me walking with a slight list, though, you'll know why.

The other day I discovered a pair of shoes in the back of my closet that I hadn't worn for a while. Overjoyed, I wore them to work (Yippee, new shoes! And I didn't even have to pay for them) without bothering to cogitate on the issue of why said shoes were in the back of the closet and hadn't been worn in such a long time that their origins and history had been lost in the mists of time. It therefore did not occur to me that there might be a reason for their obscure location and my lack of memory.

It was on the way from the parking lot to the office that I discovered why I had not been wearing this particular pair of shoes, when the sole decided to separate itself from the heel of the shoe. Rats. It all came back to me. I didn't have time to go home and change shoes, and the courts frown on barefoot employees as a safety hazard, although I'm usually a kind of walking safety hazard even on a good day. I'm the only person I know, for instance, who takes the dog for a walk and ends up with dog slobber in her eye. I know what that dog eats, and that knowledge caused me some concern, I can tell you. I could just see myself trying to explain to the doctor why I had an eye infection: "Well, you see, the dog slung slobber in my eye…" But I digress. Back to the separating shoe…

Not to fear – court employees are an ingenious bunch, as they have to be these days due to budget shortages, not that they weren't always inventive – and although I couldn't get a stapler to unhinge itself adequately to staple the shoe together (even though I'm usually quite good at unhinging things and people in general), figuring that what worked for my tights ought to work for a shoe, Sue in Family Law managed to find some clear packing tape that did the job until lunch time. Unfortunately, by lunch time the tape was starting to unstick itself, and when I revealed my troubles to the Civil Department, Er-inn, ever resourceful downriver girl that she is, whipped out a handy-dandy, bright pink toolbox and exactly the right size nails and tacked that sucker together lickety-split. Which worked just fine until that night, when the sole of the shoe became separated at the front end. But hey, I was home by then, so who cared?

The shoes are once again residing at the back of the closet, awaiting further repairs or faulty memory. Heaven forbid I should just throw the things out. They have plenty of tread on them, probably because they were rarely worn due to the fact that they fall apart every time I wear them. Perhaps glue this time… But then, there are different types of glue for different jobs, and I might not have the right type for rope-soled shoes…

I have trouble with staplers anyway. The truth is, I have trouble with all mechanical devices. But I'm not sure staplers count. Certainly copy machines do, and I've destroyed my share of them – more than my share, in fact, if truth be told.

Where was I? Oh, yes; I was thinking. But I can't seem to remember what I was thinking about. Sometimes, life is just too complicated.

To Sleep, Perchance....

SLEEP IS A DANGEROUS proposition in our family. Not for us, you understand, but for anyone around us, especially anyone who might be sleeping near us. I have been known to wake people out of a sound sleep by laughing or talking incomprehensibly. I get very cranky if you try to ask me questions, though – this is MY dream, and I don't appreciate repeating myself. If you're going to eavesdrop, get it right the first time.

My father developed the interesting gift of being able to sleep anywhere, at any time, with his eyes open if necessary. Very useful in meetings. He was awakened in the middle of the night so often during his days as a computer troubleshooter that he sometimes fell sound asleep with the phone to his ear, some poor person on the other end shouting loudly until my mother would wake up and take him back to bed.

The entire family has the ability to answer the phone in the middle of the night and make rational responses while completely unconscious. And we won't remember anything about it the next day, either, so there's no use trying to remind us what we agreed to.

And don't get too close; we tend to flail in our enthusiasm. On the rare occasions I have had to sleep with my children, I have discovered that they have inherited the family trait when I have had various of their body parts surgically removed from some of mine – elbows from ribs, knees from groins, etc. And they need the entire bed, thank you very much, even if it is the size of Texas, so they can stretch out diagonally across it and leave me in the northwest corner with the dimensions of a postage stamp, and no covers.

One of my earlier experiences with the family disorder was when my mother, father, and I went downtown to pick up my sister, who was working at a theatre. Now, we are a family who likes to sleep. A lot. Our regular habit as a family is to get together for New Year's Eve, where we promptly fall asleep in the living room at about 9:00 p.m., wake up at midnight, wish each other a happy new year, and stagger off to bed, still completely sober but comatose. Anyway, my dad parked in a red zone with the engine running, because we knew my sister would be out in just a minute. Since it was past 9:00 p.m., we all, naturally, fell asleep, my father in the driver's seat, my mother next to him with her head on his shoulder, and myself next to her with my head on her shoulder.

A hapless police officer came upon the scene, and, no doubt thinking we were asphyxiating ourselves as a form of family entertainment, rushed to open the door and save us from ourselves. Needless to say, the domino effect came into play, and all three of us proceeded to fall out of the car, frightening the poor officer out of his wits, especially when my father began his usual waking-up habit of snorting like a bull elephant in mating season. The officer contented himself with warning us not to park in a red zone, although by then he probably wanted to take us all to the loony bin.

My husband discovered the dangers early on in our marriage. We happened to be sharing a twin bed (we could manage that in those days), and we happened to have a small disagreement, over which we shall draw a veil, primarily because I can't remember what it was about, although I'm sure I was right. In any case, that night I had an extremely vivid dream. I was a snake, and I had disengaged my jaw, as I understand they sometimes can if they are hungry enough, and motivated enough, and was just about to enjoy a really tasty snake-type meal, when I was rudely awakened by my husband yelling in my ear. He was claiming, in some outrage, that I had bitten him. In the back. And left tooth marks, in fact, so I couldn't even deny it; a rather good imprint of my upper and lower dental work. The real shock came when I told my mother the story and she informed me she had done the same thing to my father the first year they were married – minus the snake part – and she also swears blind she was asleep. I'm not sure whether any fights were involved, either, but just in case, we've warned our daughter.

Sleep is a wonderful gift; I highly recommend it. Just be vigilant around this family when you try it. zzzzzzzzz......

161

Time Changes

THE TIME IS GOING to change soon, but the clocks in my house already have. In fact, we appear to be living in a time warp: I regularly lose 15 minutes going from the upstairs level to the lower floor. This would be because none of the clocks in our house tell the same time, which would be due to a sneaky effort on my part to actually get somewhere on time for once in my life by setting certain clocks ahead, although in reality, it's not so sneaky, primarily because I set the clocks myself, and am therefore perfectly aware that they are 15 minutes ahead, and therefore plan my time accordingly.

Once in a while, say, after a power failure, someone else will reset the clocks, thereby throwing my entire world into confusion and causing me to be late, since I had counted on the upstairs clock being early, only to discover, when I go downstairs, that I am in fact 15 minutes late. Ours is a confusing household.

A reasonable person, such as my beloved, might enquire why I do not simply plan to get ready earlier, but that would be too simple. Besides, there always seem to be unexpected intervening factors that make this impossible, mainly because I'm very bad at planning (I tend to forget, for instance, when planning an evening, to take into account the time it takes to cook a meal, not to mention to eat it), and also because my life seems to be full of unanticipated disasters that are completely predictable, or should be, given my usual life path.

I no longer have the excuse of the children throwing up on me just as we're leaving the house – they're in their 20s now, so that occurrence tends to be a rare one – but there seem to be no end of disasters to make me late, such as spilling my purple smoothie all over my white dress – which smoothie, of course, I am carrying to the car because I'm running late and don't have time to sit down at the table and drink it like a normal person. Never mind that I now have to take an extra 15 minutes to change clothes. Which brings us to the almost daily occurrence known by my beloved as "the clothing crisis", wherein I can't decide which color I'm in the mood to wear, and once I make the decision, realize the item is dirty, or I no longer fit into it, having gained 10 pounds the night before at dinner.

To be fair, I come by this fluid relationship with time honestly; many is the time I remember the flurry in my parents' household on a Sunday morning as my mother tried desperately to get the four of us children ready for church, usually adding a last-minute stitch or two to the home-made dresses she created for the three of us girls (I once sat down in church, only to leap us with a yelp, having discovered the hard way that my mother had, accidentally I hope, left a pin in the hem of my new dress), while my father sat in the car, "warming up the engine".

When at last all six of us had piled into the car, my father would tear down the hill, exhaust backfiring so loudly we struck terror into the neighbors' hearts (not to mention our own – I think it was his revenge on us for being late – that, and making us sit in the front pew, after wending our way up there in disgrace under the watchful gaze of the entire congregation); when my mother protested both the speed and the backfire, my father would reply tersely that the neighbors should all be in church anyway.

This was a war neither of them would win, and in fact carry on to this day, after 68 years of marriage: my father gets ready to leave about an hour early in an attempt to get my mother to panic and get dressed faster, then sits in the car, engine running, while my mother thinks "For heavens sake, he's an hour early; I have LOTS of time", and proceeds in a leisurely fashion until they are, in fact, late. All the clocks in their house are set 15 minutes early, too, which, of course, mother knows and accounts for.

One of my sisters has been known, when attending a wedding, to be so late that she accompanies the bride down the aisle, so that now people tell her the wedding is actually an hour earlier than it is. It's also led to more speeding tickets than either of us care to remember, although we're all trying very hard to be on time these days. And, of course, we blame our speed on the bad driving habits learned from our parents, who were always late and driving too fast to try to make up time, although I believe there's some law of physics that ensures you can only drive so fast, and then you actually go backwards in time and meet yourself – but I could be wrong about that. It would be an interesting theory to test, if only I had the time.

INSPECTIONS

I WILL BE THE FIRST to admit that I can be overly compliant at times (see what I mean?). I believe I must be part lemming; just don't let me near any cliffs. Of course, the other part of me, as my parents would be only too happy to tell you, is pure mule, but that's another story. Aside from the interesting zoological picture that may create, it also results in some, shall we say, difficult situations. For instance, the whole nodding and smiling in a friendly, encouraging manner when I have absolutely no idea what someone is saying approach can have unfortunate results at times. Then there's the fact that I'm a rotten liar; even if I weren't opposed to it on moral grounds, my lack of talent in that direction ensured my children found out the truth about Santa Claus and the Easter bunny way before most children their age. Recently, my eagerness to obey the letter of the law nearly caused a riot.

There is a long-standing debate amongst people I know about how to approach the bug station, or as I suppose employees there prefer to call it, the agricultural inspection station. Of course, most of us approach it in our vehicles, but that wasn't what I meant, although I suppose sauntering through on foot would be interesting; would they make you turn your pockets inside out, do you think?

Anyway, some people hold the theory that the inspectors aren't really asking if you have ANY fruit or vegetables, they just want to know if you have DANGEROUS fruits and vegetables; you know, the kind that explode on impact. No, really, they are usually looking for apples, cherries, oranges or other fruits not grown in California, or pretty much anything purchased at a roadside stand, as you never know when the fruit terrorists may inject apples with worms, or apple moths, or whatever it is they're looking for. These people (such as my beloved) feel perfectly justified in replying that they have no fruits or vegetables with them, even if they have a crate of four different types of every fruit and vegetable known to humanity in the trunk, so long as it's not one of the "forbidden fruits", so to speak, as they feel certain that they are obeying the spirit of the law if not the letter of it.

Being a stickler for letters myself, and believing that when they inquire as to whether I have ANY fruit or vegetables, and being a compliant type, as well as having a vivid imagination which assumes I will of course be found out and successfully prosecuted for lying at the very least, as I'm so very bad at it, and therefore condemned to spend the remainder of my sorry, short life in a maximum security cell in a prison in Marrakesh, I am compelled to tell the truth, the whole truth, and nothing but the truth.

So, when I passed through the bug – I mean, the agricultural inspection station (the length of this story must be excused as it's entirely the fault of the government's insistence on long names for their stations, as well as my own compliant nature – how about if I abbreviate it to A.I.S.?) the other day, I inadvertently discovered a way of telling the truth and yet avoiding inspection.

My daughter and I had done some shopping for food before I took her to the airport for Italy. Needless to say (for any mother, anyway), being terrified the Italians might not have any suitable edibles for my precious child, or, equally frightening in our family, that she might actually be forced to purchase airline food, I added eight pounds of essential foodstuffs to her twenty-pound pack, including some of the apples and oranges she insisted on (she's a strange child), but I thought I had brought a few with me as well. So, when I got to the bug – I mean the A.I.S. – I of course immediately confessed to having apples and oranges (so to speak) in my belongings. Unfortunately, I couldn't remember where they were. So, I eagerly and compliantly popped the trunk, which is never a good idea in any of my littered vehicles.

After I had been rummaging about for a while through the old clothes, engine parts, and general garbage accumulated therein, the inspector began to relent, looking nervously over his shoulder at the line of cars behind me stretching to the Oregon border. Not to be deprived of doing my civic duty, I offered brightly, "Maybe they're behind the seat here!" and began delving into the mountains of crucial items stored inside the car. I had gone through three grocery bags, unsuccessfully, when he rather violently waved me on, roaring, "Go! Just GO!!" in my general direction.

Somewhat miffed, but ever championing truth in all matters, and ever compliant, I proceeded home, convinced she had taken all the fruit with her. A week later I discovered said fruit in a dark corner of the trunk, but my conscience was clear.

Marauding Marlahan Madness

A VERY SERIOUS ISSUE has arisen lately in our household: my beloved has developed an obsession with marlahan mustard, otherwise known as Dyer's Woad. Not in the romantic sense (at least I hope not, but then, he is gone a lot), but to such a degree that I fear for his sanity at times.

When he's at home, he often takes a bike ride up the hill (he's like that – uphill rides), and along the way he's been spotting marlahan mustard for several years now. Aware that it's classified as a noxious weed, and anxious that it not take over native shrubbery, he has taken to stopping along the way to uproot it, which apparently gives him great satisfaction. I was a little alarmed recently when he revealed that he'd taken along a weed puller, and suddenly I realized he'd been carrying it attached to the bike in such a way that if he had stopped suddenly he'd have shish-kebabbed himself, but he has now fixed that potential problem before it could occur.

His campaign, however, has resulted in his bike rides getting longer and longer, and I'm beginning to get a little concerned; he's taken to wandering around the house, weed-puller in hand, muttering "Constant vigilance!" All right, perhaps I exaggerate just a bit, but he is truly obsessed. But that's not really the problem. Unfortunately, it appears now that he's gone away on business again, he's passed the torch of this mania to me (although a flamethrower would be more to my liking than the weed puller) like a communicable disease from which there is no recovery. It started innocently enough: "Oh," says I on one of my hikes, "There's some marlahan mustard; why don't I just yank it out? My beloved would be so proud!"

I'll tell you why not: because it's attached by roots bigger than my wrist that appear to dig deeper than the depths of hell into the bowels of the earth, and there clutch for dear life a rock bigger than Texas. It's probably been there (the plant, that is) since before the mists of time, and is not about to let go now just because some puny hiker is pulling feebly at it. Undeterred, and in the grip of marlahan madness, I borrowed the weed puller back from my parents and attacked it (that would be the mustard) vigorously, bending the weed puller, not to mention my back, several times, but eventually emerged triumphant, weed in hand, filthy and exhausted but content (that would be me, not the weed, or the weed puller). Unfortunately, that was just the beginning.

Suddenly, everywhere I went, I saw mustard, even when I closed my eyes, which is tricky when you're hiking. Everything yellow, or yellowish, was a mustard plant, and I had to be physically restrained from uprooting daisies, buttercups, poppies and marigolds – even moss. Yes, I do realize that moss is green, but in early spring, in certain lights, when one is suffering from an addiction to marlahan eradication…

The plant is ubiquitous; short of hiking with blinders on, wrapped in a straightjacket, I cannot seem to escape it. I've been clambering up cliffs and sliding down hillsides I would normally consider a scenic view rather than something to be even remotely approached, just to get at the nasty plants and yank them out. Occasionally this gets me into some untenable positions; I have visions of careening backwards down some hillside, only to be found years later, a skeleton, smiling serenely, mustard in hand.

I have been known to grab a plant with both hands, tugging energetically, and have the beggar come loose unexpectedly, landing me on my backside in a most undignified manner while the dog looks on quizzically. He has no comprehension of marlahan madness. My one-hour hike stretches into two, then three hours, and I drag myself in the front door, weary and aching, to drop exhausted into the nearest chair, from which I can only be roused to take a hot bath and dream of mustard.

It's a sickness, I've decided. I'm afraid to look up, down, or sideways on my hikes at this point for fear of spotting mustard in some insanely inaccessible site, and then climbing up to get it at great risk of life and limb. I live in fear that one day I'm going to lose it altogether and crawl under my neighbor's fence in the dark of night, clutching a flashlight and a weed puller, with only one aim: eradication of marlahan mustard.

But there is hope: I noticed the other day that some anonymous, probably equally furtive person further down the street has pulled a few of the noxious weeds too. Which gave me an idea for a solution (other than committing myself to the loony bin): if everyone who reads this pulls at least two marlahan mustard plants when they see them, why, we could have, oh gee, six or seven plants pulled in a day! Better yet, if we all tell our friends and half the town picked a few plants every day before the flowers turn into those nasty black seeds, marlahan mustard would be eradicated, and my sanity, or what remains of it, and possibly that of my beloved, might be salvaged. Please join me in marauding marlahan madness!

More Camping Adventures

WE USED TO CAMP all the time when I was a kid. We had a little trailer that was about two hundred years old and smelled of mold, with seats that folded down into a second bed, and an actual icebox, with space for a block of ice. My parents had inherited it from their parents, so you can guess how ancient it was.

We went everywhere: the Grand Canyon, New Mexico, Canada, and all over California. I remember lots of card games around the table in the trailer at night in the rain, waiting an eternity for my father to play his hand until we finally realized he was sound asleep. Our parents were always dragging the four of us kids off for some adventure we didn't want to go on, but always ended up enjoying, and still remember. Whether it was camping, or picking walnuts from the other side of someone's fence, or strawberries from the right side of the fence – and we paid to do it! – or a trip to the coast, or to Carlsbad Caverns, they were always fun and memorable times.

The last time we camped as a family was a reunion a few years ago at Shasta Lake. The train came through the campground exactly at three a.m., frightening us all out of our wits; it sounded like it was right next to the tent. My mother hadn't camped in quite some time, and things had changed; when she came out of the port-a-potty, she was amazed. "Gosh," said she, "Now they have sinks in those things, and even a little round bar of soap so you can wash your hands! But it's strange, there's no running water…" We stood in puzzled silence a while until the penny dropped. "Mom, those are urinals! And that's not soap!"

A little while ago we borrowed a friend's cabin, with all the amenities.

Okay, the toilet was an outdoor privy, but if you've camped the way I have, it was downright luxurious. I was, however, awakened in the night by a noise; I sat bolt upright and, in a time-honored tradition, woke up my husband so he could share in my terror (he never does, of course, but it's a comfort just to have him awake with me - when I can wake him).

"There's something in the sink!" I hissed.

"Huh?"

I repeated myself.

"What?"

"I don't know what! But it sounds like it has a knife!"

He grudgingly grabbed the flashlight next to the bed (he's organized like that) and shone it in the direction of the sink. Two beady eyes stared back at us. A mouse was obligingly licking the peanut butter off the knife we hadn't washed before going to bed. "He's fine," yawned my beloved, and went back to sleep, leaving me with an armed and dangerous rodent. How was I supposed to sleep after that? Besides, he was a very noisy eater. I did manage to drop off at last, only to awaken the next morning to the sight of a chipmunk the size of a toddler attempting to open my son's backpack. Where was I, the high-crime district of the north woods, filled with breaking and entering rodents?

When our kids were small, we ended up camping in some pretty remote spots. Generally, there was no running water and I ended up washing the kids off in the ice chest. Occasionally there was cactus in great quantities, which made me nervous.

But this was an improvement on places we had camped BC (Before Children), such as in Ecuador, in a place where you could see through the floor into the kitchen below, and I will not even begin to describe the toilets. We camped in an aptly named "hut" at 15,000 feet on Mt. Cotapaxi, where I became violently ill and had to spend a fair bit of time in the toilet; it was open-air and conveniently perched on the edge of a very scenic drop, which did not improve my already dicey stomach.

Yes, camping brings back such fond memories.

CAR TROUBLE

I WAS VERY EXCITED when my beloved decided he was tired of hearing me whine about driving old wrecks and actually bought me another car. This was the first one I had ever had from this century (new has never been an option for us). Unfortunately, I seem to have an odd chemistry where cars are concerned, and it went to work on this one immediately. I was sitting at a stop sign just a month or two after we purchased it, when suddenly the speedometer told me I was doing 140 mph. I was just taking this in when the temperature gauge, and all the other gauges for that matter, went off the charts. The car obediently started forward when I gave it some gas, and all the dials went the opposite direction, much to my astonishment, then went back to normal as if nothing had happened. We took it to the dealer, who, naturally, could find nothing wrong with it. A few weeks later it died in front of the local sandwich shop and I had to get it towed back to the dealer, who tried again, but still could find nothing wrong. I could have told them: it's possessed, like every other vehicle I've ever owned.

Then I noticed that two lights had come on in the car: one that looked like a little orange submarine, and one that commanded me to "Check fuel cap". Since I didn't recognize the orange submarine symbol, I obediently got out and checked the fuel cap, which was securely fastened – locked, in fact. Mystified, I hummed a few bars of "Yellow Submarine" and trotted back to the driver's side. My beloved informed me later that the orange submarine is the engine light, but since he didn't seem alarmed, I decided to ignore it and hope it went away, as I do with most vehicular issues.

A while later, I was taking my daughter back to school in the Bay Area when we began to smell something awful. Noses wrinkled, we commented on how unpleasant big cities are, and wondered aloud how anyone could stand to live in one, when my instrument panel went black. Did I mention it was night, and it's really hard to navigate when your dashboard lights go out? I rolled down the window; as I had deduced, the smell was coming from inside the car, not outside, and we had both bathed before we left home, so that factor could be eliminated. Fortunately, I found a gas station right away; as I had suspected, the car wouldn't start after I turned it off. When AAA arrived, the guy told us to stay away from the car, as the smell was battery acid and would be really harmful to inhale; I didn't bother telling him we'd been inhaling it for three hours already. That might explain a lot, come to think of it. At least the battery light went out. The next day, after we finally got a new battery, I locked my keys inside and had to call AAA again. I think I qualify for frequent flyer miles with them.

Not too long after that incident, I could no longer turn the key in the ignition. I tried all the usual tricks (this having happened before): jiggling the steering wheel, turning the key upside down and reinserting it, swearing at it; I even tried a little hand lotion on the key, not having any WD-40 handy. Nothing. We had to have it towed (again) and the entire ignition replaced. That was a month or so ago; it did it again the other night. I'm not even going there. However, the "check fuel cap" sign went out.

Perhaps the car is exacting revenge. We hadn't had it very long when I parked, as I always do, at the top of the drive and went into the house. A few hours later, I was calmly reading when my beloved came in, looking wild-eyed, and asked frantically, "What happened to the car?" "What car?" I asked somewhat stupidly. He took me outside, where I saw to my horror that I had neglected to set the parking brake and parked far enough back in the drive to allow the car to roll backwards down the hill, picking up enough speed to do extensive damage when it hit one of the oak trees, squarely in the middle of the trunk. Of the car, that is, as well as the tree, and necessitating a replacement of said car trunk. The tree died, too, but I can't honestly say I mourn it.

Naturally, we didn't get a new trunk, as that would be expensive; my beloved is fond of junk yards for replacement parts, so I now have a lovely white car with a black trunk, which makes it look a lot like a law enforcement vehicle – kind of sporty, I think. In fact, maybe I'll get a little red light to put on top. At least it's easy to pick out in a crowded parking lot. And in the meantime, the check engine light has gone out.

CHRISTMAS TRADITIONS

I WAS SITTING AROUND WITH a group of women friends the other day, and the discussion turned to family Christmas traditions. I listened as, one by one, they described lovely holiday practices – baking cookies together, setting up the manger scene, special ornaments made by the children hung lovingly on the tree (that is, the ornaments, not the children – at least I hope that's what they meant, although at my house, it may well have been the other way around; I get distracted at times) – and sat silently hoping no one would ask about mine. Our traditions run more along the lines of panicked last-minute attempts to get the fake tree up and the gifts wrapped, then cooking the meal we hope will stretch to feed any unexpected family members who happen to show up at the last minute, before falling into bed exhausted. Then, of course, I wake up in a panic in the middle of the night, having remembered that I forgot to stuff the children's Christmas stockings – having also temporarily forgotten that the "children" are now 22 and 24 years old – how time flies! But I go down and fill the stockings anyway, because that's what moms do, no matter how old the children are. Until, of course, they see fit to grace me with grandchildren, at which point they will be abandoned in favor of said grandchildren, as is the tradition in our family.

I've already written in past stories about many of our Christmas traditions – rearranging the limbs of the "Snoopy trees" my father brought home in good years, or waiting until after midnight services to steal a tree left in the lot in bad years; making snowmen out of tumbleweeds (this was Los Angeles, which tends to be short on snow most years); setting up the fake tree and having to vacuum up fake needles; scouring the hills for mistletoe to hang all over the house in order to trap my beloved into kissing me, etc – but I don't believe I described my grandmother's crèche scene.

My grandmother (the same beloved grandmother of questionable Christmas tree taste I have described before, who dearly loved her aluminum Christmas tree for reasons I cannot fathom) always set up her special crèche scene every Christmas, and when she died, I inherited it. I had carefully preserved the box holding her glass animals, but had not set it up until a few years ago, when I bought an actual manger to put them in. As I set up the shepherds, Mary and Joseph, the three kings – well, actually, two; we appear to be short a king. Maybe he got lost and refused to ask for directions – I suddenly picked out a goose in flight. A goose? I don't remember any descriptions of Canadian geese – excuse me, I mean Canada geese; it was recently explained to me that they wouldn't be Canadian geese unless they were passport-holding geese. Maybe it got lost during migration. In any case, I can be open-minded, so the goose went into the scene, although, realist that I am, he was confined to the roof. No need for the Christ child to share a manger with goose poop.

Next came the bear. A bear?? In Palestine? I'm pretty sure they didn't have bears out there any more than they had Canada geese, but oh well – in he goes, somewhat to the right and behind the wise men, so as not to make them nervous –he's bigger than they are, and they're already missing one; no sense in losing any more. In fact, I think, is there a connection between the missing wise man and the bear?! Nah…But the last animal really threw me – a kangaroo. Now, I'm as open-minded as the next person, but kangaroos? I'm pretty sure they don't travel much outside Australia, and besides, they were smaller than the sheep, and that just doesn't seem right. I mean, wouldn't they be about the size of Joseph? No sense making Joseph any more nervous than the wise men. But my grandmother was apparently a free-thinker, at least when it came to manger scenes, and hey, it's the season of miracles, right? So in he goes, in the back with the sheep, where I hope he'll feel at home, and we have our Christmas crèche scene and another, perhaps strange, Christmas tradition to pass down to the children.

May all of your Christmas traditions be happy ones!

Electronic Oddities

THINGS HAD BEEN SO automotively uneventful in my life for so long that I should have known trouble was brewing.

It started a few weeks ago when I walked by my car and the door locks popped up and down of their own volition. It was so quick and furtive that I convinced myself I had imagined it. A few months earlier the two CDs that had become inextricably and inexplicably wedged into my car's CD player and held hostage there for many months had spontaneously ejected themselves apropos of nothing, but this is so typical of the many electronic mysteries in my life that I had simply shrugged it off; it takes rather a lot more than that to faze me.

I should interject here that my electric door locking mechanism failed shortly after the car was purchased, and I have been manually unlocking it ever since. The car, I might add, has over 170,000 miles on it and is going on 13 years old, which makes it a veritable spring chicken in my world, with many, many good years in it, God willing. And, I add with some strained dignity, it is still all one color, also a rarity in my world.

Ever the eternal optimist, I serenely assumed that now all would be well. However, a few days later when I tried to unlock my car preparatory to going to work, the doors were already unlocked. I always lock my car, lest someone steal my valuable library books, so here was a mystery I could not ignore, although I tried. Every time I locked my car after that, I made a quick U-turn to surprise it and check to make sure it had stayed locked, but I couldn't catch it in the act; it behaved itself for a brief time, lulling me into a false sense of security. Pretty soon, every time I tried to open the doors, I found them unlocked.

Next, I would get in the car and start to drive, and the locks would start neurotically popping up and down while I shouted at them to stop; after a bit, they did, and I decided the car simply needed the voice of authority. But a few days later, as I turned off the car prior to getting out, it started beeping at me that I had left the keys in the ignition – and they were in my hand. I spoke severely to the car, explaining the obvious fact that the keys were not in the ignition, and I hadn't even opened the car door yet, ergo, it was not necessary for the car to warn me that I had left the keys in the ignition (I always find it helpful to speak in soothing, logical tones when my car is behaving badly – until I start yelling at the top of my voice in total frustration when it doesn't appear to be listening). The car appeared to take the hint and behaved itself for a few more days. But all was not well in automotive land – at least, not in mine.

The next time I unlocked my car door, a low warning beep ensued. It was not the alarm, exactly, but it sounded like the warm-up for the alarm, which did not bode well. I ignored it, and eventually it went away. But the next time I tried to get in, not having even locked the stupid door, it started with the calm alarm, then went into the full-fledged blare that frightens away burglars and me, and would not stop, no matter how many times I pressed the alarm button or yelled at it. As I happened to be outside an auto body shop, I calmly and logically went inside and yelled "Help!" But by the time someone came out, it had stopped. There is an element of "Gaslight" in my life that I find quite disconcerting at times. As I drove home, the door locks popped up and down frantically, just to make a point, I think. In any case, I continued to lecture the car and watched it with a certain amount of suspicion.

Sure enough, the other day I drove somewhere, turned off the engine, removed the key – and the doors had locked themselves and I couldn't get out. As it was quite hot outside, I had a momentary, frightening image of dying of heatstroke before I outthought the car. All right, I reasoned, it won't lock itself when I start the car, the way it's supposed to, so I'll fool it by starting it, and it will then unlock itself. It worked. It's a little frightening how Machiavellian I have to become just to get out of my car these days.

I have developed a theory that it's doing this because of the rain we've had recently. It's not based on any particular logic, but it beats the only other theory I can think of – demon possession – so I am eagerly awaiting sunshine.

FORGETTING

AS I GET OLDER, I find I'm forgetting more and more. I'm not just talking about the average every day lapses of memory, like forgetting where you put the car keys (or in my case, the car). I'm talking about having entire conversations with people you would swear blind you've never seen in your life but who appear to know not only your name, but the names of your spouse, children, and extended family members. You're smiling and doing your best to keep up your end of the conversation without giving away the fact that you have absolutely no idea who it is you're talking to, trying to gain information about just who this person might be and desperate not to hurt their feelings by admitting you haven't the first clue who they are or why they think you should know them. This is the somewhat nerve-wracking, sanity-questioning forgetting not all of us experience.

Then there are the personal hygiene issues, like when it's time to do a clear-cut (shave my legs) and I shave one leg and completely forget to do the other, or dry one arm after a bath and forget to dry the other one, then wonder why it's so difficult to get into my shirt. Or the time I went swimming and cleverly brought my work clothes with me so I could save time by going directly there afterwards, but neglected to bring my underwear – all of it. That was a dilemma. I also like to take hot baths in the winter, mainly to warm up, and, so as not to waste time, take a book I've been meaning to read with me. But the older I get, the more often I tend to fall asleep in the bath once I get warm and drop whatever I'm reading into the tub; I've ruined more books that way... Setting them on the edge of the bath until later never seems to work, either; unless you're smack in the exact middle of one, they tend to overbalance and fall off, usually into the water. So, I came up with a clever ploy, which means my beloved has often come into the bathroom to find me fast asleep, glasses on, my book precariously balanced on the top of my head.

There appears to be a grammatical component to memory loss, too: I've noticed the nouns go first. Truthfully, my grandmother told me this years ago, but I was young and didn't pay attention. Or maybe I forgot. We all forget words, but the nouns appear to be disappearing at a more rapid rate than the other parts of speech. I'm still pretty good at coming up with verbs, thank goodness, but common sense tells me I ought to be doing something, even at my advanced age, and the verbs seem to appear when needed. When I become immobile, I expect the verbs will go. Of course, my eyesight is getting so bad I can't see well enough to look up the nouns in the dictionary without a magnifying glass (another trait of my grandma's); the flip side of that is I can't see my wrinkles either, which is a definite plus.

I'm kind of curious about what will be next: Adjectives? Adverbs? Hardly anyone uses interjections anymore; they're pretty dispensable, so I'm rooting for them. Conjunctions are fairly essential if you want to have more than one thought at a time, and prepositions are really just window dressing, but I really don't see how I'll manage without verbs.

And if I don't write things down, there's no hope I'll remember them, but since I write my notes on random pieces of paper I happen to find lying around, particularly junk mail, I often can't find them later, usually because I've thrown them away without bothering to look at both sides – it's junk mail, right? - so it's pretty much a lost cause. I come by this habit honestly: my father used to write notes on his lunch bag, then eat his lunch and throw the bag away. I also (rarely) get into what my beloved refers to as "cleaning frenzies" and proceed to throw away things I'm sure I don't need, only to find later they were crucial to something or other. My beloved went off to climb a few mountains the other day, and about three minutes after he left, if you had tortured me, I couldn't have told you which ones he was going up, even though he had specifically told me not five minutes before. When someone asked, I offered up tentatively: "In eastern California, near Bishop – Thielson?" He later told me Thielson is in Oregon. Oh well, at least I knew it was some set of mountains somewhere in California.

I suppose eventually I'll forget who I am, which might be restful.

GARDEN SPOT

THE OTHER DAY I went past Klander's Deli and saw a sign reading, "OK, who left a bag of zucchini on my steps?" and it reminded me of my troubled history with gardening.

A few years ago we decided to have a vegetable garden, and ended up, as all novice gardeners do, with more zucchini than any sane person could deal with. We eventually grew tired of all the various permutations of recipes for zucchini bread, cake, soup, etc., that desperate gardeners and their friends everywhere collect, and did what all zucchini farmers do: threw them into random open car windows in the dark of night when no one was around. I hadn't thought of an unsolicited donation to the local deli; I swear it wasn't me, Ondia! We also had fruit trees at the time, and I nearly did permanent damage to myself while trying to make apricot jam. Those little suckers are so small it takes a gazillion of them to make one little jar, and the process involved in sterilizing the jars ended with my chin in a mug of cold water, which would take more time to explain than I have space.

I must admit it (if it weren't already obvious): unlike everyone else in this county, I am not a gardener. When conversations turn, as they inevitably do, to gardens and vegetables, I make myself small and try to blend into the background, and maintain a strategic silence. Fortunately, after years of dealing with lawns in other homes we have lived in, my beloved shares my dislike of backbreaking labor, and we have opted for what we like to call "zeroscape", or the "natural look", which makes us sound very environmentally responsible, when in reality we're just lazy. Well, I am – he just expends his energy on more useful pursuits, like climbing mountains.

I have been known to kill cacti. In college, my roommate and I had coleus, or, I suppose as we had more than one, at least for a while - coleii? Naturally, it developed some exotic fungus, so I decided to prune it to get rid of the nasty thing – that is, the fungus. When my roommate came home, she gasped in horror at the lonely stalk that emerged from the pot; it was a very widespread fungus. I found out later a little alcohol would have worked just dandy, and we still would have had a plant. I'm afraid I approach hair cutting in the same fashion; needless to say, no one in my house lets me near them with a pair of scissors.

For a while I cleaned houses for a living; one lady wanted me to take care of her ficus trees, too, so I dutifully watered them regularly. They developed ants which I could not get rid of for love nor money; I used some kind of pesticide that probably eliminated most of my brain cells, and still those dang trees had ants. If you ask me (which she did not), the stupid things belonged outside anyway (with the ants). You may be able to tell I never have gotten over my resentment of ficus. And what, pray tell, is the plural of that, anyway? Fici?

When I left a job, my co-workers, having experienced my rather dark thumb, gave me a plastic plant in farewell. My daughter wants to buy me the t-shirt we saw that has a picture of a wilting potted plant and the logo "Desperate Houseplants". I like houseplants, especially the ones in the store that look sad and in need of help, so I constantly bring them home, where they languish until my husband takes pity on them and occasionally waters them with the dregs of whatever he happens to be drinking when he notices them drooping forlornly, which may be plant abuse.

About all I can manage is a few pots of flowers on the deck, and even that is a challenge. I buy them in a burst of enthusiasm, then set them outside until I have time to plant them; too often they never make it into the actual dirt before expiring. Watering is, unfortunately, frequently forgotten. I do, however have one or two plants that serve as my canaries in a coal mine; I put them along the path to the house, so that I can't miss their little wilted leaves and am (hopefully) reminded to slake their thirst before they expire completely.

Weeding is problematic, too; how do you tell the weeds from the actual plants? I know; you're supposed to remember what you planted, but it's usually been so long since I planted the darn things, I can't remember what I bought, and some of those weeds have really pretty flowers.

Then we also get what my beloved refers to as "volunteers", possibly from previous years, and I find myself thinking, "Gosh, I don't remember planting marigolds (or, as my mother calls them, margaritas) – or are they marigolds, or just something that's masquerading as marigolds?" The ethical and philosophical issues can be overwhelming; I tell you, it's exhausting.

And as with people, it's often a challenge to tell the weeds from the flowers until they've had enough time to show their true colors. The weeds near the garage are going to swallow my car (or me) whole if we can't convince the kids to weed-eat soon. They're so high (the weeds, not the children) I can hardly see the top of the car; there may come a day that I get lost in the wilds between the house and the garage. The other day as I left the garage, some kind of viney thing grabbed my ankle and I thought I was a goner; visions of "Night of the Tryphids" terrorized me as, panic-stricken, I struggled to extricate myself from its grip.

The children are less than enthusiastic gardeners, too, so we had to resort to the drastic measure of borrowing my sister's horse in an attempt to reduce the wild grass (weed?) population. He's not measuring up, either, and I can't seem to convince my beloved that we need a goat or two. Since we live outside town and have regular visits from the local wildlife, including bears and cougars, he insists tethering a goat would be like offering dinner on a plate, and I am inclined to reluctantly agree. Meanwhile, the plants need watering; if I'm not back in three days, send out a search party.

FREEZING

UPON FURTHER REFLECTION, I am perfectly willing to admit that the white dress I wore to work that day might not have been the ideal outfit in which to clean out the freezer, especially when it came to the shelf with the cranberries on it; I am not, after all, a completely unreasonable person. But defrosting and cleaning out the freezer is not my ideal occupation, and one needs must strike while the iron is hot, so to speak, so when inspiration struck, who was I to be diverted from my clear duty? Thus it was I found myself in the basement on a recent hot summer day, thinking, "Ah, this would be the perfect chore for a hot summer day!"

Of course, if I were to be totally honest, as I must occasionally be, just for practice, I would admit that I was motivated more by the fact that the freezer had stopped working altogether and a large pool of water was gathering around it than by any higher moral purpose, and as my beloved gleefully pointed out from several continents away (you have to love email, where one can safely point out many facts which might be dangerous to one's health to point out were one closer to the object of the pointing, who might just deliver a pithy remark in a rather more physical way than one might like), he had defrosted it the last time, which may well have been true, but was so long ago the occasion was lost in the mists of time for both of us. When I remarked that objects (I hesitate to refer to them as "food") in the freezer were taking an awfully long time to melt, considering it had been doing a fine job of defrosting before I turned it off, my husband replied that was odd; and had I put basins in the bottom to catch the water when I left the door open? There was a short pause. "You need to leave the door open?" Maybe he had been the last one to defrost. So to speak.

In any case, I found myself on my knees in said white dress, since once I started there really wasn't any point in stopping to change clothes, vinegar-water bowl in hand (there just isn't a better cleaner for love nor money than vinegar-water), cold boxes at the ready, waiting for the adventure to begin.

And adventure it was. The things I discovered in that freezer belonged in a museum, or at least on an archeological dig; as old as some of that stuff was, it may have been excavated from King Tut's tomb. It was, at the very least, a trip down memory lane akin to looking through the children's baby books, and almost as sentimental, if a trifle soggier. There were the four dozen or so corn dogs our son decided he couldn't live without when he was much younger, only to decide the following year that they were unhealthy and refused to eat them. There were the Icee Pops, or whatever they're called these days, that we all thought would keep the children under control some hot summer years ago but which melted and re-froze in unfortunate shapes that resulted in the children distrusting their content. There was the phylo, a food product I had never heard of before my son's middle school international foods party about ten years ago (I only wish I were exaggerating), and which somehow ended up in the freezer, along with all the other mysterious objects. Good heavens! What could that orange glop be? Ah, yes: my daughter's "carrot nasty", the starving student's version of dinner.

Then there were the many mysterious frozen leftovers that I had cavalierly decided I didn't need to label because I would surely remember what they were just by looking at them, covered in ice thick enough to have originat-

181

ed in the Arctic and obscuring completely whatever resided therein. Surely those 16 small containers of home-made frozen applesauce didn't originate from the time the children were infants!

It's interesting to speculate on how long certain foods can be frozen before they kill you when you try to defrost them and actually eat them, or whether vegetables defrosted and re-frosted are actually dangerous; when my beloved and I were first married, we both became violently ill after one of my home-cooked meals, and he insisted the re-frozen green beans were the reason. I'm not convinced, but I am leery. I guess we'll find out, since it almost physically hurts me to throw food away – hence the many enigmatic items in the freezer. I would imagine that if any family members suspect how long tonight's dinner has been moldering in said freezer, they would refuse point blank to eat it, but that's why I don't go into menu details; my theory is, if it's been in the freezer, it must be all right. Or it will be once it's nuked. Or maybe the dog will eat really well in the next few weeks.

Be Prepared

IT ALL STARTED when I decided to take some expired drugs in to the Sheriff's office, having realized that the Yreka sewer system probably has all it can handle in the way of drugs.

Not having read the ad carefully, as usual, I discovered when I got there that I was required to place said drugs in a zip-lock bag for proper disposal. This put me in a dilemma: where to find a zip-lock bag without going all the way home again (a distance, I must add, of about two miles, but hey, gas prices are going up) or trekking to the store to buy one?

Naturally, I searched my purse, and lo and behold, by a miracle, amongst the other detritus to be found there, I discovered a small zip lock bag just big enough to hold all the expired drugs. There was just one small problem: the bag contained my portable sewing kit (yes, I carry one with me everywhere; if you are me, you never know when you might need to stitch an item of clothing that might otherwise leave one overexposed). I was therefore once again cast onto the horns of a dilemma: do I obey instructions and sacrifice my sewing kit, or do I break the rules? And if I decide to conform, what do I do with my sewing kit, which contains many small loose pieces, including several buttons, thread, a needle, and some safety pins?

After cogitating on the matter awhile (I have a sinking feeling I might have been taped, in which case someone watching it may either be quite puzzled at this eccentric woman's conduct, highly suspicious, laughing hysterically, or all three), I came up with a brilliant idea: I would transfer the items comprising the sewing kit into my empty glasses case (the reason it is empty is a long, boring story, like most of my life). The glasses case was not securely fastened, but this, I reasoned, would not be a crucial defect because I would take the items out as soon as I got home and put them in something else. Naturally, this did not happen, but I am the eternal optimist in such matters.

Several days later, I brought a zip-lock bag of mixed nuts with me to the car to stave off immediate starvation (a state which overcomes me at least several times a day). Naturally, we had a heat wave that day, which resulted in me needing to remove the bag from the car, as I can't have nuts without a bit of chocolate, which had of course melted; I put it in my purse to take into the house, having, as usual, fifteen other items to juggle up the stairs, and then discovered that it had opened, spilling a great many nuts, and of course melted chocolate, into my purse.

It was another few days before I got around to clearing the nuts out of my purse. I did this by emptying everything else out of the purse and eating the nuts in the bottom as I read that day's Siskiyou Daily News. The stories being particularly riveting, I did not carefully examine what I was eating (although I don't usually anyway, having a bad habit of eating as I read; I think if I didn't, I would never be able to indulge in either pursuit. However, it is a habit I cannot recommend, for reasons which will become clear).

To make a short digression, I must add that my tendency to not pay close attention to what I am eating has caused issues, including the other day, when I finally traced some digestive restiveness to the possibility that the lovely eggs and vegetables I had made may not have benefitted from sitting out on the counter. In my defense, I was waiting for them to cool off so that I could put them in the refrigerator without causing the refrigerator to work too hard to cool them down. I was, I reasoned, saving energy, not to mention saving the poor refrigerator from working too hard and dying young, or perhaps in middle age. However, it must be said that I then proceeded to forget all about them until several days later when I remembered to put them in the fridge. As previously noted, I did not concentrate much while I ate them, as usual reading while I ate, and therefore was not immediately aware of the odor until I had finished eating.

In any case, to return to the track I have derailed myself from (you may or may not recall that we left me sitting on the couch, eating nuts from the bottom of my purse), as I sat eating nuts and melted chocolate from my purse, I bit down on a particularly hard, flat nut, took it out to examine its provenance, and discovered it to be, not a nut at all, but a button – from the sewing kit.

Thus, the moral of the story is: Always carry extra small plastic zip-lock baggies in your purse; you never know when you may need one to keep you from biting down on a button.

ACHES AND PAINS

GETTING OLD, THEY SAY, is hell; they also say it beats the alternative, which is true, at least so far. Various aches and pains have developed which I ignored for a while, but which eventually sent me to the doctor, and from thence, the podiatrist and physical therapist. I must say, I'm getting quite tired of the first words out of my doctor's mouth being, "As we get older…" and then listing a host of things that go awry as we age, things I never once even thought about when I was younger.

I was trying to explain to my beloved the other day how much my shoulder hurt, saying, "I tell you, if anyone wanted to torture me to get information, all they would have to do is bend my arm back like this," demonstrating with a wince. My beloved raised one eyebrow. "And exactly what do you know that would result in your being tortured by anyone to get said information?" he inquired mildly. "Nothing, of course, but that's not the point!" I replied in frustration. His brow lowered. "Ah", he replied succinctly. Honestly, he's just so logical sometimes it's irritating. Well, all the time, really. Logical, that is, not irritating. Necessarily.

So off I went to physical therapy. First I noted the sign: "Don't let these innocent smiles fool you: these are cruel, vicious women." Uh oh. Actually, they are all incredibly sweet, when they're not torturing you to make you feel better. Laura looked at my feet and said something very close to "Whoa! I don't think I've ever seen anything quite like that before. Okay, you can relax them now." I sighed inwardly and replied, "They are relaxed. This is as relaxed as they ever get." "Whoa! No wonder they hurt. Do you wear high heels a lot?" I sighed again. "Never. I have enough trouble just walking at the best of times; wearing high heels would be like trying to walk in stilts – very dangerous to my health."

My feet, you see, are very wide and very short, with high arches and double-jointed toes. When I start to fall over for no apparent reason, which is often, my toes automatically go up in a usually vain attempt to keep me upright, thus wearing holes in the tops of many shoes. It's hard to find shoes in my wide size in the first place, so this is not a good thing. In fact, my feet are so wide, the arches so high and the heels so narrow that when I was little, my mother once remarked in exasperation that I should just wear the boxes the shoes came in. I've never minded about my double-jointed ankles, except that they're so flexible that ice-skating is out of the question, but then again, I never twist them hard enough to do any damage when I fall. We have to find the positives where we can, right?

Of all the things I might have imagined going wrong with my body as I grew older, my feet never even made the list. Really? Feet?? I was eventually referred to a podiatrist, who gazed at my feet for so long I thought he had fallen asleep, but apparently he was just impressed by their weirdness. Then he had me stroll around the room for about ten minutes, while he just sat and watched me walk. It seems he thought it was some sort of miracle I could walk at all and wanted to observe the phenomenon. When he took the impression for the orthotics I now have to wear in my shoes in the hopes of improving my plantar fasciitis (boy, does THAT make me feel old – orthotics!!), he remarked, "It's no wonder you have no balance! There's hardly any part of your foot actually touching the ground!"

But physical therapy was fun: massage, icing, and the electrical-stimulation machine (at least I think that's what it was), which feels a bit like you're being gnawed on by small vermin, then bigger vermin. After a while the vermin start to run across your shoulder, and then I was usually asleep, or maybe I was dreaming the vermin; sometimes it's hard to tell.

After much physical therapy, my various body parts began to feel better, so I joined the "Wellness Program", which means I get to play with weights, always a dangerous occupation for me. But other than whacking myself in the chin a few times and getting tangled up in the leg-lifter thing, I haven't done myself too much damage so far. I stay away from the treadmill, though – way too much for potential for harm in those machines.

The shoulder remained stubbornly painful, even after physical therapy, so I went to the doctor and got a shot in it that made my whole body feel as if it had been oiled, like the tin man, for several months. Torture me all you want, now – I'll never tell.

STORIES

I COME FROM A large family of Irish-German storytellers; the Irish side tells the story, and the German side makes sure it's punctuated and edited properly. Truthfully, for reasons which escape me, as I've met the Irish and the Germans in their natural habitats, it was the German side that told the funny stories, while the Irish side made sure the bills were paid.

My mother and her seven brothers and sisters were the German side; whenever we visited them, I laughed until my face hurt, while my father's family were the chess-playing men you talked to about deep philosophical issues and the current political situation, which I must admit didn't attract me much when I was ten. Specifically, my mother and her four sisters, known collectively as "the Aunties", were some of the funniest people I've ever met. They were all, with the exception of my mother, about five feet tall, my mother being the odd one out at a striking and very slender five foot eight or so. I remember shopping for hats with the Aunties one time; one of them handed me one with a broad brim (me being five foot nine), saying, "Here, you try it on – I'm so short it makes me look like a mushroom." They referred to themselves as "German peasant stock" and said they could probably have had their babies out in the fields and gone right back to work afterwards.

Two of my favorite stories about them occurred at their annual "reunions", which took place in San Francisco, a city they loved even though they were all from Los Angeles, and where they consumed quantities of their favorite tipple, Andre's Cold Duck. I lived in San Francisco at the time, and offered to show them the sights, a plan to which they enthusiastically agreed. I told them it was a short trip from my little roach-infested studio apartment on Pine Street to Fisherman's Wharf – I had walked it with my then-boyfriend, so how hard could it be? So we set off. Several hours later, they good-naturedly pointed out that when I had walked it with my boyfriend, I had been in love and must not have noticed the distance; one of them claimed that I had worn out the lifetime heels on her shoes. We finally gave up on the way back and took the bus, which resulted in the inevitable hours-long haggling sessions in which everyone tried to make sure they hadn't cheated anyone: "Well, I owe you, because you bought my lunch yesterday." "Yes, but you paid my bus fare just now, so you have to subtract that." "But you tipped him." "I tipped the bus driver?" "No, the waiter!" "I did? Well, was it 15% or 20%?" "I don't know! How good was the service?" "Weren't you there?" and on and on. They were old enough to find it thrilling to get a senior discount, and made sure everyone knew it: "Are you sure you gave me the senior discount? I qualify, you know!" they would state loudly before swaggering down the aisle on the bus.

On one reunion trip, I made reservations for them at a nice Victorian bed and breakfast in the Mission district, and we toured the house, ending up on the roof, where I pointed out the sights, including St. Mary's Cathedral, and told them the true, but scandalous back in the day, story about it: at a certain time of day, one of the peaks on the roof cast a shadow of an anatomically perfect female breast. There was a short silence as my elderly aunties took this in and mulled it over, gazing at the view. Finally one of them remarked thoughtfully, "I wonder what sort of a shadow St. Peter's casts?" We were lucky not to fall off the roof laughing.

On another occasion, they were discussing the fact that they all had a serious addiction to chocolate. One of them, I think it was Frieda, said, "Why, I eat so much chocolate, I think it runs in my veins instead of blood; if I slit my wrists, chocolate would come out!" At which Phyllis remarked without missing a beat, "Well, if you decide to do it, call me; I'll come right over with a spoon!"

They certainly knew how to have a good time.

THE GUN

THE GUN HUNG OVER the door in plain view. That was the idea, he told her; the children would take it for granted and ignore it. If they hid it away, it would be an object of mystery and intrigue, and they would want to do the forbidden and play with it. She hated having a gun in the house at all, but there wasn't much she could do about it. The times were so uncertain. She went about her daily tasks, glancing at it occasionally, always keeping it within her sight.

Sometimes the children went outside to pick berries, or to have adventures out in the woods, and as grateful as she was for the time alone, a few minutes' peace, she found herself wandering forlornly through the empty rooms, picking up their toys, tenderly folding their clothing, hearing their childish voices in the stillness.

Yesterday she played with them as she did every day, rolling the ball to the little one, listening to him laugh as he ran away from his sister with it, watching her run after him indignantly and once again explain the rules of the game to him. She could not imagine how she had lived life without them. When they had run outside to play, her eyes moved again to the gun, with its malevolent stare.

One night the baby woke up coughing and choking; she gathered him up tenderly and held him close, soothing, whispering, singing; rocking him in the big chair until he was calm, smelling the sweet baby scent of him, feeling the warmth of his body, comforting, while the gun looked on, mocking.

The next day the baby was fine, as always, despite her constant fear that this time it was something really serious. Her husband always laughed at her and told her that if she kept herself busier, she wouldn't have time for such foolishness. That day she swept and dusted and polished with more vigor than ever before; in the evening she surveyed the room and glanced at the gun in triumph. She tiptoed to the children's beds to watch their silent, peaceful sleep, and said her nightly prayer: "Dear God, please keep them happy, healthy, and safe, and please let me die before they do, because I couldn't bear to lose them."

In the morning, her little girl spilled her milk, and she found herself shouting at the child's clumsiness. The girl's tears ran down her face as she cowered in a corner, until suddenly they were wrapped in each other's arms, crying together, holding tight, apologising and telling each other of their love.

This was her life now, bounded by the glass walls of love through which she watched the horrors of the world. Their love alone would keep them safe. The gun above the door smiled evilly at her as she asked brokenly for forgiveness. They took a walk together, the three of them, picking flowers for the table that night; she marveled at the beauty and innocence she had helped to create, and trembled. She confessed her sin of anger to the priest that night, and was absolved, but her heart was full of fear. Later that night she held the children tightly to her, until they protested laughingly that they couldn't breathe; she smiled at them through her tears and tucked them into bed.

The next day they ran into the yard to play. Minutes later she heard the fierce barking of a strange dog, and heard the children scream. She rushed out the door, grabbing the gun on the way, but it was unloaded; she held it by the barrel and bludgeoned the animal threatening her children with every ounce of strength she possessed. Finally she became aware of the children crying, and looked down at the bloody, pulpy mess of fur at her feet. She calmed her tearful babies and put them to bed, and buried the dog's corpse in the forest, slamming the last shovel of earth on the grave with deep satisfaction. She cleaned the silent gun and replaced it above the door, and said her evening prayer with special fervor. She felt no need to confess this act of violence to the priest. She eyed the gun with a feeling close to kinship on her way to bed.

It was the middle of the night when the soldiers came. They ignored the useless gun above the door, and used their own weapons to answer the mother's prayer: they shot her before they murdered her frightened children.

"STEELIE"-EYED

IN WHAT WAS UNDOUBTEDLY yet another misguided attempt to join the 21st century (I'm having enough trouble with the 20th), I recently decided to buy a blue tooth so that I could legally talk on the telephone while driving. I have terrible struggles just trying to turn down the heat or turn on the radio, so forget texting; I could die just trying to change radio stations, it takes so much concentration, and if I wanted to text – which I definitely do not – it would be a major production: find my glasses, hiding somewhere in the depths of my purse, enlarge the print on the phone so that I can actually see it, text, making sure that I use all correct punctuation, spelling, and sentence structure, find the send button – you can perhaps surmise why I only text while sitting at home, with lots of time on my hands.

Undaunted, and with the help of my friend Tonya (what a woman), I figured out how to turn the blue tooth thing on, attach the magnet to my phone (after buying the magnet separately – note to self: read the fine print when buying this stuff on-line), and make sure they were all communicating with each other. Excepting Tonya, of course, who was communicating with me. Or trying to; I am particularly dense when it comes to manuals.

On my trial run, I attached the device that is meant to hold the phone (a large metal ball called, I believe, and for reasons unclear to me, a "Steelie") to a vent, slapped the phone on it, imbedded the blue tooth deeply into my ear, where it will probably remain until surgically removed, and proudly waited for someone to call me as I drove down the freeway.

A word of caution: these magnet things are serious business. They manage to attract every piece of metal within five yards, and they do not let go easily. It's amazing how much metal I carry in my purse, all of which ends up attached to my phone, and makes for some interesting discoveries when I get a call. The other day I answered my phone, only to discover about 50 paper clips attached to it, all of which had apparently been lurking unseen in my purse. One day at work I set my phone on a metal file cabinet and almost gave myself a hernia trying to get it off again before realizing I could slide it off the end of said cabinet. My friend Tonya set hers on her washer and almost picked the machine up with the phone, but ended up ripping the magnet off instead, thereby solving one problem, but creating a new one.

But I left myself driving down the road, happily anticipating my first blue tooth phone call. When it came, I became so excited (I don't get many calls) that I accidentally knocked the Steelie off the vent, and it and the phone flew in opposite directions, the Steelie ending up under my feet and the phone taking off for parts unknown. I groped around on the floor, keeping my eyes on the road at all times, of course, but came up empty. By now, as I had un-intentionally slowed down considerably, and people were giving me strange looks as they passed me, it occurred to me that I might make the freeway safer for all of us if I pulled over, so I did. I then located the phone and the Steelie, reunited them, and once again installed the pair on the vent.

At this point a disembodied voice announced that the phone and the blue tooth were not connected. I'm still not sure whether this was a direct hint from God, the blue tooth, or my telephone. So I argued, as I am wont to do, that of course it was connected, but by then the caller was gone. I then dis-covered that I had never actually turned the blue tooth on. This technology stuff is going to be a little more complicated than I had anticipated.

A few days later I decided to try again (I am nothing if not stubborn). I re-peated the process of hooking everything up, but this time I made sure I had the blue tooth turned on. I decided, as no one seemed anxious to talk to me, that I would call my elderly father, who will usually speak to me. I had forgot-ten that he is pretty hard of hearing, and it didn't help that I was on my way to Dorris; after several minutes of shouting so loudly that I am sure he would have heard me if I had rolled down my window, with him shouting back that he couldn't hear me, I gave up and decided to call him when I got home.

Technology is a wonderful thing – in the right hands.

Ties That Bind

THE OTHER DAY OUR SON, who is in a graduate program in geology at the University of Utah, called to inform me that he had an interview for a job. That's great, I replied enthusiastically, with visions of total financial independence (his, from us) dancing in my head. "No," he said in a panic, "I don't have any clothes!"

Once we had established that he was not, in fact, going about stark naked, but rather meant that he had no proper interview clothing, we could proceed with the discussion.

Because it was a holiday (of course) and the interview was the next day at 9 a.m. (when else?) and he was in Utah (naturally), where we probably could not Fed Ex one of his father's two jackets to him in time, our options were limited. Where and how did I fail in my duty to train him to plan ahead? Oh well, it was too late now.

Eventually, we established that he did have a long-sleeved shirt. That was a start. Did he have a tie? Silence. "Well, yes, I have one tie." Only one? Surely we had purchased one for him at some point in his life, but he reminded me that was for his eighth grade graduation, some eight years previously.

So we're not terribly formal people; it's a wonder I managed to get his father into a suit when we got married, rather than the shorts he normally wore. Well, what did you do with that tie, I enquired, "Waste not, want not" being our family motto. He explained it was long gone by now; his sister had probably made it into a skirt at some point, as she is wont to do. As a side note, I don't believe I've ever seen anyone as creative with clothing as that girl is; one day when I admired a short red skirt she was wearing; and inquired as to its origins, she casually replied that it was one of my tops. How she managed that I will never know.

But back to the family ties. At least he had a tie; this was good news indeed. "But", he remarked glumly, "it's a Burger King tie." A flood of questions run fleetingly through my brain: How do you know it's a Burger King tie? Is there a hamburger on it? Many small hamburgers? Does Burger King even make a tie? Why would they? And how did you get one?

I manage to ask one or two of these questions, which he clearly finds irrelevant in his logical, scientific way, but he does respond that there's some kind of logo that you can see if you look really hard. Well, I instruct him, being a veteran of such wardrobe emergencies myself (I remember having to borrow ill-fitting clothing and buy cheap shoes that definitely were not my size in a hurry in just such an interview emergency; not that I was unprepared of course. The details are lost in the mists of time, but as I recall I was in a strange city without my wardrobe and the interview was a surprise), turn to the side during the interview so they can't see the tie clearly.

He then tells me the name of the company with which he is interviewing, and I remark that his father interviewed with the same company some 30 years prior. I remember the occasion because his father was incensed that they required him to undergo a psychological evaluation and asked him questions about his mother. My beloved is British, and as we all know, the British do not discuss such matters, even amongst their own families, much less with complete strangers. In any case, he did not get the job. I can only hope they don't ask my son questions about his mother, or he's doomed.

Our son reported the following day that the company did not require a psychological exam, did not ask any questions about his mother, and did not appear to look too closely at his tie, as far as he could tell, but then, it's hard to say when you're sitting at an angle to the interviewer. He did correct the interviewer on a technical point regarding geology, which may not have gone in his favor, as he did not get the job, either: like father, like son.

He is currently ascertaining, at my suggestion, the location of several thrift stores where he can add to his wardrobe on the tight budget of a starving graduate student and become the picture of sartorial splendor for the next job interview. And don't tell him, but his sister is buying him a very nice tie from Macy's for his birthday.

THINGS THAT GO BUMP

I AM MORTIFIED to have to confess that I have cockroaches in my home. I would never normally admit this to anyone but my closest friends, as my mother would be turning over in her German-heritage grave with horror if she only knew, but there's a story to be had, and sacrifices must be made.

I've only ever had them (the cockroaches) once before, and that was not my fault; I was a starving student living in a studio apartment in San Francisco, and the entire apartment complex had them, so there was nothing I could do. As long as I didn't get up in the middle of the night and startle both them and myself, I pretended they didn't exist, they probably did the same thing, and we all lived in harmony.

This time, I'm blaming my daughter, who lives, as I have mentioned before, in a studio apartment (is there a pattern here?) in a sketchy neighborhood in Los Angeles, which is infested with the evil things. Of course, that's not her fault, but I am convinced that she has imported them to my home in her luggage, especially as she told me a sordid tale of going to the store and placing her cloth shopping bags near the conveyor belt at the checkout stand, only to notice a cockroach crawling out of it onto said belt. Aghast (my mother's German intolerance of cockroaches has been genetically transmitted), she rapidly dispatched him (or her – who knows, with cockroaches?), only to watch in horror as several more scuttled out onto the belt. Fortunately, she is very quick, they were soon very dead, and no one was the wiser.

In any case, for whatever reason, I have the nasty little things in my home, and they will not be allowed to live there long if I can help it. So, I called the exterminator and arranged to have them, well, exterminated. The cockroaches, that is, not the exterminators. What I did not realize (until they told me, of course) was that said extermination would require that I move all my furniture at least a foot away from all walls, and that I would have to empty out all my cupboards. This resulted in all the furniture being moved more or less into the center of the place, with the addition of all the boxes that hold everything that was in the cupboards. I have a somewhat delicate back, so I decided to splurge and have someone do this for me, which worked just dandy, except that I wasn't thinking very clearly (must have been the cockroach horror) and had it done a week early. I have since added even more boxes, filled with books from the bookcase, which also needs to be moved, but I think my helper was completely exhausted by then and had given up. He did mention to my friend that he had never in his life seen a single person with so much food. Apparently, I live in fear of a canned food shortage.

So I am now threading my way through the narrow path that leads from the front door to the kitchen, bedroom, and bathroom. This is not easy. I am covered in bruises from getting up in the night, forgetting my situation, and crashing into misplaced furniture. My new bruises go nicely with the ones I gained the other day when I tripped over a rock and landed, literally, flat on my face. Well, almost flat – it was worse on the left side, which is probably the only reason I didn't break my nose. I just rolled around for awhile, yelling Ow, until I ascertained that I hadn't broken anything, and got on with life. But I have two skinned knees, which makes me look like a six-year-old, and, of course, all the bruises, aches and pains that accompany slamming yourself into the ground with force at an advanced age.

I was writing a letter to a friend in New Zealand last night and ran out of paper; I had to crawl over a chair and a wicker trunk to make it to the copier to grab another piece, because the armoire that holds my writing paper is so close to the bed I couldn't open the door. The fridge is so chummy with the oven that I can't fully open that door, either, which means I can only eat the things on the shelves closest to the front, and anything that goes into the oven has to withstand being tilted at an alarming angle. But I don't cook often, because I can't find most of my food in the boxes scattered around the living room. Tonight I discovered the chai tea, so I won't completely starve, and the dish soap, so I'm less likely to die of botulism than I was.

Meanwhile, I decided to replace my 1970's kitchen cupboards, and why would I put everything back in them just to have to take it all back out again? It appears I may be living in chaos for some time, and the children are coming to visit. Timing is everything.

Many Thanks

THIS THANKSGIVING WAS shaping up to be a really relaxed one for me; my sister was cooking, we didn't have a cast of thousands coming, and all I had to do was make a few dips, some deviled eggs, and the green bean casserole. Such a deal!

For once, I was even organized; I made everything the night before, and was feeling pretty pleased with myself by the time I finished. I must admit that the casserole was, as my son would say, a little sketchy. It certainly didn't look like the one pictured on the bag of fried onions that go on top. It was really dark; I didn't remember green bean casserole being quite that brown. Maybe it was the cream of mushroom soup; it looked quite dark when it came out of the can, but I figured maybe it was made from dark brown mushrooms. I couldn't find a "best before" date on it; maybe it was purchased before they had such regulations. But our family motto is that what doesn't kill you makes you stronger, so I shrugged it off.

I may have mentioned once or twice that I dislike making two or three trips down my 53 stairs to the car if I can avoid it, although I'm sure the aerobic exercise is good for me. So the next day I cleverly loaded up the three dishes of dip, the deviled eggs and the green bean casserole into one of the boxes I currently have stacked in my living room (that's another story) and started out the door.

I made it as far as the middle of the living room when the bottom dropped out of the box and everything in it fell onto the carpet. The dishes holding two of the dips and the green bean casserole promptly broke, distributing dip and green beans generously over the carpet, along with many, many shards of glass. The dog, who is on a diet because not only my daughter but complete strangers have seen fit to tell me that he is, to put it kindly, pudgy, and thinks I am starving him to death, immediately began trying to lick up the dip. I fended him off and contemplated the situation. I was so stunned at the extent of the disaster I couldn't even cry – at the waste of food, the breakage of two of my favorite bowls and a practically new casserole dish, the huge mess all over my carpet, and the fact that I was now going to be late, and had only one dip left. Also, my beautiful deviled eggs had landed, of course, upside down, and even though they were in a protective, sealed container, landing face-down made them into a mushy mess. I could make more dip (this is a good reason for having multiples of many types of food on hand), but we would now be having it for dessert. I sighed heavily and began the cleanup process. Well, truthfully, I swore a blue streak, but having got that out of my system (I read recently that people who swear are good people to know because they tend to be honest and straightforward. I was very straightforward that day), I called my sister to let her know I would be late and poured out my tale of woe. Naturally, she gave me lots of sympathy.

On the plus side, most of the dip(s) fell on the carpet, which is old and ratty and soon to be replaced, coincidentally, and not very much on my favorite (and only) area rug. Also, as my beloved grandmother would have said, it's just stuff; there was no loss of life, as long as I could keep the dog away from it long enough to clean it up, whereas if we had eaten the green bean casserole, the results might not have been as positive. As an aside, my sister whipped up her own casserole, and it was far superior in every way: it contained fresh green beans from her garden, and was not at all dark. In fact, it looked just like the one in the picture. Go figure.

To add insult to injury, in one of those fiendish twists of fate you cannot make up, on the way over to my sister's house, a program was airing about green bean casserole. I turned it off and drove grimly on.

Then the next day the dog grabbed my carefully hoarded turkey leftovers and ate every bite as revenge for being put on a diet.

From the experience, I have gained some valuable insights, which I pass on free of charge:

1. Unless you want them for dessert, or not at all, do not ask me to bring dips or green bean casserole to a meal.

2. Never trust a box.

3. Do not, under any circumstances, replace your carpet just before a major holiday involving food.

And last but not least, no matter what, there is always something to be grateful for.

TRAVELS

POMPEII

I HEARD THE OTHER DAY on the news that Pompeii is collapsing, and I couldn't help but think: It figures. It'll probably be completely gone before I have the time to get over there again and actually see it.

Many, many years ago, before the dawn of time, when I was young, my best friend and I decided we'd had enough of college and wanted to live a "real life", so we took off for Europe with nothing but 40 pound backpacks, some beef jerky and a roll of toilet paper (my father wanted to be sure we were ready for anything), and high hopes for adventure. The adventure, we got. We also spent most of our time sick, not getting enough to eat, and sleeping in parks because we had no money for even youth hostels. Little did I know what perfect preparation this would be for married life.

We had a train pass on the Continent but hitchhiked all over Britain during winter; I decided a train pass would be too expensive. It's a wonder we survived at all, but I'll tell you, there's no better confidence-builder than being in a foreign country, where you don't speak the language, trying to get directions or buy food. Before we went, I had been shy, retiring, and quiet; by the time we came back, I had confidence I could survive anything, because I just had. We also lost ten pounds each, but I can't say I recommend it as a weight-loss program. Forget the spectacular scenery; all we wanted in this world was a warm comfy bed and a decent meal. I remember walking down suburban streets, looking longingly into windows in cozy warm houses, watching families sit down for dinner and feeling like the Little Match Girl. Did I mention we were there from September through December before coming to our senses? Hitchhiking in northern Scotland in the snow in December is not recommended.

In any case, at one point we found ourselves in Rome, sleeping in an actual hotel (cheap, very cheap - the kind where you whip back the bedcovers and inspect for bedbugs before crawling in, and sleep with one eye open) for a change, when I made the nearly fatal mistake of drinking the tap water in said hotel. I will not go into any detail about the resulting impact on my digestive system, except to say I may have lost all ten pounds that night. The next day, we had to check out of the hotel for monetary reasons, so my friend, who was about five foot one to my five foot nine, shouldered both our backpacks and led me, protesting, down the street to the train station; next on our agenda was Pompeii, which I had wanted to visit all my life. Despite my wails of "Just leave me here on the street to die! I can't take another step!" my friend soldiered on, determined to get me to Pompeii or die trying. Or maybe kill me in the effort; it would at the very least have been a lot quieter.

In any case, she managed to drag me to the train station, and, dumping me with the backpacks in great relief, no doubt, hiked off to find the ticket station. When she returned, she was forced to tell me that there was no train to Pompeii that day, because it was a Tuesday, and Pompeii was closed on Tuesdays. I looked at her incredulously, momentarily and rarely lost for words, and then announced shortly, "Get me out of here, please!"

Happy to oblige, she hoisted me off the seat, we donned our packs, and took a train for Germany – at least, we figured, we could sleep on the train. Unfortunately, the train we picked was packed with drunken male Italian soccer fans who, although kind enough to offer us seats in the overcrowded car, made the journey miserable by insisting on trying to talk to us and when that failed, pinching my friend endlessly. They asked if we were married, and having secured a fake wedding ring before leaving home to forestall just such an inquiry, I lied and said yes, and they mostly left me alone – primarily, I think, because the look on my pale face and the very real possibility that I might heave all over their fancy outfits put them off. My friend suffered so much that she swore that next time she came to Italy she would dress as a nun, which was more of a stretch than you might think, as she is Jewish.

Maybe someday I'll get to Pompeii.

BOSTON BLIZZARD

SOMETIMES I'M NOT SURE I even believe myself when it comes to my bad luck travel stories. The simplest trip somehow seems to spiral out of control if I'm involved, so all I can do is continue to advise everyone not to travel with me. I've said this before, and apparently most of Siskiyou County is paying attention, but I'm afraid two of my workmates were forced to come back with me from a conference, and they got swept up in the vortex of travel hell that appears to be my lot.

I needed to go to Boston for a work conference. I love conferences; they're like mini-vacations with education involved – two of my favorite things – so I was very happy to go. Unfortunately the flight, which had a three-hour lay-over in Portland on the way over, was delayed even further after I got there due to bad weather on the east coast. But five hours in an airport isn't so bad when you have books and about 400 crossword puzzles with you, as I inevitably do, so I simply settled down to read and nap. I had gotten up at 3:00 a.m. to catch a 5:00 a.m. flight, so I was tired anyway. And I had brought my own breakfast with me – cold scrambled eggs, but hey, at least I didn't have to buy expensive airport food, right? And yes, I was there an hour and a half early; I have perfected the art of getting out of bed and out the door in about ten minutes or less – the extra time is for me to convince myself to actually get up after the alarm goes off - so that was more than enough time for me. No guarantees about how I look – usually my hair, for instance, looks as if I've been dragged through a hedge backwards, and I can't guarantee that my shoes, or anything else for that matter – matches. It's still dark at 3:00 a.m. after all. But I got there, and got on the plane, even though there was so much turbulence that they refused to give us peanuts and juice, which made me resentful as a two-year old denied a snack. Still, I had, as always, my two pounds of trail mix, water, peanut butter crackers, and other assorted goodies, so I couldn't complain too much.

I arrived safely in Boston and met up with my coworkers, and a wonderful

200

time was had by all until it was time to go home and they cancelled our flight due to blizzards – that is, the snowy kind. Fortunately, we had insurance and the magnificent Ellice as our travel agent, who waved her magic wand and got us booked on a new flight a few days later, thereby ensuring we would get to see more of lovely Boston; that is, providing the lovely Boston was not covered in two feet of snow as predicted. We had already done the hop-on, hop-off bus tour, so we weren't sure quite how to spend our extra days, other than mushing through the snow, but I decided to take the opportunity to swim in the hotel pool as I finally had the time.

Down I went to the pool – it was on the fifth floor and my room was on the tenth. It was wonderful, as I was almost alone, and the water was warm and lovely – my definition of a perfect swim. I was enjoying myself immensely when the alarm went off. I decided at first it was only a drill, although I had no evidence of this since I couldn't understand a word they said over the loudspeaker. Maybe I just wanted to think positively. But staff came through and informed me that someone had spotted smoke, so I dragged myself out of the pool and headed for the stairs. Not down the stairs; no, there was no way anyone was going to see me in a bathing suit, and it would have been a little chilly in my wet suit out in the predicted blizzard. Besides, I needed to grab some snacks, just in case.

So up I went to the tenth floor. This was also no big deal – I mean, my workmate Lori had climbed from the second floor to the 29th that day because she got tired of waiting for the elevator, so who was I to quibble about five floors?

Just as I reached my floor, fighting through the crowds coming down like a salmon going upstream, the all-clear was announced. So I decided to take a hot bath to relieve my stress – my bath at home holds about three inches of water and is quite unsatisfactory for soaking, and this one was beautifully deep. Unfortunately, due no doubt to some fiendish karmic plot, I could not, no matter how hard I tried, make the plug stay down, so the lovely hot bath was traded for a cranky shower. That is, I was cranky, not the shower.

But no worries; by eating at free hotel buffets and consuming my trail mix, we should be able to survive the blizzard.

CHEAP THRILLS

I DECIDED TO BE BRAVE and visit my daughter, who is currently living in Los Angeles, and seems to love it. I don't know where I went wrong with that girl.

It was with some trepidation that I ventured to the big city by myself – the big city being Medford – to the airport. My first trauma was checking in using my not-so-smart-but way-smarter-than-me phone; the airline refused to allow me to print a paper boarding pass unless I was willing to pay extra, which of course I am never inclined to do, and so I was dragged kicking and screaming into the 20th century (some of us are WAY behind).

To add insult to injury, the airline also wanted to charge me extra for a seat assignment – what are we meant to do, stand the whole way? – and for my carry-on. Now, I am not one of those people whose carry-on is the size of Texas and takes a stevedore to heft it into the cabin, but I protest at the thought of paying to take a toothbrush and a change of underwear. I was, apparently, allowed to take a purse, however, so into that purse went everything I could cram in, much like Mary Poppins' valise. I eschewed deodorant, applying it thoroughly before I left and hoping, for everyone's sake, that it was as strong and long-lasting as it claimed to be.

My swim bag (which is what I was using as a "purse" – two can play this game, I decided) not being capable of holding all the changes of clothing it was absolutely necessary that I bring, I decided to take a leaf from Heidi's book, and wear everything I could not fit into my bag: two tops, an extra skirt, a nightgown, a bathing suit, several pairs of underwear, and a sweater wrapped around my shoulders just in case. While I may have presented a somewhat peculiar appearance, they didn't get any extra money out of me, so I declared victory.

Of course, all snacks cost extra, which I expected and dealt with by bringing several pounds of trail mix (fortunately they didn't weigh my carry-on), but they even charged for water! Thankfully, I came prepared with my own water bottle to stave off dehydration. If only I had remembered to fill it in the airport, I would have been set.

Upon arrival at LAX, I carefully checked my daughter's explicit instructions and searched for the "Express Bus" that would take me to the next leg of my journey: go downstairs, outside, walk three blocks, and look for the bus stop marked "Express Bus" to Union Station. Being the cautious, easily lost type, I asked several people the way before I even went outside the airport, and being the "directionally impaired" type, I still went the wrong way and got lost. A few more pleas for help got me back on track, but the extra layers of clothing, while helping me blend in nicely with the local homeless population, did not make the L.A. heat any more bearable once I got outside. When I finally located the bus stop, I asked several people who looked like locals if this was, indeed, the express bus stop, just to be certain, but when the bus pulled up, it not only was not marked Union Station, it had no markings at all. Everyone, weary by now of my incessant questions, assured me it was indeed the express Union Station bus, so despite my misgivings, I embarked.

I was not gratified to discover that the "express" bus made about 50 stops – and that was before we even left the airport – but never mind, within half an hour we were on the freeway, whizzing along. I was quite alarmed to see cars on the rail tracks in the center divider until I realized I was looking in the bus window reflection.

Along the way I was puzzled by a sign on a truck reading "Mobile Device Repair"; was it a mobile service, or a service for mobile devices, or both? What exactly was a mobile device? What would a mobile repair consist of? Someone running alongside your car as they repaired your device? The truck pulling alongside your car and repairing your device as you travelled, like those airplanes that refuel in mid-air? These musings took me into Union Station, where I caught the metro to my daughter's steep street, which I gasped my way up. Who knew there were hills in Los Angeles?

Having finally reached her apartment, I rested a moment in triumph before attempting the three floor summit, where I discovered to my dismay that I could not reach the key she cleverly hides above her doorframe. I lunged, I leapt, I stretched, all to no avail. In desperation, I enlisted the help of a neighbor, who loaned me his cold box without asking any embarrassing questions as to its use; I climbed up on it, obtained the key, and fell into the apartment in exhaustion and triumph – until the trip home.

THAT SINKING FEELING

MY BELOVED HAVING not yet accepted the notion that there is no free lunch, even after having lived in this country for nearly 30 years, it was with some trepidation and a definite sinking feeling on my part that we set off on a "free" vacation cruise to Florida and the island of Grand Bahama. And while it was true, of course, that it wasn't free, it was a pretty good trip, all in all, what with the alligator sighting, the white sandy beaches, the snorkeling, swimming (completely accidentally) with the manta ray, the frenetic games of table tennis to which I became addicted for some peculiar reason - up until the trip home.

We were actually on our way back to Florida from the island, having decided on the bus back to the dock to catch the cruise ship that it had been a relaxing time, but we were pretty much done with the Bahamas. We had managed to get the early seating for dinner at 6:15 rather than the 8:45 we were forced to endure on the way out (by about 6.30 p.m , if I have not yet eaten, my stomach thinks my throat's been cut and I get pretty cranky, which explains why I was travelling with about 30 energy bars, cheese sticks and crackers, many packets of oatmeal, and roughly 20 pounds of two different types of trail mix – heaven forbid I should go hungry for five minutes) and were watching a mildly entertaining (free) comedian when we felt and heard something peculiar. It could well have been the engines reversing as we made our way out of port, and no one paid much attention.

Meanwhile, after perfect weather for the entire trip, a tremendous storm had come up, complete with lightning, thunder, wind and rain, and my beloved, being who he is, dragged me up onto the top deck to experience it fully. At some point I noticed that we seemed to be very close to some metal structures (and, incidentally, an oil tanker). I looked over to see some of the cooking crew watching as avidly as we were, so I asked them what was going on. They assured me all was "normal", "no problem, madam", to which I was tempted to enquire why they were hanging on the rail looking confused and worried, but refrained. It was while we were up there that every single light on the ship went out and the engine died, pitching us into complete and utter darkness. This being (naturally) Halloween night, we thought at first it might be a prank, all in the spirit of good fun, but very quickly my beloved ascertained that all was not well. Of course not – I was on vacation, wasn't I?

Eventually the captain announced that there was a "small leak" in the ship and we were on our way back into port, having only managed to travel about a half mile out. At different times after the alarm bell sounded (and remained on, much to everyone's annoyance, for several hours even though we were by then fully aware there was a "situation", the noise making communication virtually impossible – not that anyone made the slightest attempt to communicate with the passengers for the next seven hours) we were instructed to go back to our cabins, told to come out to our muster stations (none of us had life jackets in our cabins), made to go back to our cabins, etc.

As the lifeboat drill had consisted of a steward strolling by while we were sunning ourselves on the deck and asking jovially if we knew where the life jackets were, I imagined none of us were very prepared for any emergency at all. However, I knew I could swim, the water was warm, and although my ever-present fear of sharks made me nervous, at least I was fairly certain I wouldn't freeze to death clinging to a door in the middle of the Atlantic, or wherever the Titanic hit the iceberg.

My beloved, determined that if the ship were going down, the last place he was going to be was in the hold down on the third deck where our cabin was located, continuously made his way (usually with me in tow) stealthily up to the top deck, only to be eventually discovered and ordered back below deck like criminals; after this had happened several times, I settled on the floor in a pile of lifejackets (it was so hot due to the lack of air-conditioning by now that most people who had managed to find a life jacket had abandoned them) near the stairway and watched as events unfolded.

The crew was mostly milling around eating sandwiches and drinking water (we had nothing) when not trying to shout out cabin numbers and distribute life jackets over the sound of the alarm – a pretty hopeless task – while the elderly, small children, and people in wheelchairs waited to see what would happen next. At some point we returned to our cabin and lay down, although no one was sleeping; I remarked to my husband that it felt as if we were listing, and he agreed, which did make me a bit nervous, but in the main, it was a lot of very boring waiting around after returning to port. It seemed we had to wait until customs authorities could be raised from their beds – I thought, good grief, what do you think we've been doing that we have to go back through customs – picking up illegal substances from passing boats in the dark as the ship sinks?

When we finally got to shore, feeling bedraggled, tired, hungry, and just a bit cranky, having waited in long lines until 4:00 a.m. to be processed by equally tired and cranky Bahamian immigration and customs officials, we were loaded onto buses and made the journey back to the same hotel we had been staying at before we left the island – but the adventure was just beginning. As we all (no one seems to know exactly how many of us there were – no doubt because they never got an accurate count on the ship – but we estimate somewhere between 700 and 900 people) stood around in the hotel lobby, staff announced they had run out of rooms; a mutinous murmur arose, and they hastened to assure us we would be accommodated elsewhere – so back onto the buses we were sent. Actually, my beloved, having some sort of sixth sense no doubt acquired and honed by many years of travel in developing countries, told me to wait, even as I panicked at the thought of the bus leaving without us, and sure enough, we managed to secure what was literally the last room in the hotel.

The next morning, after three hours of sleep, we returned as instructed to the hotel lobby, where we were informed (after more hours of waiting) that we would be taken back to the dock and put on a ferry to Miami; the fact that the trip did not originate in Miami, but in Palm Beach, was a small glitch, but not, we decided, insurmountable, even though our rental car awaited us in Palm Beach. At least we would be on U.S. soil. So off we went by bus – I have always liked buses, finding them to be temporary havens of safety from the elements and the realities of life, but I was beginning to hope I never had to ride another one as long as I lived - back to the dock, where there was a collective gasp of shock from the passengers upon sighting our cruise ship of the night before; there was, my beloved informed me, he being of a mathematical bent, about a 15 degree list to port, and I am convinced it wasn't more only because the dock was holding it up. So much for a "small leak". We were later told by a crew member that they were slipping in oil and water down on the first deck, where they were sent and not let off the ship nor allowed to sleep all night.

We settled down to wait again. By this time, there having been very little food available at the hotel (they did supply a few mini-muffins and some pastries which many passengers were unaware of and so missed out on), and many not having eaten since lunchtime the day before, people went off on foraging missions. Unfortunately, as was explained to us by port authorities (we still had had very little communication from the cruise line), this was not a day cruise ships would normally be in port, so only two snack shops were open. There were lines several hours long for limited supplies of food; hot dogs, I was told, were selling for $14. I began to distribute my supplies of cheese and crackers and trail mix to a few grateful, hungry passengers nearby.

At about 4 p.m. we were loaded onto a ferry going, not to Miami, but to Bimini. "But I don't want to go to Bimini", I wailed to my harassed husband, "I don't even want to go to Miami!" But go we did. We were finally given a meal voucher on this ship (although drinks, of course, were extra). It was very cold, the storm having only slightly abated – the wind was quite strong and there were few sheltered areas, and exhausted people were scattered about, trying to sleep on the floor. So when I saw people with blankets and towels, I dispatched my beloved to try to secure us one or two. He returned to tell me that we could have one – for a $10 rental fee. We declined the generous offer and shivered in wooden chairs on deck.

When we finally arrived in Miami, we were once again loaded onto buses, this time for Palm Beach, where our rental car awaited. I engaged my seat-mate in conversation, as survivors of disasters are wont to do, and discovered that he was not only a lawyer (lively discussions of liability theories ensued; they had by now missed two flights home and had to book a third, at their own expense), he was on his honeymoon. We decided it would be a memorable one.

In Palm Beach at last, our journey was not yet complete; we had reservations in Orlando and had to drive there that night, arriving at 5 a.m. I was not in the mood to visit the Pirates of the Caribbean, so we passed on Disneyworld. As we drove to the airport, a friend texted me, "Hey, I just saw a story on the news about a sinking cruise ship. That wasn't you, was it? LOL!" As a matter of fact, I replied... She knew me better than she realized.

As we packed for the flight back to Medford, where we had booked a room for the night, I came across our car keys in the bag we meant to check and, on a whim, put them in my hand luggage, which turned out to be a good thing because when we got to Medford airport we discovered they had lost our luggage. It didn't arrive until almost noon the next day.

My only regret is that while on board the ship we chose not to purchase the T-shirts which read "I Survived the Halloween Cruise!"; if they give us one, I promise not to sue.

OF HORSES AND HAIR

IT WASN'T VERY LONG after we left the Paris airport on our recent vacation that I became aware of a disturbing fact: everyone was speaking French. Much to my chagrin (a French word; I'm afraid they wore off on me), I speak French not at all, having cleverly opted for Latin and ancient Greek in school, secure in the knowledge that I would never have to engage in conversations in those languages and thus embarrass myself. Needless to say, I was mortified to observe toddlers who spoke French more fluently than I; in point of fact, it became clear that even household pets comprehended the language better than I, and I began to rethink this determination to remain ignorant of spoken languages other than my own.

On our way to the store to buy that most necessary accoutrement (another French word – is English littered with them?!), a hair dryer, I discovered that my beloved, who, having been raised in England and therefore fluent, more or less, in French, did not have a French vocabulary that extended to feminine accessories. From this realization, it was a short journey to the lowering prospect of playing charades (more French) in order to secure the crucial item. My beloved, however, always game, so to speak, began working to put together the words necessary to keep me from despair.

It did not take long for the awful truth to emerge: not being the best of spellers, to put it mildly, he was uncertain whether the word he wanted was "chevaux", "cheveu", or even, if we wanted more than one, possibly "deux chevaux", all of which are virtually interchangeable in their pronunciation, but which were vastly different in meaning. The last, we finally worked out, was actually a model of car, and eventually puzzled out that one was a horse, and the other might mean "hair", but I was fairly nervous about getting a car, two horses, or possibly a wig when we at last broke our huddle and approached the saleslady, with some trepidation.

Even when my beloved at last requested what we hoped was something to do with hair, the clerk looked at us blankly, and we had to resort to charades after all, me holding out strands of my hair while my hubby blew vigorously on them. The clerk looked at us as if we had just escaped the asylum, and pretended to speak no English (as the French often do, although honestly, I would have done the same in her place), and we left the shop, defeated. We went to a larger, anonymous store, where we were able to find what we needed without discussing it with anyone or causing any unnecessary scenes.

French really is a diabolical language, I must say, even if it is beautiful to listen to. Granted, English is a horrible language to learn, even for native speakers (how many meanings can one word have? And how many ways can we find to pronounce the same word, after all, much less spell - just ask my husband), but I really cannot understand the French habit of tacking a lot of extraneous letters on to the end of words, apparently just for show, that no one has any intention of pronouncing. I mean, what's the point? You're usually safe in spelling any French word if you just add -eaux on the end, in my experience, but for heavens' sake, don't try to pronounce it.

And the French are so very emphatic about everything; it's difficult to know, when one is eavesdropping, which I am in the habit of doing, whether people in conversation are seriously angry and you'd better run for it, or they're just discussing last night's soccer match. Of course, in France, as in most of the world outside the U.S., soccer is a very serious issue, and it might erupt into violence – you just never know. With the English, even if you can't understand them (and I usually can't unless they speak very slowly and carefully), even if they were telling you the world was about to end, they have a way of making it sound as if they're inviting you to tea.

In any case, we are safely back in the land of English once again, but our daughter has gone off to Italy (although, unfortunately, her luggage did not follow her), having first diligently listened to Italian tapes beforehand. How do you say, "Where is my luggage?" in Italian?

I Meet the Equadorian Navy

BACK IN THE EARLY days of our marriage BC (Before Children), my husband took me and a couple of his friends to Ecuador to climb a mountain called Cotopaxi. Well, of course I wasn't going to climb it, I just went along for the ride, or more accurately, the hike. We rented a vehicle and drove to about twelve thousand feet, where we set up camp, and the guys decided to climb higher as a practice exercise. I was left in the base camp, which consisted of me and three tents. It was next to a small lake, so I decided to wash the dishes and the laundry, having nothing better to do. As I knelt next to the lake, totally deserted except for me, a huge truck drove up, and about thirty men poured out, heading straight for me and my little camp. Great, I thought frantically, here I am, with the guys up some mountain, thirty strangers coming straight for me, and all I have is a fork. Prepare to die.

Fortunately, when I bravely stood up to meet my fate, I discovered I was at least two feet taller than the most strapping, robust of them. This instilled confidence, and we began trying to communicate. Unfortunately, other than menu items, my Spanish is fairly limited, and there's only so long you can go on about tacos, tamales, and chili rellenos. Their English wasn't much better than my Spanish, but we did manage to establish that they were members of the Ecuadorian Navy. What the Ecuadorian Navy might be doing at 12,000 feet I couldn't be sure, and they couldn't make clear to me given the language barrier.

They were, however, fascinated with the shoes outside our friend's tent. Dave is about 6'4", so his shoes are pretty big, and they were very impressed indeed; I don't think they believed the shoes belonged to a real person. I managed to convey that the "muy grande zapatos" belonged to a "muy grande amigo", and they commenced to all have their pictures taken with Dave's shoes. Then, undoubtedly realizing their lapse of courtesy, and not wanting to hurt my feelings, they proceeded to have their pictures taken with me and the grande zapatos.

Eventually, after much hand shaking and good feelings all around, they piled back into the truck and headed back down the mountain, to the Naval Academy no doubt, and I returned to my laundry.

But I am convinced that somewhere in the hallowed halls of the Ecuadorian Naval Academy is at least one photo of a tall gringa with many short Ecuadorian men and a pair of muy grande zapatos.

SOMEWHERE IN THE MIDWEST

I DECIDED TO GO to Wisconsin for the wedding of a dear friend, which brought up memories of a previous trip there. At least, I think it was Wisconsin; it might well have been Minnesota. I'm still not actually sure where I was at the time, which might warrant an explanation.

A while ago I was traveling with a small group of people to attend a training; they had all the details, so I just tagged along, not feeling it necessary to actually figure anything out, like which state I was traveling to. After completing the training, we decided to drive around a bit. I remember being in a gift shop, looking for mementos to bring my children, when I became frustrated at not being able to find anything that had "Wisconsin" written on it (or maybe it was Minnesota). I complained about the odd shortage, when a shop clerk looked at me strangely and replied, "Maybe that's because you're in Minnesota (or, perhaps, Wisconsin – I'll never remember now)".

I was repeating this story to my sister and father the other day at a restaurant, saying that all I could remember was that we went to the Mall of America, when a woman at the next booth said, "Michigan. The Mall of America is in Michigan." I was in MICHIGAN? How did that happen?? I didn't think we had driven that far. Someone else later assured me that the Mall of America is in Minnesota – at least, I think she said Minnesota. I don't even care; I never wanted to go to the Mall of America anyway, but it would be nice to know where I was.

In any case, on this trip I was on my way to Wisconsin; I was sure of it. I arrived at the Medford Airport and happily told the clerk at the United desk that I had a flight booked. She looked it up and said, "Yes, the flight to Minneapolis." Now, as I have just proven, my grasp of geography, especially Wisconsin and Minnesota, is tenuous, but I did know that Minneapolis is in Minnesota, and I was going to Madison, Wisconsin. "No!" I cried in a panicked voice. "I'm supposed to be going to Madison, Wisconsin!" I mentally added: at least, I think I am. "Oh, sorry, yes", she replied calmly. "Madison. All those "M" towns. We have so many going to Minneapolis." I could definitely relate.

The flight went smoothly, except that after we landed in Madison, as people were getting their luggage down from the overhead compartments, the pilot announced that we were going to be towed, so "Just kind of brace yourselves". "Just kind of brace yourselves"????

I had contracted a nasty cold, so although I enjoyed the wedding very much – it was held in a park, the lovely bride in a beautiful long white gown riding up the aisle on a moped, then proceeding to kiss the groom often and enthusiastically throughout the ceremony until he was covered in red lipstick - I slept throughout most of the weekend and arrived at the airport about nine hours early for my flight home. It's a good thing, too, because when I got to my gate, the waiting area was empty. I found a staff member and explained my dilemma. She looked at my boarding pass, then at me, then replied, "That's your seat number, not the gate number." Fortunately, my gate and my seat number were quite close, or I might have missed the plane anyway. I'm blaming it on the cold.

I boarded the flight to Denver at last. After a while, the captain announced that it seemed we had a piece of rubber hanging from somewhere – that is, the plane did – and we would be delayed while a mechanic came out to inspect it and, presumably, fling it back where it belonged. This did not seem too awful, but I had a pretty short turnaround time until my connecting flight, so I was a bit nervous. Anyway, what's a bit of rubber among friends? It's not as if we would catch it on anything 10,000 feet up in the air.

Unfortunately, announced the captain a bit later, it was a Sunday, and the only certified mechanic capable of effecting the repair lived an hour away. We all groaned, and the crying babies seemed to pick up the volume a little. The steward whispered to the man next to me that he could have all the free beer he wanted, and the crowd at my end of the plane was somewhat mollified. An hour or so later, we were informed the rubber was no longer an issue, but reports must be sent to appropriate parties far away – more wait time. At last we were cleared for takeoff, but I had, of course, missed my connecting flight and there was, of course no other flight to Medford until the next day. I had visions of sleeping on the airport floor, hacking and sneezing all night, but we were mercifully given a hotel room and meal vouchers, so all was well in my world.

I'm just not sure how soon it will be before I fly to Wisconsin again. Or Minnesota.

TIRED

I DECIDED TO GO down to the Bay Area to have Thanksgiving with friends this year, where I managed to spot fugitive wild turkeys (of the non-alcoholic type, at least as far as I could tell) making their stealthy way across Skyline Boulevard in Oakland, where I used to live, before the actual feast day. My car having behaved like no other vehicle I've owned in quite some time, by which I mean it has exhibited very few oddities, other than some electrical eccentricities - I think the last good one I had was a little exploding blue Pinto – I expected no difficulties, which is almost always a fatal assumption for me to make, my life being what it is.

So, off I went. I had made it as far as Redding – actually, only six miles from Red Bluff – when I began to hear, over the sound of the oldies on the radio at full volume, an odd sort of knocking sound. Frowning in concentration, I turned the radio down to listen, but could not ascertain either the source of the noise or its exact nature. Within minutes, however, the car began to shake as if in terror, until I thought it was going to fall apart. Having experienced many such events in my driving career, I pulled over and stopped. I noticed a rollover accident directly across the highway, complete with three highway patrol cars and two tow trucks (but no partridge in a pear tree), and, thankfully (it was Thanksgiving after all) no injuries. I called AAA, thinking at least one of the tow trucks might be free, but no, mine had to come from Redding, 30 miles away. At least one of the highway patrol officers was kind enough to check on me, and he was very friendly, even if he was a bit put off by my pit bull; the only danger that dog poses to anyone is in licking them to death.

So, I was towed, not to Red Bluff, which you may recall if you were paying attention, was only six miles away, but to Redding, for reasons unknown. The mechanic said I had lost a weight, which made me feel pretty good until he explained he meant a weight had fallen off my tire; he said it would be simple to have Les Schwab (or one of Les's associates, presumably) replace it, and I would be on my way, which is indeed what happened. I was feeling very thankful, as none of this had cost me a penny, other than dinner, as my theory is you can't eat on an empty stomach, and I was feeling pretty hungry by then, and three hours of delay. But hey, I didn't have to rent or buy a new car, so I was feeling pretty good about the whole thing.

This would, of course, be a very short story if that ended the matter, but this being my life, it was not to be. I had a lovely Thanksgiving and started back up the highway. I was, oddly enough, about an hour and a half away from the Bay Area (the same distance I had been from Yreka on the way down; a friend has suggested I drive no further than an hour and a half from any one place at any time) when exactly the same thing happened. This time I skipped the mechanic and went straight to my old friend Les Schwab, in Vacaville as I recall (they all blend together after awhile) who, naturally, could find nothing wrong. However, the car, apparently needing just a short rest, drove beautifully all the way home. Ah, the mysteries of my vehicular life.

Upon my return, I realized I needed to change into my snow tires – that is, my car needed to do so – that is, my car did not change into a pumpkin or anything else, this being after Thanksgiving, but it needed to have snow tires put on - which naturally necessitated transporting them from my father's garage to the back seat of my car (the trunk being too full of other garbage – that is, important materials). It wasn't until the third tire that it occurred to me that said tires could be ROLLED to the car rather than carried, which had resulted in me straining my back. So the tires stayed in the back seat, so awkwardly placed that I couldn't completely shut the passenger side door, which made all future journeys even noisier than they had been with the radio turned up, until I could get to Rob Coppi, who, kind man that he is, not only put them on, but replaced my wiper blades and checked for my car's mysterious malady, which did not, of course, manifest itself; that would be too easy, and would make this someone else's life instead of mine.

The non-snow tires now rest comfortably in the back seat, so it's back to tire removal operations. This time perhaps I'll try to remember that round objects tend to roll easily.

TORS AND MOORS

WE'VE BEEN GONE awhile, having travelled to England, Scotland, Wales, Northern Ireland, the Republic of Ireland, France (briefly) and, just for good measure, Iceland. In trying to decipher my notes, which I wrote in longhand despite the purchase of a tablet, bought specifically to allow me to type in a move towards efficiency, I discovered that, for reasons I cannot explain – jet lag, perhaps? – I wrote in it from back to front, as I read magazines, for which I also cannot find any logical reason. Jet lag is a very handy excuse for many lapses, I find, but unfortunately it wears a little thin after the first month or two.

My beloved was born and raised in Britain, so we had lots of people to visit there. I expected the weather; in fact, I was quite looking forward to cool, smoke-free skies, and I was not disappointed. Although we did have some lovely sunny days, mostly it rained like a son of a gun, which made me very happy, although hubby was none too pleased, mostly because he had to do all the driving.

Cheddar Gorge seemed like an interesting place to visit, and if you think it sounds like an exercise in binge cheese-eating, you would be correct. Yes, this is where the famous cheddar cheese originated, but as it was stuffed with tourists crowded into twee cheese shops, we by-passed the village, although we did drive through the gorge itself, which was a bit harrowing, especially with all the climbers hanging from cliffs next to the road. It reminded me a bit of the Clifton Suspension Bridge we had just left (near Bristol), where I entertained myself and gave my beloved far too many ideas by imagining ways in which he could toss me over the edge and never be discovered or brought to justice.

We had to visit Dartmoor for several reasons, one of which involved a stomp across the moors to climb the tors (a rhyming hike, apparently), which are best described as large untidy piles of rock, and a wander through the woods, followed by a cream tea which immediately clogged our arteries and caused us to stagger off to rest.

Next we saw friends in Wales, which is a lovely country: the sheep, the lilting accents, the friendly people… At least, I think it's a lovely country. We went sight-seeing with our friend at the wheel; she was born and raised there, and so drove with great confidence – and swiftly. I was still jet-lagged, so hurtling at heart-stopping speed down two-way roads narrower than my driveway, with tall hedgerows completely obscuring the view of said sheep-covered hillsides, coming to the occasional screeching halt when we met a car coming towards us from the opposite direction at equal or greater veloc-ity, was still a little unnerving, although I got used to it in time. Well, truth-fully, I just learned to close my eyes.

Moving on to another friend's brother's dairy farm in Shropshire, I learned about "robotic milking", which sounds alarming but is actually pretty neat: cows wander through fields at their leisure until the urge to be milked, or at least to have a tasty snack, strikes them, at which time they stroll over to a machine that automatically hooks up to their udders, guided by lasers, and dispenses special food the cows like. Everything is recorded by a computer, so should a cow try to cheat and get herself milked early in order to get ex-tra treats (do any of us relate?), she is rejected and sent out to wander and browse until she's due for a milking. Maybe everyone else in America knows about this, but it was new to me. I spent the rest of my time at the farm killing thousands of flies, which did not affect the fly population one little bit, but was entertaining.

At another friend's house we had a barbeque – one of the rare British summer barbeques when you don't have to huddle under umbrellas – and discussed the Royal Canadian Mounted Police. I forget how or why they came up, but it was probably on the television, because this was a visual. We noticed that one of them was not, surprisingly, on his horse, to which a friend remarked, "He must be a Dis-mountie!"

Then we all tried to play croquet, which I had not played since the last time I'd been in Britain many years ago. My game had not improved. Despite making a remarkably good hit too complicated to explain, I contrived to miss the ball entirely on most of my swings and actually uprooted several hoops with wild tries, managing as usual to come in last. At least I didn't acciden-tally throw my mallet into the air on a rather vigorous swing, as our friend did, frightening several low-flying birds.

We then travelled through a driving rain, appropriately, to Scotland, from whence we left for Ireland, which is another story entirely.

ADVENTURES ABROAD

SO OUR DAUGHTER finally returned home from Europe (after missing two planes, but that's another story) having had many adventures, which tend to happen when you're young, traveling alone, speak no languages other than English, taking trains everywhere and sleeping rough out in fields because you're too cheap to spend $30 on a youth hostel.

I would know this because, other than the traveling alone part, I did the same thing at age 19, with my best friend. It must be genetic. Mind you, I had my underwear with me the entire time, as I recall, but that wasn't her fault. That is, her not having her underwear wasn't her fault, as you will know if you happened to read a prior story on the subject.

In any case, she had many stories with which to regale us once she was safely home and not worried about sending her mother into fits of terror – she's a wise girl. There were the obligatory tales of sleeping in a field under the stars until the heavens opened, lightning flashed and thunder rolled, bringing with it the heavy rains that usually accompany such phenomena. Being a thrifty, careful girl, our daughter whipped out the large plastic bag the airline had thoughtfully wrapped her backpack in (which was useful, I'm sure, for keeping it safe for the two weeks it wandered Europe without her) and wrapped herself and her sleeping bag up in it, feeling smug and prepared, until she shifted her position and discovered by way of the cascade of water down her back that the bag had acquired some holes along the way. Oddly enough, I had the exact same experience, minus the plastic bag (we had a "tube tent" we sarcastically referred to as the "supersonic garbage bag"); I was convinced we were going to be struck by lightning and die, being the tallest items in the field, even lying down, and loudly expressed this belief to my friend, who stoutly ignored me. In the morning we discovered I had been sleeplessly residing in a water-filled ditch, and was thoroughly soaked, while my friend at least had, so to speak, the high ground, but I still wince at the thought of all my complaining on that trip.

From the sound of it, our daughter got very little sleep (or food, judging by the massive quantities I watched her consume when she arrived home) the entire five weeks she traveled on her own, especially when lying in the fields, which was often. There were the usual nettle beds, dodgy neighborhoods, and large barking dogs just as one is about to bathe in a nearby stream.

My favorite Europe story of hers, though it's actually a visual, occurred when she was on a train in France traveling with a couple of other young ladies she met along the way. They were discussing how embarrassed they were that they spoke no other languages, and how difficult it was to pronounce French (a subject I've weighed in on myself), when the Frenchman in the seat in front of them turned around and said (in a very strong French accent), "Eef you sink pronouncing French ees difficult, try saying" and here he apparently screwed up his face in a way that only my daughter (or a Frenchman) can do justice, and with some difficulty spat out "SQUIRREL"! and faced front again, clearly satisfied that he had forever settled the matter.

How Do I Kill Thee? Let Me Count…

ON OUR LAST NIGHT in a hotel before setting out for the wilds of New Zealand in a camper van, my husband and I made the mistake of watching a deeply disturbing television show about a serial killer (I guess there's a reason we don't watch television). I spent the next week meditating on creative methods my beloved could employ to knock me off should the marital glow begin to dim. Not ordinary, dull means, you understand, but imaginative, diabolical ways. Not for us the run of the mill, "Oh, officer, I got out to take a picture of this lovely scenery, and I was so overwhelmed I must have forgotten to set the parking brake! Surely it happens all the time! What cliff?" Not even the slow asphyxiation from the gas leak in the propane tank – much too pedestrian. No, these were location-specific, and took some serious thought.

The first night, I fell asleep trying to work out how my beloved might have managed to locate a serial killer, give him our planned location that night (which even we didn't know until we spontaneously pulled off to the side of the road), and set it up to look like a random attack in a country with strict gun control laws and a very low rate of violent crime. He, of course, would survive with only a few broken bones to tell the tale. When I told my beloved my speculations the following morning, he objected to being physically damaged, came up with a few thoughts of his own, and continued to enlarge upon his theme for the duration of the trip. Not exactly reassuring.

There was the stop at "Pancake Rocks", where a person might easily hurl another into the boiling ocean cauldron some 200 feet below with slick rock walls and no clear escape route. He could probably have lost me along the "Glow-Worm Trail" if we hadn't gone in broad daylight and the trail hadn't ended six feet from the start.

The old gold-mining towns offered some interesting possibilities, with their long-abandoned mining shafts several hundred feet deep; when I suggested he might toss me in and throw in a few boulders, just to be sure, hubby pointed out that this would be – you guessed it – overkill. He almost got a little boost over the edge himself for that one.

Moving south on the island, we came upon several suspension bridges. Now, the ordinary killer might simply heave his victim over the edge and call it a day, but we are not your ordinary murderers. No, to be creative one would really have to cleverly disconnect the bridge at one end and wait until we had several other hapless tourists goggling over the edge of the swaying, swinging rope contraption into the roaring inferno below, and… And while we're on the subject (and the bridge, still – just hold that thought), doesn't anybody read signs? Several times I found myself in the middle of one of these flimsy constructions (and that term is giving them more credit than they deserve), smile frozen in place, waiting for my beloved to take a picture to document my bravery, fortitude, and trust that he hadn't put any of our schemes into place, and here would come twelve or fourteen galumphing tourists, completely oblivious to signs clearly stating the maximum capacity of the bridge was ten – TEN people!! As the bridge sways precariously from side to side and undulates like a hula dancer, I find myself speculating about who works these things out - some guy in an office with a dartboard? And we're not even asking them whether they meant ten people of average weight and height, with no backpacks, purses, cameras, or heavy clothing, mind you! I found myself shouting, "Walk! Do not run! Walk slowly! This is not the Golden Gate!" And who tests their theory? Us? Did I mention I'm afraid of heights? No matter; I emerged unscathed, but highly nervous.

Then there were the aptly, if unimaginatively, named "Clay Cliffs", where rocks perched precariously in odd places, and the only way to get a really good look is to stand right underneath them and look up… We have photographic evidence of that little attempt, too, if needed.

I began to be quite thankful there are no snakes, poisonous or otherwise, in New Zealand (just the sight of one would undoubtedly have sent me into cardiac arrest, just as it does here), much less any other kinds of natural predators – other than man, of course. Nevertheless, I informed my beloved that I had been keeping notes, just in case, in a hidden place known only to me and a few close friends; I didn't like the way he kept inspecting the emergency door on the plane on the return trip. I fear his enthusiasm for murder most foul and its various permutations has continued unabated since our return; perhaps it's the questions he keeps asking about my life insurance policy…

FLYING

I'M AFRAID TO FLY, which is a shame because I've had to do a lot of it in my life. I didn't used to be afraid; it seems to have come with old age and good sense. I used to revel in the speed and power of the take off; now I remember that's the most dangerous time because there's so much fuel on board and find myself mentally calculating consumption rates of jet engines. I stare at my fellow passengers, wondering who's going to crack first and make a break for the exit door.

When you could see into the cockpit, I always looked at the pilot's and co-pilot's eyes, not in a romantic way, but to see if they were bloodshot; I wanted to be sure they had had enough sleep the night before. These days, none of them look old enough to drive a car, much less fly a jet. All of us passengers look pretty tense, but one woman on a flight not long ago pulled an almost life-size statue of what I assume was St. Christopher out of her hand luggage and began audibly praying the rosary, which was not exactly confidence-inspiring; did she know something I didn't?

And I am convinced that every airport in the world is permanently under construction – why is that? They're hard enough to navigate without all the detours, and for someone who gets lost in the parking lot, hopelessly confusing. I once searched for hours for my car because I forgot to note where I parked it; I was ready to set up a tent and spend the rest of my life camping out.

Sometimes it's a challenge even getting to the airport. Once I decided to take a bus to save myself the aggravation of driving; it seemed like a great idea at the time. I was late, of course, by the time I finally found a place to park. For some reason, everyone else had left a huge central part of the lot empty; when I got out of the car, I discovered why. I sank to my knees in mud, and when I tried to remove my leg from the morass, as the bus to the airport had just arrived, it sucked the pump right off my foot and into the depths of the mudpit. I frantically waved my arms at the bus as I searched for my shoe. Retrieving it, I moved forward and promptly lost the other shoe the same way. I grabbed them both and sprinted to the bus, mud flying.

The bus driver opened the door partway, studied me dubiously, and remarked that he was pretty certain there was some sort of code violation involved in allowing me onto the bus in my current state. I begged, he relented, and the other passengers moved as far away from me as they could manage given the narrow aisle. Making my way carefully down the seats, I headed for the tiny bathroom in the back, where I managed to remove my nylons and wash both them and my feet in the miniscule sink while hurtling at warp speed towards the airport around tight corners. I never realized I had training as a contortionist, but I was a lot thinner then. I returned to find a seat, hung the nylons out the window to dry, and settled down for a nap, ignoring the bemused stares of my fellow passengers.

When the kids were little, we traveled back and forth between West Africa, where we were living, and California – about a thirty-four hour trip altogether – interesting with a three year-old and a five-year old, especially if you're the only parent and you get sick on the plane on the way over. There's nothing quite like wrapping yourself around the toilet in an airport and trying to keep an eye on the kids, or lining up the little airsick bags in front of you on the plane and watching the airline stewardess pick them up in disgust.

My son had the unfortunate habit of locking himself into the toilet on the plane and forgetting how to get out; more than once, I fell asleep waiting for him and had an indignant stewardess bring him back, ready to nominate me for Worst Mother of the Year.

Once, we were traveling through Heathrow Airport with two carts full of luggage; my beloved couldn't make this trip and it was just me, two little kids, and six trunks. My five-year old was pushing a cart so loaded with baggage she couldn't even see over the top, and the three-year-old was precariously perched atop my equally mountainous pile. The elevator door opened, my daughter pushed her cart in, and just as I prepared to follow her, the doors closed. The realization dawned on me that I was in a foreign airport with three trunks and a toddler, and my daughter had just disappeared. Eventually I found her in the midst of a large and happy group of Middle Eastern women, holding forth as only a five-year old can do, not a care in the world. Kind of put flying into perspective.

FLYING AGAIN

I REALLY DON'T KNOW why I bother to fly anywhere. It's expensive, you're packed in like veal, you don't get any goodies, you have to pay extra to take luggage, and in my case, I rarely arrive anywhere without incident. It's gotten to the point that I now buy travel insurance every time I fly, because chances are excellent I'm going to need it. I think by now, I have earned the title "The Typhoid Mary of Travel"; friends and relatives refuse to go anywhere with me for fear of infection.

This time, I flew because my daughter, who lives alone in a colorful neighborhood of Los Angeles – well, alone except for the cockroaches – got sick and needed her mommy. She's a very tough young lady, so when I offered to come down and she didn't immediately say no, I knew she was really ill, and off I went. Since I brought rice and chicken stock with me (groceries are expensive in LA) and stopped off at a Pollo Loco for the chicken along the way – if they'd let me bring a chicken on the plane I would have, but since they were already highly suspicious of my Gatorade, I knew that wouldn't be happening – I was able to make her home-made chicken soup, with which I plied her –well, to say I force-fed her like a Christmas goose would be a more accurate description – and soothed her fevered brow.

The trip down went smoothly, other than leaving my scarf on the plane, but it should have been a warning to me; when things go smoothly, it's because something diabolical is coming. Getting to her apartment is a somewhat complicated journey, involving a bus ride from the airport to the metro, and taking the metro to a location several uphill blocks from her apartment, to be repeated on the way home, but I pretty well have the hang of it now, having navigated it several times, other than the panic I inevitably suffer over how to find the ticket machines at the metro station, and having discovered them, how to make them work. Having finally sorted out these details, I was able to congratulate myself on my own cleverness and eventually board the plane from Los Angeles to San Francisco, and thence back to Medford. At least, that was the plan.

I generally hate flying through San Francisco, lovely as it is, because it inevitably has weather issues, and I have missed too many connecting flights there. It's odd, for a place with such a mild climate, but as I had been in a hurry, I didn't have time to be picky about the route. All went smoothly until the San Francisco to Medford leg of the journey. While I am generally nervous about the San Francisco airport, I tend to forget that Medford, too, has weather issues, generally involving fog.

Sure enough, the pilot no sooner put the wheels down to land in Medford than she abruptly brought the nose up sharply, and we were airborne again. So close, and yet so far away from home. About the time my stomach had settled, the pilot announced that, regretfully, the landing had been aborted due to fog, and we were on our way back to San Francisco, amongst a chorus of groans from the passengers. I don't know about the rest of them, but I was groaning because I knew this would result in a night in the airport. When they cancel a flight due to mechanical problems, you generally get a night in a hotel courtesy of the airline, but when it's weather, it's the airport floor unless you're rich enough to shell out for a hotel on your own dime, which I am not. It's kind of sad that I know these things from unlucky experience.

By the time we had deplaned and walked the 12 miles to the customer service desk, it was about two in the morning, and we were all pretty tired. I was also wet, because I had accidentally knocked my cup of water into my lap on the plane, but that was a minor irritation compared to sleeping on the floor. I'm really way too old for sleeping on the floor.

Much to my surprise, we were offered a hotel, but as the next plane left for Medford at 10 a.m., and I was confident that my own personal Murphy's Law of Travel was in full effect, I refused to leave the airport. In my world, there is way too much scope for disaster in trips to and from the airport in San Francisco, with only a few hours' sleep in between trips, to risk leaving the area. So, I grabbed a few free snacks on offer, as well as a breakfast voucher, and settled down in one of those diabolical airport lounge bench chairs, designed specifically to keep you awake, draped myself to one side over my backpack, and had actually drifted off for about 30 minutes when a family – or maybe several families, it was hard to tell in my groggy state – with about 13 very noisy children decamped next to me. Having thoroughly awakened me, they proceeded to board the next plane, leaving me in a quiet area, although too alert now to allow for any more sleep; I was bright-eyed, if not bushy-tailed, for the rest of the morning.

Due to some miracle, I was able to catch my flight back to Medford without further incident, but I think I might stay home awhile.

LOST LUGGAGE

OUR DAUGHTER RECENTLY LEFT for Italy, much to her mother's trepidation. In my experience, mothers always feel anxious when their children leave home, even when they're 40 years old, living on their own, come home to visit and go out to buy a gallon of milk. But our daughter is only 21, and an artist. While this may not seem relevant, believe me, it is; as an artist, she's much more interested in and more likely to notice things like colors and shapes than in reading, say, written instructions, street signs, guide books, or flight arrivals and departures. She hasn't traveled much on her own, which is a good thing because twice now when we've been travelling with her and staying in cheap hotels (the only kind with which we have any familiarity), I've awakened in the middle of the night to find her, in one case, sound asleep, trying to get out the door, which was, thankfully, securely locked, and in the other case (just a week or so before she left) half way across the parking lot in her nightie, going who knows where, fast asleep.

Her brother decided to set a trap for her the next night, with a suitcase in front of the door and some kind of weird arrangement with a hanger in the lock mechanism, but other than breaking her leg by falling into the suitcase, we had no assurance any of these security measures would stop her. Fortunately, she slept soundly through the night, even if the rest of us were pretty jumpy. This behavior is fairly nerve-wracking for an already nervous, over-protective mother, so we began to solicit ideas from friends about what we might do to keep her from wandering out into strange Italian streets in the middle of the night. However, other than spreading Vaseline on the floor near her bed or tying cans around her ankles, which I suspect might have interfered with her ability to sleep, not to mention everybody else's, nothing particularly useful was suggested.

So, off she went to Italy. I waited anxiously, praying fervently that she would make the numerous connecting flights, since as far as I knew they weren't color-coded, and was relieved to finally get an email – until I read it. She began with those dreaded words: "Mom, I don't want you to worry, but…" It seems she had made it all the way to Rome – but her luggage did not. Unfortunately, her luggage, in this case her backpack, contained the information she needed to tell her not only where she and her fellow art class students were staying, but the instructions for getting there. She was, therefore, stuck in Rome with no idea where to go or what to do, not speaking the language, having only the clothes she stood up in and no personal toiletries essential to your average 21-year old, such as hair conditioner. Unlike most 21-year olds, she is techno-phobic, and therefore had no cell phone or computer with her, despite our pleas that she take SOME means of communicating her status to us.

Remembering that her teacher had forewarned them to take ONLY the red and white taxis, she naturally could not find any, and so got into the taxi of the first man who came up to her and offered her a ride. Are you still with me, mothers, or have you fainted dead away by now? Because it gets worse.

He then proceeded to ask her where she wanted to go, and when she said the Vatican (remembering the hotel was near there), he asked if she had an address for it. Scusi? You live in Rome and drive a taxi, and you need an address for the Vatican? Worse yet, he then asked her if she were travelling alone, at which point she flashed the fake wedding band we had thoughtfully provided her with, and airily replied no, she was meeting her husband in Munich. The logic (or lack thereof) of this reply apparently not fazing him, he actually took her to the Vatican, presumably after consulting his GPS, and delivered her there safely without making any detours to sell her off into white slavery.

She then managed to somehow find an internet café, from which she sent her plaintive plea for help, and then solved her own problem by walking over to the Vatican museum and waiting outside for several hours until, in a miracle I can only attribute to her proximity to the Vatican itself and thus divine intervention, her class walked by and she was reunited with them.

They have moved on to Venice, she still sans backpack, the Italians apparently being unable to decide: 1. If her suitcase is anywhere in the country, and 2. Whether or not they are going to get it to her anytime soon if it is there. In the meantime, she assures me she is borrowing conditioner and washing and blow-drying her one pair of underwear on a daily basis. She has, in her usual creative way, found an amazing variety of methods of wearing the one long skirt she had on when the plane landed – as a dress, then a skirt, then one side hiked up, etc. borrowed a few tops from others, and has thus quadrupled her wardrobe.

In the end, she was finally reunited with her luggage at long last, after two weeks, on the last day of her class tour, and coincidentally on the day she bought "five, count them, five" new pair of undies, just before she was to leave her classmates and strike out on her own for a month. She has emailed me that she is getting "reacquainted with her lingerie". I should have known she would be just fine.

Travels Abroad

SO, WE JUST GOT BACK FROM a vacation to New Zealand. We (or rather I – my beloved had to leave home to go to work before the vacation started and join me later by way of Mali, but that's another story) hopped on a plane for San Francisco, where I was making my connection to New Zealand.

There I was, happily ensconced in my seat on a plane the size and weight of a kite, securely seat-belted in just in case we had a mishap on the runway while still stationary, when the stewardess cheerily announced we were on our way to Arcata. That's interesting, I thought; no one told me we were going to Arcata. Still, I'm a pretty flexible traveler (you get that way when you're used to traveling 36 hours alone with two small children and six trunks to West Africa. As long as the plane lands somewhere eventually, I'm good to go), so I took this in stride until I began visualizing being shot out of the sky by some paranoid rocket-launcher-carrying dope grower in Humboldt county mistaking us for a law enforcement flyover. Still, what were the chances?

I settled down with the airline crossword puzzle until the obligatory crying baby erupted; having had my share of crying babies in my possession, I made faces at the baby to help calm it down, but apparently I was too scary and it just cried harder. Never mind; the baby got off in Arcata, but was unfortunately replaced by a coughing baby. It was going to be a long trip.

And it was. I don't mean to complain, really I don't, but on the flight over we were jammed together like veal, or maybe battery hens – and when you don't even know each other, it's a little close for comfort. Naturally, I was stuck in the middle, but I felt far sorrier for my seatmates; the woman on my right had to crawl over me and the man to my left to go to the bathroom, and the man on my left had to put up with both of us crawling over him. Unless you're a contortionist, you're bound to hurt somebody's body parts, not to mention their feelings. Still, we managed, miraculously somehow, without even discussing it ahead of time, to synchronize our bathroom trips, causing less anguish than might otherwise have been the case. And once they got my movie screen running (they had to reboot it twice – what is it about me and electronic devices?), the films were great.

Upon arrival at Auckland Airport, I was stunned to discover someone who looked just like Lyle Lovett waiting for his luggage. Wait - my former seatmate confirmed (after all the crawling over one another, we were on a first-name basis) – it WAS Lyle Lovett. The clincher was when he picked up a guitar case (Lyle Lovett, not my seatmate). He certainly looked a lot shorter in person, but then the few famous people I have seen in person always did (OK, I've only seen two other famous people, but they were both really short. One was Dustin Hoffman, who looked like he was standing in a hole, and the other was Mother Teresa, who was really short. Oddly enough, I saw them both at San Quentin Prison, but that's another story).

Upon arrival in New Zealand, one must cope with the language barrier. I know, they speak English there, but with an accent that's somewhere between Australian and South African that enabled me to catch about every sixth word. For days I thought two of my hosts were nicknamed "Tid" and "Kin" for some unfathomable reason, until I saw their names in print and realized they were actually Ted and Ken. I was quite alarmed one day to hear a radio announcer urge us to "learn to skydive with the beast!" until I worked out she'd said "with the best"; it's not fair when you can't even read their lips. And personally, I'm not skydiving with anyone, best or beast.

Then there were the long-legged, dark blue birds I thought were called "pooh-kickers" until somebody straightened me out (they are actually "puke-kos"). It's no wonder foreigners think Americans are strange.

And speaking of poop, the quaint local expressions, like "Rattle your dap!" can be confusing, too. Trust me, you don't want to know. All right, if you insist: Apparently sheep, of which there are a few in New Zealand, are not tidy poopers; what's dried out and left behind on their behinds, so to speak, is referred to as "dap", and when they run, it rubs together and makes a sound like a rattle (at least to some people). So, to be told to "rattle your dap" is Kiwi for "hurry up!". Now aren't you glad you know?

I was thrilled to see a sign for "Big Manly Beach", and next to it, "Ladies' Walk", but they were only street names. I had less interest in "Little Manly Beach" down the road. We passed a barn with a big sign on it reading "Jesus is …"; the rest was obscured by another sign that said "For Lease" with a phone number. If we'd been driving less than 100 kilometers an hour, I would have taken down the number and called it, just to see who answered. And this was only the first part of the trip; things got even more interesting when I was joined by my beloved (as they always do with him) and we went out on our own in a camper van.

Driving on the left is always a challenge, but my husband grew up doing so, being from England, so I assumed he'd fall right into it. My beloved, who is a geologist, tends to become distracted by interesting rock formations, of which there are many in New Zealand, trust me, and forget where he is, but I only had to scream "left, left!" a few times to get him back into the correct lane. Of course, everything in the car is reversed, including the steering wheel being on the right, and the turn signals and windshield wipers are on the reverse side, too. You can always tell the tourists like us: we would be the ones turning without signaling, but with the windshield wipers going madly. I'm sure we had the cleanest windshield on the island.

On the first night out, we discovered in a torrential downpour that we had a leaky roof – or rather, our van did. So hubby, ever resourceful, rigged a Rube Goldberg contraption to capture the rainwater and keep it off us (naturally, the leak was just above the bed) which involved stacking everything we could find, including our suitcases, high enough to then wedge a bucket under the roof. We traveled this way, keeping a wary eye on the leaning tower as we drove some very windy roads.

The rain, of which there was quite a bit (our spring is their autumn), caused some wardrobe issues. My hubby, of course, is known for wearing shorts in any weather imaginable; he has a perfectly reasonable explanation, of course, being the scientist that he is. His theory is that if you (or, in this case, he) are in long pants, and it rains, your pants will, of course, get wet, and you will then spend the rest of the day (and possibly the night, if you're with him in some forsaken outback only lunatics frequent) wet and miserable, whereas if you wear shorts, your skin will dry and you will be cozy and comfy – or at least your legs will be (but please see the note above – this is always unlikely when you travel with my beloved). I, being the disorganized, optimistic person that I am, had forgotten my rain jacket, and was forced to buy a replacement. Clothes are very expensive in New Zealand, and I really didn't want to buy yet another rain jacket, so I settled for what was basically a plastic garbage bag with sleeves. I tell you, we were a picture of sartorial splendor: my beloved in his shorts, boots, and lovely New Zealand knit woolly hat with earflaps, and I in my garbage bag over some mismatched outfit, soaking wet.

As we drove, we were treated to what I was forced to categorize as an un-interesting, over-orchestrated, non-musical, repetitive, American-Idol-win-ning, self-indulgent mashed cat noise some people are pleased to call music; other than that, the radio stations were fine, and I am an old fogey, as my beloved will be all too happy to tell you, so pay no attention to my crankiness on the subject.

I generally have no sense of direction in any case, but in New Zealand, apparently everything is reversed: the sun is in the southern hemisphere, or something, I guess, and the water all goes down the drain in the opposite di-rection than you're used to; that is, if you spend time watching water go down drains and note in which direction it is moving. I, for one, do not, but I can name someone in my immediate vicinity who does, and comments on it for my edification. In any case, in New Zealand my already diminished sense of direction left me with absolutely no hope whatsoever of finding my way, and I had to be led by the hand from one location to another everywhere we went.

On the second night, after buying copious amounts of groceries, we dis-covered the propane tank for the stove had a leak, which meant cooking would be a challenge. I watched as my beloved, ever the ultimate fixer, gath-ered twigs, leaves and various other forms of unspecified vegetable matter and somehow made it work. I'm telling you, if you have to be marooned on a desert island, this is the man you want with you. He'd have a five-star hotel built within a month. Of course, you wouldn't be able to actually sleep in it, because he thinks that's not adventurous enough, but still.

Sometime after we fell asleep, and I was discovering that the mosquitoes of New Zealand had a taste, so to speak, for my blood and voracious ap-petites, we were awakened by a most peculiar noise. Roughly, I would have to compare it to the sound some creature, perhaps a cow or a sheep, might make if it had swallowed a clarinet and then tried to breathe, or play the instrument. As it didn't seem to be getting any closer, and we were really tired, we went back to sleep and resolved to investigate further in the light of day. When morning came, we discovered (as I madly scratched mosquito bites, which continued to be an Olympic event for me for several weeks) our neighbors were a herd of domesticated elk (hence the noise, which was them bugling, or singing love songs, or whatever it is they do), which are raised (according to a local cattle rancher's wife, looking quite disgusted) solely for their velvet, which is harvested and sold as an aphrodisiac. Go figure.

After we'd been camping for a few days, I began to notice how good people smelled as they passed me on various hiking trails. Since I had somehow punctured my deodorant bottle and had it drain its lifeblood over my clothes early on in the trip, and I hadn't even brushed my hair in four days, much less showered or changed clothes (what would be the point? And besides, all my clothes were covered in deodorant!), I began to realize this was probably a bad sign. I didn't even want to speculate about what sorts of odors were wafting back to them after I went by. I finally convinced my beloved we were a toxic waste hazard, and we camped in an actual campsite for a night. Hot showers! Soap! Flushing toilets! Bliss!

TABLE DECORATIONS

IN THE FIRST YEAR OR TWO of our marriage, my beloved and I decided to take a trip to Baja. But we did not want the usual tourist trip; no, we wanted adventure! So we drove our car, which was, as usual, some beaten-up monster no one would want, down the highway ourselves.

As we began to grow tired and looked for a place to stay in the middle of nowhere, my beloved spotted a sign for the "Agua Caliente Hotel"; even with my limited Spanish, I was able to ascertain that this translated roughly to "hot water", which boded well for our happiness and comfort, and we enthusiastically headed down the sandy road to rest. If it is possible for a road constructed of sand to have pot holes, this one would win the prize; we bounced and jounced down the completely deserted lane until I thought we must have driven into Mexico itself, teeth nearly forced into our foreheads by the ruts.

After driving for what seemed forever, we finally spotted the hotel in the distance: while somewhat unprepossessing in appearance, it had a pool! I was ecstatic. When we pulled up, however, my enthusiasm abated immediately and completely. The pool, although very deep, was only half full of very green water and had many plants of unknown origin growing in it; it appeared swimming was off.

Next we decided to have a bite to eat, and wandered into the café, which contained about four tables and zero tourists. Never mind; we would have the place to ourselves. When we sat down, however, all thought of a romantic evening on our own immediately vanished when I worked out that the table decorations consisted of large jars containing either a rattlesnake or several tarantulas. I made a hasty exit, any desire for sustenance gone; escape from poisonous entities was now on the top of my bucket list.

We repaired to our room, where we discovered it held only one twin bed. Never mind, we were newlyweds, and in those days could both still fit in a twin bed. After brushing our teeth with bottled water, we snuggled into bed (snuggling being a necessity if we wanted to both fit) and dropped off to sleep.

As my husband tells it – and I have to believe him because I was peacefully asleep and have no first-hand knowledge – he suddenly found himself flung onto the floor (by me, he says) and me, wide-eyed, pointing at the ceiling and yelling, "Tarantulas!" Not unreasonably, he asked, "What? Where?" At which I allegedly replied, pointing even more forcefully upward, "On the ceiling!" He being a patient, logical sort of man, my beloved went to the trouble of turning on the lights so that I could examine said ceiling carefully for my-self, at which point (I am told), finding no marauding arachnids, I lay back down and went calmly to sleep. Although chances are good, since I have no memory of the event, that I was never actually awake. He says he thought it best not to point out to me the rat he had espied scurrying across the floor while the light was on; after all, he would be driving the next day and needed to get some sleep that night.

THE ANACONDA

DURING OUR TRIP TO ECUADOR, after my beloved had climbed the nearest mountain, of course (in this case, Cotapaxi), we traveled up into the Andes and down into the jungle, just so that we could get the feel of the place. This was after I had, according to my beloved, tried to poison us all by cooking a somewhat sketchy version of a local dish which made us all rather violently ill while at 15,000 feet, but I swear that, like most of my culinary misadventures, it wasn't on purpose. Hey, I got sick, too…

In any case, we drove up further into the Andes and the boys (there were three male mountaineers, all Brits, and myself) decided to humor me by taking me to a local market to shop. Knowing how paranoid I am about getting lost, they made a detailed plan for meeting up later and finding each other in the market should we get lost, and emerged from the vehicle. This was when I realized that there was no danger of losing each other, and that we were definitely not going to blend with the locals: we were all at least two feet taller than anyone in the market.

Next we descended to the jungle, where my beloved promised to treat me to a stay in a hotel. I was so excited to actually have a chance to bathe that I didn't even mind too much when the night before we left, we stayed at a "hotel" that was beyond sketchy; I can safely say that this place was the worst we had ever stayed in, and that's going quite a ways. Maybe it was a ploy to make me appreciate the accommodations at the later hotel, but where else can you find a room where you can see through the floorboards into the kitchen below? And the "bathroom" does not even bear remembering, much less speaking about, but of course, misery loves company, so I will: It consisted of several holes lined up, and I will just say that no one had very good aim, or had escaped from some sort of digestive disorder, and I hadn't even fed them.

So I was quite relieved to catch the boat upriver the next day to stay in our hotel. I use the term "boat" loosely; it was actually a dugout log with a motor attached. But the river breezes were nice, and it was wonderful to escape the confines of our dubious lodging.

Then we arrived at the hotel, which some bright spark had dubbed "The Anaconda"; this is not a happy association for a woman who hates snakes of every size and description, but I still clung to hope. That is, until I saw the rooms: they were on stilts, there was no electricity, and the "shower" was a hose snaking (unfortunate word, but appropriate nonetheless) into a concrete enclosure. They were roofed in thatch, which sounds romantic until you realize things live in the thatch, and they are not things with which I care to fraternize. Call me a snob. But I am the eternal optimist; at least I had a hose to clean myself up with.

As an aside, rooms on stilts became a theme in our travels; several years later, when we traveled to Kenya (Mt. Kenya needed to be ascended) with our eight-month old daughter, I took along my parents and sister as backup and support system while my husband was conquering the mountain. We traveled in style on a "safari" tour while he roughed it, but even the Hilton was on stilts. My father had great fun trying to sell off my sister, my daughter and I, as the locals felt he clearly had some women to spare and were happy to trade him a few goats or cows for us.

But back to the Anaconda: we had a good dinner in the open-air restaurant, as I recall, but it was unfortunately eclipsed by later events. After we retired for the night and I was just about to fall asleep, I heard an alarming noise. Though my beloved attempted, as usual, to ignore it and sleep, I made him get up and investigate, which he had to light a candle to do, there being no power. It was probably a mistake for me to insist, because what he discovered with the candle kept me awake all night: cockroaches the size of tour buses were running up and down the wall next to the bed. My beloved made a valiant effort to chase them away using the candle, but I was not fooled; I knew they would crawl back the instant the candle was doused. Still, it was entertaining to watch him try. In the morning, the half a banana I had left on the counter had been hauled away...

There was a pet monkey on the grounds that was fed beer and took a liking to one of the other few tourists in residence; he (the monkey) had to be physically restrained from making his home in her (the tourist's) hair. And karma did not fail me: a pet ocelot kept on the compound developed a crush on my beloved's ankles, and spent the entire stay rubbing on them and nibbling on them, much to my beloved's alarm.

A word of advice: stay away from hotels sporting the name of reptiles...

Going Where the Wind Takes You – Or Doesn't

WHEN MOST PEOPLE, including me, think of a vacation in Baja, the image that springs to mind is of a lovely resort on the beach, perhaps at Cabo San Lucas; long vistas of white sand stretching as far as the eye can see, someone handing you a fruity drink with an umbrella peeking over the rim as you bask on said beach, skin turning a golden brown… but most people do not travel with my beloved.

You would think I might have learned after 30 years, but no; I am rudely jerked from this happy daydream of relaxation by the reality of life with hubby. To begin with, we travel to Baja via Salt Lake City, Atlanta, Mexico City and La Paz, thereby turning what should have been a five or six-hour flight into an epic journey that takes the better part of two days; we could have driven there faster. At one point I find myself so exhausted in one of many airport terminals that I sit hunched over my backpack, which rests (as I have been unable to do) in my lap, and, to my astonishment, fall soundly asleep. When we actually arrive here in Baja, my feet are so swollen by all the air time that they look like unbaked bread loaves.

And where, you might enquire, is "here"? Not Cabo; no, we drive (the taxi is way too expensive) for an hour or so to a tiny village called La Ventana, which I thought meant "the wind", where in actual fact, it means "window". Who goes to countries where they cannot speak the language? Other than, of course, the menu, to some degree; it's amazing the number of languages in which I am able to somehow work out how to feed myself. Along the way, not a single sign indicates which direction to go in order to reach the village, of course; I cannot imagine why the road map manufacturers bother to label the highways, as the highways themselves remain mysteriously silent on the matter of identification. It would have been so helpful to see a number, a name, even an arrow with the words "La Ventana"... Part of the map is even printed upside down, which is singularly unobliging of it. My beloved, thankfully, has an unerring instinct for geography, and manages to get us to the right place, despite my insistence that we travel in the exact opposite direction. He learned long ago to nod and smile when I am navigating, and go his own, correct, way.

After sleeping a good ten hours, we awake in our little room, which is, admittedly, very near the beach; so near, in fact, that we can hear the raucous sounds of the bar all night. By morning, my nasal passages are completely clogged, which tells me I am probably allergic to the lovely thatch that covers the roof, although the fronds are covered in so much shellac I thought they were wooden at first; I can't imagine how my nose even detects any vegetable matter, but apparently it manages.

But I lie; we have actually awakened many a time during the night. Once, we were dragged from happy slumber when it seemed every dog in Baja gathered outside our room to howl and bark at who knows what; I decided someone must have been prying open our car in order to steal it, but was too tired to care. Many times we groggily woke to the roar of hundreds if not thousands of trucks bombing past at speed, as our room sits right next to the road, and when those sounds became more widely spaced, we were treated to the dulcet tones of cock crow and bird song, including some sort of pigeon I would have happily throttled had I only been able to locate him or her. It was probably hiding in the thatch; a lot of creatures I would rather not think about undoubtedly make their home in the thatch. At least we didn't, as far as I know, hear whatever noise the pelicans, of which there are numerous in the water nearby, make; given their size, I imagine when they become irate, the racket is unbearable. I suspect we may find out before we leave.

We are here so that my beloved can once again indulge his passion for kite-boarding, but of course, with our arrival, the wind ceases and we are all becalmed. I say "all" because given the size of the village; it's amazing how many gringos are here, all apparently waiting for the wind to come up. The "local" market, staffed almost exclusively by expat Americans and other for-eigners, has nevertheless shut down just in time for lunch, or possibly siesta, so we have nothing to eat; breakfast was a meatless tamale, which has not stuck to my ribs, and I am getting hungry and cranky as my beloved snores contentedly next to me. Maybe I can find that pigeon after all…

Back From Baja

I HAVE BEEN BACK from Baja for some time now, recovering from the trauma of yet another vacation with my beloved. I believe there are a few points about Baja I have not yet divulged, and perhaps recounting them will have a cathartic effect, so here we go.

One thing that stands out about the little place we stayed in was a small feathered annoyance, a bird that sat on a metal structure just outside our room and which we began referring to as the "striped-backed, lesser-brained metal-pecker" because he insisted on pecking the aluminum strut as if it would someday, if he kept at it long enough, yield an edible bug. He ignored every effort we made to re-direct him to more savory fare, and as far as I know, he is still there, hoping against hope that his endeavors will yield fruit someday, and irritating everyone within audible reach.

On one of several days of becalmment (yes, I know that's not a word, but I like it) (we were there so that my husband could practice kite-boarding), we decided to go to an old mining town (that's what happens when you're married to a geologist), where we stumbled across the grandly named "Museo de Musica". The title was accurate, as far as it went, which stretched to about a dozen old pianos that looked as if they'd been through The Flood, at least, if not several fires - a guitar or two, and random photos of famous singing stars. Wait – my beloved reminds me there were a few old record players and an organ, too. Well, that certainly made all the difference.

We moved on to the Cultural Center in La Paz, where we wander upstairs to peruse more exhibits. This excites the guide, as we are the only people in the building, and she proceeds to describe the scenes in front of us in enthusiastic Spanish. Although I speak no Spanish, my polite smile encourages her, apparently, because she expounds further on more exhibits as my eyes glaze over, dragging us from one display to another as I respond with the only Spanish word I can think of, "Si", which I repeat as necessary, nodding sagely, although this becomes quite dangerous when she asks questions, as I assume she is asking if we understand, but of course, for all I know, she may be asking if we would be happy to transfer our life savings to her personal bank account. Occasionally I turn to my beloved and explain in English some aspect of what we are looking at that only an idiot wouldn't understand, and he nods, too, because he appears to be afflicted by some malady that enables him to communicate solely in French while in Baja; no matter what anyone says to him in Spanish, he replies in French, which leaves all of us confused, including him.

Having carried on this exhausting charade for what feels like an hour, no well-intentioned deed apparently going unpunished, we make our way to the front door, where a sympathetic security guard smiles knowingly and says in English, "You don't speak Spanish, do you?" We flee before the museum guide can discover our calumny. This makes being hauled into the boat like a giant tuna on our "Swimming with the Whale Sharks" adventure seem like a swim in the park, even if I definitely did not feel like the catch of the day on that occasion, either.

When it is finally time to leave Baja for the epic 12-hour trip back home, which naturally begins at 4 a.m., we discover that, true to form in Baja, there are no signs directing us to the airport, and it is too dark to try my usual plan, which is to follow the big planes landing somewhere which might be the airport. Instead, we stop to ask several different locals for directions. I have cleverly brought our Spanish phrase book in the car, and am able to grandly ask, with a flourish, "Donde esta el aeropuerto?", which is, naturally, followed by a volley of Spanish, none of which I can understand.

I then sit mute as every vestige of Spanish I have ever accidentally acquired rapidly flees my brain, only to be replaced by the very word I am so desperately searching for in every other language I have been exposed to, words I never knew that I knew, in French, Italian, German – even, occasionally, Latin. When a few Spanish words do miraculously make their way into my head, I attempt to string them together into a sentence, managing to come up with something akin to: "I Spain to be very bad. Please to forgive." Followed by, in English, the pleading "Do you speak English?" They do not, and many hand gestures and active pantomimes ensue until, by accident, we stumble upon the airport just in time to catch our plane home and resolve to take Conversational Spanish the very next time it is offered.

Swimming With the Fishes

WE DECIDED TO GO to Baja California so that my husband could practice kiteboarding, which he had recently taken up in Maui. At least it's a sport
that tends to take place in warm tropical climates close to water, if not actually in the water, as opposed to, say, the tops of mountains, or in the middle
of a desert.

Life here in Baja is about as I expected it to be, only cooler and noisier.
Our room is fairly close to the beach, but right on the road. After the first
noisy night, things quieted down and I lived in hope that it would remain so.
Silly me.

Last night I was awakened by the dog next door incessantly barking at
something I certainly couldn't hear; I was just dropping off when something
that sounded suspiciously like a street-cleaning machine jerked me back
awake, except that given the state of the streets, it certainly was not that.
Then the roosters, awakened no doubt by the dogs, started in, followed by all
the other birds in the known universe chiming in, minus the pigeon from last
week for some reason. This was followed by hubby's phone buzzing on the
windowsill above our heads, and then the alarm clock, which I had somehow
accidentally armed, went off. Next, some guy in a truck drove past, loudspeaker blaring who knows what, or cares, in Spanish as he drives by - and
he's the only one who drives slowly, of course. Despite some sizeable speed
bumps, everyone goes at warp speed right up to them, when you hear the
screeching of brakes or the "whump" sound as they hit it, and no one in Baja
appears to have a working muffler by the sound of it.

After a few days of good kite boarding, hubby was again becalmed, so we
decided to go "swim with the whale sharks", as the ad urged. Now, the words
"whale" and "shark" have never inspired me to accompany them with the
words "swim with"; I can only plead extreme boredom in my defense. So,
I hopped into the boat with Jorge, the boat driver, and a woman even older
than I, neither of whom spoke English, and off we went. My beloved and I

changed into our bathing suits on the boat, which was quite a feat in itself, donned flippers, mask and snorkel – another act involving much squeezing, tugging and yanking – and waited with bated breath. That's bated, not baited.

After some time of searching the sea in a state I would not quite describe as anticipation, there it was: a spotted behemoth swimming past our boat in a leisurely fashion, as well he might, being pretty much bigger than the boat, and definitely bigger than us. Jorge yelled something in Spanish and shoved me into the water, and suddenly I was about six inches from the biggest fish I had ever seen in my life, thinking about the word "shark" in whole new ways. Let me tell you, gasping under water, even with a mask and snorkel on, is not advised, and by the time I could breathe again, he was gone. Feeling relieved, I endeavored to haul myself back into the boat, as hubby was off following the shark, which, as it turned out, would have been the easier task.

I was reminded of the time, many years ago, that my beloved and I went to Hawaii and took a tour around some cliffs or other in a rubber dinghy. We motored into a cave of sorts and were urged to jump out and swim, which we happily did, but when it was time to get back into the boat, issues arose; I could not, for love nor money, get myself back into the boat, even with my beloved tugging strenuously – and I was at least 25 pounds lighter then. Finally, he grasped both my wrists firmly and heaved – and my head connected with his knee with a crack I remember to this day; I literally saw stars and began to subside underwater, but fortunately we were young and in love and he rescued me.

This time, hubby was off with the shark and it was up to poor Jorge, who unsuccessfully yanked and tugged until I thought I would end up swimming back to port alongside the boat with two dislocated shoulders. We finally managed it, but not without incurring bruising – to me, anyway, both physically and to my battered ego; I shudder to think about what poor Jorge looks like. This act was repeated several times, as the bloody fish kept coming back, clearly having no sense of pity for me; my beloved was thrilled, describing a huge gaping mouth with, he assured me, no teeth, but all I could do was shudder, and heave myself back into the boat, time after time, until it all mercifully ended.

We then motored back into port, where I lurched back into the boat while attempting to disembark, prompting Jorge to shout good-naturedly, "No mas tequila!", and shove me back out; he was getting good at this.

We were met with the sad sight of what appeared to be a sick sea lion lying on the dock – until the woman with us bent down to pet him sympathetically, when he rose up sharply and almost bit her hand, thereafter looking considerably revived and perky. Having survived the whale shark encounter as well as multiple boat encounters, I was feeling pretty perky myself.

A FEW NOTES ON TRAVEL

LAUNDRY: WHEN TRAVELING, I occasionally find it necessary to do some laundry, especially since I save room in my luggage for important souvenirs by bringing as little clothing as it's possible to take without freezing to death or violating public decency laws, and my recent trip to Eastern Europe was no exception. Being far too cheap - I mean thrifty - to use expensive hotel or laundromat services, I prefer to wash it myself, even on a luxurious tour. Thus, I would wait until I was going to be in a hotel for a few days, as I had discovered that clothing took a long time to dry in the humid air, dump some shampoo in the sink or bathtub if they had one, and start scrubbing.

Bathtubs, I discovered, were problematic, as they were usually as huge as an ancient sarcophagus made for a giant, and so hard to climb in and out of that I needed a stepladder to get in and out, so I usually used the sink. If at all possible, I would then hang larger items outside to dry, but this depended on several factors, such as whether or not I had the requisite hangers – the kind you can actually remove from the closet – and a balcony or private courtyard in which to hang them without shocking the neighbors. Even though I can tell myself I'll never see these people again in my life, I try to maintain some decorum. Smaller items could be hung on deck furniture, if there was any, which is why the chairs outside my room were so often festooned with underwear; it had to be anchored between the wall and the heavy metal chair in high winds, which were wonderful for drying but tended to result in me having to collect various items of clothing from nearby bushes if precautions were not taken.

Electronics: Before leaving home, I cleverly bought a mobile charger – or whatever they're called – and it worked a treat the first time I used it to charge my phone. But it didn't work the next time I tried to use it, and I decided my charger needed charging. In a move that reminded me of the time my friends in college had to explain to me how eggs become chickens (me: "But there's no hole in the egg. How does the rooster…?"), I hunted industriously for the place to plug in the cable that I could then plug into my power converter, but I found only two connection points, both too big for my phone cable connecting/charging thingy. Puzzled, and out of ideas (it doesn't take long), I messaged my tech support – my son, in graduate school in Salt Lake City. He was puzzled, too; he was also certain there must be a place to connect the charger to the charger, so to speak, so he asked me to send him pictures of the charger from every possible angle, close up, which I did. Then we both waited. And waited. When it eventually became clear that the photos had not made it through the ethers peculiar to Croatia and Utah, I tried again. Before he could respond, and after I had donned my glasses and turned on a brighter light, I realized I could actually see another, smaller opening that he had described to me perfectly – success at last.

So I plugged it in to charge, notified my long-suffering son, and settled down to sleep. I had no sooner turned off the light than my potential golden slumbers were interrupted by a pulsing blue light that seemed to fill the room – had aliens landed? No, it was the charger, happily and enthusiastically publicizing its message: "I'm charging!" Pulse. "I'm charging!" Pulse… I frantically hid it under my notebook, then the covers, and finally a pillow before dropping it into a drawer in frustration – still attached to its cable so that I could find it in the morning, when I searched madly for it, not remembering where I could possibly have put it – before the problem was solved and I could sleep.

Swimming: The next day, exhausted from the technological problems of the night before but determined to swim in the Adriatic, as I had never done so before, I wandered down to the "beach", which is all rock with a metal stepladder down into the water, wondering why no one else was taking advantage of the lovely weather. My dip was brisk, brief and bracing: the water was quite cold, and the surf was quite rough, and I bobbed like a cork atop steep waves, struggling to stay afloat. As no one else was braving the water with me, making me the default shark bait, I beat a hasty retreat as soon as I could drag myself up the slippery stairs and mossy rocks. Swimming in the Adriatic may be slightly overrated.

Go Croatia!

PEOPLE HAVE ASKED me what my fondest memory is of my trip to Eastern Europe, and my answer surprises even me: it was the two soccer games I was able to watch.

Now, I am not a huge sports nut, and I like soccer, but I would never have guessed that, for the first time in my life, I would find myself caught up in the magic of a fervently enthusiastic crowd of soccer fans. But this was the World Cup, and by a complete coincidence, I found myself in the central square of Zagreb (the capital city) in Croatia for both the semi-final and final matches of the World Cup, in which Croatia was playing. In a country of only about 4-5 million people, the fact that they made it that far is close to a miracle, and the Croatians treated it like one.

The games themselves were incredibly exciting, and I found watching the national hysteria over their team to be indescribably uplifting. There was no violence, just complete devotion – to their team, to each other, and to their country. I have never witnessed more emotional, enthusiastic patriotism and glory in one's nation as in this small, proud country.

I went down to the town square for the semi-final game against England with three other women from my tour group: one thirty-year old and two teenage soccer players. We stood jammed together in a crowd of thousands of cheering, singing, smoking, beer-drinking fans, mostly young men, but some women, too. Croatians are unnaturally tall folk, and it was almost im-possible to see the giant screen, but you knew whenever England scored by the groans and looks of despair on their faces. There was absolutely no doubt when Croatia put a number on the board, because everything anyone might be holding went straight up into the air, along with their entire bod-ies – streamers, flags, confetti, beer, hats, empty bottles, and the occasional lit cigarette – and came down on us all. There was jubilant screaming, chanting, crying, jumping up and down, flag waving, flare lighting, and more singing.

It was hard for me to tell who was doing what on the field, because to my unaccustomed ears, all the players' names sounded the same. "Ic" is generally pronounced "itch" in Croatian, and herewith I list the team names: Modric (the team captain), Rakitic, Mandzukic, Subasic (the goalie), Persic, Rebic, Kalinic, Kramaric, Kovacic, Brozovic, Strinic, Kalnic, Pivaric, Livakovic, Bradaric – and the odd men out, Vida and Lovren. There might have been a few more, but I gave up by then. By the end of the game, there was so much smoke from the flares I wasn't sure anyone could see, but there was no doubt who had won, given the eruption of cheers and mania. I was grabbed and hugged by complete strangers, as were my compatriots, and I'm not sure I've ever had so much fun or witnessed as much emotion in my life. I came back to my hotel room reeking of beer and cigarettes, bruised on every part of my body from the jumping up and down all around me, and completely content.

Fans wore an amazing assortment of headgear and costumes to celebrate their team, all in the red and white checks that adorn the national flag: horned hats, cat in the hat hats, scarves as hats and headbands, checked caps (red and white, of course), weird flat things that resembled earmuffs and tied under the chin, flags as hats and capes (the horse statue that sits in the town square wore a long flowing cape of red and white), ties, jerseys, scarves worn as scarves, and a bizarre suit of checkered headgear that I later saw were actually car side-view mirror protectors. Walking back to our hotel room was an experience in itself – honking cars, young people hanging precariously out car windows and popping up out of sun roofs, waving impossibly large flags, everyone waving, laughing, yelling, and singing as they raced by. I heard cheering in the streets outside my hotel window well into the night.

I happened to be in Zagreb again for the final game, again by a complete coincidence, for which I will always be thankful. The crowd was even bigger this time, and if possible, even more enthusiastic. I don't think anyone, even the Croatians, really thought they would make it this far, and their pride in having done so was immeasurable. The crowd was so dense this time, however, the smoke so thick, and the screen so completely obscured that by half time I had slipped away to my room to watch the rest of game. If they had scored more goals, I'm convinced the entire crowd would have been asphyxiated and the town burned to the ground by fireworks before game's end. While Croatia lost to France in the final match, there was no rioting, no boos, no violence of any kind – just celebrations that they had gotten so far and done so well. It was refreshing to see.

244

Later, still in Croatia, I watched the team's homecoming parade on television: through the same streets I had walked a short time before, the team rode atop a large bus, waving to the wildly cheering crowd; you would never have known they had actually lost the final game. The square was packed with even more people than ever, and the bus made very slow progress indeed - about half an inch every half hour, it seemed, as adoring fans greeted their heroes. The police alternated between gently pulling people off rooftops and joining them to wave national flags, a fighter pilot doing a flyover and a nun in the crowd were both bedecked in the team jersey, and one player held another by the back of his shorts to keep him from falling off the bus into the arms of the crowd. Everyone was clearly having the time of their lives.

And everyone was still singing and chanting, much to my amazement – I was sure the entire country must have shouted themselves hoarse by the final game. I found myself singing along with the national anthem, which I had practically memorized – in Croatian – having heard it so many times.

A never-to-be-forgotten experience.

Stairways to Heaven – Or Not

SOON AFTER ARRIVING in Croatia, still jet-lagged, my first tour group stayed in a hotel in Dubrovnic that had a fiendishly complicated route to get to our rooms. I am, as many of you know, hopelessly directionally challenged, but this system confused even my fellow tour members, all of whom seemed to be of at least reasonable intelligence and abilities.

This is, quite literally, the path I had to take to get to my room: Up some stairs, down the hall, turn right, down some stairs, turn left to get to the elevator, go down a floor - I had no idea what floor I was on by now, so I had no idea what button to push. Fortunately, room numbers were also helpfully printed next to each floor number, so I managed to work that one out. Then it was out of the elevator, turn right, up some stairs, turn left, and down the hall. The porter who gave me directions in the elevator actually said to go to the end of the hall. I therefore kept going past my room (having long ago forgotten my room number), down more stairs and into a bar, but eventually

I worked out that I was in the wrong place, as it was a bit crowded. I wanted to drop bread crumbs, but it was forbidden. It was like being in some real-life version of that famous Escher painting, continually going up when you think you're going down, and vice versa into eternity in an optical illusion of hotel travel, condemned to never reach your destination.

In an interesting, Dante-like twist of fate, I found myself in the same hotel two weeks later with my second tour group. Fellow travelers, knowing I had been there before and finding the route as confusing as the rest of us had, asked to follow me. Despite my sincere and fervent warnings not to do so, they persisted, and soon we were all wandering up and down stairways and halls like the lost and the damned.

This time, I was in a different room, of course – just when I thought there was a slight possibility I could find my way to my old room - and again, I only wish I were making this up, my route was as follows: turn right, go down the stairs, turn left, and take the elevator down a flight. You will see stairs, we were instructed, but do not, under any circumstances, take them, as even though they appear to be going up, or down, whichever direction you need to go, they will not, somehow, take you to your destination. I later had the opportunity to prove the warning correct, unfortunately, when I lost patience waiting for the elevator, but around that we shall draw a veil. By the same reasoning, we were instructed, do not, repeat do not take the elevator if you are told to take the stairs, or you will, believe me, be punished in the inferno of wandering forlornly and forever in this version of hotel hell.

For breakfast, I had to go back to the lobby, take the elevator to the bottom floor, go down some stairs, outside and across the street into an entirely different building.

In another hotel, room numbers did not match floor numbers, and just to make my life complete, the floors were indicated by 1ROT, appropriately enough, as this was what I thought I might do there, trying to find my room; 1 was the top floor, but the rest was a mystery. In that hotel, the elevator nearest the lobby didn't work at all, which at least saved me from taking it to the wrong place.

In writing these notes, at this point I became so confused about how to get to my room that I completely forgot the route, and decided in a panic that I would be lost in the hotel the rest of my life, or just stay in my room until someone came looking for me when I didn't get on the bus the next day, which is reason enough to travel with a tour group. My luggage had already been delivered outside my room, so I couldn't even find a bellboy to follow down to reception.

In Sarajevo, there was an entirely different system. While there were no stairs, thank heavens, you went to the elevators and punched in the floor number your room was on before getting on. If you didn't do so, you might wait there forever, because there was not a chance said elevators were going to open their doors, figuratively crossing their arms and waiting with a glower for you to get with the program. After you had, a letter would appear that corresponded to a particular elevator, you got in it, and it would theoretically take you to your floor, but this was not a sure thing; occasionally it would take you to a different, random floor, or God help you if you made a mistake, because in either case you would have to start all over. This was trickier than it might sound, because once on the elevator, there was not a single button to push. Ingenious when it worked, but frightening when it didn't. Another chance to spend one's life, not even in a room, but in an elevator, and there was so much to see…outside.

THE TUNNEL OF HOPE

WHEN MY TOUR OF EASTERN EUROPE went to Sarajevo, I was keen to learn the history of the place; I knew that there had been a war there, but I was vague on the details and wanted to learn more.

The states comprising the former Yugoslavia had been occupied over the years by the Italians, the Greeks, the Ottoman Empire, and the Austro-Hungarian Empire, among others. After World War II, Croatia, Serbia, Montenegro, Bosnia, Macedonia, and Slovenia were united to form Yugoslavia under General Josip Broz, known as Tito, a former member of the Resistance movement (the Partisans) against the Nazis, and a communist. This union was perhaps always a bit uneasy, given the variety of ethnicities and religions involved, but Tito managed to keep the factions from breaking away while he was president, prime minister, and marshall until his death in 1980.

After the death of Tito, no one emerged as his natural successor, and the states making up Yugoslavia began to assert their independence; in June of 1991, Slovenia and Croatia declared their independence. Slovenia was allowed to secede without much trouble, as its population was not as diverse as the other states, being mostly Catholic, but Croatia was a different story, as it contained the majority of the coastline, more money, and a large population of Serbs. It was shelled by the remainder of the Yugoslavian Republic in an attempt to bring it back into the fold. Nevertheless, Croatia managed to become independent in 1993.

Next to declare its independence was Serbia, which voted to be independent in a referendum on February 29, 1992. The vote was rejected by the Bosnian Serbs, although it was formally recognized by the European Community and the United States in April of 1992.

The Serbian government, led by Slobodan Milosevic who commanded the "Yugoslav People's Army", attacked Bosnia and Herzegovina and perpetuated "ethnic cleansing" of the ethnically "non-Serbs", including the Bosniaks (Muslims). The Serbs destroyed 296 villages and murdered thousands of people between April and June of 1992. In a particularly horrific act, the Serbian Army besieged the town of Srebenica, which had been declared a "safe area" by the United Nations (UN) in April 1993, for almost three years, from April 1993 until July 1995. During a visit in March 1993, French UN General Morillon visited the city and promised the inhabitants that they were under United Nations protection, and that he would never abandon them. Conditions were crowded due to the many Muslims who had fled to the city to escape the ethnic cleansing in other areas of the country; food became scarce, there was no water, and there was very little electricity other than that provided by some generators, and a number of people starved to death. In July 1995, the Serbs rounded up approximately 8,000 Muslim men and boys who had taken refuge in the city and executed them, as well as raping many women and children and killing other residents. This act was later declared by the United Nations to be a genocide, a decision upheld by the International Court of Justice in 2007.

In addition to this, the Serbs besieged Sarajevo, where the 1984 Olympics had been held, from April 5, 1992, until February 29, 1996: almost four years. During this time, the city, which sits in a valley surrounded by mountains, was constantly shelled, and snipers sat in the hillsides, shooting civilians as they foraged for food and water within the city. A street our bus drove down

248

had been dubbed "Sniper Alley" during the war, and many buildings retain the scars of bullet holes and mortar rounds, kept purposely by the residents as a reminder of what occurred there. In a town of approximately 300,000 people, more than 11,500 were killed, including over 1,000 children; 60,000 people left. It is estimated that an average of 329 mortar rounds and shells landed in the city every day. Our "local specialist/guide", Samara, pointed out red paint patterns on the ground all over the city and told us that everywhere we saw one of those, called "Sarajevo Roses", at least three people had died.

I met Samara during my tour of Sarajevo. She had grown up there and lived there currently. Samara was a slight, boyish-looking woman in her early thirties with short hair and a serious expression. She gave us some of the facts about the town's history, but didn't say much about herself. Our "regular" tour guide filled us in a bit the day before we met Samara, explaining that Samara had been in second grade when the war started; her father disappeared at some point, and she and her mother had escaped through the tunnel (dug between March and June 1993 – in four months and four days) during the siege. They lived in New Jersey for most of Samara's third grade year, but then returned to Sarajevo. Our regular guide told us that Samara probably wouldn't talk much about those days, at least not about her personal experiences, and for the most part, she didn't. Samara showed us a movie at the tunnel museum detailing its construction and other aspects of the siege, including footage of shooting in "Sniper Alley". She also informed us that the war left approximately 60% of Sarajevo's buildings in an uninhabitable condition.

Samara took us on a tour of the very tunnel through which she and her mother had escaped Sarajevo, "The Tunnel of Hope", in what must have been an eerie experience for her; it certainly was for me. Although in total the tunnel is 800 meters long, we only went into about 20 meters of it; most of it, Samara explained, was now inoperable due to the fact that it was under the Sarajevo Airport. The tunnel, variously called "The Tunnel of Rescue" or "The Tunnel of Hope", was dug by hand, 24 hours a day in eight-hour shifts by men paid with a pack of cigarettes a day, cigarettes being more valuable than the currency. Rails and cables donated by Germany were later added to make transportation, electricity and communication easier. 1,200 cubic meters, or 2,800 square meters of dirt, were removed by men working from both ends of the tunnel to link Sarajevo with Bosnian-held territory on the far side of the airport, land which was controlled by the United Nations. Food, oil, war supplies including ammunition, and humanitarian aid were all transported through the tunnel, and occasionally, people like Samara and her mother were able to escape through the tunnel, mostly at night. But it was very risky.

Samara told us that if the Serbian snipers spotted people trying to escape out the tunnel exit, or even going towards Sarajevo (with supplies for the beleaguered city), they shot them. If United Nations personnel caught you, they might shine a spotlight on you, enabling the Serbs to shoot you, or sometimes they would simply return you to whichever direction you had come from. Therefore, she related, the thing to do if you were caught by U.N. personnel as you tried to escape the city, for instance, was to simply face towards Sarajevo, so that they would "return" you back to the villages outside Sarajevo, where you were trying to go in the first place.

One day I found myself walking alone next to Samara, and told her that I had hiked up a hill in Sarajevo on my own and had seen a huge cemetery stretching up the hillside, thousands of crosses and other grave markers, some with pictures of young people, and asked her if the tour would be going there. She said in a tone of some surprise, "You went there? No, we won't be going there." She was silent for a moment, then said, "My father is buried there."

Another time, as we all hiked to the site of the 1984 Olympics, I found myself next to her again. I mentioned that I hiked most mornings with my dog at home, and she said shyly, "I have a dog also that I walk with", and showed me his picture. I felt a connection to her that I hadn't felt before, over a simple thing like a shared love of dogs and walking.

There was something about Samara, a seriousness, a gravitas perhaps, that told me she had seen things no child should see, that no person should ever have to see. While she smiled on occasion, and had a wonderful dry sense of humor, she never lost that air of gravity. Samara also possessed a toughness that told me she was a person you would not want to cross. She clearly retained some bitterness at the lack of attention to Bosnia's civil war and the atrocities committed, by both the world in general and the United Nations in particular, but she was kind and considerate, and an excellent teacher.

Today, Bosnia and Herzegovina, as it is called, contains approximately 44% Muslim "Bosniaks", 31% Orthodox Serbs, and 17% Catholic Croats, all living in peace together once again. Clearly, most of the population has made great efforts to put the past behind them and create a strong country. But like the mortar and bullet holes in the buildings, scars remain: scars felt by people like Samara.

WALLED IN

I HAVE RECENTLY BEEN LUCKY enough to travel to Eastern Europe. This was a guided tour, with all the convenience you could imagine, which I could not, always having traveled in something approximating poverty-level travel, if there is such a thing – and there is, because I've done it. Not being used to the luxury of actually having someone carry my baggage for me and having all (four-star) accommodation booked in advance, with even some meals laid on, it took me a while to overcome the shock. The down side was that not having disasters occur on a regular basis cut down on the number of stories I was able to write; I hardly knew what to do with myself. But I managed somehow.

I found myself in Dubrovnik one day (well, actually two days, on different occasions, but that's another story), a beautiful ancient walled city in Croatia, and decided I would walk the wall. This was a brave feat on my part, not only because the wall is high and I am afraid of heights, but also because it was so hot the sweat was running off my nose already, and the wall is about one to two miles around. But, determined to get the most out of my vacation, I paid my fee (that they can get away with actually charging to allow us to punish ourselves in this fashion is an astounding testimony to tourist determination) and climbed to the top of the wall, where I was joined by quite a few other masochistic tourists.

I ambled about for a while, enjoying the beautiful views, and then started my journey around the city. What I had not counted on was how many stairs there were – up and down, up and down I went, clutching the handrail and hanging on to my billowing skirts; it was very windy up there, which provided a lovely relief from the heat except for the sail-like effect it had on my clothing, which threatened to blow me right off the ramparts.

About half way through my expedition, I came across a guard who pointed to a sign stating unequivocally that this was a one-way system, and I was clearly going the wrong way. How could this have happened? When I started walking, everyone was going every which way; I saw no sign stating that there was only one way to go. How could I have missed that memo? I suppose in the last bit of my hike, I had noticed that I was doing a very good impression of a salmon going upstream, but as that is not unusual in my life, I hadn't really paid much attention. I remember noting that it seemed an odd coincidence, but nothing more, as my life is full of mysteries, little and large.

In any case, when I wailed to the guard that I was already halfway round, and couldn't possibly go back and start over, he seemed to take into account my age, state of hysteria, and the possibility of my keeling over and causing an international incident by falling off said wall, and waved me to go ahead, commenting sagely, and accurately, as it turned out, "You will meet 1,000 people going the other way!" If the number of times I had to apologize to compliant tourists coming towards me on the rest of the walk is any indication, he was remarkably accurate in his estimation.

Clearly, it's a one-way system for a reason: the path atop the wall is so narrow that it can barely accommodate one person, much less two, especially two people going in opposite directions, one of whom is wearing a billowy skirt.

About three quarters of the way through, I was again confronted by a guard with a sign telling me I was going the wrong way. I share at least one trait with my pit bull – stubbornness – and I was not about to give up now. Perhaps it was the look on my face, or my wildly bedraggled appearance – all in black, hair flying everywhere in the wind, even though I had done my best to contain it – possibly he decided I was demented, concluded that discretion was the better part of valor, and decided this was not a hill he wanted to die on, so to speak, or maybe it was just too hot to argue, but this guard, too, waved me on after an exasperated casting of the eyes heavenward. The people here have been successfully repelling all boarders from this ancient fortification for hundreds, if not thousands of years, but thankfully they surrendered to this wrong-way Corrigan. Maybe it's the entertainment value.

I then refreshed myself with a mini-birdbath in Onofrio's fountain, although I strongly suspect from the looks I got that this was not the purpose for which Onofrio intended it, and headed back to the air-conditioned bus. Bliss. All the same, I think I might pass on the Great Wall of China; I'm guessing they're less flexible there.

252

A Length of Chain

YEARS AGO, WE LIVED IN GHANA, West Africa. About two weeks after we arrived, Kojo (our driver) and I were sent on a mission to buy a length of chain with which to secure our front gate.

But this was not America, where such an endeavor involves driving down to the local Ace Hardware, selecting a chain of the appropriate size and length, and going home. No; this was Ghana. We drove to downtown Accra, the capital city where we lived, which involved many detours to avoid the long lines of traffic always to be found on any main street at any given time of day.

We park the car at a gas station and begin our chain odyssey, walking down the street, dodging the odd chicken, goat, child, and street seller. I do my best to give the appearance of a submissive female, eyes downcast, behind Kojo; the reality is, I cannot walk fast enough to keep up with him and look down in order to avoid stepping into an open sewer, tripping over the occasional chunk of concrete or falling into a pothole (since there was nothing resembling a sidewalk, I suppose it is fair to say that the potholes were merely extensions of those in the road).

We trek down a long alley full of lean-tos and filth and more car parts than I have ever seen in my life: the automotive department. I am the only woman for miles, it seems, let alone the only obruni (white person), which appears to excite some speculation. I try to look knowledgeable, just as I do in similar circumstances in the States, although I wouldn't know a transmission from a radiator. Mercifully, we pass through the automotive department and on to scrap metal, where we briefly confer with a merchant who advises us that although he himself has no chain, he knows where we can get some.

We follow him down maze-like passages until I am sure we are in Zaire; I mention this to Kojo, who has a good laugh but keeps moving. We finally arrive at a shady junk-yard where, after some discussion, we are led to what looks like gigantic rusty anchor chain, at least 2 inches thick, which secures some three dozen tires. Kojo explains politely that this is a trifle larger than we had in mind. Not to worry; we are led further, to a well-dressed man who appears to be some sort of management personnel.

By now we have attracted a small crowd of some 2 dozen men; there is more debate, and we are led to yet more unsuitable chain.

This appears to exhaust the market's entire stock of chain. No problem, however; we are directed to Timba market (another trek all the way across town) where there is sure to be something suitable.

We hike through the 'wood department' at Timba, narrowly avoiding being whacked in the head by passing boards, and filling our shoes with sawdust. Kojo explains to the various wood salesmen who hiss at us and make kissing sounds (the common practice for attracting attention to one's wares, but fairly disconcerting) that we are not in the market, so to speak, for wood today. Eventually we locate the 'metals department' down another long and narrow dirt alley full of scrap metal.

Wonder of wonders, we locate a suitable length of chain almost immediately, and even more miraculously, shortly negotiate the price from 10,000 to 6,000 cedis (about $6.00)

Just as I am about to pay the merchant, a man arrives; there is a heated exchange in Akan (one of the native languages), and we abruptly move on. When I ask Kojo what happened, he explains that the man who sold us the chain was not, actually, by a technicality no doubt, the real owner; the man who arrived at the scene was the real owner, and not happy with our negotiated settlement. End of deal; end of chain.

We move to the next alley, several runners preceding us and a crowd following behind, where I am invited to inspect more varieties of rusty chain than I hope to ever see again in my lifetime. After much consultation by everyone, we decide on a suitable length of chain, the links of which are about half an inch thick. The owner brings out a hacksaw. I sit down; I may not know much about chain, but I have a rough idea how long this is going to take. After much advice from the crowd, and much unsuccessful sawing, an alternative is brought forth - a large railroad spike and a chunk of metal with which to beat it.

Eventually, the chunk of metal is exchanged for a sledge hammer and in a relatively brief time - voila! We have a length of suitable chain, and for only 4,000 cedis! We carry our prize back to the Land Rover in triumph. Buying our simple length of chain has taken three hours. Welcome to Ghana.

BLIND JUSTICE

AFTER HAVING BEEN IN GHANA for about six months, I was invited to accompany my husband's attorney, Benson, to court. We met in the National Supreme Court Building, built by the British in the late 1920's and apparently unaltered in any way since then. It was strongly reminiscent of a stable in its structure, except for the steep stairway with no elevator. As I waited, I was amazed to see lawyers and judges pass by in 100+ degree heat and almost 100% humidity in the traditional British court dress of high starched white collars, black wool suits covered by black robes, and white wool wigs. A woman lawyer I knew there related a story to me one day regarding these outfits: It seems that a Supreme Court Justice had died, and all members of the Bar were encouraged to attend the funeral in full court dress. The procession then exited the church and began the two or three mile walk to the cemetery. About half way there, my practical friend took off her robe and wig, and when criticized for doing so, replied tartly that she had no intention of joining the deceased in his grave. As it happened, one of the other justices, dressed in red velvet robe and wig, collapsed of heat stroke before reaching the cemetery and had to be taken by ambulance to the nearest hospital for treatment.

But back to my day in court: Benson drove me to court, and we parked in a spot reserved for a judge, apparently not concerned with parking niceties. We fought our way through a persistent swarm of flies and climbed a set of rickety outside stairs to a courtroom, where I sat with other spectators, defendants, lawyers and supporting family members on a backless wooden bench. I was able to trace the decorating history of the courtroom through at least four coats of peeling paint as a ceiling fan made painfully slow revolutions above our heads and lawyers conferred hurriedly before the judge's arrival. There was no air conditioning. As it happened, Benson discovered in conversation with other lawyers that his case had been called in his absence, so we left before the judge arrived. Benson showed me the calendar taped to the wall downstairs: all cases for the day are scheduled for 9 a.m.; attorneys arrive at 9 and wait, all day if necessary and sometimes into the next day, for their case to be called.

We went to another courtroom to observe a case in progress. Although English is the official language in Ghana, it is not the first language of most Ghanaians. In fact, quite a number of local dialects are spoken, so it is necessary to have translators in the courtroom at all times. I noticed Benson muttering to himself; eventually, even though it wasn't his case, he began whispering advice and instructions to the defense attorney, much to the annoyance of the prosecutor (a police woman), who hissed at him to stop helping the defendant. Benson whispered back that he was entitled to help if he wanted to, and suddenly the bailiff announced that the courtroom would be cleared. I wondered if Benson was about to be held in contempt of court, or if there had been a bomb threat or a military coup (you never know). Benson informed me, however, that the (female) judge needed to use the toilet. I stared at him blankly, until he elaborated: there was no toilet near the courtroom, or in the entire building, for that matter, so the judge would need to decamp to another building to use the facilities. When I expressed my surprise, Benson merely shrugged and remarked, "She's lucky; one of the other judges has to go all the way down the street to find a bathroom."

Eventually, court was reconvened. The case appeared to involve a charge of fraud; a woman claimed that the defendant had taken a sum of money from her with the promise of either buying diamonds or procuring a visa – I wasn't clear on whether the charges meant one or the other or both. After a great deal of discussion it was still unclear to everyone else, too, as far as I could tell. Suddenly, I noticed the absence of a court reporter. This omission was brought to my attention when the judge, after listening to the defendant's statement, held up a hand. The entire courtroom sat in silence as the judge copied down what the defendant had said into a large bound notebook. The prosecuting policewoman's questions, witnesses' testimony, lawyer's points, everything said in court was slowly, painstakingly copied in longhand by the judge into the book. Now I knew why every case was set for 9 a.m.; there was absolutely no way of predicting how long a hearing would last, except perhaps by timing the judge's writing speed. Benson informed me that there was some court-reporting equipment donated by the U.S. government sitting in a warehouse; it seems because the equipment was procured through the efforts of the Ghanaian Bar Association, and the Bar and the current Chief Justice were at loggerheads over something to the degree that the Bar was attempting to have the Chief Justice recalled, the government would not allow the equipment to be released. So, in every courtroom in Ghana, every proceeding is recorded in longhand by the judge. Upon reflection, it may not be practical for Ghana to have electronic recording equipment anyway; electricity is so intermittent here that court reporters would probably sit idle a great deal of the time. While we sat in court, the power went off, the fan went still, and the judge removed the proceedings to her chambers behind the courtroom – a dilapidated tiny room about five feet by 20 feet – because it had enough light through a small window to allow her to see what she was writing. When we left, a bailiff called Benson back into the judge's chambers; it seems my presence as the only white person in the room had been noted, and she wanted a full explanation as to my purpose in the (open) courtroom.

Some time later I had the opportunity to attend family court with my female lawyer friend, where the judge allowed me to sit in on some hearings, primarily child support and custody matters. These sessions were not recorded in any form, and were conducted in local dialects rather than in English for the most part, but at one point the judge interrupted a child support hearing to question the woman's lawyer regarding an entirely unrelated matter. The lawyer was a member of FIDA, an international association of female lawyers, and the judge wanted to berate her about a case in which a man was arrested in the middle of the night for spousal abuse; as a result of his arrest, the children's school fees had not been paid. This, said the judge, was disruptive to the family system, and attorneys in general and FIDA members in particular (who concentrate their efforts on indigent women) should be very careful about interfering in family relationships. "But, your worship," responded the attorney calmly, "the woman was severely beaten with an object, resulting in her hospitalization." "Yes, well of course, he should not have used an object to beat her, but…" Apparently it's all right to beat your wife, as long as you don't use an object to do it. I was reminded of the old English law that you could use a stick to beat your wife, but only if it was no bigger around than your thumb – hence the expression "rule of thumb", which I ceased using after learning of its origin.

Occasionally I reflect back to the brief time that I was a law clerk in Nevada, complaining if the temperature in the office varied more than five degrees from my comfort zone, or if a case were delayed or had to be rescheduled, or a particular transcript wasn't available when I needed it. We have no idea how lucky we are here in the United States.

COMMUNICATIONS

SHORTLY AFTER WE MOVED to Ghana in April, my husband opened negotiations for a telephone. I say "negotiations" because, although he thought he was ordering a telephone system, he was actually only beginning the process by which one obtains a telephone there - if one is lucky enough to get a telephone at all. Where we're from, it's a simple business; you generally call the telephone company and ask them to connect a line. They give you your new number, and within a few days - voila! The rest of the world is at your fingertips. But this was Ghana.

First, my beloved ordered a telephone system from Seatec (a private company which installs telephone lines): six lines and eight extensions, for the business and our home, which happen to be in the same building. Next, he ordered three telephone lines from Post and Telecommunication (P&T). Upon inquiry, however, a slight complication arose - good news, and bad news. The good news was, a line to the house already existed; the bad news was that the previous tenants had left an outstanding bill of three million cedis (about $2000) which we would have to pay to have the line reconnected. It was actually cheaper in the long run (one million cedis) to pay P&T to install a new line, so this was done. Seatec was paid $5,000 to install their system as well.

By the time we showed up in mid-July, there were still no telephones. By August, after much more negotiating, P&T delivered a cell-phone, a crackly, cranky device that worked on alternate Thursdays if it was in the mood and tended to cut you off altogether in the middle of a conversation when it felt like it. Two tin cups and a string would have been just about as effective. In fact, we had friends in the next block that we could hear more clearly if we both got on the roof and shouted back and forth.

258

When informed of this unsatisfactory situation, P&T assured us ("By all means") that a new system was forthcoming. Meanwhile, Seatec did, indeed, install their promised system (consisting of eight extensions and three lines). My husband and his business manager, who claimed to be close friends with powerful people at P&T, paid them a visit. They were directed to chairs at one end of a room full of other people sitting in chairs.

About every half hour someone would be summoned to the inner sanctum, and the rest of the group would rise and move up one chair. In time my beloved and the business manager were interviewed briefly, assured a telephone line was forthcoming, and ushered out the door.

Innumerable visits to various P&T offices throughout Accra yielded no observable improvements in the situation. My hubby was finally persuaded to hire a "fixit man" (read 'crook'), who shall remain nameless, to procure telephone lines. By September, at a cost of about $500 each, four phone lines were installed, and the cell-phone was discarded.

Unfortunately, this was not the end of our troubles.

In December we began to notice a lack of incoming faxes. After waiting a week to be sure this was not due to an oversight, we checked with P&T and discovered they had, apparently arbitrarily, changed the fax number without bothering to notify us of this fact. They were, however, kind enough to give us the new number when we enquired.

The following July, the main international telephone line suddenly stopped working. When anyone tried to use it, a recording would come on stating that the line had been disconnected due to non-payment of the bill.

Now, we get eight separate telephone bills from P&T, one for each of the four local lines and also one each for the four long distance lines. These are not itemized or detailed in any way - simply a total figure owed is supplied for each - although we've heard a rumor that for a large fee, you may be able to get an itemized long-distance bill. When my beloved's new business manager, Rosemary, researched the matter, it appeared that we had not yet received this particular bill. She went down to P&T to explain the situation and get the bill and was told, to her surprise, that the bill hadn't been prepared yet. But she was informed, if she would pay the bill, they would be happy to give it to her. How Rosemary sorted all this out I will never know, but sort it out she must have, because the line was shortly re-connected.

It is now September and the fax line is once again dead. Ominously, we have received no communication regarding its demise - not even a recording. This is not, of course, unusual; after a while you get used to telephone numbers being changed or disconnected, seemingly at random, whether bills are paid or not. Almost weekly, friends get together to update telephone numbers; business cards generally leave a space for the telephone number so that you can fill it in as needed. All of our personal telephone books are in pencil, and the first and last official phone directory is now six years old. It's also quite common to get a recording: "All lines to this area are busy, or the customer has temporarily turned off his phone. Please try again later." Although the recording, like most Ghanaians, is invariably polite, you get to hate the sound of it so much that it's generally easier to just drive to see those you want to talk to. Anything, any missed appointment or social gaffe, can be explained by merely referring to a problem with either the telephone system or the traffic.

If by chance you should get through, your troubles are not yet over. Ghanaians, as I've mentioned, are invariably polite, so prepare yourself for the following conversation:

Callee:	"Hello"
Caller:	"Hello"
Callee:	"Hello"
Caller:	"Hello"
Callee:	"Yes, what is it you want?"
Caller:	"Hello - good morning"

You grit your teeth, growl "Good morning", and generally, if you're lucky, you get down to business at this point. Unless, of course, the caller kindly inquires as to your health, or wishes to discuss the weather.

A friend reported a conversation wherein she asked our secretary to take a message for me. My friend gave her a rather complicated message, and asked if she'd gotten all that. The secretary replied, "No, Madam." (All white women in Ghana are referred to as "Madam". It's quite unnerving). My friend asked why. The secretary replied that she had no pen. My friend asked if she had a pencil. "No, Madam." "Well, go and get one then." The message was repeated. "Did you get that?" "No, Madam." "Well, why on earth not?" "My pencil lead has broken, Madam." "Never mind, I'll just come 'round to see her."

It is best to take comfort in the fact that someone manages to get through occasionally, and to realize that at least it's faster than the mail service. Usually.

CULINARY DELIGHTS

THE COOK WAS SCHEDULED to arrive in September, but this is Ghana after all, where goats wander at will down the middle of the highway, you trip over chickens about every other step, and it takes six months to get a telephone installed and then it only works alternate Thursdays, if it's in the mood. The rest of the time it rings twice and disconnects when you pick it up. Alternatively, when you dial a number, it mulls it over for a while, and then disconnects. It's diabolical, and threatening it has no appreciable effect. Electricity is intermittent, water is haphazard and it took me a solid week of looking to locate a bottle of propane. This was crucial as the gas-powered stove works, but not the electric oven, and as we have no cook yet, if I don't want to starve the children, I need the stove for the 87 variations on a theme of macaroni and cheese I make in one of the two pots I own at present, as our things haven't even left the US yet after six months, let alone made the ocean journey or sat on the docks while we haggle with customs agents. We might even get our own belongings back from them by Christmas if the price is right.

In any case, the cook, Stella, finally actually arrived. It didn't take her long to assess the situation; I could almost see her rolling her eyes. She clearly has developed a deep and abiding disdain for my total lack of culinary skills and utensils. She is less than thrilled with the refrigerator and her accommodation (we converted the garage), but so far deigns to stay, no doubt out of pity. She knows, as an animal senses your weaknesses, that I would commit any act short of murder (and maybe even that) to keep her here, and cooking, such is my desperation.

She is the only person I've met who can actually recognize a ripe papaya when she sees one. Most of the time I don't even know what I'm eating, much less how to cook it, although the universal recipe here appears to be "mash it up, boil it, and make a soup out of it". I've eaten cocoa-yam leaf stew (quite tasty), yam balls and yam chips (yams are one of the few indigenous crops, as you may have guessed). I have not, however, succumbed to the attractions of fufu, which is best described as roughly equivalent to bread dough. Another local delicacy is kenke - all I know is that it is something wrapped in leaves and have so far resisted any impulse I might have felt to investigate further. The only other thing I've seen that comes wrapped in leaves is snails, but they're easily recognized, as they appear to be stretched to abnormal lengths while still attached to their shells. For a treat, I suppose one could try "grass-cutter", a local delicacy that you will find being sold by the side of the road; look for what appears to be a flattened squirrel or some other large, paper-thin rodent on a stick.

In order to placate Stella, we invested in a small freezer; unfortunately, the day after we stocked it the power went out for 36 hours and we discovered what poor insulation a freezer can have. As the pork roast slowly thawed and the ice cream melted into oblivion, Stella frantically cooked everything she could find. She is not impressed with the freezer, either.

Menus are a problem as well. Every morning she corners me in the kitchen, looks me in the eye and throws down the gauntlet. "What would madam like for dinner tonight?" I smile feebly, "Why, anything you'd like, Stella. You're such a wonderful cook, everything you make is delicious," which is true, but it does not satisfy her. She raises her face heavenward in despair of me and proceeds to whip up one of her many specialties: pizza, curry, cakes, cookies, chicken dishes, burritos - the list is virtually endless. I have been known to scour the town for ingredients I've never heard of to keep Stella, if not happy, at least mollified. Either she has a naturally morose disposition or working for us has sent her into the depths of a semi-permanent depression.

In the interests of defraying costs and possibly getting semi-fresh produce, we have started a garden in the back yard. While we undoubtedly feed the entire city through our generous staff, who distribute it liberally, we may also get carrots more than two inches long. In addition, I plan to have a chicken coop built and begin chicken farming in earnest. Fresh eggs would be lovely, and when the chickens are through laying, we have a source of cheap dinner, providing I can convince someone to wring their little necks; I can guarantee it won't be me. Upon reflection, we may start the world's first chicken retirement home. Perhaps we should become vegetarians.

FEATHERED FRIENDS

WHEN WE HAD BEEN in Ghana a few months, I decided it would be a good idea to raise some chickens. Of course, the closest I'd ever been to a chicken was the meat counter at the supermarket in America, but no matter. Besides, my father's family had been ranchers - it must be in the blood (they raised cattle, mind you, but these are petty details; chickens are smaller - they should be even easier to deal with). I saw chickens of every description wandering the streets of Accra, the capital city, looking fat and happy (the chickens, that is) - how difficult could it be?

The first task, of course, was to build a coop - even I knew that. Unfortunately, I hadn't the slightest idea how to construct one. Research - that was the sensible approach. I remembered seeing a picture of one somewhere. Suddenly, it struck me where I had seen it. I raced to my 5 year-old daughter's room. Yes, there it was, in one of her books, - "Spot's First Easter" - a chicken coop. I studied it carefully - no problem: simple, comfortable, practical.

I spent the next three months trying to locate a carpenter who spoke English well enough to comprehend my explanations without charging me a fortune. When I finally found Victor, he was sick or busy every other day and had to be fetched from the heart of Accra in heavy traffic, but never mind. In a mere three months, I had my coop, and a magnificent coop it was - a veritable poultry penthouse. Covered with a lovely tin roof, with separate compartments upstairs for laying and downstairs for socializing, chicken wire (what else?) on the front hinged door to keep the dogs out - what more could any self-respecting chicken desire? Which reminded me - now I needed the chickens.

I proudly installed the coop in the back yard and began researching the project - what type of chickens to buy, and where to get them. Well, that was easy; I wanted layers. The whole idea was to get fresh, cheap eggs, right? The next question, apparently, was how old I wanted the chickens to be. Certainly not too young - I didn't want to spend a lot of money on feed before they started to lay. And not too old, or they wouldn't lay either, I'd been told. Besides, the beauty of my plan was that after a year or so of laying, when production showed signs of slowing, we would simply dispatch them and eat them - how beautifully economical and thoroughly ecological! So, I told Kojo, our driver and the fountain and source of all knowledge, that I wanted sort of post–pubescent, adolescent chickens. He looked at me blankly. You know, teenage chickens. Comprehension dawned.

Yes, of course, he knew just the place to find them. Downtown. I sighed. I knew what that meant - hours of fighting Accra high street traffic. Never mind - we'd done that before. And I was so close to my goal at last! Fresh eggs, the gentle clucking of contented chickens, the sweet "peeping" of the babies - a cottage industry would no doubt be hatched. Kojo thoughtfully rounded up a few boxes, and downtown we went.

Naturally, the chicken sellers had been moved by police order from the corner they had inhabited since time immemorial, but after a few inquires, we bumped down a red dirt road with potholes the size of Sherman tanks, parked, and continued our journey on foot past open sewers, over a raised railroad track, and into an open market, where a few scrawny chickens were held up for our inspection. Upon enquiry, however, they were discovered to be broilers, not layers. We were given further instructions on how to find laying chickens.

We hiked back to the car and honked our way down a maze of narrow lanes to another market where, we were assured, there were chickens of every size and description, and sure enough, there were. When I enquired as to whether these were sure to be layers, the seller flipped a chicken upside down and began moving aside feathers from her nether regions, pointing and insisting vociferously that these were indeed laying chickens - healthy, happy, motherly types. After requesting the chicken be turned upright in order to insure her future happiness, we began bargaining in earnest. Eventually we ended up with six layers - presumably imported, as the next two we purchased were described as "local" - and, just for good measure, two guinea fowl, which I had been told made excellent eating, as well as laying quite tasty eggs.

Our negotiations complete, Kojo stuffed the chickens into the boxes and then the car, and we were off. The chickens were obviously healthy; in no time at all they had freed themselves from the confines of the boxes and were fluttering maniacally about the car, pooping indiscriminately. Sitting in traffic in a small car with no air conditioning in 100+ degree heat with six cackling, pooping, loose chickens and two guinea fowl is enough to put a sensible person off eggs for the rest of his or her life. Needless to say, we proceeded with the plan, and finally reached the house. Kojo off-loaded chickens and parked the car while our three dogs decided they were born to hunt feathered fowl. They went straight for the hens and pandemonium reigned as Kojo and I beat on dogs and pried open their jaws to remove various chicken parts. When the dust and feathers finally settled, we had one slightly wounded chicken and three abject but hungry dogs.

When we finally, triumphantly bore our prizes to their new home, we discovered a small flaw in the coop design - it was several feet off the ground, and the chickens had no way of getting into the coop. We stuffed them in their laying boxes to recover from their ordeal and sat down to contemplate this new hitch in the plan. Obviously, we didn't want to spend our lives acting as chicken elevators, but how else to protect them from the dogs and get them into their little home after a day of contented pecking? The veterinarian we enlisted (and should have consulted in the beginning) came up with the ideal (and obvious, to anyone with a brain) solution - stairs. He also suggested several other practical alterations to the coop, along with a more reliable carpenter, and (at more expense) voila! A chicken apartment block with a ramp! And a fenced yard, even!

Our travails were not yet over, however; the chickens began to look a bit peaked (distinguishing a peaked-looking chicken from a normal-looking one is not my area of expertise, but the staff seemed to know). One by one they began their inevitable deterioration and eventual demise (the chickens, not the staff).

Frantic, I prevailed upon Dr. Tettey, the vet, to make a coop call. He diagnosed a respiratory disease and an antibiotic that cost more than our malaria medicine. Only I would end up with chickens with a respiratory infection - ever seen a chicken gasp for air? It's not a nice thing to see – or to experience, I would imagine. Dr Tettey also informed me that our two local layers were actually broilers (the fittest and healthiest - looking of the lot, naturally) and that the layers were well past their prime and would probably never produce more than the one egg we'd had from them. My theory was that I'd bought geriatric chickens and they'd died of old age.

I am now left with two broilers, one sniffly, non-laying chicken and two guinea fowl, one of which is a male. The one egg laid, as a last gasp effort by one anonymous chicken, is probably the most expensive egg ever produced, when the cost of feed, coop and renovations to same, fencing, antibiotics, veterinarian consultations, to say nothing of the original purchase price, are factored in. I could have, for the same amount of cedis, undoubtedly supplied the entire population of Accra with eggs for life. The one female guinea fowl, on the other hand, has laid ten tasty eggs in two weeks. I have the distinct feeling I shall shortly be making a guinea- fowl purchasing expedition.

GETTING THERE

GHANAIANS SEEM TO BELIEVE with an almost religious fervor that the shortest distance between two points is a corkscrew. The "direct" routes are tortuous enough to make the average person insane, but in order to avoid the ubiquitous traffic jams, even more devious detours must be taken. In the end, I haven't the slightest idea where I am, much less how I arrived there. Admittedly, I am a person who gets hopelessly lost in department stores (I appear to be "directionally impaired", according to my husband, or perhaps "geographically challenged"), but it really is too much to ask me to find my way in a city where they don't even bother with street signs most of the time, and if they do, the name changes half-way down the road anyway. If you stop to ask directions of a local resident and they happen to understand what you're asking, it usually transpires that they don't know the name of the street they live on, much less the number you happen to be looking for.

Many roads on the map appear to have no name; sometimes the ones that are marked are closed, and occasionally we stumble across roads that don't appear on the map at all. People tend to give directions in terms of landmarks or named or numbered roundabouts: "Go to Akuafo Circle." "Is that the 47th military roundabout?" "No, I think it's the 37th. Whatever. Anyway, you go straight across there, past the Four Flowers fruit stand..." Or: "Go to Danquah circle, to the Flash Photo Shop (there are two, directly across from one another, naturally), past the banana seller, turn left at Kwatson's."

The directions to our house, for instance, are as follows: Route (1): Take a right at Gold House. This will put you onto Patrice Lumumba Road, although there's no sign to inform you of that; turn left on Ridge Road (or the "Hydro" sign, whichever you see first); take a right on Sir Arku Korsah (your first right, and the street, not the person); left on Nortei Ababio (whatever happened to Elm street, Main street, something I can spell? I suppose I should be grateful I'm living in Accra instead of Ouagadougou); take the second left after that (I've never been able to find out the street name); your first right after that is Nme Lane - we're number 85, but there's no number, so look for the green gates, providing we haven't painted them by then. Alternatively (and probably more successfully), follow the signs for Frandesco + Partner all the way; we're between them and an empty lot. Route Number Two is simpler but involves turning left when you see two red trucks on your right, which appear to be permanent fixtures; however, this may be a risky assumption, so we will dispense with this route for the time being. Besides, that road is now closed.

No one bothers to signal their intentions, which is just as well as they would, in all probability, not do what they've indicated they were going to in any case. Most people tend to be hesitantly aggressive drivers; they pull out in front of you, then stop and wait for your permission to cut you off. Taxi drivers are notorious risk takers, darting in and out in front of everyone in order to pick up and drop off passengers, especially near signs reading "Military Zone - No picking of passengers "(presumably this means they must take whomever they can get, with no discrimination allowed). Taxis also have slogans painted on their vehicles, such as "I am covered in the blood of Jesus", which I found rather alarming. Conventional wisdom is that if you see an accident, you'll find a taxi in the near vicinity; he's either directly involved, or he caused it.

First aid boxes are required in all vehicles, although rumor has it that the taxi drivers just paint an empty box white with a red cross and display it prominently in the back window. It seems to work. One day a taxi stopped in the middle of an intersection - an almost suicidal action here - and refused to move despite the acrimonious response from the other drivers. Eventually it became clear that he couldn't continue because his right front wheel was stuck in an open sewage drain about 2 feet deep. No problem; all six or seven passengers - men in business suits carrying briefcases - hopped out, picked up the taxi, literally lifting it out of the hole, climbed back in, and continued on their way. The potholes are truly impressive. It's gotten to be quite a challenge to avoid them; a bit like driving an obstacle course at top speed. As my father pointed out gently once when we were traveling in Kenya, it would actually be easier to drive if they would simply remove the small bits of pavement between the potholes.

The horn serves a variety of functions: it is used to frighten the life out of pedestrians so that they will get out of the middle of the street (it's considered bad manners to not at least give them a sporting chance to get out of your way); to warn parked cars not to pull out in front of you as you drive past; to open a gate to let you in; to indicate that you wish to make a turn in front of someone, or alternatively, by them to signal that you may do so; and even occasionally when another driver has done something particularly stupid and annoying, and you wish to convey the impression that you are not pleased. One of my favorite signs is a variation on "Quiet; hospital zone": "Hospital: no hooting" which presumably means either no honking, or else no owls allowed unless they are appropriately muzzled.

Everyone is also required to carry warning triangles and fire extinguishers, which is a handy excuse for the police to graciously accept a bribe to avoid giving you a major fine if you haven't got the required items. Rarely have I seen the triangles used, however; usually the technique is the same one I saw in Kenya: a few tree branches in the road held down by large rocks at intervals before the scene of the breakdown. And breakdowns are common; what is truly amazing is how a great many of these vehicles manage to keep running at all. In fact, I am convinced that if taxi drivers spent half as much time maintaining their vehicles as they do in cleaning them, the number of broken-down (but clean) cars in Ghana would decrease dramatically. I have driven behind an amazing variety of wobbling wheels, black smoke pouring from the exhaust, car barely able to creep along, bits falling off practically as I watch; its purely miraculous that they're moving at all. Some of them proceed sideways, in a crab-like fashion, due to some serious chassis problem that will probably never be repaired.

At least I can see them; there are plenty of what my husband calls "stealth vehicles". These can be anything from a taxi to a tractor, traveling in the pitch-black night with not a single light to be seen, and no such thing as a street lamp to be had. It's truly vitalizing to come upon one of these invisible vehicles at sixty miles an hour on a highway late at night.

My goal is to become more independent by obtaining my driver's license. When I go to the local equivalent of the DMV, however, I discover why the driving in Ghana is so erratic: no one actually takes a driving test. A driver's license, like most other things here, is a commodity you buy.

Going Bush

WE STARTED OUT ONLY an hour and a half late for our trip north, which meant that we were late for our landlord's father's funeral; although we've never met him (that is, the landlord's father, not the landlord; him, we know), it is considered a mark of respect to attend, so we fit it into our schedule. Although we missed the actual burial itself, we did arrive in time for the rest of the proceedings. Apparently, the rest consists primarily of shaking hands with everyone in town in an anticlockwise direction, which appears to be quite important, although I never did discover why. Although our landlord, Mr. Amoako, was "chief mourner", it became unclear who were the actual guests of honor, Mr. Amoako or ourselves, as the only obrunis (white people) present. After a few rounds of handshaking and sitting in the sun, surrounded by people dressed in black and red (the colors of mourning here), shaking hands some more and making small talk, we moved across the street to where the band was setting up (for what later evolved into a sort of afternoon karaoke program). We were ceremoniously seated under an awning; a crowd of small children materialized to stare at us and smile shyly, some goat poop was removed, and drinks were served all round.

Large groups of men made the epic journey to the toilet when our young son announced the need, and it was conveyed to us discreetly after an interval that our duties had been fulfilled. We were presented with a bill for only 15,000 cedis (about $15) for the honor of helping with the funeral expenses, at which point I was immensely relieved that we were not guests of honor and chief mourners; that position is apparently reserved for the richest person involved (in this case, Mr. Amoako, fortunately), and is based on ability to pay, as the chief mourner picks up the entire tab. Our respects duly paid, we moved on to the camp at Nsawkaw and the company geologists' home sweet home.

It has all the mod cons (my beloved's phrase for "modern conveniences") now - an outdoor non-flush toilet, open air shower, candlelight (no electricity), and one room with screened windows. And the cook, Benjamin, makes excellent ground-nut stew, oatmeal, and yams with mushroom sauce.

We drove up to Bui the next day, to the end of the road, and inspected the place where the Russians had intended to build a dam but gave it up some 30 years ago. We visited a very tidy village, where as always the children were entranced and not a little frightened at the sight of our white children. They showed us the traps (wooden cages) and dugout canoes used for fishing and were thrilled when I took their pictures.

Next day we headed for the game park at Mole, hoping to see wild animals in the flesh. We hadn't even made it to the outskirts of the park when we saw our first "wild animal": a 10-foot long python stretched along the road. I gabbled incomprehensively enough to communicate that I'd seen something unusual, and we backed up (not over the snake, I might add) for a better view. It hadn't moved, and after careful and extended examination (from a safe distance, of course), we concluded that it was dead, having been shot. We all piled out of the car to admire and exclaim (although I share the almost universal Ghanaian indiscriminate loathing and distrust of all things reptilian) over the enormous snake and had the children stand near it "for scale" so we could take photos "Stand a little closer, dear, so we can see you and the snake together". Suddenly it moved and six bodies of various sizes hurtled faster than the speed of light into the Land Rover where we sat, doors locked, quaking in our sandals. While the python may have been mortally wounded, it was most definitely not yet dead.

I am forced to admit to having no memory of grasping my beloved children to my bosom before scrambling to the safety of the car, but my husband assures me they were there before we were. Their memories of the incident may vary, but they were very young and no doubt do not have clear recall of the event.

After arriving at the game park, we gratefully unloaded our belongings at the motel and went off to what would be the first of many variations on a theme of chicken: chicken and rice, chicken and yam chips, chicken and pasta, etc. We arrived at this conclusion after asking for various items on the 8-page menu, only to be told, "Sorry, madam, it is finished", meaning they did not at present have that particular dish, although I began to realize after the fourth or fifth time that these items were never going to materialize. Finally my beloved cut to the chase by simply enquiring what was available, to be answered with the above three or four variations on a theme of chicken.

Unfortunately, we had made the mistake of leaving the light on in our room while we were at dinner, and discovered the infinite variety of insects that can mange to crawl through a screen toward the lights, where they promptly die and land on the bed. After a night spent sweeping off sheets and swatting bugs, we had breakfast and headed off to see some wild animals in the morning.

At about 9 am we saw some elephant tracks in the mud. We were able to examine them quite minutely for about 12 hours, as a matter fact, as the Land Rover sank up to its axles in mud and we became immobilized. While Nelson the driver, my beloved and the other geologist accompanying us sweated, slopping around in mud up to their ankles, jacked up the car (several times), shoveled mud and wedged various objects under the tires, the children and I sang Eensy Beensy Spider, 99 Bottles of Beer on the Wall, The Ants Go Marching One by One, and The Twelve Days of Christmas until I actually remembered all the verses. When the jack slipped and the car fell the wrong way for the last time, Nelson and the geologist set off to walk the five or so miles back to relative civilization, killing a potentially poisonous snake on the way.

Having run out of the water we always brought everywhere with us, my beloved went off to get some ditch water to drink, surprising the only other wildlife spotted on the outing - a three foot crocodile who was a little too close for comfort and decided to leave as abruptly as my hubby did - thankfully in opposite directions. I would like to add that while I became nauseated even drinking filtered water from the tap at home in in Accra, swallowing much ditch water formerly occupied by a crocodile did not even phase my beloved's digestive system, which I found truly impressive.

By nightfall we decided help wouldn't arrive until morning, so we settled down for the night. Between slapping mosquitoes, I began an epic made-up tale in an attempt to put the children to sleep, but it backfired; even my husband became interested, and when I started to drop off to sleep or silently tried to decide what happened next, they all clamored to hear more.

Fortunately, help arrived before I became completely befuddled: a Land Rover with bald tires containing nine Ghanaians who literally lifted us out of the mud. When we returned to the hotel, tired and hungry at about 10 p.m., they had actually kept dinner for us. Chicken never tasted so good.

We emerged from the adventure no worse for the experience aside from the fact that the mosquitoes had found us so tasty that it would be three weeks before I could shave my legs without requiring a blood transfusion. The family still nags me to finish the story begun while in the truck, and the children, much to their father's mortification, still stop complete strangers to regale them with the tale of being stuck in the mud and attacked by poisonous snakes and crocodiles. Their last words to us before falling asleep at night are invariably "Don't get stuck in the mud!"

HIGHER LEARNING

I DECIDED TO APPLY to the graduate program at Legon University in Accra while living in Ghana, having not much better to do to fill my time. After several unsuccessful trips there I actually manage to speak to the head of the English Department, one Mr. Denkabe, who tells me there will be no problem admitting me to the program. I hasten to inform him that although my undergraduate degree is in Psychology, not English, I do have a strong background in English. He stops me. "There will be no difficulty. I will recommend that you be admitted, and they will admit you." Gee, I think; no resume, no letters of reference, no transcripts, no copies of degrees or credentials, no begging essay to write; this is the easiest application process I've ever been through! Little did I know that my troubles were only beginning.

Although I had heard the easy-going Mr. Denkabe briefly mention 'buying the application', the words at the time did not have the ominous ring they later acquired. When I inquire as to where I might obtain the application, I am directed to the registrar's office, logically enough; a Mr. Kornu will be happy to help me. And where would I find Mr. Kornu? No problem - up the stairs, turn left down a long corridor, left again, up more stairs, down another long corridor, and look for the sign on the door. Several wrong turns later I arrive, puffing, at Mr. Kornu's office (now knowing why everyone here is so thin). Regrettably, Mr. Kornu is at a meeting. By now, it is close to lunch, so I give up for the day.

Next day I return to the fray. Regretfully, Mr. Kornu is still not in, but someone helpfully informs me that he is not the person I need to see in any case. I am directed to the cashier's office at the opposite end of the campus. When I arrive there and request, between gasps, an application, there is a brief conference. It appears the cashier's office is not the right place, either. I am instructed to go to academic affairs, which is, of course, back in the area I have just left.

I get directions, arriving breathless once again, only to be told to go to the cashier's office. No, no! I protest, I have just come from there! Oh, well then, you must go to see Mr. Kornu in the registrar's... no, I have just been there too, I insist. Casting about desperately for a place to send me where I have not already been, they have an agitated discussion and happily suggest the Graduate Studies Department. I trudge to this locale (mercifully, only half-way across the campus) where I discover that I need to speak to Mr. Datay. Unfortunately, Mr. Datay is in a meeting (with Mr. Kornu and Mr. Denkabe, no doubt). When shall I try again? Tomorrow morning. I go home and set aside 9 am to noon every day for a week for Legon University.

By now I am in what my mother refers to as my 'bulldog' mode; I am a woman with a mission. I don't even care whether I get the damn degree any more, but I will be admitted, by heaven! I will, at the very least, obtain an application!

Next day I arrive bright and early at Mr. Datay's office in Graduate Studies. He is, regretfully, not in just at the moment, but his assistant will be happy to help me. When I explain my situation, the assistant frowns, looks harassed, and tells me in no uncertain terms that applications are no longer being ac-cepted for this year. "But Mr. Denkabe said it was all right," I wail. Then I must get Mr. Denkabe to write a letter to the dean explaining why there are special circumstances existing in my case to make an exception, he responds unsympathetically. I am beginning to feel crass and frustrated enough to wave a checkbook and yell, "Name your price!" Instead I simply grit my teeth, smile politely, and return to the English Department.

By this time Mr. Denkabe's secretary, Agnes, and I are on a first-name basis. She looks up in some surprise and says "You have returned!" I assume that by this time most prospective students have fallen into an exhausted heap somewhere along the well-worn path between the English department and Graduate Studies. But I am made of sterner stuff - pioneer stock, by God! I explain my current difficulty and Agnes sends me to Mr. Denkabe. He shakes his head and clucks sympathetically; by now, I have learned my lesson and have obtained the name of Mr. Datay's obstructive second, Mr. Adumuah, which I give to Mr. Denkabe. "It would have been better if you had spoken to Mr. Datay". I am sure this is true, which is, no doubt, precisely why he employs Mr. Adumuah: to frighten the faint-hearted into abject failure. It is clear, as I remain seated and silent, that I intend to become a permanent fixture in Mr. Denkabe's office in true Ghanaian style; with a sigh, he drafts a letter and dispatches me once again to Mr. Datay's office. Mr. Adumuah heads me off with a mean smile; Mr. Datay's meeting is an extensive one, it appears. I give him a shark smile in return and produce the letter from my pocket. He grins in capitulation and tells me to come back tomorrow morning. I do so, and am actually admitted to the inner sanctum - to the presence of Mr. Datay himself.

In great excitement, I hear him say that he will give me the forms - triumph! It is short-lived, however; he informs me that I must complete three applications, obtain three letters of reference, send for my transcripts (from five different universities in two different states, fees to be paid in US dollars, which I don't have). Never mind; I fill out my forms in triplicate over the weekend, obtain passport photos and 30,000 cedis, and take everything into the cashier's office on Monday. Sorry, the cashier tells me, we cannot accept cedis from foreigners. I stand mute, monetarily stunned. 'But I live here. All I have are cedis!' 'Are you paid in cedis?' he inquires. - Well, no; we are paid in dollars in an American account, which are then transferred into a cedi account here in Accra, so I have no dollars. No matter; I must pay in dollars.

So I drive in pouring rain to the nearest bank, which is, naturally, closed, continue on to a forex (change bureau), where at great cost I exchange 36,150 cedis into $30, return to the University, and pay the application fee. My application is duly stamped, and I return it to Mr. Datay, who will process it appropriately, I am sure. I await word from on high.

Meanwhile, all the professors are on strike; there may not even be a fall semester. A luta continua (the struggle continues)!

ONE DAY

THE FOLLOWING IS A DIARY entry made when our two children were small and we lived in a very nice, 10-bedroom house in Accra, Ghana. In fact, when my husband called me from Ghana to announce that he had found a house for us, and that it had ten bedrooms, I was aghast; were we going to open an orphanage, I enquired? But he hastened to inform me that the lower floor would be used as office space, while the basement would house unfortunate visiting geologists. Each bedroom had its own bathroom, with the toilet on a pedestal, but it's not quite as luxurious as it sounds. Our bathroom, for instance, was in such dire need of renovation that when I called in a friend to help me decide on décor, she gazed about for a bit, then remarked, "Well, I know one thing: you don't need a magazine rack, because staying in here for any longer than is absolutely necessary is not going to happen." I suppose the fact that the blue toilet did not match the green tub or the teal washstand might have put her off, but I'm guessing it was more likely the brown walls with large orange circles.

Accra, Ghana, West Africa, about 1996:

My husband left yesterday afternoon, and at 7:30 this morning the power went off and has stayed off all day. Stella, the cook, can't cook without power, so we eat yam balls and watermelon.

The computers are down, of course, so no office work is done.

The freezer we bought this week and promptly filled is slowly defrosting, as we still have no generator (of course, this happens in the States, too, but not nearly as often). At about 6:00 pm. the power comes back on, and I get a phone call from someone in Houston trying to send a fax just as the children erupt into hysterics. Houston, we've got a problem. I've just about calmed them down (the children, that is) and explained our troubles to Houston when our secretary calls to tell me not to answer the phone as someone is trying to send a fax.

The security guard (yes, we have a security guard – several, in fact, and for good reason; the day after we arrived, someone broke in and stole all of my husband's work computers) comes upstairs to announce: "Madam (all Ghanaians refer to all white women as "madam", despite repeated entreaties not to), the French teacher is here".

French teacher? I don't know any French teachers. I don't remember asking for a French teacher, and my memory is not yet nearly as bad as it will become later. But this is a place where bizarre random events are commonplace. In any case, I decide, why not? I interview him and decide French lessons might be a good idea. I tell him to come back Thursday night when my husband is here. Meanwhile the three new puppies have pooped diarrhea all over the mat, so I rinse it off. Two strange men show up in the living room requesting something to drink.

"Who are you?"

"We have been working on the radio. We have eaten our dinner and now we are thirsty."

What am I, the neighborhood soup kitchen? I didn't even know we had a radio, much less that people were here fixing it. I open the cupboard to get cups (why not?) and the door falls off. I hand out the water and cups and tell them to leave the cups downstairs when they are through; it would be so nice to have five minutes alone in my own house. Well, my rented house.

I still don't know how to set the computer to fax or transfer the phones upstairs, and I feel nauseous (a common occurrence – you never really know why; it could be the water, or the malaria medication, or it could be malaria. Or it could be intestinal dysentery – hard to say); my daughter (age five) is running around in her undies and my son (age three) is shouting that he has to go potty right now! Suddenly the two strange men appear in my living room again—although by now they're beginning to feel like old friends—water bottles and cups in hand, asking for 4,000 cedis (local currency – about $4) for taxi fare. We're not that friendly yet, I decide.

"Why?"

"Because we have finished our work and our master has not come back to take us home."

I cruelly send them off empty-handed, although I discover later that our staff has donated 4000 cedis to the taxi fund, so I reimburse them. I lecture the watchmen about the inadvisability of letting strangers into the house. My son falls asleep on my shoulder in his T-shirt as I read the children a story. I put them to bed, lock up, and fall into bed.

Another day in our tropical paradise.

RENOVATIONS

ONE NIGHT AS I LAY reading in bed in our home in Ghana, I detected a fishy odor; surely it hadn't been that long since I'd had a shower. After a while I began to smell something burning, and I deduced someone had now overcooked their fish. Suddenly, I heard odd popping sounds on the other side of the room. When I investigated, I discovered flames shooting from the outlet into which the air conditioner was plugged. Advancing cautiously and trying desperately to remember which materials were non-conductors, I grabbed a towel (great insulator), switched off the air conditioner, and began yelling for my husband. As he commenced attacking the outlet with a volt-meter and screwdrivers, I timidly suggested that he might want to turn off the power at the fuse box. "I can't be bothered." Kapow! More smoke and flames. "Darling…" Blam! Repetition.

I began wondering whether his life insurance was paid up. After the third explosion he went in search of the fuse box. But first, he handed me his tools, which were attached to various objects in or near the outlet, telling me to be very careful not to move one tiny instrument off a screw the size of a pin-head, and to let him know if the needle on the meter moved. I sat, un-comfortably rigid, sweat pouring down my face, eyes glued to the needle, wondering what my life insurance policy was worth, until the lights went out: wrong fuse.

Naturally, the right fuse was the second-to-last one of eighteen. Somehow he managed to remove the melted bits and get the air conditioner working for the night until the "master electrician" could be called in the morning, when we discovered that the wiring does not extend through the walls - that would be too simple. No, it lies under the firmly-cemented tiled floors, which are now being dug up. So far, part of the wall, the bedroom floor, and a room outside the bedroom look as if we have a bad infestation of tile gophers moving toward the hall. They're noisy ones, too - lots of banging and hammering. I tiptoe through massive piles of sharp bits and pieces of tile, over stray wires, around scattered baseboards and tools.

Meanwhile, we have "master carpenters" from Togo working on the reception area; lots more banging and hammering going on. They speak only French, which makes things interesting. Yesterday I used up my entire stock of French saying, "Good morning" and "I don't speak French", which earned me an enthusiastic volley of speech of which I could not comprehend a word. I told my beloved, "I think, although I can't swear to it, that I've just had a conversation with the carpenters." God knows what we agreed to. My beloved does better but there's still a lot of dictionary consultation going on. At least he has a grasp of grammar and vocabulary. I'm better at intuition and charades, however. And my accent is better, when I can think of the words, which isn't often.

Having temporarily rid the house of various plumbers and electricians and their hangers - on who descend like a veritable plague of locusts (no, scratch that, we had the insect-spray man in too), I coped for awhile with painters upstairs and down, a man who speaks only French re-tiling my bathroom, and others turning the garage into living accommodations for the cook, Stella. I am planning a large party for Tuesday evening, so naturally we have a persistent (and smelly) leak under the sink, the cupboard door fell off its hinges, and the light in the guest bathroom has fallen apart, and do you think I can locate a single handyman when I need one?

After having the water in the kitchen turned off every evening for a week and discovering the only way to flush the toilets is to permanently remove the tank lids, it seems the plumber has become ill and disappeared. I can't say that I blame him.

I came home last night to find water covering the floor of my son's bedroom from a leak in the ceiling and a puddle in the kitchen from the leak under the sink.

I have been trying to track down the carpenter for a week. He's actually our second carpenter, not counting the Togolese "master carpenters" - the first one took a good look around and disappeared, presumably forever. So much for my chicken coop, not to mention the broken cupboard door. At least the tile man finished the bathroom quickly - beautifully, I might add - a very pleasant change from large orange and brown spots to a really rather restive plain greenish-blue tile. And the plumbing works, as long as you remember to turn on the water heater and, of course, remove the lid from the tank before flushing. And leave plenty of time for the tank to (very slowly) refill.

They finished digging up the concrete patio within a week - not bad for six men with sledgehammers, pickaxes, and shovels. Of course, then we discovered why they had put in the patio in the first place; it covered the swamp nicely. Never mind; with a little engineering from my beloved (including finding PVC pipe and then drilling holes in it for a drainage pipe - no such animal ready-made to be found here), a fancy French drain was achieved. After another 3 weeks' wait for topsoil and grass clumps (no seed either), we now have nice dark soil with the occasional tuft of grass emerging. Apparently it's crabgrass - I've never seen it spread so slowly.

Someday when I have the energy and can recapture the painters, I might have the living room ceiling painted; I spent a lot of time staring up at it while I was ill and decided I can live with blue squares, or even blue and white, but not blue, yellow, and olive green squares. Maybe I'll just put candles in the guest bathroom and call it romantic; the power, with its usual predictability, will probably be off in any case, adding atmoshphere. And, after all, it is a Halloween party.

SHOPPING

I'M NOT A BIG FAN of shopping; I'm more the get in, get what you need, and get out kind of person these days.

I used to love to shop, and of course buy stuff, but a combination of factors has conspired to make shopping and buying things more of a chore than the enjoyable, Olympic sport of former days. For one thing, I'm older and have less energy; I have to conserve what little I have for important things, like getting out of bed in the morning, remembering who I am, where I am, and where I'm supposed to be that day. Another factor is that being older, I'm closer to the stage where I want to get rid of stuff, not accumulate it; it's too hard to dust things and vacuum around them, and the thought of moving it all one more time into a new house, should it become necessary, is enough to put me, babbling, into a care facility. I'm more into the Zen thing these days: no furniture or rugs to get in my way. My mother constantly threatened my father with all kinds of dire consequences should he predecease her and leave her with a houseful of his "stuff", unsorted and unorganized; important things (to him), like cash register receipts from 1972, family photos no one can identify, catalogues for items no longer in existence, and old computer data cards. But the major reason I no longer like to shop is that I lived in West Africa for two years and did the grocery shopping, which put me off the activity for life.

Although we lived in Accra, the capital city of Ghana, things were not as easy as one might expect as far as shopping goes. First, there was getting downtown; not a fun prospect in traffic jams that rivaled Los Angeles at quitting time, in a non-air-conditioned car, over potholes the size of Texas, in humid, 100+ degree heat. Next, there was finding a store that was open; Ghanaians were not big fans of the "all day, every day" approach to business hours – it's just too hot, and everyone with any sense shuts up shop and takes a nap during the heat of the day, which is most of the time after noon. It's just a matter of finding out everyone's schedule, which can take some time.

Then there was the fact that there was no supermarket in my section of the city, just little "corner shops" with a variable inventory and no air conditioning. Some days you went to four different stores in search of the item necessary for dinner that night, and still came up empty. Some of us developed an intelligence system to rival that of the CIA; you might get a whispered phone call from a close friend at 8 a.m.: "Don't tell anybody, but Four Flowers has cream cheese! Hurry up and get it before all three packages are gone!" "Did you hear? The place on the corner near the butcher's has celery, in fresh this morning!" At, I might add, $7 a bunch, and this was 20 years ago. Or perhaps another little spot might have real milk (we drank boxed, unspoilable, no doubt irradiated milk – not a tasty experience) for a small fortune, if you were quick, a few times a year; our kids got it for dessert. Wherever you went, there was only one brand of laundry soap: Omo. You didn't even ask for detergent, you asked for Omo; everyone knew what you wanted. This was not Wal-Mart, with its hundreds of brands to choose from, and I can't say I minded; it certainly made decision-making a lot easier.

Fruit and vegetables were bought at road-side stands, and everyone had their favorite "fruit and veg lady" (they were all, without exception, run by women). Not that she gave you any special deals; you were expected to bargain. You would ask the price, she would name it, you would look shocked and shake your head slowly and sorrowfully, murmuring that surely she did not mean for your family to starve. She would cock her head to one side, meditating on the vicissitudes of all our lives, comparing your particular hardship with hers, while you waited hopefully. Another price would be mentioned, everyone would reconsider, and on it went; Ghanaians are a patient people. When I did make the occasional, desperate trek across town to the (only) major supermarket, I found it a disappointing experience; there were rarely any more brands to choose from, and it lacked the elements of surprise and challenge inherent in bargaining.

Meat was purchased at the butcher's, adding yet another stop on the epic shopping journey, and good luck finding anything else. I made the trip home to the US at least once a year, and learned to pick up on all toy sale items for the inevitable children's birthday parties; toys were imported in Ghana, expensive, and hard to find, and I wanted to be prepared. I got so good at it that I had a cupboard full of extra brand-new toys; friends would come shop in my closet, and we could have our own bargaining sessions.

On the other hand, Ghanaians could make clothes from a catalogue photograph (my friend's gardener made our girls' Halloween costumes without any patterns – a princess and a goldfish), any furniture you wanted, and toys from wire, all cheaper than anything back home, and easier to find. They were amazingly inventive folks, generous to a fault, and the world's best recyclers. Nothing, and I mean nothing, went to waste: plastic bags were used until they were useless, and then they were bundled together to make soccer balls; plastic bottles were used endlessly for a myriad of purposes. There was no trash to be seen anywhere, because it was all being used somehow. Shopping became less of a necessity because you used everything, in a variety of creative ways, kind of like the Old West pioneers.

Shopping in America just doesn't seem to offer the challenge and excitement to which I had become accustomed.

WOMAN'S BEST FRIEND

THE THIRD NIGHT we were in Ghana, someone walked through the front gate past two night watchmen and stole my beloved's laptop computer. The next day we hired new watchmen, put metal spikes on the walls, and told our staff to be on the lookout for a guard dog.

When we returned from a trip to the bush, we found not one, not two, but three four-week old puppies awaiting us. They are all of a breed euphemistically referred to as "African bush dogs", which translates to dogs having nothing in common but an absolute instinct for survival. One bears some resemblance to a Doberman with short, skinny legs, while the other two, a brother and sister team, are vaguely white with brown markings. None of them are likely to be admitted to the S.P.C.A. any time soon, much less the American Kennel Club.

I suggested they be named Lucky I, II, and III; they were sold by the side of the road and are therefore lucky to be alive, rather than chopped (eaten) by the locals, who are not fussy about their source of protein, there not being a lot to choose from. However, our six-year old daughter was allowed to christen them, and being the highly imaginative child she is, the sister and brother became Patch and Shady, while the short-legged Doberman is now Skylar, also affectionately known as "The Psychotic Dog". He has a look in his eye that ought to repel any sensible person, but if it doesn't he is famous for growling in a seriously menacing way at anyone foolish enough to approach him in a friendly manner. Shady insists on growling and snapping at our friends, while showing her adoration of complete strangers by throwing herself lovingly at their feet and then peeing on them. She must love us, too, since she gives us the same treatment.

By comparison Patch, the other male, seems almost normal, except that we never heard him bark until about six one Sunday morning, when we couldn't get him to be quiet and noticed him staring fixedly and menacingly in one direction. My beloved stumbled downstairs to find that Ayubah, one of our watchmen, had passed out in the guardhouse. He (Ayubah) was taken to the hospital and treated for malaria. About a month later, we were awakened at 2:30 a.m., again by Patch barking (never having heard him utter another sound until then). Again my hubby investigated, only to discover Ayubah once again unconscious in the drive. Upon further inquiry, Ayubah appears to be epileptic and so now works a day schedule; Patch is once again silent but we feel confident that should Ayubah have another seizure, Patch will be sure to let us know. Burglars may come and go with impunity, but Ayubah has his own personal watchdog.

When the dogs were almost a year old, I decided it was high time they learned some manners. Being the lazy type, I decided to hire a professional dog trainer, Peter.

Unfortunately, Peter believes in interactive dog training, between owner and dog(s), and I was sent into the pen to retrieve a dog on a leash. This was not as easy as it may sound. First, Peter spent hours trying to explain to me how to put on a choke-chain without strangling the dog; he finally gave me up as a lost cause; apparently singling out a virtually wild dog from a pack and getting it to allow me to put a choke-chain and leash on it were feats well beyond my capabilities. Peter and my friend Leslie rolled around in helpless laughter as I chased dogs, cajoling and threatening by turns. They (the dogs) ran between my legs, jumped up just as I leaned down, thereby inflicting severe damage to my nose, tripped me, and knocked me flying. Leslie caught her breath long enough to express a deep desire for a video camera in order to make her fortune on "America's Funniest Home Videos".

I threw obscenities in her direction and returned my attention to the fray. When I finally cornered a dog long enough to slip the chain around his neck - Patch, I think - he slunk around as if I'd beaten him and he was forever my abject servant. I would have been happy to have beaten him by then, but Peter doesn't approve of violence. Peter also swears there's no such thing as a stupid dog, but I'm willing to bet good money he's wrong on that count.

Once I dragged Patch outside the pen, however, he suffered an abrupt personality change and became The Acrobatic Dog, flinging himself straight up in the air above my head, doing triple back somersaults and sideways standing broad jumps well beyond the length of the leash, and managing somehow to always land up against me in the most painful manner possible.

Within five minutes I was covered in bruises, scratches, and mud and had sweat streaming off the end of my nose. Leslie and Peter were by now in convulsions, I still had two more dogs to train, and I couldn't even get this one to stand still for ten seconds so I could at least beat it into some half-dazed semi-conscious semblance of exhausted motionlessness, much less submission. They certainly had me beaten.

Miraculously, under Peter's guidance the dogs were actually heeling within three days, although I was barely ambulatory. They now behave beautifully while on the leash and completely ignore me otherwise, unless I have food, which gains their instant, intense, and focused concentration.

Peter suggests I spit into their food bowls to prove to them that I am leader of the pack, which seems pretty peculiar to me, but as I am desperate, I comply, although I never let anyone see me do it. How they can notice anything as miniscule as some spit in the five seconds it takes them to inhale their food is beyond me, anyway. Besides, they seem to show a marked proclivity for chicken - specifically, the chickens we are trying to raise in our back yard. At the moment, Patch has the run of the yard and the chickens are, you should pardon the expression, cooped up in their tiny pen, because The Acrobatic Dog can now easily clear the four - foot fence constructed specifically to keep him in. I figure we'll keep building it higher until he either loses his taste for chicken or they're ready to add dog fence-jumping as an Olympic event. It's nippy-tucky which will happen first. And I've yet to hear any of the three of them bark at a stranger.

ICELANDIC FEASTS

WE SPENT OUR 30TH wedding anniversary in Iceland, where we had always wanted to go, having dinner in our spacious room at the Mar Guesthouse. Lest you become carried away by romantic visions, let me clarify, which I can do because we took a picture of the meal. It consisted of reconstituted dehydrated soup, cheese and salami and peanut butter and jelly sandwiches, with olives on the side, beer for my beloved and lemonade for me, and canned peaches for dessert. This was a real feast compared to our usual fare of bread and cheese, and the room was spacious because it had a high ceiling and was mostly empty of furniture.

Fortunately, I had ascertained before we left home that Iceland would be very expensive food-wise, it being an island and all, with no discernable seasons other than winter, and had cleverly planned ahead by packing lots of said dehydrated soup, a seemingly endless supply of oatmeal packets, dozens of energy bars, several pounds of trail mix, and seasonings. I felt very clever until I realized I had inadvertently packed the soup mix entirely too close to the soap; even the addition of curry powder and all the seasonings I had brought was not enough to disguise the faint smell of toiletries that permeated it, and several other items as well. Food was so expensive that we never ate out, but bravely soldiered on with our bread and cheese and soapy soup.

The Mar Guesthouse was located in the industrial section of a town called Grindavik, our first stop in Iceland and a name that carried a faint tinge of "Beowulf". It appeared to be in an industrial area, located next to a fish-packing plant, but fortunately the wind was in the southeast, so I could never be entirely sure. Icelandic décor is Spartan, to say the least; we found that it mostly consisted of a bed, a light, and a wardrobe. The toilet and shower were always down the hall, and if we were lucky we only had to share them with five or six other guests.

Most guesthouses provided a breakfast of sorts; the usual meal was bread, cheese, ham, tomato, jam, the occasional boiled egg, and tea or coffee; creating different versions of a meal with those ingredients always made me feel as if I could be on one of those cooking shows with mysterious, limited and bizarre ingredients. But in one town, we hit the jackpot; at Uxi's Guesthouse in Hella, Uxi himself cooked "semi-traditional" Icelandic meals of such substance that after the first morning we had to warn new guests to pace themselves: course after course of home-made vegetable pasties, muffins, eggs Benedict, cereal, toast, etc, paraded across the table until I suspected Uxi was stuffing us like geese for Thanksgiving dinner, if they had celebrated such a thing. He was also a wonderful, eccentric conversationalist with a friendly, helpful manner who, when we lost our room key, left the dinner he was having with a friend to let us into our room, not only not charging us for the extra key, but giving us two more for good measure, cheerfully remarking that he had a bag full of them. When we discovered a day after leaving that we had left a small jar of mayo and some olives in his fridge and asked if we could come back to retrieve them, he happily met us at the door to hand them over.

While almost every Icelander speaks English very well, learning it from about age ten through high school, very little is actually written in English, which made grocery shopping a challenge. I was never quite sure what I was buying, sometimes even after consuming it. Once, we studied containers for what seemed hours, trying to purchase egg salad. There were many possibilities, so we read contents carefully, or as carefully as we were able to in Icelandic, triumphantly carrying home from the field of battle a package of, as it turned out, shrimp salad. Another time we ended up making sandwiches with, instead of the elusive egg salad – cole slaw, although to be fair, there may have been eggs involved. Eventually we gave up and went back to bread and cheese; at least we knew what we were getting. At least "tunafisk" was pretty clear, and I especially liked the Icelandic word for ham, "skinke", which was really quite evocative – perhaps too much so.

By the time we got to our rented studio apartment in Reykjavik, which had a two-burner stove, a microwave, and a fridge, I was actually almost happy to cook. That's when I discovered just how expensive food really was in Iceland. A very small head of broccoli was over $5, so we settled on canned veggies and some pasta and chicken – and, of course, bread and cheese. When asked what people eat in Iceland, I can only say that there's a lot of cole slaw.

ICELANDIC RAFTING

I KNOW: WHO GOES river rafting in Iceland?

Apparently, lots of people with more of a sense of adventure than sense, which would include us, because there are people who actually make a living taking nut cases out on the river. Besides, the brochure made it look fun, like a little trip down the Klamath in the summertime: lots of white water and people smiling. But then, the world is full of mentally unstable people, not that I count my beloved and myself among them. Necessarily. On a good day.

We had just finished visiting a geyser called, appropriately, "Geysir", which is the origin, if not the spelling, of our word geyser, and in Iceland is pronounced "geezer", at which I tried not to take offense, when it was time for the river rafting trip. It was mid-August; summertime at home, but apparently not so in Iceland. We had been enduring cold weather and fog for some time, and today was no exception. And the company is named "Arctic Rafting" for a reason.

The first step, unfortunately, involved putting on a wetsuit. I believe I have mentioned in a tale of caving long ago that I am not a huge fan of these items, which, while they do keep you marginally warmer than you would be without them, are a torture device of which the Inquisition would be proud. The last time I donned one, I was thirty years and many pounds lighter than I am now, and it wasn't a fun thing to do even then. These wetsuits, not being my beloved's, were newer and nicer than his, but even smellier than I remembered. Having skinned my knees a few days before on our volcano epic, I was feeling even more recalcitrant and cranky than I would be normally about squeezing myself into one. But, determined to be a good sport, come hell or high water, both of which I was expecting to encounter, I took on the challenge and began the process. I had just about tugged it over my thighs when I belatedly noticed that I had forgotten to take off my leggings; off came the wetsuit, and then of course I had to pull it on all over again while everyone waited. By the time I got it up to my hips again, I realized this was going to have to be a group participation activity, and enlisted my beloved's aid. With much heaving and ho-ing, huffing and puffing on both our parts, I was stuffed like a sausage into the thing. Then, with more help, came the wetsocks, the helmet, a jacket, and a life-vest. I looked like the Pillsbury doughboy, I could barely move, and I had to be heaved onto the bus by several strong guides, but by golly, we had done it.

So, off we set in our big yellow school bus, down a typical Icelandic dirt road, which is to say pot-holed, boulder-strewn, and corrugated, with a sharp drop on either side I would rather not think about. I clutched my paddle as if I were already on the raft, managing to clonk myself on the head with it several times along the way, until we got to the river. We were fully instructed as to safety, including the use of the O.S. rope, the meaning of which I immediately grasped, having been there before in the Grand Canyon when we rafted down the Colorado and I thought every day would be my last. By comparison, this felt like a slow day on the Klamath River, only a lot colder and in a very uncomfortable wetsuit.

Our guide, Esther, insisted we name our boat, but immediately ruled out our suggestion of "Titanic" as being unnecessarily gloomy, even for Iceland, which is not exactly filled with happy-go-lucky types, so we settled on "Go-Fast". Then we played trust games involving everyone standing on the edge of the boat holding hands, or later with our paddles hooked, and leaning back until everyone fell in except my beloved and myself – me only because I was clutching him. I'm not sure where the trust came in, but maybe it's an Icelandic thing. Esther also told us a favorite Icelandic story: In Iceland (not known for its tall trees, or really, any trees at all), if you're lost in a forest, stand up! Along the way we were informed we would be privileged to jump off a 25-foot high cliff; my beloved, of course, felt impelled to leap along with the other nutters, not once but twice, just because it was so much fun. I, naturally, remained safely clinging to the shore.

Then it was back on the bus, into the changing room for a reversal of the wetsuit procedure, and on to a heavenly soak in a geothermal pool called the Secret Lagoon, which I can only hope stays secret, as it was relatively uncrowded, and a perfect end to the day. Although it would have been warmer in Siskiyou County, and I wouldn't have had to wear a wetsuit.

Icelandic Road Trips

I FOUND THE ICELANDIC language to be pretty nearly indecipherable. Apparently deciding the inadequacies of the English alphabet were too much to bear, Icelanders have added a few letters of their own, which are impossible for me to reproduce here without a competent calligrapher. Town names are so long they take a foot and a half of space and tend to fall off the page and the map, having used every consonant in the alphabet at least three times while needlessly conserving vowels. To prove my point, I herewith list a few of the most colorful, areas called, I kid you not: Hrunamannahreppur; Rangarvallasysla; Gnupverjahreppur; Hraungerdishreppur; Kirkjubaejarklaustur (which translates, if you're interested, to "church floor") and Geldingadalsfjall; and I am leaving out the ones, even longer, whose use of letters foreign to English prevents me from typing them. I was told that when the volcano Eyjafjallajokull (yes, really) erupted in 2010, the American military found the name so (understandably) difficult to deal with that they simply referred to it as "E-15", presumably for the 15 letters that follow the beginning "E". And just so you know and can brag to your friends, that "jokull" on the end means glacier, not that we would know about them; the weather was so bad while we were there (in mid-August, mind you) that the glaciers generally blended into the fog in an indistinguishable blur.

When I felt I was starting to get the hang of reading the names, I began to worry, and rightly so. I was lulled into a false sense of security at one point by a town called "Hengill", only to discover it is actually pronounced something like "Henglit" with a fishbone stuck in your throat, but that cannot do justice to the glottal stops and other mouth and throat sounds involved in Icelandic. The volcano called "Hella" appears to be closer to "Hekla", but that's one of the simpler ones. After a while, when plotting our route, I would simply say to my beloved, for instance, "It's something beginning with H and ending with "hraun" (meaning lava field, and therefore quite widely used) and we would take it from there.

The road signs, being mostly in Icelandic, also proved mysterious, involving flying birds and other potentially ancient runes unknown to American tourists – or at least to this one. And speaking of roads…I'm becoming convinced that road signs indicating "4-wheel drive only!" are actually a clever plot by Icelanders to preserve the best roads in the country by keeping them untraveled by tourists. It also appears that if there is a road sign stating, in large, ominous letters: "Warning!!! 4-wheel drive vehicles only!!! Rental car owners note: Road not recommended for rental cars!!! Serious damage to cars may result from road conditions!!!" that is the road we will take in our small, rented, non-4-wheel drive car. Hopefully the statute of limitations on our rental agreement has passed by now.

More than once, we take the gravel road that isn't even marked on the map, searching for the elusive "vertical cliff" (is there another kind?), which we never did find. Occasionally we take a road no one else is on, for reasons which become clear the further we travel: no sane person other than a desperate sheep rancher could be persuaded to use it. At times we found ourselves driving for hours on roads uninhabited by anyone but sheep, which look up, surprised to see us. Sometimes we find a gravel road in better shape than some of the paved ones, but mostly it's a teeth-jarring ride. Now and again they are so bad, in fact, that you want to get out once in awhile to check, not only to see if you have a flat tire, but to ensure you still have wheels.

One day, instead of gazing rapturously at Gullfoss, possibly the most famous waterfall in Iceland, I found myself focused on a desperate search for a toilet (waterfalls will do that, and there are a LOT of waterfalls in Iceland, take my word for it). I finally found one (toilet, that is), only to discover that there was a fee of about $1.50 for the privilege of using the facilities; of course I hadn't a penny on me and my beloved was miles away, searching for the perfect camera angle. For the waterfall, I hasten to add. Besides, I object on principal to the "pay to pee" policy. So I braided my legs until he showed up, we drove about 200 yards, and I made my "door privy", created by parking the car at the correct angle for maximum privacy, opening the front and back doors on the same side of the car, and doing the necessary. Or at least I thought it was private; I was just about done when half the tourists in Iceland drove up, either for the same purpose or to take photos of the river below; I was never quite sure, as we high-tailed it out of there as quickly as possible on the next corrugated, pot-holed road we found.

INTO THE GLACIER

WE WERE SO BUSY looking at "fosses" (in Iceland, words ending in "foss" generally indicate waterfalls, of which there are innumerable examples; at one point, debating whether or not to drive to see yet one more, my beloved shook his head sadly, declaring he was "all fossed out") that we were late for the tour we'd booked to go see a cave. At least, that's what I thought we were going to do; my distinct recollection, disputed by my husband, of course, was that we would casually drive to a "show" cave geared for tourists (as opposed to a "caver's cave", which would involve getting into wet-suits and performing uncomfortable contortions known only to die-hard cavers) by the side of the road, wander around a bit, and move on. I was only mildly alarmed by the sign on the side of the bus exclaiming in large letters: "Into the Glacier!!"; hype for the tourists, I figured. I was a bit miffed by the snickers that greeted us as we climbed onto the bus; everyone else was dressed in clothing appropriate for an Arctic expedition - woolly hats, boots, waterproof pants and tops - and they apparently felt my long skirt was not quite the thing. So back I ran to the car for my tennis shoes. That ought to do it, I thought with some satisfaction, although my beloved's usual outfit of t-shirt, shorts and sandals didn't seem to impress anyone, either. The driver took a long look at the two of us, but tactfully refrained from commenting on our attire.

When I had settled back into my seat, the driver announced that he was only our first guide; when we got to the glacier, he said, the next leg of the journey would be led by someone who would drive us across the glacier itself to the ice cave. "Glacier?" I squeaked. "Ice cave?" My voice was rising with every utterance, and I began to frantically poke my husband. "What glacier?" I hissed. "What ice cave? You didn't say anything about any glacier, or an ice cave. I never would have worn a skirt if I'd known there was a glacier involved!" He shrugged. "I forgot about that part." Furthermore, the driver continued, when we got to the glacier, we would be provided with crampons to wear into the cave. "Crampons?!" I screeched. A brief discussion ensued between my beloved and myself as to which had the potential to do worse harm: me with no crampons, careering across the ice, or me with crampons, which, for those of you who are unaware of the devices, are sharp pointy metal things you attach to your boots should you find yourself crossing glaciers, which I had, thankfully, avoided doing my entire life for very good reason until, apparently, this very moment.

After a drive of some distance, we arrived at "base camp", a rather Spartan place still under construction consisting of a collection of disgusting porta-potties (at least there was no charge) and a platform, where we were loaded onto the most enormous vehicle I had ever seen; the driver cheerfully announced it was a former military vehicle – a rocket launcher, in fact – towed by what looked like a Mack truck. The tires alone were taller than I was. We took off up the glacier, stopping occasionally so that the driver could inflate and deflate the tires, depending on the conditions. I was so relieved that I didn't have to trek across the glacier myself, ice axe in hand, crampons on my feet, and skirt billowing over my head, that I didn't even mind too much when the truck lurched occasionally, pausing while, I assume, the driver dragged our wheels back out of whatever crevasse they had just fallen into.

We finally arrived at the ice cave, where it appeared there was a slight breeze blowing; we had a short wait until we could actually enter the cave, the guide said, so we were free to exit the vehicle and stretch our legs. I got out, and had I not grabbed ahold of one of the formidable truck tires, the gale force winds would have filled the sails of my skirt and blown me right over the edge of the glacier; yet another reason, had I needed any more than the obvious ones, not to wear a skirt to climb a glacier, or even to visit an ice cave.

I was quite relieved to have Guide #3 take us into the cave, where, thankfully, we were out of the wind, and instruct us to put on the crampons, which, as it turns out, were just those rubber and wire doohickeys you slide over the bottom of your shoes. We were then treated to a wonderful tour of the cave, complete with a view of a crevasse said to extend downward for 30 meters, magnificent icicles, and a chapel, icy and drippy and available for weddings, should you wish to be wed in an ice cave in Iceland, for a small extra fee. I can only recommend that any dress worn to such a wedding be tight, or be pants, and include festive crampons.

INTO THE VOLCANO

SO, WE HAD BEEN in Iceland a few days when we took our pre-booked tour, called, naturally, "Into the Volcano!!" Let me hasten to assure you, lest you should either worry, or think me far more adventurous than I am, that this was not just an inactive, dormant volcano, but a totally extinct, dead volcano – in fact, an ex-volcano altogether. My beloved being a geologist, it seemed required that we take the opportunity of a lifetime to actually descend into a volcano and examine its interior. That was the easy part; actually getting to the volcano took more effort than I had counted on.

We rode a small bus from the heart of Reykjavik, the capital of Iceland – a lovely city of about 100,000 out of the 300,000+ total population of Iceland – to the "base camp" (a popular euphemism, I discovered, for a really primitive hut where you can, if you're lucky, have a cup of tea or coffee and defrost). Here we were all given standard-issue yellow rain slickers which were hooded and extended to our ankles; this was a good thing, as we then ventured forth into yet another howling gale, accompanied by horizontal rain that hit your face like glass shards. Fortunately, by then we all (there were about 18 similarly unhinged but friendly folk in our group) had no part of our bodies exposed other than a few necessary inches of nose and eyes, so it wasn't too bad.

We were led off by our guide across a lava-rock-strewn field, and after a while the wind became our friend, as it actually propelled us along the route. Very soon, my shoes and socks were wet, and the rising damp made its way up my leggings until I was pretty much soaked under my cheerful yellow slicker. I kept my eyes on my beloved's feet and stumbled along after him for about 3 kilometers, until something, possibly exhaustion, or maybe the wind, knocked me to my knees. My beloved, totally unaware (I hope) that his wife had just collapsed, marched on, but a nice young man behind me politely hoisted me to my feet and inquired after my health, probably because I was blocking the path. Embarrassed, I assured him I was fine, but I never could pick him out later to thank him properly, as all I could see, other than the raincoat, was a generic nose and half a pair of what may have been blue eyes. I sustained only minor injuries: a few scrapes and bruises to the knees - but noted that my already tattered leggings would require yet more stitching.

We had soon squelched our way to yet another "base camp", and I just had time to sit down for a brief rest and cup of restorative tea, when we were hauled off for the final leg of our journey, a hike up the mountainside to the actual mouth of the volcano. This involved an exhilarating climb up the volcano itself, clinging to a flimsy rope (and each other) to avoid being flung off the side of the hill by the wind as we made our way up the precarious path to the summit.

By then, it was almost a relief to undertake the next phase of the trip; I say "almost" a relief because the descent "Into the Volcano!!" was accomplished by means of two planks, a couple of steel bars, and a motorized pulley system which lowered us about 400 feet onto the floor of the volcano itself. This contraption, which my beloved assures me was perfectly safe, is enthusiastically described in the literature as being a machine of the same type as those used by high-rise building window washers - as if this were a recommendation. Did I mention that I'm afraid of heights? I held my breath and closed my eyes as the machine jerked and clanked its way down, us strapped to it like unwilling sacrifices to the volcano gods, rubber wheels keeping it off the rock walls lest we be scraped off before we reached the bottom.

I must admit that once we reached the bottom and safely disembarked from the torture machine, the view was amazing: the multi-colored rock formations, and raindrops from above glittering their way down like diamonds to meet the cave floor, were spectacular. It just about made the trip back worth it. Besides, it briefly sheltered us from the pelting rain and fierce winds outside – always a recommendation in my world.

After a fortifying bowl of hot soup, we were cheerfully sent off once again into the howling gale, across the rubble field of lava rocks; at least this time I didn't disgrace myself by toppling over. We reversed our trip back into Reykjavik, where we were able to finally wring out our sodden socks and other sundry items of clothing, dry our shoes atop the radiator in our room, and sit down to the sumptuous repast described in another story.

If there is a better way to celebrate your 30th wedding anniversary, I can't imagine what it might be.

CELTIC KNOTS

ON A RECENT TRIP abroad with my beloved, after a brief stay in Scotland, we moved on to Ireland, where we toured the "Causeway of the Giants", which are rock formations (columnar basalts, in case you were wondering; you see a lot of rocks when you travel with a geologist), walked along the cliffs, and ate sandwiches in the car, as it was, yet again, raining. In the interests of historical accuracy, I asked my husband at one point if he knew whether the marauding Romans had made it as far as Ireland, to which he replied, after some thought, "I don't think so; that would have been a Celt too far."

We then ventured onto the aptly-named "Wild Atlantic Way", a route down the west coast of Ireland. I'm not complaining, really, but I have to say the wind blew very hard - so hard, in fact, that we dubbed them "Gael force winds", and it did rain exceptionally enthusiastically, even for Ireland, especially for July. In fact, at one point I commented to my beloved about a dog I saw that had very short legs. "Yes," he responded glumly. "He'd have to have short legs, wouldn't he, or he'd be blown off the island entirely." He then pointed out that another dog with more conventional-length legs was lying flat on the ground, presumably to avoid that very fate.

Arriving at the bed and breakfast hotel we had booked, we discovered the establishment did not look quite as advertized; it would be a kindness to say it had aged somewhat since the picture had been taken, but then, as the nice young lady explained as she showed us the way up the shabby-genteel staircase, the place was rumored to be haunted by the lady of the house, which made up for its genteel shabbiness – at least, in my mind, avid as I am about murder mysteries. I shall spare you the gory details of the story, but suffice it to say I did not sleep easily that night.

We noticed several tents in the yard which were, by a miracle, still there in the morning, but only because they had ballast inside (from the looks of it, heavy dressers), which kept the howling winds from blowing them off the cliff. When we went outside to take a photo, the wind was blowing so hard we actually saw birds flying backwards. How do we find these places? This is a rhetorical question; my beloved finds them – cheap.

Our next bed and breakfast was in a lovely, secluded spot, so secluded, in fact, that I began to get nervous. It didn't help that when we asked directions to the place before arriving, a few doors down from what we later discovered was the B & B, no one seemed to know who we were talking about, or that although all our communications had been with a "Margaret" over the internet, the door was answered by "Sean", who explained that "Marcy" (Marcy? Who is Marcy??) had a family emergency and couldn't be there. I know I have an overactive imagination, but I began to be suspicious.

Sean very kindly directed us to the local ruin, which was one of the spookiest places I've ever seen (but in all fairness, my opinion might have been influenced by the fact that it was getting dark, and I tripped over a root and fell flat on my face), and by the time we returned to the house, I was trying to convince my beloved that we had wandered into the realm of the perfect murder. It was the ideal set-up, really: no one knew where we were, Sean could easily dispose of our rental car, not to mention our bodies, in the deep surrounding woods, and tell anyone who asked that we had left for parts unknown. Another sleepless night. The next morning when it came to making comments in the log book, I wanted to say that Sean really was the perfect host, apart from that whole potential serial killer thing, but my beloved restrained me.

Our last B & B was with a lovely lady named Mary, who had clearly not been lucky in love, as she had a sign which read, "Grow your own dope: plant a man".

The winds did not abate, but when my husband grumbled I reminded him that this was Ireland, after all - what did he expect? As a Brit, he ought to know better than to expect good weather in Britain in any season. At least on this trip we were able to actually see the Cliffs of Moher.

I must end with one of my favorite things about foreign countries: their traffic signs, which never fail to bring pictures to my mind. In Ireland we had "Traffic Calming", and in Britain were "Hidden Dip", "Men and Van Removals and Deliveries" (which I can't help but feel might be enthusiastically received in some quarters – like Mary in Ireland, for instance), the slightly risqué "Humping Next 180 Yards", and my personal favorite: "End of Diversions". There's nothing like traveling to broaden the mind and end your diversions.

EIRE ADVENTURES

I MAY BE THE ONLY PERSON I know who comes back from vacation perilously close to developing an ulcer. You might have thought that having survived two weeks on a sailboat off the coast of Turkey and another two weeks of touring in the country itself, two weeks in the relative civilization of Ireland would be easy; that is, you might think that if you weren't aware of my travel history. Besides, in Turkey I was with my beloved, who is known for his calm approach to travel, as well as disasters of every sort, and his remarkable sense of direction, while in Ireland I was on my own – a very frightening proposition when you are me, not to be too metaphysical. After all, I had booked bed and breakfasts through a travel agent in all five major cities I was to visit, and I had a train pass; how hard could it be? This is always a dangerous and rhetorical question for me to ask, and I should have known better. Having had a train pass in Europe in my youth, I might have remembered the trip and its accompanying traumas, but I am old and it didn't come back to me until it was too late. Besides, I made the mistake of thinking I was older, and therefore wiser now.

My first, unavoidable, error was choosing to lug around a fifty-pound suitcase. I say unavoidable because, when you are going to two very different climates for two months, including two weeks on a sailboat, even when you strip it down to the bare essentials and off-load everything you can possibly think of to your longsuffering husband's luggage, there is a certain amount of baggage that simply must be brought along, like toothbrushes and, I admit, a hairdryer. Also, when you travel to Ireland in November, a certain amount of very warm clothing is essential. As it was, I had only two pairs of shoes, which suffered greatly, and not enough socks. I wore so many layers I looked like a walking thrift store, and they all got very wet; after one particularly precipitous day wherein I never did see the Cliffs of Moher due to heavy cloud and much rain, it took my boots two days to dry – and that was even with housing them on the radiator every night, which turned out to be not the best of ideas, as they burned. They still smell funny, as does every pair of socks I wear with them.

In any case, so to speak, my suitcase, although on wheels, proved unwieldy in the extreme when I attempted to haul it onto buses, trains, and trams, and was not easily lugged up the inevitable two to three flights of steep narrow stairs to the room at the top into which I was booked at every single bed and breakfast. At one point an older gentleman shorter than I by far, watching me try to lift the cursed thing onto a seat next to me on the train, muttered, "You're not goin' to be doin' that, now. Never mind about getting' it down - we'll just let it fall down at the last stop!" and proceeded to fling it into the overhead storage. I could have kissed him, first for calling me "Miss", which I am clearly not, exceeding that title by several decades, and secondly for taking the thing off my hands; at that point I would not have objected had he flung the thing off the train entirely. I cursed that suitcase roundly every day, several times a day – especially on the stairs.

My next major error lay in forgetting just how directionally impaired I am. Having caught a taxi to my first bed and breakfast outside Dublin, I attempted to find a bus back into the city, where I had a tour booked the next day. First problem: no exact change, which was required. This became a recurring theme, which caused me no end of troubles. I got change from the singularly unhelpful landlady, who seemed to think every tourist new to the country should be able to find their way into the city without effort.

Then I asked the bus driver to tell me when we got to my stop, as I asked every bus driver in Ireland, with the same result: he forgot to alert me. I walked several blocks back, asked directions from every person I met along the way, and learned my next Irish lesson: very few people actually knew where anything was that I asked about. So I took my best guess of three out of four replies (or seven out of eight) and slogged onward. Occasionally when I asked more than one person, especially if they were sitting next to each other or even in reasonable proximity to each other on a bus, an argument would ensue, sometimes involving most of the bus, and I would slink off at the next stop, afraid I had just re-opened the civil war.

Just about the time I had acquired a map and begun to get a feel for getting around in a city, it would be time to move on. In one city, I asked taxi driver after taxi driver for a particular part of town where my B & B was located, and none of them were even willing to try to find it – a first for me. Even the bus drivers seemed clueless. Just as I was beginning to think I'd be spending the night at the bus station, I found a cab driver who seemed to know exactly where I needed to go, and took me there. And it's a wonder, too, as I discovered later I was asking for the wrong district altogether.

And why is it that there appears to be a shortage of working clocks all over Ireland, and those that do exist invariably give conflicting times? I realize most people use their cell phones to get the time, but as I didn't have one that worked, I was obliged to carry my alarm clock everywhere, which got me some odd looks. One bus driver suggested I duct-tape it to my wrist. A few days before I came home, I managed to find a cheap watch – which lasted almost until I boarded the plane home, so who's complaining?

In addition, "R" is pronounced "or" by the Irish, leading one to suppose, when they spell a word for you, that somewhere in the middle the current spelling becomes optional, with a second possibility mentioned, just for your convenience. Like French, there are always lots of extra letters included that are never pronounced, or are slurred together so as to make them completely unnecessary. One day, I asked a lady at the train station if she were going to Tralee and understood not one word of what she replied. The announcements in the train are in Gaelic first, then English, and I swear when they say the train company's name, it sounds like they're saying "Here and there", which may be appropriate, but probably not accurate.

Everything in Ireland, like most places in Europe, was quite expensive; I don't know why they're not all running about naked and hungry with these prices, other than the cold, naturally. And of course, everyone in Ireland can knit, and there's no shortage of sheep, so there you are.

Radio news, Irish-style: "There's a report of a swan walking down the road to the Minuth roundabout." "Why didn't he take the bus?" "Also, there's a dog, accompanied by a pony, on the road to Galway." Me: Does that make it a dog and pony show?

Then, of course, there are the bus schedules: they run less often, and sometimes not at all, on weekends, which I had, of course, not counted on. So there I would be, waiting several hours outside at night in the cold to catch a bus to a place I had never been before, suitcase partially blocking the stiff breeze. The pinnacle of this experience was the night I caught the bus, standing all the way and attempting to keep both myself and the case upright, asked two different women where the B & B was (they disagreed with one another, naturally), made my best guess as to where it was, hiked a few blocks (having, as always, guessed incorrectly) in the dark, dragging my 50-pound case behind me, until I finally located the B & B, and hoisted the suitcase up a flight of stairs, only to find the gate locked. Muttering imprecations under my breath, I prepared to climb back down the stairs when a man came out and informed me that they never used that gate; the entrance was around the block. I stood there, utterly defeated, until he remarked, "Never mind, I'll get it open", after which there ensued much banging and swearing on his part, the trip to get a hammer and screwdriver, and the employment of said implements until the gate was opened. I could have walked the block by then, but I was tired and therefore grateful nonetheless. Of course, there was still the inevitable climb up to my third-floor room at the top of the house, suitcase banging behind me.

On public buses: Good Lord, madam, do teach your child to chew her gum (if she MUST chew gum) with her mouth CLOSED. As if that's not bad enough, I sit bracing myself on the outside of the seat, trying to avoid being flung into the aisle on sharp turns, when I become aware of the laughing drunk behind me, babbling to himself, and begin to earnestly pray he won't hurl down the back of me before I get to my stop.

"If y'get lost in Adare, darlin', I'll give ya a medal!" says the friendly bus driver who drops me off in said village. He was wearing sunglasses, which I thought was very optimistic of him. Have your medal close to hand, sir – you underestimate me! They are used to it, of course, but this habit they seem to have of changing street names can be confusing. You'll be happily perambulating down, say, Flood Street, when suddenly, without warning or the slightest curve in the road from one block to the next, it's managed to transform itself to Augustine Street, without so much as a by-your leave or explanation of any sort. Whereupon, no doubt exhausted by its efforts, it abruptly ends entirely. Since it's on the end of the street nearer to the river, perhaps there's a reason Augustine becomes Flood, but as I'm a stranger here, the history of the thing is lost in the mists of time for me – if there is, indeed, a history.

And if while in Galway you cross Wolfe Tone Bridge, Quay street becomes High Street which transmutes to Shop Street, which, chameleon-like, turns into William Street, which is then mysteriously, and for reasons apparently known only to itself, renamed W'gate Street. I can only assume that in the great circle of life that is Irish transport, this is a contraction for the hopefully related and geographically akin William Street, from whence it becomes Prospect Hill, upon which, one assumes, having transformed itself more times than a shapeshifter and confused any tourist foolhardy enough to walk it, it gives its shoulders a shake and leaves town in triumph. At least on MY map it does; I wouldn't have dared try it on my own, or I would probably still be there.

Things got so bad at times I lit candles in churches all over Ireland – and I'm not even Catholic. It seemed to work, though. When I got to my lowest points, I strongly considered throwing myself onto the neck of every bus driver in Ireland, weeping copious pitiful tears and begging them to help me; they're a nice lot, Irish bus drivers, even if they never do tell you when your stop is coming up. I often had the same tour drivers, who sometimes even recognized me; and why not, when I wore the same outfit for two weeks solid? The bus tours were havens of safety; it got to the point that I didn't even care if I saw the sights, because I didn't have to worry about anything once I was on the bus; they were safe and dry and provided a running history of Ireland.

And as it happens, my vehicle difficulties at home appeared to travel with me and infect even Irish buses; one of our tour buses had its windshield wiper (on the driver's side, naturally) stop working, but he was a clever lad and simply swapped them over so we could continue. On the next bus, the driver announced that we were not to be alarmed, but he'd lost first and second gear, but no worries, he could manage without them both – and did, all day. My last tour bus developed a major water leak, and we had to wait 45 minutes for a new bus to arrive, but the town was charming and it wasn't raining that day, so who cared?

Then there was the "Connemara pony incident". As we flew past a field, a lovely white pony raced the bus, and I had an actual magic moment in Ireland. The driver, in what seemed like a moment of spontaneous inspiration but which I later realized was a planned and frequent move, pointed him out, stopped the bus, and suggested we go "pet the pony". A lovely idea, thought I, and as I was in the front seat, was first to hop off the bus. Reaching out to pet the lovely beast, I was stunned when he bit me hard on the arm, eying me with malice. "He bit me!" I cried out in shock, to which the driver cheerily replied, "Oh, aye, they do that; here, feed him a bit of apple." Inspecting my now red, soon to be black and blue and swollen wound and wondering if the ill-tempered animal had had its rabies shots recently, I backed away; I'd be damned if I rewarded the thing for attacking me and considered punching it in the nose, which I might well have done if there hadn't been witnesses. I took photos to document the event, as is my habit, in case I should die and my near and dear ones decided to sue.

I will admit that the Irish, like the Brits, have the most civilized custom known to humanity: tea. No matter how bad things get, the exhortation to "There now, luv, 'ave a nice cuppa, you'll feel better" does seem to make everything look brighter. My rooms invariably contained the kettle, tea bags, milk, and sugar necessary to making everything all right, often with the added bonus of a biscuit (cookie) or two - sometimes even homemade. Such luxuries almost made it all worthwhile to be on vacation. As an added bonus, when I had no money, the bread provided at breakfast often went towards feeding me for the rest of the day.

My next error was not having any electronic devices with me. I don't have a cell-phone that works overseas; I refuse to carry my heavy laptop (even more weight for the luggage), and clearly, the world no longer functions for a person without either. Although I did manage to find, in the village of Cong, what a bookshop owner declared to be "the last working phone booth in Ireland", my bank, which declares itself able to accept collect phone calls, refused to do so, naturally. So I was reduced to hunting down internet cafes, which my daughter did a better job of at age 21, and in Italy, for heavens' sake, than I did in a place where they speak English. More or less.

Eventually I hit upon the idea of libraries, where the computers are free, which helped quite a bit, and it's a good thing, too, because near the end of my trip I discovered I was out of money and the bank refused to give me any; apparently my failure to tell them I was going abroad resulted in them deciding someone had stolen my ATM card and gone to Ireland. So there I was, more than ready to go home, with no money in a foreign country, wondering how I was going to pay the bed and breakfast and find change to catch the next bus to the train station and thence to the airport. I was contemplating begging on the streets when I tried an old trick: fooling the ATM by asking it for 20 euros rather than the 100 I'd been requesting. It worked, and I felt that I'd won the lottery.

Now all I had to do was find my way to Dublin and the airport without getting lost.

Taking a Cat to Okinawa

IT ALL STARTED when I had to take a cat to Okinawa.

My nephew is a Marine stationed in Okinawa, and he and his wife had to leave the cat behind with relatives when they left about a year and a half earlier. I had rescued the cat for them, because the people who had him were keeping him in a shed outside. He is declawed, so this was clearly not a good idea; he'd been in some fights and had wounds that needed tending, so I volunteered to take him on for my nephew's wife, who missed him and wanted him back with them. I also said I'd be happy to accompany him to Okinawa. Unfortunately, he was not a well cat, besides being quite elderly, which necessitated several trips to the vet – one an emergency visit to Medford undertaken by my sister, who spent most of the day with him there. In the end, my vet declared him unfit and too old to travel, but I went anyway, as no one was allowed to tell me the same thing, and was warmly welcomed, despite my lack of cat, who is as I write happily relaxing in Los Angeles with my daughter, where he is no doubt enjoying the warm weather, movie stars and cockroaches, even if he is not well-traveled, although Oregon to Yreka to Los Angeles is probably as far as he wants to go at his age. My daughter seems to have made a specialty of caring for cats in their dotage. I rely on her expanding that talent to elderly mothers soon.

In any case, I went to Okinawa without Meow (his name), adding Japan just for the heck of it. I'd never been there, which is always justification enough for me to go anywhere.

I knew it was going to be an interesting trip when I noticed the young man behind me in line at the Medford airport hauling an industrial-sized vacuum cleaner behind him. I just had to ask, being the enquiring sort, and he related that his mother had moved to Hawaii and didn't want to buy a new vacuum, so she had asked him to bring it to her. As this flight was heading for Portland, I was confused, but it seemed a small detail compared to the whole concept of lugging a vacuum cleaner along on a flight, but who was I to argue the matter? Fascinated as I was, I was able to obtain closure when I overheard an airport employee get the OK from someone higher up to go ahead and check it in. At least he wasn't trying to take it onboard as hand luggage; I seriously doubt that it would have fit into an overhead compartment, or even two or three, and the effect of it falling out mid-flight and landing on some unsuspecting passenger didn't bear thinking about. Mind you, some of the objects I have seen crammed into overhead compartments are every bit as scary as an industrial-sized vacuum, and probably more dangerous.

I had virtuously limited myself to a smallish backpack stuffed with egg salad sandwiches, just in case; I like to travel light, but you never know when they'll feed you next, and I hate being hungry. So far, no one has mistaken them for plastic explosives, but there's always a first time, especially with my egg salad, and then I would have to consume them on the spot rather than waste them by throwing them away.

The next surprise was that I had somehow decided my flight departed at 6 a.m., and so had, with difficulty, roused myself from a peaceful slumber at 3:30, only to discover at the airport that my flight actually left at 8 a.m., so I was hours early, which is actually a good thing, as I tend to run late. I was definitely not late, but I really could have used the extra sleep. Trying to get breakfast down my throat (you guessed it – egg salad) at 4 a.m. does not qualify as one of my top ten activities.

I slept all night on the flight and arrived safely in Okinawa. However, I hit a snag at Immigration.

Immigration: At what address are you staying?

Oops. I had no earthly idea.

Me: Uh – Okinawa?

Immigration: (reasonably enough, and very patiently) Which city in Okinawa?

Having only recently ascertained the location of the island on the world map, I was stumped as to any cities that might be located there.

Me: Uh – no idea (helpfully, having been struck by inspiration), I'm visiting my nephew.

Immigration: (making an amazingly logical leap) On a military base?

Me: (beaming) Yes, that's it! A military base!

Immigration: (long-suffering) Which military base?

We were back at square one.

Me: Blank look. There's more than one?

Immigration rattles off about a dozen base names. None of them sound familiar.

Me: (helplessly)I don't know. My nephew is picking me up.

Immigration looks heavenward in despair, sighs, and lets me through.

I have arrived.

A FEW FACTS

HAVING ARRIVED SAFELY in Okinawa, I was faced with a series of distinct shocks:

1.They speak Japanese in Okinawa. I mean, of course they do, as they are part of Japan, and I knew that in some deep recess of my brain, but it was a surprise to discover that not so many people spoke English as I had thought, and almost every sign was in Japanese, and not in English, making menus, store names, train stations, instructions - everything, in short – very confusing. Now, I'm pretty good at unraveling words in other languages (one time that taking Latin and ancient Greek comes in handy), but Japanese, of course, does not share our alphabet; it uses complicated characters, and I was familiar with none of them. I had, in fact, exactly two words of Japanese to my name when I arrived, one of them from doing the crossword in the Siskiyou Daily News: hai (which means yes, and was the one I got from doing the crossword puzzle), and arigato, which means thank you (no idea where I got that one). Thank you is fine, but only being able to say yes can get a person into some serious trouble. Fortunately, I'm pretty good at charades, and even more luckily, the Japanese are pretty good at interpreting them. I picked up (and this is phonetic, as I've no idea how it's spelled) ko-nee-chi-wa, which seems to mean welcome, glad to see you, have a nice day, and a variety of other things I'm not sure of.

2. It gets pretty cold in Japan, even in Okinawa. Having not done the research I usually embark upon before going to another country, I reasoned that I was going to an island, and most islands are warm, right? Conveniently forgetting that another island I'd been to recently – Iceland – was pretty darn cold, even in the summer when I was there, I packed mostly summer clothes. The night before I left, my friend Tonya called. "You know, Virginia, I'm looking at the weather in Japan right now, and it looks pretty cold." "How cold?" "About 45 degrees." Whoa. I threw in a long underwear top, some leggings, and a sweater. I wore said clothing, along with my scarf, gloves, jeans, a fleece jacket and a rain jacket – simultaneously, in layers - almost every day for three weeks, and borrowed a woolly hat from my niece for good measure. They did not smell nice when I got home. It snowed in Japan while I was there, more than once, and was pretty darn chilly in Okinawa. Maybe next time I'll check the weather before I go somewhere. Or not, knowing me.

3. They drive on the left in Japan and Okinawa. This was not such a big deal, as I was not driving, but it gave me a turn at first, so to speak. I've spent a fair bit of time in Britain, so it's really just a matter of adjusting your mindset, but my head still swiveled as if I were demon-possessed at every crosswalk. And the sidewalks and stairs have a yellow line down them to remind you to walk on the left. People obey rules in Japan, and look at you askance if you forget and walk on the right. But they are very polite, and no doubt make allowances for idiot tourists such as myself.

4. Japan and Okinawa are incredibly clean, and did I mention that everyone is very, very polite? No one litters, even though there is not an abundance of garbage cans – I got used to carrying my garbage around with me in a plas-

tic bag in my backpack until I could find one – and everyone recycles every-thing. When you do find a garbage can, it's almost never just a regular recep-tacle: there is a hole for cans, another one for plastic bottles, another one for newspapers, and yet another for "combustibles". I was somewhat mystified by that category, but as I generally saw a hodge-podge of miscellaneous items in it, I usually threw the remainder of my garbage in there.

And polite – oh my goodness! Everyone bows to each other; I got in the habit and was still bowing occasionally for a week after I arrived home. When you buy a sandwich, the clerk bows to you when you bring it to the counter. You bow back. They bow when they give you your change, and thank you for the privilege of dealing with you (at least, that's what it seemed like they were saying). You bow back. This can go on for hours. Walking down the street one day, I saw a young woman approach an elderly one; they clearly knew each other, and were overjoyed to see one another, but they did not throw their arms around each other. No, they bowed to each other, smiling widely, back and forth as I walked past. I looked back, and they were still bowing and smiling. It was lovely to see.

Kimonos, Obis and Toe Socks

Remember the cat and Okinawa? Back to that story…

One of my first few days in Okinawa, my niece treated me to a luncheon with her international expat women's group, who were meeting with a Japa-nese and Okinawan women's group. For the occasion, we opted to experience the full cultural spectrum by dressing in kimonos. My niece, having lived there for a year and a half by now, had already done this, but I had not, and certainly did not expect what followed.

Dressing in a kimono is not a simple matter of throwing on a robe and tying it shut, as I had imagined. No, it took several women and about an hour and a half to get me into my kimono, and I don't think it was just because I was particularly awkward and difficult to fit, although I was both of those things. In fact, my niece, at 5'10", is even taller than I am, but it took her about the same amount of time.

First, you have to have the appropriate undergarments. I, of course, did not, but my nightgown was a reasonable substitute. At least, no one looked down their nose at me, but as I have said, they are very polite people. And pretty short, for the most part, so it would have been difficult anyway.

Next came the sort of under-kimono; it looks sort of like a kimono, but not quite. It's white and rather like a plain cotton version of a kimono. This garment is then folded and held up by various pieces of elastic done in exactly the correct way – everything in Japan and Okinawa, I was to learn, is done carefully and exactly, from street-sweeping to dressing to the amazing artwork.

Next comes the kimono itself, which is also folded and tucked and placed on the body in the particular way it should be. I had no idea what way that was supposed to be, of course, which is why I had several women conferring – no one would call it arguing – anxiously, probably about my weird American body and how in the world they were going to make this work without embarrassing themselves and me.

At last they had the whole thing draped and folded to their satisfaction, which made me very happy, as I was beginning to be very hungry, but then came the obi, or sash, that tops the whole affair off. We do not just tie the kimono closed with a simple sash; no, that would not be appropriate. Instead, the obi is brought out: about 12 feet long and gorgeously decorated, it is wrapped around the body as tightly as a boa constrictor; they had to ask me several times if I could breathe. "Yes, just about" I replied, weak but smiling politely (I was beginning to take on local manners). "I'll certainly eat less lunch, though!" Upon further reflection, this may have been the point; I certainly didn't see many overweight people on either Okinawa or Japan. I saw one fairly obese guy on a train in Japan, but I figured he was a sumo wrestler.

Having wound the obi around me until I felt like a maypole, they commenced to tie an intricate series of folds in the back which apparently means something, although I'm not sure what. I couldn't see it, of course, but I saw others, and they are lovely. Plus, you could hide all sorts of things in there if you needed to, like an extra hankie or jewelry.

I saw some women whip out a napkin at lunch, but didn't see where they came from, so I had to ask, but it seems they came from their sleeves. At least I think that's what they said. So, I discovered yet another hidey hole for extraneous items which eliminated the need for a purse. I was impressed. In fact, single women wear long sleeves, while married women wear shorter sleeves, so I figured there was a definite advantage to being single, but all our kimonos, which were brand new but rented, had short sleeves, so I didn't get to hide anything extra up, or more accurately, down my sleeve. Rats.

Last but not least came the toe socks. I had seen these before, but never tried a pair on. I don't like things between my toes – it's one of my little foibles – but I found the toe socks surprisingly comfortable, and they helped keep my feet warm on the tatami mats. And, as a bonus, we got to take them home.

People asked me if I brought a kimono home, and although I found some stunning examples in a thrift store for less than $30, after giving it some thought, I refrained. After all, I don't know anyone who knows how to put them together properly, and I really don't have the time to spend an hour and a half getting dressed in the morning. I did bring home a couple of obis that I can use as table runners on a 12-foot table, though, and I can just about manage to put on my toe socks.

TROUBLE WITH TRAINS

WHILE IN OKINAWA, my niece took me everywhere by car, so I didn't have to worry about transportation at all. When we flew to Japan, however, it was a different story.

Some of you know that if it's possible to have a negative sense of direction, I have one. So when we had to take the subway to our hotel, I was in serious trouble. I've been on subways in London, Paris, Los Angeles and New York, and I have never – let me repeat that, never – seen a more complicated subway system than the one in Tokyo. The map is a hopeless tangle of knotted yarn, and I could make no sense of it whatsoever. Fortunately, my niece could, and she also had a working GPS on her phone, which I did not (that's what happens when you have the cheapest phone plan available). It didn't help that every time we came up out of the bowels of the earth to return to the hotel, we seemed to come out in a different place, even though it was always the same stop. Or usually, anyway.

Our first night in Japan, we wended our weary way through the subway, up into the street, down the street for about ten blocks, up a long set of stairs (and just to make the picture complete, I was hauling a 50-pound suitcase behind me), across a bridge, back down the stairs, and up the street to the hotel. After that, we found a much simpler route – having dumped my suitcase in the room so that I was traveling with only a light backpack by then, of course. Well, pretty light – I always had plenty of food in it, just in case.

After a few days of observing my blank expression every time we entered or exited a subway, my niece became understandably concerned. "What are you going to do when I leave?" she exclaimed (I had another six days to survive after she left). "I'm afraid I'll lose you forever in the Tokyo subway system, and I don't want to be responsible for that. It will be so awkward at family reunions! "Oh, you're the one who lost Aunt Virginia in the Tokyo subway!"

But, knowing myself as I do, I assured her I would be okay. Just find me a cheap hotel within walking distance of the train station – NOT the subway – and I'll be fine, I said. At least, I will be after a few days, which is how long it will take me to remember the route, if I'm lucky, but I didn't tell her that part. And sure enough, after a few wrong turns in the first few days, I mostly had it down.

The trains were another story. Japan is famous for its "bullet trains", or Shinkansen, and they seemed relatively straightforward compared to the subway. However, everything, including both verbal and written announcements of upcoming stops was, of course, in Japanese, which made matters complicated. Also, the trains were so fast that any photos I tried to take came out a blur, and I got a little seasick when I tried to do the crossword puzzle. But hey, they sure get you there in a hurry!

For starters, you had to know from which platform your particular train was leaving. I had been lucky enough to have an itinerary printed out for me by a travel advisor in the hotel, but not all my train platforms were on the schedules she gave me. Also, I had splurged on a first-class train pass before I left home, thinking I might end up sleeping on the train, while Beth, my niece, was relegated to steerage, so we had to sit in different cars.

Then, you stand in the place on the platform indicated by your ticket, which sounds very organized until you realize that there are many train lines, color coded, and you have to know which train line you're boarding, what color it is and its destination, and find the appropriate car number. Occasionally, such as the first time we took the train anywhere, there were duplicates, which meant that, when I thought I had the right train and car, I did not. Thankfully, I dithered long enough that I missed the train, and Beth had some sort of sixth sense that told her not to get on the train, since we were miles apart on the platform, or I really would be wandering the streets of Tokyo for the rest of my life.

First class was amazing. It was never crowded – in fact, there were times when only one other person shared my car – and the seats were so roomy and comfortable that, if I hadn't been terrified into rigid watchfulness by the prospect of missing my station every day, I would have been able to enjoy the ride. As it was, I did not exactly look like a first-class passenger, with my ratty backpack and generally unkempt appearance, due to the fact that I had been wearing the same clothes for three weeks because of the unexpected (for me, anyway) extreme cold. Even when I accidentally ended up in the wrong car and/or seat, which happened more than once, the conductor was unfailingly polite, asking me apologetically to move to the car/seat clearly indicated on my ticket, accompanied by much bowing on both our parts.

By the time I left Japan I had taken so many trains that I swayed when I walked. At least I felt confident I could find my train. But I steered clear of the subway.

CUSTOMER SERVICE

I HAD MANAGED to get myself to Hakodate in Hokkaido, the northernmost island in Japan; it was about a six-hour journey by bullet train, and it was snowing pretty hard by the time I arrived. I don't believe I've ever seen snow on a beach before. I wandered around town for a while, taking pictures of manhole covers and other interesting things, and then decided to buy a few souvenirs for my niece and nephew's children. I also needed to sharpen the pencil I had brought with me to work on the backlog of crossword puzzles I take everywhere when I travel, lest I be stuck somewhere with nothing to do. I thought I might pick up a cheap manual-type sharpener such as the one I have at home.

When I mimed my need for a pencil sharpener, or even a new pencil, the young clerk in the first store at which I made my inquiry indicated that, regretfully, they had neither item in stock. However, suddenly seemingly struck by inspiration, she disappeared into the back room, returning in short order with a box cutter. When I had gotten over my alarm at this development, I watched her carefully place a tissue under my pencil and proceed to painstakingly, artistically carve the tip of my pencil until it was almost as sharp as the box cutter. An electric sharpener could not have done a better job of it. I bought more items than I needed just as a tribute to her craftsmanship and superior customer service skills.

You learn to wear nice socks in Japan, because chances are excellent that you will be asked to remove your shoes somewhere along your journey. They very politely provide slippers to wear, but the Japanese were not prepared for my weirdly shaped feet (neither are Americans, for that matter; it's really hard for me to find shoes that fit anywhere), and the slippers never fit my feet. Himeji Castle was particularly memorable for this, as the slippers provided refused to stay on; as the castle is seven stories high, and all floors are reached via very steep wooden stairs (more like ladders, really), the situation became downright dangerous. I would climb halfway up the stairs, doing my best to grip the slippers with my toes, at which point one or both of the slippers would fall off my feet, and I would do a balancing act to keep from tumbling down the stairs after them; some kind person would retrieve them for me, and on it would go. Eventually I got so frustrated I simply took the slippers off and proceeded in my stocking feet; it was slippery (so to speak), but still not nearly as dangerous as those slippers.

After touring the castle, I was approached by an elderly Japanese man who must have seen the confused look on my face (I was trying to find the exit and was, as usual, directionally impaired). He indicated that I should follow the route he and his wife were taking, which appeared to be off the beaten path. His English was very good, and he explained that he wanted to show me something special. We went down some steep steps, and then he told me that this exit was a secret one that couldn't be seen from the front of the castle due to the angle of the walls. Thus, if the castle were attacked and invaded, the defenders could come out this way and the attackers wouldn't see them until it was too late. He also showed me places in the castle walls where later shoguns had added on to the castle. It turns out that he was a volunteer guide whose workday was over, but who loved his job so much he was perfectly willing to show an interested visitor a few sites she wouldn't otherwise have seen. When I asked how to find the gardens (which were next door, as it turned out), we both struggled a bit trying to work out the directions until his wife kindly pointed out to both of us the map on the back of my brochure.

When my niece and I went to a town near Mt. Fuji, we decided to take a cable car, or as they call them, a rope car. This name did not inspire confidence in me, especially as I am afraid of heights to begin with, and intimating that we were suspended by nothing more substantial than a rope did not help. When the attendant bowed to the empty car before we got in, we began to imagine all sorts of frightening things. Was she bowing to forestall disaster? Was she praying for us? Saying silently, "So sorry to lose you, but thanks anyway for riding with us"? She did the same thing when we came back; was this "I'm thanking the gods you made it back after all"? The mind – or at least my mind – boggled at the possibilities. But make it back we did, so maybe it worked. Customer service at its best.

SOUP AND SNAKES

EATING IN JAPAN and Okinawa was an adventure, as it generally is when you don't speak or read the language.

There was a delicious, inexpensive noodle soup available in most train stations called soba, of which I became very fond. There is also a highly poisonous snake (called, according to my niece, the "cigarette snake", because by the time you finish your cigarette after being bitten, you're dead) on Okinawa called a habu, and unfortunately, I kept getting the two confused, calling the soup "sabu" and generally confusing and alarming large segments of the dining establishments. Who knows if "sabu" is even a word, and if it is what it might mean. But I was not alone in my confusion; we passed a sign stating "Let's be careful of hubs" with a drawing of a cheerful looking fanged snake on it that amused my niece so much she took a picture of the sign with her husband standing next to it. Happily, I never ran into any. Snakes, that is.

Equally disturbing, if not more so, were the many bottles of alcohol containing said deceased habu, mouth open and fangs exposed, sort of like a very nasty, larger version of the worm in a tequila bottle. I never could figure out what the attraction was – to either.

I fell in love with the vending machines, and they became a staple in my diet. Not the machines themselves, you understand; I was never quite that hungry. These were not your ordinary vending machines; besides cold drinks, hot coffee and hot milky tea, they dispensed hot chocolate and even hot soups, including my favorite, corn soup, and my not-so-favorite, bean soup. They couldn't hold a candle to the soba, but in a pinch, they filled up the empty spaces.

A very fun discovery was a restaurant called "Sushi-Go-Round", which, precisely as described in the name, sent individual dishes of sushi and other treats to each table on a conveyor belt. You simply snag whatever looks good, eat it, and slide the empty dish into a slot on the table. Staff keeps count of the dishes, no doubt in the bowels of the restaurant somewhere, and charges accordingly. If you don't see what you want, you can order on screen, which doubles as a sort of children's game with prizes, but I never did quite work that one out.

My nephew took me to dinner one night at a hole-in-the wall place apparently beloved of the locals. Run by three elderly women who brook no nonsense from anyone, the restaurant has fantastic, cheap food. You come in the door, select what you want from a chart of pictures on the wall, move to what looks like a vending machine, locate your dish by finding the same picture on it, and press the button. Out comes, not the dish, but a ticket, which you take to one of the owner-operators, who proceeds to cook your selection for you. The dish I wanted had a red light under it, indicating they were out of that item, but my nephew, who eats there often, said, "Oh, don't worry. That light is always on. I think they just haven't gotten around to changing the bulb." Sure enough, he got the ticket and gave it to the cook, and she prepared the dish, which was delicious, without hesitation. It pays to be with a local.

TEA CEREMONY

I HAD HEARD a great deal about the Japanese tea ceremony, but did not have the opportunity to experience one while I was in Okinawa. We did have tea quite a bit though; it seemed as if every time we visited a castle or a tourist spot, we were offered tea, which is a lovely custom. Sometimes it was quite spontaneous, as in the time we visited the aquarium; when we went outside, we discovered a reconstructed ancient village which was completely devoid of tourists, or anyone else, and wandered about enraptured until we came upon an elderly woman who urged us to have tea with her in one of the huts – for free. It was one of those magical moments that is completely unexpected and charming. We also indulged once or twice in one of the tourist-oriented tea houses, which were inexpensive, authentic, and very tasty. The tea, that is, not the teahouse itself, of course; I wasn't that hungry.

It was not until I was wandering around a garden site in Kyoto, having purposefully lost the rest of my tour group, as I was wont to do, when I stumbled across a sign indicating that inside the building one could experience a tea ceremony, so in I went, having decided I had enough time before the tour bus left to at least observe. I was ushered into a lovely, open room with an older Taiwanese couple and a French mother and son; the latter were sitting on the floor, being instructed in how to hold the tea bowl properly. The older couple were seated on chairs, looking slightly alarmed, as was I by then. I don't sit well on floors, being old and crotchety, and I do especially poorly at folding my legs under me like a small child – I wasn't able to do that even as a small child, and my abilities, and my knees, have not improved with time. The Taiwanese lady whispered to me that she wouldn't be able to sit that way, either, so at least I had a fellow geriatric on my side. We quelled our fear of failure temporarily to watch as the mother and son were firmly told how to stir the tea.

One would think this would be a fairly simple operation, but it was anything but that. First, the tea was unlike any tea I had ever seen. To begin with, it was green, but not like green teas I had seen and drunk in America; this tea bore a strong resemblance to the kind of slime you would find under a river rock, with the sludgy consistency of a green smoothie, but warm. So, it really, really needed to be stirred, and the stirring had to be performed in a very particular way, while on one's knees, with the correct implement. This implement looked a lot like a whisk, except that it was made of bamboo rather than wire, and was open on the bottom. It had to be held in just the right way, and to be moved back and forth rather than in circles around the bowl (the tea was prepared and drunk in a bowl, not a cup). By this time, the lady next to me and I were becoming quite concerned that we would abjectly fail the tea test and live in ignominy the rest of our lives. If I could have crept quietly and unobtrusively out the back door, I would have at this point, but there was no back door, and the women in charge were watching us carefully, no doubt to forestall just such a breakout. We were given sweets to keep us in check, and then it was our turn, the mother and son having finished their tea duties and escaped. At least the Taiwanese couple and I had each other for company and no audience, which would have made me so nervous I probably would have dropped everything in a panic and disgraced myself forever.

We were shown how to hold the bowl just so, hand placement apparently being very important, and commenced to stirring, having carefully observed what not to do by the example of the mistakes made by the mother and son before us; it appeared from the kimonoed (somehow I doubt that's a word) ladies' smiles that we had not completely disgraced ourselves, as we were allowed to drink our tea, which was, unfortunately, was not an experience I would care to repeat, or normally count as a reward, but we were so relieved at this point not to have spilled, or offended everyone's ancestors by stirring the wrong way or holding our bowls badly, that it counted as a prize of sorts.

And I had at last participated in a real Japanese tea ceremony! Now all I had to do was arrange for a crane – a mechanical one, not the bird – to lift me up off my poor, cramped knees in time to hobble my way back to the tour bus and resume my tour of Kyoto – City of 1,000 Gardens and one genuine Japanese tea ceremony.

THE BEEHIVE

WHILE I WAS ON OKINAWA, I was lucky enough to stay with my nephew and his wife; he is stationed there, and they had been there about a year and a half when I got there, so they definitely knew their way around the island and showed me a wonderful time.

When my niece and I decided to go to Japan together, we were able to stay at a hotel for military families which was quite elegant and very reasonable, so I was getting spoiled by the time she left and I was on my own. Before she left, she had noticed my tendency to become disoriented, and was quite concerned that I would be lost forever in Tokyo when she left me to my own devices. But I had a solution: find me a cheap hotel within walking distance of the train station, and I'll be fine, I said. So she researched – I did not have access to the internet on my cheap phone plan – and found what is referred to as a "capsule hotel". I had heard of these places and was a little alarmed; they were said to slide you in and out of a drawer like a cadaver on a morgue slab, and while I do not generally suffer from claustrophobia, I did get a little breathless the last time I had an MRI. It was fine as long as I kept my eyes closed, but still…

So we decided to check it out before Beth left, just to be on the safe side. It was pretty easy to find, all things being relative for me of course when it comes to directions. Unfortunately, we marked one turn by noting a large crane, and when I came back alone I discovered the hard way that there was lots of construction and more than one crane in operation in this part of town, but still, I worked it out. The hotel was called the First Cabin Kiyoboshi, Kiyoboshi being the area of Tokyo it was in, First Cabin sounding vaguely aeronautically comforting, and was next to a restaurant I couldn't afford to eat in, but at least there was food nearby in case of emergency. I have a lot of food emergencies.

The hotel was reached by taking an elevator to the second floor, where the very polite receptionist offered to show us a sample room. We took the elevator to the ninth floor and were told that the rooms were segregated by gender; men and women were housed on different floors. We were shown the shared bathroom on my floor, which included showers and just about every toiletry one could want - for free.

Then came the room itself. It was not a morgue drawer, but it was close. The bed took up the entire room, which wasn't hard because the room measured about five feet by eight feet. The bed was a little hard, but as I had to stand on it to get dressed in the morning, that was useful. There was a light on one wall and an air-conditioning control which, as far as I could tell, never worked, as it was always hot. A small locking storage area was on one side of the bed, and a large-screen television was attached at the foot of the bed. A few hangers were provided for clothing, which I hung from the TV. There was no door as such, just a screen very much like a window shade that you pulled down when you crawled into bed at the end of the day. The rooms were right next to each other, a bit like post office boxes. My suitcase was stored out in the hallway, locked to a brass rail, and I stored food in the kitchen fridge manned by staff in a back room on the reception floor. It was perfect.

When I checked in the next day, I found on my bed a bag containing a set of pajamas, a pair of slippers (mine to keep), toothpaste and a toothbrush, comb, washcloth, and several other toiletry items, just in case I might need them. They were replaced with fresh ones every day. Headphones were provided so that one could listen to the television quietly.

The one thing I was nervous about was noise levels; I had images of loud, partying teenagers shouting throughout the night, as has happened to me even in very nice, large American hotels. To my total surprise, the only sound I heard in the six nights I stayed there was a woman unzipping her suitcase early one morning; as I had to get up anyway, it was not a problem. I cannot imagine such a system working anywhere in America, or much of the rest of the world, but as the Japanese people were the most polite, considerate, respectful people I have ever come across, it worked a treat.

I did notice that the issue of poorly translated written materials ran rampant even in the hotel. I quote directly from the document I had to sign to stay there: "Article 5: Cancellation of Reservation. When applicant of reservation cancelled all or a part of the rule to determine particularly. Day in response to notice of contract cancellation:

Two days ago: 30%

The day before: 50%
On that day: 80%
Non-night: 100%
When we do not arrive even if hotel guest does not in form…"

It was at about this point that I gave up trying to understand the contract and simply signed, as I was tired and wanted to sleep.

I affectionately referred to the hotel as "The Beehive", and I would stay there again in a heartbeat – a very quiet heartbeat.

TOILETS AND MANHOLE COVERS

WHILE IN JAPAN, I developed a fascination with manhole covers and toilets.

This is not quite as nutty as it sounds – really; the manhole covers were varied and quite beautiful. It seems that everything in Japan is done with tremendous care, precision and workmanship – even the manhole covers. They were so beautiful, in fact, that while other tourists were busily taking pictures of things like shrines, temples and gardens, I would find myself crouched over a manhole cover, eliciting some odd looks. In fact, one day as I stood over a very fine specimen of manhole cover in Himeji, a town renowned for its quite gorgeous castle, to which I was completely oblivious, at least while my fascination with this particular example of sewage equipment lasted, I looked up to see a Japanese woman looking at me with some bemusement. After a while, she shook her head, laughed, and moved on, no doubt thinking to herself, "These crazy American tourists will take a picture of anything!", much as I had thought on various occasions about Japanese tourists in America, proving we humans are really all alike.

But the toilets were magnificent. Of course, not all of them were, but the majority were impressive. They ranged from the hole in the ground that you had to stand over, which I encountered in a parking lot in Okinawa (I know, it would not be my first pick, either, but at least they had one, and I was pretty desperate), complete with illustrations of how to use it properly, to the ones in the first-class train car and those in fancy buildings, which I did not often have occasion to enter, being on a very tight budget. The first-class train restrooms were so impressive that I took pictures; royalty would have been quite comfortable in them. Some were so large you could have fit a family of six in one. They were tastefully decorated, with hot water, soap, towels, and every other amenity you could possibly desire. There were, of course, mysterious (to me, anyway) items in some of them whose purpose I never could work out, but at least I could usually figure out the flushing mechanism.

The fancy toilets had, if you can believe it, warmed seats. It was a luxury I am sorely missing now that I'm home and as I write it's a bitterly cold, late winter. However, most toilets also had cryptic instructions in poorly translated English that left me completely stumped about how to flush them. There was normally nothing so straightforward as a handle; that would be too easy. These were such high-tech toilets that they had a variety of ways to flush them, and at least once, after spending ten minutes or more trying to suss out what they had in mind, I had to leave without ever puzzling it out. Or flushing, for that matter.

In addition, on the sides were pictures that baffled me. It appeared from the illustrations that one could bathe, listen to music, and call for the assistance of a young woman if in dire need of aid, and I was afraid to push any of the buttons related to the pictures in case something untoward should occur. Occasionally, immediately upon entering the stall, soft flushing sounds would ensue before I had even sat down. Was this an encouragement? I did once find instructions that read, clearly and simply, "Push the button to flush the toilet", but the arrow pointed down to a bewildering array of buttons, and again I was stumped. My favorite sign read, verbatim: "Thank you for having you always use it neatly. Please carry away the toilet paper to the restroom. Please do not stroll around thing except the toilet paper. It causes trouble." What caused the trouble, and exactly what kind of trouble "it" was, I did not care to discover. But then, bad translations ran rampant; I would have a lifetime job if I applied to be the national editor/translator into English.

Other helpful hints included such instructions, with illustrations, as "Please sit down to use the toilet." "Do not throw toilet paper away in the trash bin. Please place the toilet paper in the toilet and flush." "Please use up the toilet paper til the last." The last what, I dared not ask.

And then there's the toilet paper. At one tourist spot, they wanted you to pay for the toilet paper; hah! I thought – never! It is for just such occasions I carry Kleenex. At other places, there is so much toilet paper on display that it was clear no one ever thought of carrying it away for personal use – "to the restroom", or anywhere else.

Now that I'm home again, I must admit: I've been completely spoiled, and I'm finding our toilets rather boring. Even if they are easier to use, the seats aren't warmed.

PARTING SHOTS

MY BELOVED AND I FINALLY REALIZED a long-standing dream of visiting Timbuktu, which is, as it turns out, a real place, in Mali to be precise.

It appears that the journey to Timbuktu begins even before it begins. I went in for eight, count 'em, eight shots before leaving – not including the tetanus shot I had in my left arm the week before, which made my arm so sore I could hardly use it for a week, but hey, I'm right-handed, so who cares?

After having avoided flu shots my entire life, I decided what the heck, as long as I'm doing my pincushion impersonation, what's one more? So I went for that one, too. My beloved, of course, scoffs at all vaccines other than yellow fever, which is required to get into the country, or he'd probably skip that one, too; it certainly would be cheaper. After all, this is the man who drinks from puddles recently vacated by crocodiles and doesn't even get stomach cramps (my beloved, that is, not the crocodile, although I can't really vouch for the crocodile).

So they covered my puncture marks with carefully labelled Band Aids, all eight of them, in case I swell up like a big toad and keel over from allergic reactions to one or more of them, no doubt so they can tell which one it was for future research purposes ("Whoa, Carl, don't give that one again!").

Speaking of Band Aids: I have Band Aid issues. While some brave souls subscribe to the "Rip 'em off all at once and get it over with!" school of thought (these are the same people who, I am convinced, hold to the theory that one should leap into a cold swimming pool rather than gingerly test the waters one toe at a time), I admit that I myself am a total Band Aid wuss. This means that when I'm not lucky enough to get that stretchy Ace bandage stuff that sticks to itself and not your skin (and I didn't get it this time, but I don't blame them a bit, as it would have taken an entire roll of the stuff to cover all my punctures and cost the county more money than they can afford), the Band Aids stay on until they basically rot off. There aren't enough hot baths in the world to soak these puppies off; some, but not all of them are currently hanging from one end, which makes me resemble a sort of fugitive character from an undead film, but I just wear long sleeves. Hey, its' winter, right?

Anyway, I held up the vaccination line in town for half an hour while Public Health, bless them, sorted me out. A woman I talked to a while ago who's going to Ghana said her doctor advised her to get a rabies shot (at more than $400); having lived there, I suggested she not worry too much, as in my experience most of the animals over there have already been eaten. I certainly intend to stay away from any fauna that might remain in Mali, especially the bats. I'm not overly fond of bats, for some reason, and I don't even watch that "True Blood" series or read the books; life is scary enough as it is, especially with all these Band Aids hanging from my arms.

Meanwhile, much to my beloved's amusement should he find out, which he will soon enough, I have packed water purifying tablets, a treated mosquito net (although as far as I can tell I won't have anything to hang it from), copious amounts of insecticide with DEET (I fully expect to reek of eau de bug juice the entire trip), and enough energy bars to last me the entire three weeks if I ration myself to two a day (yes, that's 42 bars, plus a few in my hand luggage should the plane crash and/or I become separated from my luggage) – you never know. Also Immodium, about which nothing more need be said, laundry detergent, and powdered Gatorade (see "Immodium"). I only hope I don't confuse the Gatorade with the laundry detergent, or I'll really need the former). I've also started taking the malaria preventive medicine, which doesn't always work and sometimes only masks the symptoms when you've actually contracted the disease, and causes a psychotic reaction in some people, but what the heck. I warned my coworkers to be on the lookout for symptoms of irrationality, but they just shrugged and remarked they probably wouldn't notice the difference.

The last time we traveled in Africa, the children were small and I was a lot younger and more optimistic (or just dumber, I'm not sure which), and I, too, scoffed at such preventive measures. Of course, that was before the children managed to be infested with two different types of worms, my beloved contracted malaria, and I came down with bacterial dysentery. These days, I want as many preventive measures and as much insurance as I can find and pack into my already bulging luggage.

TRAVEL TRAVAILS

SO, THE TRIP TO TIMBUKTU did not work out quite as planned. My life being what it is, this should surprise no one, least of all me, but I must admit I didn't expect the problems to start even before I got out of the Medford airport.

There was fog in San Francisco, apparently, which caused a delay in my flight for that destination. Not an unusual occurrence, but I had a connecting flight to Paris, so I was a bit nervous, I will admit. However, the travel gods smiled upon me, albeit briefly, and I made it to San Francisco in time to make my connection.

Unfortunately, we sat on the tarmac at the San Francisco airport waiting, it seems, for a parking place. I knew parking was bad in San Francisco, but really? At the airport? On the tarmac, for the airplanes? It's not as if we were waiting to get into the parking lot at a San Francisco Giants game. In the end, we were delayed just long enough for me to miss my flight to Paris – they held the domestic flights for everyone else, of course – which meant I was stuck at the airport, as there were no more flights to Paris that day, naturally. It seems Air France shuts up shop and goes home the instant the last flight leaves, which was about 4 p.m.

I frantically called Air France customer service, which gave a figurative Gallic shrug and said they'd be happy to re-book me on a flight the next day, for a small $800 fee. I explained that it wasn't my fault I missed the flight, it was an air-traffic controller/parking problem, at which they gave, I am certain, another shrug, and told me it was United's fault, not theirs, and I should speak to United.

Off I went to United, at another terminal, naturally, which involved a trip on the tram from hell, as I came to think of it, where United shrugged and told me it wasn't their fault, either, or their problem, and I'd better go back and talk to Air France. This went on for awhile until I began to feel I was in the eighth or ninth circle of Dante's Inferno, a flaming badminton birdie being batted back and forth between airlines for the remainder of my natural life, when someone warned me I ought to check on my luggage.

The status of my luggage having not even occurred to me yet, I now had another potential crisis to worry about. So down I went to the bowels of the airport to check my luggage, which, of course, no one knew anything about, and discovered to my horror that I was now outside the secured area of the airport, and would not be able to get back in, because, of course, I now had no valid boarding pass.

Resisting the urge to sit down and cry, I realized I could call my daughter in Oakland and throw myself on her mercy for the night, at which point I discovered my cell phone was missing. Looking and feeling no doubt like a lost waif from "Les Miserables", or more likely an escapee from an asylum, which was exactly what I felt like by now, I asked a stranger if I could borrow his cell phone, and although he looked at me suspiciously (I could hardly blame him), he gave it to me long enough to arrange my rescue.

Back I went to the tram from hell, which I was now beginning to regard as an old friend, and which fortunately got me to BART and from thence, all the way to my daughter, who calmed her elderly, hysterical mother and got her back to the airport the next day. I also discovered my cell phone, buried deep in the recesses of my hand luggage, which was a relief.

I made it safely to Mali, where there was another delay once I actually got as far as immigration – so close, and yet so far away once again. I was pulled aside, and after waiting in a small room with about 50 other people for what seemed like hours, watching money in many denominations change hands, I wondered if I was missing something crucial – like a bribe. All of us were apparently having visa issues, although it's hard to tell when you don't speak any of the languages being spoken all around you, but determined not to be separated from my passport, which they had taken from me. I was the last one left and was beginning to think I might spend the rest of my life in said small room. I was finally informed that my visa was not an original, and I therefore could not enter the country.

At about the time I was ready to have another sinking spell, someone handed me a cellphone with my beloved on the other end of the line. He told me to step outside the office (no problem – they had already kicked me out), and sure enough, there was a stranger holding up a sign with my name on it. I rushed over, he handed me an original visa, and I fell into my beloved's waiting arms, free at last.

Rats and Other Vermin

MALI IS A French-speaking country. I had been there about four days when I realized I was beginning to think in French. Since the sum of my French vocabulary consists of about ten words, conversations were guaranteed to be short.

After about a week, I managed to think of needed words in every language but French; thereafter I spoke to the English-speakers in French and the French speakers in English, and then subsided into total silence (very restful for my husband, he assures me), as I couldn't think of the words for things in any language at all.

And rest is hard to come by at times. One morning in camp I was awakened, in turn, by the cockerel (4:30 a.m.), the call to morning prayer (5:30 a.m.), the cockerels again (6 a.m. – they must have got the time wrong the first try), donkeys braying their displeasure at assuming the day's burdens (6:10 a.m.), the obligatory dawn chorus of birds (6:20 a.m.), half the population of the village starting up their motorbikes (6:30 a.m.), and the other half banging their breakfast cooking pots (6:35 a.m.), at which point I surrendered – clearly, it was time to get up.

One form of wildlife we got to observe was found at the sacred crocodile pond, and it was fully occupied. It's fairly unnerving to watch lots of beady eyes staring intently at you from just above the surface of the water. There's very little doubt about their intentions, and I noted that the biggest one was gazing fixedly at my beloved, and while I do the same often, it had a very different look in its eye. It was time to evacuate the area.

One of my most vivid memories of the trip actually occurred at the end of it, at our first (and last) hotel. It was a pretty good hotel, but for some reason the swimming pool was located on the far side of the of the outdoor restaurant. Seeking to spare the patrons the sight of me dripping through their meals in my bathing suit after a swim, I slipped into a back alley to reach my room, where I happened upon the largest rat I have ever seen in my life, coming straight towards me in a rather more determined manner than made me comfortable.

This rat was bigger than most of my cats at home, put together, and I began to understand why I had seen so few cats on the trip: they had no doubt all been eaten by the rats. I'm not overly fond of rats to begin with, so I whipped off my towel and began "shooshing" him with it in an effort to change his direction, while hissing "Go away!" under my breath, not wishing to alarm those dining a few feet away from the scene. He actually complied – "shoosh" apparently being a universal word, even to French-speaking rats, or else the sight of me in my bathing suit was more than even an African rat can handle – but just when I thought it was safe to breathe again, a waiter entered the alley from the opposite end. The rat, no doubt confused by this development, turned hopefully in my direction and came towards me once more. I resumed "shooshing", and the rat reversed direction towards the waiter, who did some "shooshing" of his own, or at least the French version of it, resulting in the rat, for whom I was beginning to feel sorry, heading back towards me.

He (the rat) was desperate and fast by now, and managed to whizz past me (not that I really wanted to sidetrack him at that point), while the waiter explained the saga in some detail to another waiter (at least that's what I assumed he was doing from all the hearty laughter that ensued, since it was all in French), while I beat a hasty retreat to my room. I can't imagine what the guests on the other side of the wall made of it all.

I didn't see much else in the way of vermin, truthfully – it had all been eaten – although I did spot a few ground squirrels at my husband's camp that had somehow managed to escape the cooking pot – so far, anyway. Fortunately, I missed the appearance of the scorpion in the tent; he (the scorpion) had the good sense to hide out until I had left for home, which is a good thing, as I'm sure you would have heard my response all the way back home had he had the nerve to show himself to me. I am no more fond of things that sting than I am of rats – possibly far less so.

My beloved has managed to take pictures of the widest array of insects imaginable while living in Mali, and even a stray, very nervous hippo, which he enjoys showing me when I get bored here at home. They are fascinating, but I like them so much more from a distance.

Driving Me Crazy

THE BEGINNING OF our trip to Timbuktu in Mali was explained previously, but from there it's a bit of a blur, probably because of the driving.

I had forgotten what driving was like in Africa, or at least in the parts I have seen, which are, admittedly, limited. Mostly because no one takes what we would call driving lessons, and licenses are generally obtained by means of a few judicious payments to the appropriate government official, driving habits tend to be somewhat, shall we say, erratic. The preferred method appears to be to go as fast as possible, honking like mad, and hoping everyone and everything gets out of the way.

We had a car and a driver, Salif, while we were in Mali, and our car horn had gone from two tones to one, no doubt from overuse. Salif was a very good driver – so good at gauging distances and getting us out of tight situations that my husband described him as having whiskers – but I think I'm getting more timid in my old age. After my first few gasps on the way from the airport to the hotel, my beloved leaned over and whispered kindly, "I find it's really better not to look." Which proved to be very good advice, and I employed it for the remainder of the trip, except when I forgot and terrified myself.

Malians have developed a very effective method of slowing vehicles down: outside every village are enormous speed bumps, which will send your car flying into the stratosphere if you don't take care. Occasionally they will strategically place a few tree branches beside the speed bumps to give you a heads up, so to speak, as the speed bumps tend to blend into the color of the road. Nothing like giving a driver a sporting chance, I say. A few of those speed bumps placed outside every school in America would go a long way to eliminating injuries to children, I'm certain, even if some of us had no chassis left. On our cars, that is.

We spent a week or so in Dogon country, where there was lots of sand in places. Driving there was a lot like being in a dune buggy at the beach, as there's no pavement at all - but without the water. We appeared to be driving randomly in first one direction, then another, and I began to wonder if our guide was as directionally impaired as I am, but it all seemed to make sense to them, especially when it was explained that we were avoiding a huge sand dune. Since none of the roads were paved anyway, this seemed a minor issue, but I had faith in Salif. At one point we encountered several overturned carts clearly and intentionally blocking the road, but Salif wasn't going to let a little thing like a road block stop him; a turn of the wheel and voila! Ne c'est problem (they speak French in Mali, which I have no doubt just massacred. The French, I mean) - we go around, off road! Loosely speaking, as there is, of course, no road to go off. No one seemed to care about why the road might have been blocked off, which was just as well, since we never did come across any issues – at least, not that I noticed during the brief periods that I had my eyes open.

I thought after this little excursion that I had experienced the worst that Mali had to offer in the way of roads, but I was, as usual, wrong in that assumption. The next day my beloved decided (wisely, as it turned out – he has an instinct for these things) to hike over the hill to our next destination, while Deo, our guide, and I opted for the drive with the faithful Salif. Although I had by now christened our four-wheel drive vehicle "Le Mouton Montaigne" (roughly, I hope, "The Mountain Goat", but given my lack of aptitude for French, who knows?), even it struggled; it was without a doubt the worst road I had ever been on (at least before we drove the road to my beloved's camp site. I use the word "road" very loosely for that particular goat track, which no self-respecting goat would dream of using). As my father thoughtfully commented on our trip to Kenya, "If they would just remove the asphalt between the potholes, it would probably improve the roads."

But I digress. Aside from being straight uphill – but no, I misspeak, since there wasn't a two-foot straight stretch on this road – the hairpin turns and breath-taking drop over the all-too-near edge would have terrified anyone – the relatively short pieces of spine-jarring, teeth-loosening cobblestone were punctuated with potholes the size of Texas, no offense to Texas. Nerves of steel were required of passengers as well as the driver (to keep us from leaping out and abandoning the vehicle altogether), door handles were gripped with white-knuckled iron fingers, and there ensued a stark, eerie silence for the duration of the trip. I'm not sure any of us even inhaled. My beloved met us at the end, cheerful and oblivious to our ordeal.

In a small village I was astounded to see three people crammed onto one small motorbike, but my beloved said that was nothing; he had seen as many as six people – three adults and three children, but one of them was an infant, so maybe that doesn't count – stacked onto one motorbike. At least there wasn't a goat onboard as well. That is, he didn't mention one.

MOUTON IN MALI

I HADN'T BEEN in Mali very long before I fell in love with every goat I saw, and there were more than a few. On the rare occasions that I actually looked up ahead out the front windshield (driving being what it is over there), it was usually to see a goat use up one of its nine lives dodging the vehicle.

Goats and livestock of all kinds wander at will throughout Mali (if not the entire continent), and it's definitely a case of "the quick and the dead" – if you're not quick, you'll soon be a goner. By some miracle, only once did a goat not quite make it out of the way of our vehicle and meet with an unfortunate accident; Salif, our driver, insisted that he (the goat) was better off going to that great pasture in the sky. Apparently if you're not a quick goat, you're a sick goat, and rather than see any of God's creatures suffer unduly, they are rapidly dispatched – one way or another.

Soon after connecting with said goat, we were, coincidentally, stopped at a checkpoint. When my beloved enquired why we were being stopped, I muttered, "He's probably looking for the goat murderer", which caused great hilarity all around, except in my corner of the vehicle (having become quite attached to every goat on the continent, I took this one's untimely demise personally).

By the end of the trip, some two weeks after we started, the tally was: Salif, one goat, one bird, and as my beloved put it, "plenty bugs" on the windshield; local fauna: nil.

Goats and vehicles figure prominently in my recollections of Mali, for some reason. Other people remember museums, the renowned mud-built mosque in Djenni (the largest mud building in the world), the charming children in the villages, the handicrafts, the manufacture of shea butter, the grand escarpment in Dogon country, but from me you will hear about the goats, or as they say in this French-speaking country, "mouton". I vividly re-member driving behind a very small motor scooter and seeing a goat strapped across the back. Then there was the man sitting on the roof of a bus, facing us, with a goat on one side of him and a sheep on the other, everyone apparently quite content, and last but not least, passing another bus with about 40 goats stacked like cordwood atop the roof, on their backs, feet straight up in the air and heads lolling over the side, tongues out, looking pitiful. I can't make any guarantees about their level of happiness, but no one was complaining. The poor things are massacred en mass during Tabasci, a Muslim holiday. I was fortunately spared witnessing said massacre, it having occurred shortly before my arrival, so I suppose all in all a short ride on their backs atop a bus isn't so bad. It's a tough life for Mouton in Mali.

There are lots of sheep as well, in case you were tired of goats, and they seem to have adapted nicely to the heat; they have very short coats, which is good as no sane person wants to wear anything like wool at any time of the year there, especially the sheep. They also keep cattle and have a great abun-dance of chickens and roosters, if the early morning racket is any indication, and they're all very quick indeed.

The cattle are herded by small boys, this not being considered women's work. The women are confined to raising crops of maize and millet, harvest-ing them, pounding and cooking them, doing the washing (in the nearest river), caring for the children (not to mention bearing them all: Mali has the third highest birth rate in the world, at almost seven children per woman), panning for gold in their spare time and, as far as I could tell, anything else not concerned with herding or sitting down discussing the problems of the world, which important business is strictly reserved for the men. But I was discussing sheep, wasn't I?

Actually, I also fell in love with the little donkeys that pull fully loaded carts everywhere and have a very hard life indeed. Occasionally you will see a two-donkey-powered cart for extra heavy loads, but generally it's just one lowly little donkey hauling a cart loaded ten feet high with firewood or who knows what. My beloved, looking meaningfully at me, remarks that he hasn't decided whether the donkeys or the women have it tougher in Africa. I'm voting for the goats, personally.

SCALING THE HEIGHTS

FAIRLY EARLY ON in our trip to Mali (at least it felt like right away), I was introduced to an interesting local implement referred to (in French, of course, in an effort to disguise its purpose from me) as "l'escalier". This was loosely translated (and I mean very loosely) as "ladder", but it seems to be my fate in life to never be able to use an implement in its normal fashion, or else never to use a normal implement in the fashion in which it is meant to be used, or both. Alternatively, I am expected to use implements that sound like something with which I am familiar, but have taken on some strange and creative new form that does not lend itself to whatever use it is meant to have. If you followed that twisted logic and grammar, you deserve a prize, although it all makes perfect sense to me, of course.

So I was presented with my first "l'escalier" in the middle of a challenging "hike/scramble" (my beloved's word; mine would be more like "forced march with acrobatic leaps", but I guess that's more than one word) up several hundred feet (and that's just the vertical climb. I won't go into the length of the hike; there's not enough time or space) over the escarpment in Dogon country. An "escalier", it transpires, much like a caving ladder, bears very little resemblance to any ladder I've ever seen; it is in truth a log with notches cut out of it. I have enough trouble with regular ladders, and they did not provide two of them, one for each leg (that being considered too extravagant in a country with very little wood to spare), so I had to affect a rather pigeon-toed, cross-legged stance in order to get up it, all while carefully avoiding looking down into the yawning chasm beneath me. And I did this several times, not being very quick on the up-take – or on anything else.

But I was assisted by my able sub-guide, a young man whose name I never got, probably because I was in shock at the sight of all those escaliers. Yes, I had my own personal sub-guide, although technically I suppose he was my sub-sub guide. We had our primary guide, the aptly-named Deo, who contracted out to our local Dogon sub-guide Omar, who was then joined by several hopeful sub-subs when we got to the village.

Eventually, I'm not sure by what method, but I'm pretty sure it involved lengthy assessments of physical ability, my size and degree of klutziness, and some bribery, I was assigned a very nice if quiet young man who did very well. I may never have caught his name, but he caught me from falling more than once. I was embarrassed to be assigned my very own personal helper until my beloved pointed out another female tourist who had not one but two healthy young men hauling her over the rocks, one on each side of her.

My young man more than earned his tip that day as I teetered over boulders and hovered over gorges, defying gravity if only briefly as I searched anxiously for the next foothold. How do I let myself be talked into these things?

I had opted, in deference to local custom, as I thought, and in defiance of any kind of common sense I may once have possessed, to wear a long skirt, this being a largely Muslim country, but my error was soon brought home to me. Even under the best of circumstances, I am not a nimble kind of person, and climbing over boulders, up l'escaliers, and across cliffs, I am here (barely) to tell you, does not lend itself to long skirts. In case you were silly enough to want to try it, I can definitively report that I do not recommend it. Needless to say, for the next day's rock-hopping I donned shorts and a light shirt, carried a walking stick, and even, at one point, an umbrella someone handed me. I ended up with a sunburn anyway. It's hard to walk with all that stuff in your hands, much less climb.

So when we stopped in a little village along the way, I sat down in exhaustion – apparently in the one place forbidden to women. Fortunately, although there was some gasping (aside from my own as I fought to catch my breath after my exertions), I was quickly hustled off to the side, no one decided I needed to be sacrificed to the gods in expiation of my blunder, and we moved on – rapidly, or as rapidly as I could manage, in case they changed their minds.

Against all odds, I managed to survive all the escaliers, chasms, climbing, hiking, and sweating, and we made it back to the car, where our driver Salif was highly amused when I declared my undying love for him, and more importantly, for the air-conditioned car he drove.

If I never see another escalier, I shall die a happy woman.

Homeward Adventures

OUR PLAN TO GO to Timbuktu, a lifetime dream, or at least a dream from the time I realized there really is such a place, was cut short by the unfortunate kidnapping of two French geologists. Well, truthfully, that probably wouldn't have stopped us, as it took place some distance from Timbuktu, but the kidnapping soon after of three tourists and the murder of a fourth, in broad daylight in a restaurant frequented by foreigners, did slow us down a bit.

We were going to board a boat the next day to start the three-day journey from Mopti, but the government decided to round up all the tourists in Timbuktu and fly them back to Bamako, the capital city, so even though we reasoned it was probably pretty safe to go to Timbuktu at this point, the terrorists having presumably left the area, we were persuaded not to continue, much to the relief of our guide. It's not as if we were going to be able to blend.

Along the way back we were, by chance, interviewed by a very brave French journalist, who was going into the area despite government warnings. Although my beloved later found the news clip, we have no idea what we said, as the entire five-second interview was dubbed in French. But that would be me in the headscarf and sun glasses, doing my best to fade into the background and failing miserably, experiencing my 15 minutes of fame.

Timbuktu now being off the menu, I ventured off to familiarize myself with my husband's tent camp in the southern part of the country, to get a feel for his way of life and share in the hardship of earning a living in the geological fashion he loves so well. This being experienced to my satisfaction, if not his, in a matter of minutes, especially after the seven-hour, bone-jarring road trip to get there, I determined it was time to go home a little early. While he does have a flush toilet, showers and an air-conditioned tent, the stomach ailment I had picked up along the way made me long for the comfort of my bed at home, so off I went.

My husband, being an expert in all things travel-related, cleverly suggested that rather than stand in the long, hot, crowded lines at the airport in order to check in my luggage, we take it to the Air France office in Bamako and check it in. Never one to turn down an opportunity to be comfortable, I concurred, and off we went to town. Unfortunately, as soon as we got there, I remembered I wanted my bathing suit out so I could swim at the hotel, so instead of the cursory check the Air France employee had in mind, I was able to give everyone in range a full view of everything I had brought with me, especially those items, like underwear, I would have preferred to have kept private, as I flung everything out in a mad rush to find the suit, which was, of course, on the bottom of the bag, and then toss everything back in.

After the usual hour-long delay on the tarmac for unspecified reasons in Bamako, and the stressful plane change in France, where of course they speak French, which leaves me with jangled nerves, I arrived in San Francisco, where I discovered they had, naturally, lost my luggage. Having already, I thought, undergone the worst that could happen in airport disasters on the way to Mali, I determined to remain calm, even though I was once again in the San Francisco airport, my own version of Dante's Inferno.

I called my mother and sister, who were going to pick me up in Medford, and calmly informed them that I was once again on American soil and would be in Medford soon (optimistic soul that I am), and began the laborious process of filling out the lost luggage claim form. When I had almost completed the form, I mentioned that I needed to hurry, or I would miss my connection to Medford, and the woman taking my information threw her hands in the air and informed me that if I had a connecting flight, I couldn't fill out the report with her. But we just did, I pointed out helpfully. Oh no, this is no good, she replied, and proceeded to tear it up. No matter, I responded, breathing deeply, I'll just go get the plane to Medford and worry about the luggage later. Oh no, she replied; my flight to Medford had been canceled due to fog. As one of my fellow frustrated passengers muttered through clenched teeth, "I thought they were flying with instruments these days?" But by now I knew the drill: I called my daughter in Oakland, negotiated the tram from hell and BART, spent the night with her and flew home the next day. I was beginning to feel that I could guide people through airport disasters professionally by now. At least this time, I'd had the sense to put my toothbrush in my hand luggage.

At six in the morning after I arrived home, waking me from a sound, jet-lagged sleep, a cheerful airline employee brought my luggage to my door.

Coincidentally, a week after my beloved left Mali to come home, a coup erupted which overthrew the government completely, although he claims it's because they couldn't manage without him. He is now on his way back there, coup or no coup, so I can only hope he has better luck traveling than I do.

BROKEN

BROKEN BUT UNBOWED

HAVING RECENTLY BEEN CURED of the plantar fasciitis that had kept me from hiking for some time, I had once again begun happily roaming the hills behind my house with the dog as soon as the snow melted enough to present less of a health hazard to someone as klutzy as I am.

On Valentine's Day I had a lovely hike and was only a few yards from home when I slipped on a small patch of frosty grass on a downhill slope, and down I went. I felt my right leg twist under me and heard a small crack as I fell. I shrugged mentally and thought, "Coulda been a twig." I waited a few minutes, but it didn't hurt much, so I started to get up and move on. Not happening. The dog and I sat and enjoyed the view for a few minutes, contemplating the scenery, although he was a little hungry for his breakfast and probably wondered why we had chosen this particular moment to take in nature's splendors. I had plenty of time to wish I had carried my cell phone as many people had recommended. After a while I located a small bush and used it to heave myself to my feet, and we proceeded into the house, where I made muffins and carried on with life, eventually heading into work, although I will say the 53 stairs to my car presented more of a challenge than I had anticipated, as my leg kept giving out, and driving a stick shift was trickier than I would have thought. I had considered grabbing one of my walking sticks to help with the trip, but as I would have had to climb a step ladder to retrieve it, decided not to.

By the end of my work day at 6:00 p.m., I felt a definite reluctance to walk; in fact, two strong men had to support me to my car, and driving a manual transmission with only one foot is a trick I do not recommend. By this time my friend Tonya, who had been telling me all day that I had broken my leg and was simply in denial about it, drove me to emergency. What a woman.

After x-rays, the doctor came in and announced with medical enthusiasm, "You have a very interesting fracture! It's a..." and here he rattled off something long and French that I was by now in too much pain to write down. Much preferable, I suppose, to having a boring, garden-variety fracture, but just as uncomfortable. I had sprained my ankle for good measure, but that was barely a blip on my radar screen.

Things have changed since the days of plaster casts, I discovered, having miraculously never broken anything before. Well, there was the shoulder, but that didn't hurt much either at first, and the doctor and I were almost equally surprised to discover that I had chipped pieces of bone off after falling while on a hike in the Grand Teton. It only hurt weeks later, when the bone chip migrated into the shoulder joint, and besides, it didn't require a cast. In any case, for the leg I was fitted with what I have not so affectionately christened "Das Boot", a huge, heavy black monstrosity with more Velcro straps than a straitjacket, and I haven't seen my leg since, which is probably a good thing.

About crutches: ouch. The armpits are not happy. Also, I am discovering what might have been muscles had I ever bothered to develop them, but are now just painful areas of my body: my left leg, shoulders, and, of all things, stomach muscles – who knew? I am such a klutz that I am way more dangerous on crutches than I ever was without them. When I get some momentum going, I'm pretty much unstoppable, and not in a good way. Another problem with crutches is that carrying anything is problematic; liquids are out of the question, and at work all my reports sport teeth marks.

Rolling chairs are another hazard; when I sit down at work, I'm halfway across the room before I can stop myself. Also, when I tried to get up from a walker, it rolled away before I was ready, and down I went. The fall isn't nearly as bad as trying to get back up from the ground, which requires engineering feats I can't describe.

As I am unable to negotiate the stairs to my house, I have moved in with my 91-year old father, who has a ramp and a one-level house. It's hard to say who is taking care of whom. The first night I was there, he fell flat on his face in the bathroom and by morning was sporting a lump the size of a goose-egg on his forehead, two black eyes, several band-aids and a sprained wrist. It's pretty scary when we go out together; we look as if we were in a bad bar fight – with each other. Fortunately, my sister has been taking Cross-Fit classes and is able to not only make endless trips up my stairs to retrieve loads of necessary belongings, but manage both our care. Maybe I ought to look into Cross-Fit… when I can walk.

COOKING WITH CRUTCHES

IF I HADN'T BEEN LIVING with my father until recently, I'm sure I would have starved to death by now. Cooking is a special challenge with a broken leg.

One of the major issues with being on crutches, I find, is the inability to transport anything. While I can carry a certain amount of produce in my teeth (and I hope my dentist is not reading this), there is a maximum weight limit, I find, and when that limit has been exceeded, items tend to get dropped to the ground, where they scatter and remain until, with a great deal of maneuvering, I can pick them up. Open bags of chopped kale, when dropped, make me particularly testy.

My backpack works a treat up to a point, but it's such a hassle to put things in it, then get it onto one's back, travel across the kitchen, then take it off again and root around inside, take items out, then replace it on the back, all while balancing on one leg, crutches leaning on some handy object from which they invariably slip and crash to the floor, that it really is unworkable in the kitchen. So I've had to develop tactics for other items. Yogurt, for instance, is a test of ingenuity; I generally plant myself halfway between the refrigerator and the counter, grab the container, toss it onto the counter, and slide it along slowly until we both reach our destination. Lighter weight items in bags I simply fling in the general direction I want them to go, usually several yards away, and hope for the best. The other night I heaved a can of beans and an opener from the kitchen to the living room couch and called it a meal. I cannot, however, recommend this method for liquids.

Having recently moved back to my abode with the 53 stairs and a very small kitchen, I find that other tricky situations now present themselves. While the kitchen is cozily efficient, it contains a rug. Having acquired the heretofore unknown - to me, anyway - abilities of hopping and pivoting, I have discovered that it is very easy to twist said rug into tight little knots that

I get caught up in, catch a crutch in, then try to hop over and nearly break the other leg – or maybe the same one all over again, or both. And I can only hope my orthopedist is also not reading this.

While I've become a dab hand at sailing through large open spaces with the crutches, small maneuvers are more risky; I tend to catch a crutch or two on chairs, doors, items of clothing (mine and others'), steps, and pretty much everything else in the vicinity. But having had plenty of time to do so, I have by now developed the soon-to-be patented "armpit crutch clutch" maneuver, to be used when forced to carry objects while poised on crutches, which I will pass on free of charge: one grips the crutches in each armpit while holding an object or objects in one's hands, swings one crutch forward with heretofore unknown armpit muscles, then the other crutch, does a quick hop, and repeats the process until one has reached one's destination. This trick is not, however, recommended for long journeys, as it will likely take several days to cross a room.

Walking, or, more accurately, not walking, with an impaired leg presents a few sartorial challenges as well: I am wearing out only the left shoe of every pair, as my right foot is so swollen from the sprained ankle that I can fit nothing over it other than a rather unattractive thick white sock, which, I might add, goes with nothing in my wardrobe. On the up side, I highly recommend long skirts as a fashion statement (sorry, guys), as then one does not need to worry about what to do with the extra pant leg that cannot be fitted over "Das Boot".

I was recently told to begin putting 25% of my weight on the broken leg, to be gradually increased to 50% and then, I suppose, 100%. Math not being my strong point, I am having some trouble working out the percentages, weight ratios, etc, but I feel sure it will soon result in me walking on both legs.

The other day I found myself taking a brief bodily inventory: Right leg: broken. Left leg: tired. Armpits and hands: bruised from crutches and now sporting calluses. On the other hand, or leg, while my right leg, on the brief occasions it sees daylight, may be scary-looking, the left one is definitely stronger than it used to be. And of course, I shall always have, to go along with the crutches and so many other items of a rehabilitative nature that I could open a shop, as a sentimental keepsake, since I paid for it: "Das Boot". What more could a woman ask for in the way of attractive accessories?

Opening Doors

USING CRUTCHES, I have discovered, presents numerous opportunities to test one's logic and ingenuity. For instance, when confronted with a curb, I stand for awhile, flamingo-like on my good leg, contemplating the many options it provides: Do I put the crutches up on the curb first, and drag the rest of me up after them? Or try to put my foot up before the crutches? Bad leg first, or good leg? Leg before wicket? Sorry, that's a cricket reference – it just slipped out.

The thought of a trip to the Post Office is exhausting in its tactical issues: get out of the car (which I, of course, am not driving), wrestle the backpack and crutches into position, up onto the curb, with its attendant aforementioned difficulties, up the step, which raises the same logistical problems, through the doors, wait in line, over to the counter, and back again. Going down a step or curb, of course, raises the same issues as going up; some of us are slow learners, which would explain why you might come across me staring at a step or curb for quite some time, as if I were organizing a trip across the Gobi desert.

Doors are fun, too. I had never noticed how really heavy they are before I broke my leg. Now getting through one takes a feat of planning and engineering that rivals a tactical military operation: throw my weight against the door, hoping it's not a light door, which would result in me falling on my face on the floor, plant one crutch inside, heave half my body inside, lean heavily on the door some more in order to open it wider, trusting no good Samaritan inside or outside, perceiving my struggles, now kindly flings it open wider for me while all my weight is on it, again resulting in the distinct possibility of me ending up on the floor (and bathroom floors are not a place to find yourself face-down on). Having the advantage now, I use a series of little shoves to get the door open wider, get both crutches inside, and throw the rest of myself through the opening.

Now there is the issue of the stall; one hopes the toilet is high enough, or at least has bars sufficient to get oneself up and down, but various muscles have been drafted into action that have never seen the light of day before now, enabling me to accomplish feats heretofore unknown: As a result of using crutches, I have actually developed stomach muscles – who knew?! - as well as improving muscles in my left leg, back and both arms. I should be quite buff by the end of the six weeks in Das Boot, although the broken right leg, I suspect, will be quite puny by comparison. Then at the end of the operation, I get to repeat the process. If it weren't a necessity, it would hardly seem worthwhile.

Not being able to drive is probably the worst problem; I never realized just how complicated my schedule is until I had to start arranging other means of transport for myself. Friends and family have been incredibly generous – let me just take this opportunity to thank them all profusely – but I do believe I could organize the invasion of a small foreign country by now. Getting from Point A to Point B, then C, D, and E all in one day, only to repeat it the next day with a different schedule, trying not to impose on any one person too much, is quite the challenge, and brings with it humility at the kindness of so many good people. I have managed to climb in and out of several different types of trucks and various cars, and now have it down to a fine art and a routine that works pretty well, unless I get the seatbelt tangled up with the crutches, the crutches caught in my clothing, or my sweater caught on a lever, all of which seem to occur on a regular basis.

Once at work, it appears to take everyone in both of my offices to help organize me; how they find time to get their work done amazes me. One person gets me in and out of doors, another one carries files for me to avoid the imprint of my toothmarks on them (that would be the files, not the person), someone else makes sure I am not dehydrated or starving to death, another kind soul makes copies for me – I am a full-time job.

As I believe I may have mentioned, not able to live at home due to the many stairs (53, but who's counting?), I am staying with my 91-year old father; I can just about make it up the ramp on my crutches as fast as he can get up the stairs to the front door, but I think I'm gaining on him. After two weeks, I'm barely huffing and puffing when I get to the top anymore, either, so progress is definitely being made.

But my armpits, I fear, may never be the same.

Frozen Fruit and Airports

I ABSOLUTELY PROMISE that this will be the last of the broken leg saga, primarily because my leg has now healed and I am finally off crutches. Well, all except the sprained ankle, which, despite several weeks of physical therapy, still has a tendency to blow up like a giant puffer fish for no discernible reason. I tried to follow my physical therapists' advice of icing said ankle, but among the myriad medical items I possess, there is not an ice pack to be found. As a rule, I use frozen vegetables (in the package, of course – I'm not completely stupid. Really.), but my freezer having limited space, veggies did not make the cut. I did, however, have a selection of frozen fruit for use in the smoothies I make, so I experimented with the strawberries. Upon further reflection, I decided perhaps the mixed fruit would have been a better choice. Truthfully, frozen peas are the best, but beggars can't be choosers. In any case, my physical therapist sensibly suggested making my own ice pack of rubbing alcohol and water in a zip-lock bag, which worked a treat and allowed me to restore my frozen fruit to its original purpose.

In any case, I decided to fly to Los Angeles once again to visit my daughter while I was still using one crutch. A discussion ensued with my physical therapist as to whether to take one crutch or two. I would be taking two carry-on bags in order to save baggage fees, one of which was a shoulder bag (oh, how I hate the misnamed shoulder bag! They never stay on my shoulder!), so I decided on two crutches, just in case my leg became fatigued at an inconvenient time and place and I collapsed in a heap on the tarmac with two bags to contend with. She suggested that a crutch or two might come in handy, although I was too dim to realize what she meant at the time.

So, I stood at the end of the longest line I have ever seen in the Medford airport, waiting to go through security while balancing on my good leg, struggling to get the "shoulder" bag to stay on my shoulder (my daughter later showed me the sensible alternative of slinging it around behind my back, but I was already in Los Angeles by then), and cursing my need to take so much heavy stuff with me, including home-made muffins and Easter candy for her.

Suddenly one of the TSA guys approached me. Nervous that I was going to be told that I had too many bags, that my flight had been cancelled, that I personally exceeded the weight limit, or that I had been bumped from the flight (I am an optimistic soul), I watched in some trepidation. As he neared, he asked if I had a pre-check boarding pass, and I had to admit I hadn't even looked at it. He examined it and told me I did, and that I should follow him. He exclaimed, "Here, let me take that", and proceeded to relieve me of not one but both my bags. Deciding this was definitely an advantage, I followed along docilely behind him as he opened up the security tape, remarking, "You just come right through here. Don't worry, you don't need to take your shoes off." Better and better. When we got to the metal detector, he asked solicitously, "Do you think you can make it four or five steps through there without your crutches?" Deciding this was not the time to explain that I had been walking without either crutch at home occasionally, I worked up what I later came to christen my "pitiful but brave" face and replied, "Well, yes, I … I think I might manage that." Meanwhile, he manhandled my luggage through the x-ray machine and accompanied me over to the seating area. Soon he was back, looking anxious. "Pre-boarding is beginning soon. Do you need a wheelchair?" I graciously declined, at which he asked kindly if I would be able to make it up the few stairs outside and up into the plane. I allowed as how I might be able to, feeble though I was.

Upon landing, friendly staff in Los Angeles marshaled extra help to handle my baggage and crutches until I was inside the building; I was beginning to feel like visiting royalty. As I stood looking for the right door to find my bus to Union Station, a man on a luggage cart pulled up and asked where I was going; when I told him, he said, "That's too far for you to walk; let me take you", grabbed my luggage and tossed me aboard. We passed a little girl walking with her mother who asked plaintively, "Why does SHE get to ride, mommy?" I waved a crutch at her.

I will admit the fairy tale ended abruptly on the journey back, mostly because I couldn't find my ID, even though I spread all my belongings over the check-in desk (I found it in my shoulder bag when I got home), but I'll be keeping those crutches for the next trip.

My Sporting Life

Beached

HAVING BEEN ENTHRALLED by watching kite-surfers in action on the beaches of California and Oregon, we (we being my beloved and I, although truthfully, mostly my beloved) decided we needed to try it for ourselves. Visions of soaring into the air twenty feet or more with every jump filled our heads, and I convinced myself I could do this; I can swim, after all, so how hard could it be? Why do I always ask myself the same question, always with the same, inevitable result?

Off we flew to Maui, because after all, chances were good that even my beloved might spend some time in the water while learning, and at our advanced age, as our son so kindly and often reminds us, we wanted the wait to be in warmer rather than colder water.

On our first night we discovered how expensive food is in Hawaii when we went out to eat, so we took most of our pizza home and proceeded to eat it every night for about five days. Then I cooked at the condo, to save money. My journal reads something like: "Went to the beach. Came home. Ate pizza." This later changed to "Went to the beach. Came home. Ate curry." for several days, and then to "Went to the beach. Came home. Ate burritos." for the rest of the trip as my culinary skills deteriorated. But back to the kite-surfing.

The next day we arrived at "Kite Beach" as it's creatively known, anxious to begin our new sport. Or just anxious, on my part. I was instantly glad to be there after getting a look at our instructor: Alex bore a strong resemblance to a Greek god, with his curly hair and big brown eyes, and let me tell you, kite-surfing for a living does no harm to the physique. His Italian accent was charming as well – so charming I could almost forgive him for looking at me as if I were an idiot after about ten minutes of giving me lessons.

Kite-surfing lessons, I learned, are begun on the sand (and in my case, end on the sand), probably for safety reasons after too many experiences with people like myself. The first thing they try to teach you is how to "self-rescue", also essential for someone like me. The theory is that, should you find that you have tangled your lines to the point that you cannot put the contraption back together, you simply hold the kite in a particular way so that you can sail it and yourself back into shore without having to use the board, which means you're being dragged bodily through the water rather than actually surfing on the board. Since my two major fears at this point were either 1. Being eaten by a shark, or 2. Sailing off to Polynesia because I couldn't figure out how to turn around and come back, or both, this was a great comfort.

But before any sailing in the actual water is done, they try to teach you how to "fly the kite", also on the shore. This, I discovered, I was completely incapable of doing. I kept falling over backwards in the sand every time the kite took flight, much to Alex's disgust. At some point, I felt sick to my stomach and realized I was taking only short, panting breaths, at which time I told my beloved and Alex to go on without me (where, of course, my beloved excelled at the sport very shortly) and toppled over into the sand for the last time, eventually falling into a deep sleep. First, however, I discovered I was still wearing my helmet, which I removed and used as a pillow since my neck was already aching (and which continued to ache for the following few days). Unfortunately, I forgot I was still wearing my wet-socks, which resulted in some very strange sunburn patterns as well, but at least I hadn't been eaten by a shark.

After that, I confined myself to swimming in the pool, although I almost had heart failure when I discovered that some idiot had decided it would be nice to tile the bottom of the pool with dolphins, which look surprisingly like sharks when you're as paranoid as I am. I also consented to snorkel, eventually, even though my previous experience of the sport resulted, when I pointed out a pretty fish to my beloved, in it latching onto my finger and biting enthusiastically while I yelled underwater, "He bit me!" thereby almost drowning myself. Every time I stepped into the water, all I could hear was the theme music from "Jaws". And that was even before my beloved informed me (after we got home – he's no fool) that there had been a shark attack off the coast of Maui the week before we arrived. At least we managed to get back before the hurricanes struck …

Down The Slippery Slope

I AM FORCED TO ADMIT that the first time I affixed skis to my feet, conditions were ideal. I had managed to put off this dubious experience until just after my thirtieth birthday, having had many valid excuses to avoid it: It was expensive, I had no health insurance and would be unable to pay for the hospital care necessary when I undoubtedly broke every bone in my body, and I hate the cold. Then I got married. Our first ski trip was to sunny southern France, where we stayed at a beautiful resort. My husband had thoughtfully provided a week's skiing lessons, and the resort provided no easy means of escape other than skiing out, which was definitely not an option. Bright and early, I approached the slopes, skis slung casually over my shoulder and terror in my heart.

Fortunately I had some time to practice before my lessons began that afternoon. We began with the basics. Husband: "Put your toe into that clamp in front, then press down with your heel and it will latch onto your boot." The foot circled slowly like a buzzard approaching prey. I thrust it towards the toe clamp, missed, lost my balance, and fell over. When I got the skis on, I felt like Bozo the Clown in his over-sized shoes, and waddled like Donald Duck on drugs.

We proceeded to The Lift. It is aptly nicknamed the "button lift", and consists of a long pole, or rope, with a circular "seat" attached. The idea is to grab the pole, fit the "seat" between your legs, and be pulled smoothly up the hill. I must confess that I was warned not to sit on the lift. I fully intended not to sit on it. But it picked me up with vicious force, and I suddenly sat. Unfortunately, the more weight you put on it the more it stretches, until I found myself on my hands and knees in the snow, being dragged more and more slowly. Eventually I fell off, in the path of other novice skiers, all of whom skied into me and fell over, until we had an untidy heap of skis, poles, and skiers. Finally the ski lift operator's sadistic tendencies had been satisfied and he stopped the lift. Suddenly, it was time for lessons.

Instructors want to check your skill level, which they do by having you ski slowly towards them. It was a gentle slope, but no one had taught me the rudiments of stopping. I rocketed down it, heading straight for the ski instructors. I responded to this emergency in the classic style - I leaned back, thereby increasing my speed, waved my arms and poles frantically (and dangerously), and shouted "Oy! Oy! Oy!" at the top of my lungs. Although I'm told they're really good at this sort of thing, one instructor wasn't quite quick enough; I nailed him and we both went flying. He was French and very cute, but possibly not at his best as he dusted himself off and gave me The Look and remarked, in his charming French accent: "You owe me a beer, madam."

We were allowed to progress to the chair lift. We painstakingly positioned ourselves - "ski tips on the line, poles inside, bend knees, sit!" What else can one do, I ask, when the bench hits the back of one's legs at 45 miles an hour, except sit? With a loud "Oomph!" I might add. For the first several yards I was so busy untangling poles, skis, gloves, legs, etc., from my seat-partner's that I had no time to admire the scenery. After sorting ourselves out, however, I began to notice that we were suspended several hundred feet above the ground, dangling and rocking like some mad ferris-wheel ride. Did I mention that I'm afraid of heights? My teeth chattering from cold and fear, I prepared for the exit from the chair lift - how hard could it be? Scoot forward, they said, skis flat, push off, and "Voila!" (or some other frivolous French phrase). Needless to say, I followed these instructions scrupulously, landed in a heap, and took out fourteen skiers behind me until I could scuttle crab-like to the side. Another twenty minutes of untangling followed.

Now it was time for the real test - down the slippery slope. We stood in varying states of terror at the top of a green run. It felt as if our charming, handsome, and obviously sadistic French instructor had taken us to the top of the Alps and was now ordering us, in his romantic accent, to throw ourselves off a precipice. We had all developed a "zig-zag" technique by now - ski across the slope at an angle, fall over, get up (a major undertaking, in my case requiring several helping hands, both ski poles, and a large crane), face the other way, repeat. This pattern was occasionally varied by the odd death-defying trip straight down the hill out-of-control when one of us forgot to traverse. I myself won the group prize for managing to ski straight through the outside café, poles flying, diners diving for cover.

I discovered an alarming "homing" instinct in myself, heretofore useless when attempting to find my car in the parking lot. At the top of a hill I carefully noted any potential obstacles in my path, and then proceeded to ski straight into them. I destroyed five slalom poles, ran over twelve other skiers, and did major damage to my ski pants when I ran into a large boulder.

Another class member had threatened all day to simply remove her skis and walk down the hill if the instructor insisted on dragging us up one more hill; by the end of the day, despite the instructor's protests, she did exactly that. As a matter of fact, she and I ended up on the chair lift together one day. We chatted merrily until suddenly we saw a cliff looming ahead that hadn't been there the day before. It gradually dawned on us that the reason it hadn't been there the day before was that we were on the wrong chair lift. We panicked; we couldn't possibly ski down whatever black run this was, and it would be an awfully long walk back down through three feet of snow from the top of the run. So we did the only logical thing: we held our collective breath and jumped off the ski lift. Mind you, we were only about five feet off the ground at this point, so it wasn't much of a daredevil feat, but for people like us who found it difficult to disembark from the chair lift under the best of circumstances, it was risky. It was, if anything, easier this way - no tension build-up before-hand. We then proceeded to duplicate my friend's epic of the day before; we simply walked down the slope. In fact, it is my firm opinion that this is the only sensible way to descend the slippery slope - slowly and on foot.

Ah well, at the end of the day's skiing, I discovered the true reason for the pastime: boots off in front of a warm fire, drink in hand, recounting stories. But I continue, on the rare occasions I am coerced into repeating the experience, to wear black, so they can find me in the snow.

INTO THE DEPTHS

MY BELOVED AND I recently took a tour of the Shasta Caverns, a lovely spot which I highly recommend, if you don't mind a few stairs and aren't claustrophobic. Personally, I don't mind the dark or small enclosed spaces, as long as I'm relatively certain I can get out at some point, and as long as no one turns on the lights so that I can actually see what I'm headed towards. It all reminded me of my first caving trip, many years ago in England...

For my 30th birthday, several months into our marriage, my husband invited me to go caving. This seemed a fairly safe venture; how much trouble could I get into underground? Of course, every effort on my part to undertake any sort of physical endeavor invariably ends in some sort of disaster, but I decided not to listen to the small still voice of reason. Thus it was that on my birthday, which happens to fall on the first day of winter, I took my first caving trip.

We drove out to some soggy moor in Yorkshire, England (we were living in Scotland at the time). It was raining, or more accurately, sleeting. "Bit cold, isn't it?" I inquired hopefully. As always, he responded cheerfully: "Much warmer underground. Besides, the hike will warm you." Hike?

We hiked to what was euphemistically referred to as a farmhouse to change. First comes the wetsuit. Perhaps there is a less comfortable, more excruciating instrument of torture in the world; I, for one, am not interested in seeing it. Threaten me with a wetsuit and I will tell you anything you want to know. My husband, who is of a somewhat smaller build than I, had loaned me his wetsuit. By means of a great deal of yanking, tugging, groaning, sucking in, and cursing, the thing was put on me. I felt like a wheel base wearing a Goodyear tire several sizes too small. In fact, my husband is a frugal soul, so where the rubber of the wet-suit had been ripped, it had been patched with pieces of innertube. Since most caving tends to be done on the hands and knees (when not flat on the belly or sideways down a slot), these areas wear out first, which means that is where the patches were. Two facts now emerge

- one of physics and one of physiology. First, the point of physics: tire rubber does not bend much. Next, the point of physiology: knees and elbows bend a lot. Now, when we put these two facts together, I had a difficulty. Nothing bent easily where it was meant to. In fact, as I discovered during the course of the trip, when these joints were bent, it resulted in a loss of feeling from the knees and elbows down.

Although I had no desire to move in any direction at this point, we set off across the sodden fields. We hiked for miles (I use the term "hike" loosely: "forced march" springs to mind more easily) through potholes so deep and thick with oozing mud that I occasionally sank hip-deep and had to be yanked out, usually leaving behind at least one shoe.

At last we reached the "cave" (how they managed to distinguish this particular hole in the ground from all the others I shall never know), consisting of an aperture about two feet in diameter. Before descending, however, I was introduced to the ritual of lighting the carbide caving lamp (the curious will find one in the small museum at Shasta Caverns, which will tell you about how long ago this was). I observed in fascination as my husband poured crystals of some mysterious substance (carbide, no doubt) into a small container, sucked up some water and spit it in, poked it with what appeared to be a long stiff hair, and attempted to light a flame with a (by now) wet flint. Apparently an electric battery would have spoiled the ritual fun of it all. Then the entire affair was affixed to the front of my helmet, which promptly fell down over my eyes. Actually, the majority of the trip was completed in darkness, as very little can be seen with one's helmet over one's eyes. In retrospect, this was probably a mercy. This astounding piece of technological achievement does have occasional side effects. I was told of a caver who accidentally leaked water into his supply; it exploded, making a large number of bats very unhappy, not to mention the caver. The lamps also have an irritating habit of going out about every five minutes, necessitating a repetition of the above-described ritual, usually at the most inconvenient of times.

Now it was time to descend into the depths. My husband had referred in passing to "ladders" in order, no doubt, to pacify my terror of abseiling into the cave on a rope. I have a literal mind, and when the "ladder" was produced I argued this was not a ladder as anyone sensible would define the word. The object he produced was rolled (no self-respecting ladder in my experience was ever able to roll; they were without exception rigid structures of wood or metal which could be extended, collapsed, tilted, or propped, but never rolled). When it was unwound, it was about four inches across - enough to hold one (narrow) foot or one hand, but not both simultaneously. It was - there is no other word for it - flimsy. I immediately discovered four uncomfortable truths: 1. The "ladder", not being of the sensible, civilized, rigid type, swung with me on it. 2. Not being of the aforementioned rigid type, the ladder conformed itself to the cave wall upon which it rested, thereby making it impossible to get a foot or finger-hold on it. I was able to swing myself and the "ladder" away from the wall briefly, enabling me to wrap my fingers around the rungs, where I had time to briefly congratulate myself before discovering: 3. If one does manage to get a finger-hold, the "ladder" will then promptly swing back to the rock wall, consequently mashing one's fingers. 4. I have amazingly weak arms and legs that tend to shake when I am frightened; this was accompanied after awhile by the stiffening of the limbs into a rigidity of which any self-respecting ladder would have been proud.

After climbing down a distance of 15 feet, the real caving begins. This can apparently only be accomplished by means of squeezing oneself into improbable openings at every conceivable angle, normally in one or two feet of water.

As my husband explained to me at about this point, caving involves expanding and contracting muscles in order to keep one's body upright (or sideways) and to avoid falling down into various holes and "slots". After examining several of these at close view, it was my firm opinion that nothing short of dynamite would blast me out if I should fall in, which provided a valuable incentive. They told me later of cavers who had not sufficiently expanded and contracted at appropriate times who did, indeed, have to be blasted out, resulting, needless to say, in injuries which might put one off caving forever, or sometimes in death by slow starvation. As I say, they told me this much, much later.

Suffice to say that for three days afterwards every muscle in my entire body ached – muscles in places I had never known I had muscles: knees, elbow, hands, ankles, ribs, back, shoulders, shins, thighs, feet - have I missed any? All this to gaze in exhaustion at a few nice stalactite and stalagmite formations. I shall draw a veil over the tears, the pleas to leave me there to die rather than force me to climb back up that evil twisting metallic snake of a "ladder". But finally the caving was over; a trip normally completed in two or three hours had taken me seven.

At last I emerged, shaken, exhausted and tear-stained, but triumphant, and ready for the promised pub. Unfortunately, the farmhouse was closed, so we were able to enjoy changing out of clammy wet-suits in the sleet by the side of the car in pitch black. Warm dry clothes never felt so heavenly in all my life (I am gradually becoming convinced that the real reason my husband participates in these activities is because it feels so good when you stop - and, of course, he doesn't mind the odd pint, either). Our friend assured us that he knew of a good caver's pub nearby. When we opened the door, conversation immediately ceased. Instead of the expected hearty companionship of similar lunatics, we gazed upon a crowd of nattily dressed, business-suited and angora-and-pearl-studded "trendy types", who gazed back at us with expressions of horror akin to those you might observe upon the faces of people who have turned over a particularly well-entrenched rock and discovered nasty things underneath. When we stepped forward, a path opened before us in a manner reminiscent of Moses parting the Red Sea.

I was surprised, as I had taken particular care to "wash up" in the cave water; snotty group, I decided, and proceeded to the bathroom, where I got the shock of my life. Not only did my hair look as if I'd been dragged through a hedge backwards, my attempted ablutions had succeeded only in smearing an amazing quantity of mud over my entire face. I did my best to repair the damage in the sink (doubtlessly stopping up their drains for a week with mud), skulked back into the pub, and drank up.

Amazingly enough (is there no limit to the body's resilience and the brain's stupidity?), within a week I was warm, ache-free, and enthusiastically ready to descend once more into the depths.

NEPTUNE RISING

WHEN MY HUSBAND SUGGESTED I try waterskiing I did not immediately panic, although, not being athletic by nature, neither did I embrace the idea with the enthusiasm he felt it deserved. He knows that I enjoy the water, and that I actually even know how to swim, having nearly drowned only twice that I recall - an excellent average for me. Due to my mother's foresight, all of us children took swimming lessons at an early age. She herself is deathly afraid of the water and doesn't swim, and did not want my father distracted by having to choose between her and one of us in case of an accident; since, technically, we could all swim, he could concentrate on saving her and leave us to our own devices.

In any case, as I am more or less comfortable in the water (due, I think, to the temporary suspension of the laws of gravity), he thought I would quite enjoy the experience. In a moment of temporary insanity, I had visions of smooth, graceful arcs through glassy water with the sun setting in glorious technicolor behind the hills. I could not, try as I might, envision any specific disasters which might befall me. My silence was taken as an assent (he is quick to follow up the advantage) and I was whisked off to a nearby lake.

The boat to which I was introduced was not exactly awe-inspiring. The owner was on a tight budget (he had, in fact, traded it for an old Chevy and a dirt bike, as I understand it) and did not waste money on frills. The seats had been salvaged from a wrecked Toyota and were unique in having head-rests. As I was to learn upon further acquaintance with boat and owner, the head-rests were not optional; whiplash was a constant threat. Holes in the floor where passengers had fallen through were pragmatically converted into removable hatches so that the amount of water leaking into the boat through holes in the hull could be conveniently ascertained as necessary. At high speeds (and for all its faults it must be admitted that, when running, the 350 Chevy engine could reach high speeds) the boat's passenger seat had an

352

unfortunate tendency to come loose from its moorings, so to speak, and tip over backwards. At one point, in fact, the seat came loose altogether on a particularly tight turn, and the passenger, a cooler, and other miscellaneous objects flew through the air and into the water. Priorities are well-established in such an emergency; the all-important cooler containing the beer was rescued first. The passenger sustained only flesh wounds and made his own way back into the boat. Passengers, of course, are optional, but more disturbing was the steering wheel coming off in one's hands at inopportune moments.

A hole in the exhaust system warned everyone of our approach. The boat came equipped with three mismatched wooden skis covered in what appeared to be kitchen linoleum and/or shelf paper. The boat owner contributed to the colorful scenario by wearing a somewhat ragged wet-suit; as unessential parts tore, he would simply cut them off, resulting in one sleeve being shorter than the other and one pant-leg ending several inches above the ankle, with the other just below the knee. Essential bits that tore were left to flap in the breeze, giving the overall effect of a scarecrow being dragged behind us, or driving the boat, depending upon his mood.

All in all, I imagine we presented a rather alarming picture to the trendy jet-setters in their matched outfits and powerful, color-coordinated speed boats. I believe we were cast in the role of the Hell's Angels of the boating set. At least they usually gave us a wide berth. Every situation has its advantages. I endeavored to remember this as I was jolted and bounced across the lake, mentally moving my next chiropractic appointment up by two weeks. At last we arrived at a little cove considered suitable for my first water-skiing effort.

Then came the "gear" (why is it that every sport my husband manages to finagle me into involves "gear"?). I was strapped into a safety vest that came up to my chin and cut off my air supply. Next came gloves with velcro which, as always, stuck everywhere but where it was supposed to, and I was ready. Almost. Everyone has their own method of getting into a body of water, whether it be a lake, an ocean, or a bathtub. My husband's method is the well-known "Kamikaze" approach: take a breath, yell encouragingly, and leap in. My approach, on the other hand, is a more cautious one - I put one toe in, wait for possible cramps or hostile marine life reaction and, if neither results, venture in up to my knees. Naturally, this method takes some time. Well aware of my tendencies, my husband did not allow me to proceed in the usual way, but sneaked up behind me and unceremoniously threw me in.

Just as the sputtering and teeth-chattering had ceased, two of the mismatched wooden planks were tossed in after me, narrowly missing me. These I was expected to attach to my feet. I tried - Lord knows I tried. It seemed quite simple - my husband assured me it was - just lean back in the water, he said; the life jacket will keep you afloat. What he neglected to explain was the fact that while the jacket was quite capable of supporting me, it wasn't at all particular about what direction I was facing. I therefore ended up face-down in the water, rolling like a barrel every time I attempted to turn upright and get a hold of a ski. In the end it became a two-person effort - hubby had to jump in and assist. If you think snow skis are difficult to put on, try water-skis; at least you get to stand on solid ground (more or less) in the snow.

In any event, both planks were eventually strapped on and we were ready to proceed. As the boat takes off, hold on to the handle, my husband instructed me, lean back, take a deep breath, bend your knees, and if you start to fall over, step hard in the direction you're falling. Right. For a person who finds it difficult to walk and chew gum at the same time, no small feat. Being terrified that my arms would be pulled from their sockets didn't help. With luck, I thought perhaps I could manage two of the instructions at any given time. I took a deep breath and shouted "Hit it!"" with more bravado than I felt.

I heard the Chevy engine roar into life and immediately felt a wall of water hit me in the face. I responded in the natural way - I gasped. I had to let go of the rope in order to cough and choke more effectively, and the boat slewed sharply around so that I could try again. The effect of slewing around, of course, is to form a giant wake, resulting in more bobbing up and down, gasping and choking. After twenty minutes of repositioning myself and another twenty for putting the skis back on (with help), I tried again. This time I snorted half the lake before starting to break the surface.

Gradually I began to notice that all was not well. My skis were going in opposite directions, causing me to do a form of the splits - not something I am normally capable of. I let go again. A rope was tied between the skis to (hopefully) prevent this occurring again. On about the fifth or sixth try I actually managed to get up; for about five seconds I was totally exhilarated, but unfortunately blind - the rope between my skis caused a constant stream of well-aimed water to hit me in the eyes. I didn't have time to enjoy the view in any case before I hit the water again.

This time, because I had actually managed to get up on the skis, I was going, as my husband says, at a fair rate of knots (probably five miles an hour at most). The result was that upon hitting the water (literally, I felt), my eyelids were peeled back into my head until I thought surgery would be necessary to restore them to their normal positions (fortunately I was wrong. I learned - post facto, as usual - that this is a fairly common occurrence). I practiced falling over forwards, backwards, and sideways - I like to be well-rounded and experienced. I got my legs tangled up in the rope, was nearly run over by the boat, and ended up floating helplessly on my stomach, legs and skis floating serenely out behind me. On the rare occasions in which I did "get up", my husband shouted instructions at me (useless, as I couldn't hear above the roar of the boat engine) and pantomimed the correct position (also useless, as the water still sprayed consistently in my face, effectively blinding me).

However, like many other sports my husband has coerced me into trying, I ended up, of course, hooked; not good, or even competent, but definitely hooked.

NOVICE CLIMBS

LET ME BEGIN BY stating categorically that I am NOT a climber. My husband is a climber, and a good one, they tell me. I wouldn't know; it gives me sweaty palms just to watch him. What he views as my groundless (ahem) aversion is actually firmly rooted: I am terrified of heights. To be accurate, I'm not afraid of heights, but of falling from them. There is no rock, no bridge, no cliff so stable it might not someday decide to collapse, and will undoubtedly do so the day I am on it. Why tempt fate? However, in the first blush of marital bliss, soon after we married, I threw caution to the winds and actually tried.

We went to the Dolomites in Italy. Quite frankly, I was bored to tears with hiking and card games in the tent while it poured rain outside. My husband, enthusiastic, naturally athletic soul that he is, encouraged me. It is perhaps helpful to explain that I am the most uncoordinated, unnatural athlete that ever lived. I fall off sidewalks and up stairs, trip backwards over walls and other harmless inanimate objects, and have been known to lose my balance and slowly topple over while simply standing. Sports, as they say, are not my strong suit, or as one of my friends says, it is one of my lesser strengths. I relate to a sign in a friend's office: "My idea of exercise is a good brisk sit." The only reason I haven't broken every bone in my body is that I decided at a young age not to chance it, and refrain from most forms of sport. The sole exercise forms I have pursued are swimming and horse-back riding. Suffice it to say I have seen the underbellies of more horses than their saddles.

My husband, undoubtedly to prevent my escape, escorted me to a large, rocky cliff. I looked up. I looked at him. He smiled. "See? Piece of cake!" I looked again at the cliff. It was amazingly vertical. My husband, sensing my hesitation, immediately began strapping me into a climbing harness and cramming my feet into shoes three sizes too small. "Wait!" I yelled. "These shoes are the wrong size." "No, it's O.K.," he assured me. "They're supposed to be that way." I immediately began to have grave doubts about any sport that required excruciating discomfort to be fun. "Why?" "Helps you to climb better," he replied. I failed to see why having uncomfortable feet was helpful, except perhaps as an encouragement to get up the climb faster so that I could take the horrible things off sooner and enjoy the bliss of stretching my toes.

The harness, a Whillans, is well-known to climbers. I know a man who fell while wearing a Whillans, got tangled in the rope and ended up hanging 20 feet down a cliff by one leg - and all he could do was breathe a sigh of relief that it was his leg that took the brunt of the fall. I had no intention of falling; I had no intention of going up. Love prevailed. I took a deep breath and started up.

At first, it was easy; then I got stuck. I could go neither up nor down. "Let me off!" I yelled. "I'm frozen - I can't move!" My husband yelled back, "You're only two feet off the ground!" He pointed out holds to me. I resisted. "I can't reach that! Do you think I'm a gorilla?" "Lean away from the rock." "Are you completely crazed?" I was, in fact, developing a very intimate relationship with the rock; I was glued to it like a starfish. "Don't use your knees!" Forgetting myself, I looked down at him in disbelief (I immediately regretted it. Rule Number 1: Do NOT, under any circumstances, look down). "Why ever not?" "It's not good form." Form! Who cares about form? This is survival! "Why do you suppose God gave us elbows and knees if not to use them? See how conveniently they fit into these holes?" "Use your feet!" "I can't!" "Why not?" "I can't see where to put them." "Why not?" "I can't look down!"

I began to think logically and consider my options. Point One: There were only two ways to go: up or down. Point Two: I was already three quarters of the way up the cliff. Point Three: Climbing down would probably be just as awful as climbing up had been.

I climbed up, actually making it to the top. After awhile, my body stopped shaking. I even stopped cursing my husband. I looked down (carefully, from a great distance, while wrapped firmly around a tree). It seemed like a very long way. Suddenly, I experienced a great sense of accomplishment. I had made it. I swaggered back down the hill. "Piece of cake!"

RAFTING

I RARELY CONFESS that I was, for a brief period one summer, a rafting guide on the Klamath River. I don't talk about it much because what I don't know about rafting, boats, nature, and the Klamath River would fill volumes, but I was desperate for a job and the guy who hired me was under the mistaken assumption that because I lived on the river, I might actually know something about any or all of the above (he was from down south - Los Angeles – what we on the river affectionately referred to as a flatlander).

Needless to say, it was a brief, disastrous affair for all concerned. We were both disillusioned early on; I, when I discovered his real intent was that I and the other young woman he had hired were expected to be in camp by five a.m. to cook breakfast and not leave until 10:00 p.m., when dinner had been made and eaten (although we were not allowed to eat – we were the hired help, after all) and dishes done, after a very long day on the river with tourists even more clueless than I, rowing upwind in a howling gale after having been sunburnt to a crisp. I have never been enthusiastic about getting up in the middle of the night (anything before 9:00 a.m.), cooking is one of my lesser gifts, and waiting on people is not likely to garner me any praise or tips. I'm not bad at doing the dishes, though. He lost faith in me the first day on the river, I believe, when I became involved in a spirited discussion with the other guide, lost track of where I was, and instead of neatly turning into the selected "take-out" spot, hurtled past it and the assembled slack-jawed tourists, yelling "Help!" in a panic-stricken screech as I approached the next set of rapids.

Fast forward to many years later, when my husband managed to convince me to take a rafting trip down the Colorado River. It did not bode well that the starting point was reached by hiking what seemed like a twenty-mile trail into the depths of the canyon to get to the river itself. When we arrived, I was fairly crabby, but that's not unusual, since I hate to hike in the first place, and it was hot. The guide, however, more experienced than I with physical exertion, sensed I was dehydrated and exhausted (probably when I snapped at him) and forced me to drink a lot of water and rest awhile, resulting in an immediate improvement in my temper. It did not last long.

When we approached the first rapid, the guides stopped to carefully explain the procedure should the boat "high-side", i.e., end up vertical in the air with one side higher than the other: we were to paddle furiously in order to get through the rapid as quickly as possible (hence, I learned, the origin of the term "rapid", which had until now escaped me). I began to sense I was out of my depth.

As long as I live, I will never forget the sight of the misnamed "Lava Falls". The lava part was certainly not accurate, as there was nothing remotely hot about the water I was witnessing, and there was no sign of a "fall", unless it was what my stomach was now doing. What I saw was an opening in the water the size of Texas, drawing our little boat and all the others into it like a magnet.

The first raft into the roaring din lasted about six seconds before all the occupants except the guide were tossed unceremoniously and violently into the drink. When the first one emerged from the riverbed, gasping from his near-death experience, the guide gripped him firmly by the back of his life jacket, lifted him into the boat with one arm, and shouted, "Break's over – get paddling!" The rest were dragged out like so much flotsam and jetsam farther downriver as they floated to the surface, stricken numb with cold and terror.

My husband's boat went second. The six men in it were pulled inexorably into the hole and the raft turned completely around – they were going down the rapid backwards. No worries; in a move looking like it had been choreographed by the backup singers for the Temptations, they rose in unison and turned around so they were all facing front, and went down like pros, paddling furiously.

I was by now trying to find a way out of my raft and back to shore – I would have swum if they'd let me – without success. When the first wave of water hit us like a freight train, I tossed my paddle with abandon and wrapped my arms around the man in front of me – I think his name was Chuck. We hadn't spoken before this, but we were suddenly intimate. Something jarred my death grip loose, I grabbed a stray rope, and suddenly, Chuck was gone. My hands scrabbled around in terror in the bottom of the raft under a foot of muddy water for the straps they think you're going to put your feet into, as chaos ensued around me and three more people went for an unexpected swim. Now it was just me and the guide, who smiled encouragingly at me. He was actually enjoying this death-defying experience.

By a miracle, I somehow remained in the boat all the way down the rapid. When we finally reached shore, I dragged myself onto the warm sand, limp as a dead jellyfish, and breathed sweet air.

I had seven days to go.

Riding into the Sunset

EVER SINCE I was a little girl, I've loved horses. I used to picture myself astride a horse, galloping through the pounding surf, wind blowing through my hair. Like every little girl, I wanted my own horse, but since that wasn't possible, I contented myself with cleaning the hooves of my sister-in-law's horse. Not quite as romantic, but much more practical. Of course, I wasn't allowed to actually ride him, as he was a cantankerous Appaloosa (is there any other kind?), but I did get to take him on walks. Since I was deathly afraid of him, that was about as good as it got for many years. Finally, however, I got to ride my first equine.

At about age sixteen, my best friend and I decided to go to a riding stable and rent a horse (two, actually – we weren't interested in doubling up). Not being conversant with horses, so to speak, we didn't realize that this was probably the worst possible way to acquaint ourselves with the species. So off we went, happy and excited to realize our childhood dreams.

The first thing I noticed was how huge they were. I was tall, but these beasts towered over me, and once I was assisted into the saddle, the ground was very far away indeed. The instant mine moved, I was terrorized, but I had heard that they can tell if you're frightened, and will take off with you if they think you're not in control, so I faked it as best I could. I kicked him in the flanks with my (spurless) heels and said, "Let's go" confidently. He turned around, gave me a long, measuring look, sighed heavily, and slowly walked up the hill.

As soon as we were out of sight of the stable, my friend and I decided to be daring and go off the trail. Urging our very reluctant mounts by kicking, yanking on the reins, and yelling encouragement, we finally got them to turn off the track, but it was short-lived. Mine immediately turned around to go back to the stable – this sort of behavior wasn't in his contract, and anyway, it was late in the day – then thought better of it. Suddenly I found myself, feet still in the stirrups, horse prone under me, apparently taking a nap. My friend helpfully screamed, "You've killed him! You've killed the horse!" and rode off at a brisk walk (all she could get her horse to do even though he was heading home) back to the stables while I pondered the possibilities of mouth-to-mouth resuscitation on a horse. Of course, the stable hand merely commented that the horse was just being stubborn and yanked him back onto his feet, but I was too traumatized to continue the ride, and it was a while before I tried again.

The next time, the same friend and I again rented horses (some people are slow learners), but this time from a different stable, being too embarrassed to go back to the same one. And this time, my horse actually trotted! Encouraged, I again tried to go off the beaten track, but the horse, also apparently overexcited, took off into a dead run. Naturally, I immediately lost my stirrups and parted company with the saddle. Knowing instinctively that hitting the ground at this rate of speed was bound to be painful, I held on to something – I've never known quite what – as I slipped slowly down the side of the horse, until I was eventually contemplating his underbelly. Realizing at last that this had to come to an end, I let go, and yes, it really hurt, but infinitely more painful was the sight of my friend's hysterical laughter and subsequent description of the scene to anyone who would listen after I got my breath back.

Many years later, I married and we moved to Scotland, where I decided to take riding lessons. My balance issues were compounded by the instructor's Scottish accent, which was virtually incomprehensible to me, and cultural differences. And of course, there's the saddle, if you care to call it that. At least a western saddle gives those of us who are balance-impaired something to hang on to; English saddles are roughly the size of a postage stamp, with no horn for security, and with your knees up around your ears, believe me, you need some security. So there I was, shakily ensconced on the back of yet another mammoth beast, trying not to panic as he walked slowly around the ring, when the riding master calmly instructed me to take my feet out of the stirrups and cross them in front of me on the saddle. I looked at her, mouth agape. "You want me to do what?" She repeated her instructions. Did she think I was a circus rider? Yes, I was from California, but did I look like a rodeo trick rider? Still, she was a stern woman who brooked no nonsense, and the truth was, she scared me almost more than the horse did, so I did my best, shakily removing both feet from the stirrups and attempting to cross them on the tiny piece of saddle in front of me. "What are you doing?!" she screeched at me. I looked at her and repeated, "You told me to cross my feet on the saddle." "Not your feet, the stirrups!" Needless to say, it was a short lesson.

I have yet to ride into a pounding surf, but I live in hope.

SWIMMING

WHEN I WAS A CHILD, my mother insisted all four of her offspring take swimming lessons. This was not, as you might imagine, born of an excess of maternal solicitude. My mother was deathly afraid of water; she was of the "Let's throw them into the deep end of the pool and see how quickly they learn to swim" generation. Needless to say, she not only didn't learn to swim, she was left with a determination to never go into water deeper than her bathtub, and even that made her nervous. In fact, she related to us that her worst fear wasn't even drowning, but being on an airplane (she's also afraid of flying) that catches fire and lands in the ocean. She's not overly fond of sharks, either. So the swimming lessons for us were more to do with self-preservation; it was clearly understood by all of us, including my father, that in the unlikely event we were all on a boat somewhere and it began to sink, we kids were on our own, and dad's job was to save mom. I can't swear to it, but I have a firm conviction that his having been a lifeguard as a teenager had a lot to do with her acceptance of his marriage proposal.

When we were very young, we lived near the beach, and my mother was persuaded to go into the ocean in a small rubber raft with my father. He carefully explained that should the raft capsize – highly unlikely, he added, seeing the look in her eyes – all she had to do was firmly grasp the rope and hang on until help came, as it surely would. Leaving the four of us kids on the shore with an auntie, they embarked on their adventure. As an afterthought, my mother called out to my aunt that if anything should happen to her and my father, my aunt was to care for us kids. Ignoring my aunt, who was by now frantically racing up and down the beach, waving her arms and shrieking for my mother to come back, they paddled into a calm sea a few hundred feet from shore.

We don't know what happened or how it happened, but suddenly the boat flipped over and my parents were unceremoniously ejected into the water. Everyone, including my father, who had reached shore safely, now frantically searched the beach for my mother, calling her name and looking in the most unlikely places, until some bright spark thought to turn over the raft. Sure enough, there was my mom, clutching the rope, eyes shut tight, waiting for rescue – in two feet of water.

In any case, my swimming lessons started out well enough; water is the only place on earth where I feel anything close to graceful, and as long as I wasn't in over my head, so to speak, I was fine. However, I had an aversion to opening my eyes under water –the chlorine made them sting – so I refused to do it. Since my right arm was stronger than my left, this resulted in my swimming in diagonals across the pool, ending up with me whacking my head against the side of the pool at the other end and knocking myself almost unconscious, much to the amusement of my fellow swimmers.

I refused to do any stroke other than ones that kept my head above water, such as the sidestroke and backstroke, as breathing is also an issue for me, as in I like to do it and don't like anything that might interfere with it, like the crawl or scuba diving, but even then I tended to get distracted and smack my head into the pool edge. Still do.

And I don't need help from anyone else to hurt myself in the water, but sometimes someone volunteers. My husband and I went to Hawaii, which was very romantic, except that every time I got into the water I heard the theme music from "Jaws". Snorkeling didn't ease my fears; I occasionally got glimpses of creatures whose existence I could easily have lived without knowing about. Once as I excitedly pointed out a small colorful fish to my husband, he turned around and bit me (the fish that is, not my husband), and I almost drowned.

So we decided to take a motorized raft tour of the coast, which was lovely. When we stopped and they invited us to get out and swim around, I did so, not realizing how difficult it would be to heave myself back in. My husband, chivalrous as always, offered to help me back in, grasping my arm firmly and pulling me forcefully upward – and directly into his knee. I saw stars and sank slowly back into the water, almost unconscious, until someone, I don't remember who or how, pulled me successfully back into the boat.

As my mother knows, water can be dangerous.

Raising the Bar

IT WAS A VERY HOT July about 20 years ago. I was sitting in a steamy fifth wheel on my parents' property in Horse Creek, studying for the Bar Exam while my mom looked after my two kids. I was having trouble concentrating. I should have been asking myself what in the world I was doing, but as usual, I didn't.

I went to religious school for my first eight years, where creativity was not encouraged. But that didn't matter to me, as creative was the last way I would have described myself. I remember eagerly answering questions, only to have the teacher get this look on her face and say no, that's not the right answer Virginia. I couldn't seem to get the right answers, so I decided I was stupid. I stopped talking, stopped answering questions, and retreated behind a wall of silence.

I spent five years in college trying to figure out what to do with my life. For the first few years, I didn't declare a major. Then I decided to be pre-med, but I was terrible at math and science. Needless to say, that idea was a failure. Although I loved to read and wrote things occasionally, I only took two English classes in my entire undergraduate career. I couldn't see the point of an English major – how would I earn a living with that? And besides, I felt it would be too easy – I wanted a challenge. I finally decided to major in Psychology. When I graduated, all I knew was that I didn't want to listen to people's problems all day without telling them how to solve them.

But I'd volunteered at San Quentin Prison, teaching reading during my last semester in college, and I was offered a job teaching English there. I loved it, so I got my teaching credential and taught there for a few years. But I decided that wasn't enough; I wanted more of a challenge. So I decided to go to law school.

I went to school at night and worked full time during the day. I wanted to help people, and I decided that in the poker game of employment, a law degree would beat out a master's degree like a full house beats two pair.

But law school was hard. I was a good writer, but I didn't seem suited to the study of law. It felt as if my brain was a bonsai tree, being twisted in unnatural ways. I remember taking a test on civil procedure, and getting a bad grade. I was surprised, because I thought I'd done OK, so I took it to the professor, who read it for a while, looking puzzled. Finally he said, "You've got all the right words and phrases here, Virginia, you just don't have them arranged in a way that makes any sense." But I had spent too much money and time by then, and I was too stubborn to quit, so I kept on with it. I didn't really know what else to do, and I didn't get the message the universe was trying to send me.

Meanwhile, I fell in love with the man of my dreams and got married. A few years later, feeling as if I'd left something unfinished, I decided to take the California Bar Exam. Because it had been awhile since I graduated from law school, I took a Bar Review class. The first night of class, I sat down with about 400 other hopefuls, and the professor drew a circle inside a square on the board, then asked us to write down what we saw, which we dutifully did. Then he asked how many of us saw a circle with a square around it. Lots of people raised their hands, and he said, "You are big picture people; when you take the Bar Exam, you need to be sure you don't miss the small important details in the questions. Now, how many of you saw a square with a circle inside it?" About half the class raised their hands. "You are detail-oriented people. You need to be careful that you don't miss the picture when you're answering questions on the test." I sat with my hand covering my answer, thinking that perhaps l should rethink a legal career, and wondering if any-one else had seen what I did: a front-loading washing machine. I still refused to get the message; I took the Bar Exam and failed.

I had two children, moved around a lot, and worked a variety of jobs. I actually passed the Nevada Bar while we were living in Winnemucca and worked as a lawyer for about thirty seconds before realizing that the stress was going to give me an ulcer, if not kill me, but about then my husband got laid off and we moved to Horse Creek where I could find other work. But I was still dissatisfied and driven, wanting something more.

Instead of taking the time to explore other possibilities, discover who I was or what I wanted, I wrapped my world around whatever job I was doing and my family; my husband and children were such interesting people that, like a lot of women, I immersed myself in their lives and forgot about me. I taught my children to follow their passion, to do what they loved, but I had no passions of my own. But I wanted more, so many years later I decided to take the Bar Exam once again.

So, there I was in that trailer studying and miserable, and not just from the heat. I was so stressed that my back went out, and my doctor gave me Vicodin for the pain. About 20 minutes into the first day of the test, my leg started to bounce, my clothes felt tight, my head hurt, and I discovered that Vicodin does not agree with me – off I went to the bathroom to throw up. I threw up all day and into the next, wrapping myself around a potted palm on the floor during lunch breaks. I failed the test again, but I still didn't get the message.

I'm stubborn; it seems God had to hit me over the head with a two by four, so God did.

After 31 years of marriage, about the time I thought we were going to ride off into the adventures of retirement, my husband decided he didn't want to be married to me anymore. A month later my beloved mother died. I didn't think I could survive the pain; I kept saying to God: "I have nothing." I realized that I had a huge hole in myself that I had filled with my husband, with my children, with work, with law school, but that wasn't who I was. I had no idea who I was, or what I wanted, even after all these years. One day I saw two clear pictures in my mind: in the first one was a torso with a huge rock, covered in vines that had been wrapped around it for a very long time, holding it in place. In the next frame was the same torso, with a gaping hole and the vines trailing outward. The hole, what was missing, was my identity, who I was, what I wanted.

Another day I was out hiking, crying over the loss of my marriage, when I heard a voice in my head, clear as day, say "I have something better in mind for you." A few months later I was out hiking and crying again, when I heard the same voice in my head say, "You have to let go of this marriage." I discovered that I had to weave myself anew, fill in the empty space with me.

I probably should have been an English major. It wasn't too easy; I was too scared. Scared to try my best at something I loved and fail, never feeling good enough, filled with self-doubt. I went to law school because I felt the need to prove to myself that I was smart, worthwhile, worthy. I was drawn to the creative, but afraid I wasn't creative, afraid I wasn't good enough, so I never tried. Instead I took another path, for all the wrong reasons: the wrong path.

So now what? Well, I don't know what the future holds for me any more than I did forty years ago. But I'm open to the possibilities. And I guarantee you one thing: I will never again spend long hot summer days or nights try-ing to be someone or something I'm not. I'm no longer trying to pass the Bar; I'm trying to raise it for myself, and fill in the hole of who I am. I've finally gotten the message.

POEMS

Beauty and the Beast

What do you know of pain?
You with your careless beauty
Your thoughtless heart
Your flawless everything
Drawing all into your golden light
While the dark one sits in the corner
Unnoticed and alone
Filled with fear
And rage
And what do you know of love
Always so freely offered
To you
You never even notice
But the dark one kneels in supplication
Longing but never having
An ache never soothed
Watching you
While blood spills out in rivers
To feed your bright days
And you will never see
The carnage beneath your feet.

Breathing Fire

Take a deep breath
And dive into the pit of despair
Blow on the banked fires of rage
Spark them into the flames of life
Let it burn off your clothes
And dance naked round the inferno
Do not fear the heat
Embrace it
It will not destroy you
It is you.

Bruja

No one will ever know you

As well as I do

She said

And no one will ever love you

As much as I do.

That was her curse

And it worked.

All he could see

Were her green eyes

The rest of his life

However far he ran.

The small kindled flame

Had flickered

And died.

Hard as he tried

He never felt that warmth again.

The comfort of her fire

Burned his life

To ash.

But Not My Son
(For Masheeda)

I have the cold medals in their velvet-lined box
But not my son
I have fine words of commendation
Written on watermark paper
But not my son
I have the green grass above his grave
To kiss
But not my son
I have the hard unyielding granite
Of his tombstone to hold
The fierce wind to which I howl my grief
Kind words of family and friends
Meant to comfort
But not my son
Never again will I see him smile
Never see his children play
I watch the birds
I read the clippings
I have my memories
Dreams of what might have been
But not my son

Dream of Love

I once had a dream of love

A softly sighing river

Golden skies

Velvet violet nights

Ancient castle keep and high stone walls

To lock up happiness

The deep earth of your eyes

Queen Street Station and the Walk of Life

You wore all white

Coming off the field

I caught your smile

Forever in my lens.

Mountain heights and deepest depths

Round the world we went

But sweet dreams shatter

In the light of day.

Now I have another dream

I see it

Through the glass

I am on the edge

Of another universe

Light all around me

Colors everywhere

Stars

Other planets

Peace at last

Efforts

I'm doing the best I can here
Hanging on by my fingernails
To this piece of flotsam
Or is it jetsam?
In the wild sea of despair
Hoping it can carry me
Until the storm is over
Hoping I'll survive
This time.
The keeper of my heart
Flung it back to me
And I've nowhere to put it
I'm too busy
Searching for land
And there's no room for it
On this piece of wreckage
I cling to.

Gold

Gazing at that empty place
Where the gold used to shine
Impression still on my skin
So slow to fade
As the months pass
Years
Mortally wounded.
Thief of life
Stealer of dreams
When you left with my future
You took my past
For good measure
And left me holding
The ravaged present.
You walked away whistling
Without a care
Down the path of least resistance.
You never cared to learn who I was
I knew your every breath.

Gravity

Like gravity
God exists
Independent of our belief
In her
She smiles
And shrugs
At the vagaries of humans
And goes about the business
Of holding the world together
While we agonize
About it all.
If we were listening
We would hear her say
It's really not as serious as we think
It just is.
Get over it
Move on
In your orbit
I've got this
Me and gravity
Your job
Is to love.

He
(for F.S.)

His hold on life is too tenuous

His roots are shallow

Like the grass

His hands are gentle

Too gentle to hurt

His spirit serene and calm

His mind tranquil

His manner

Quiet and melancholy.

When I am swallowed up

By fears and troubles

He is full of compassion

He tenderly eases

And soothes me.

He is consolation and comfort.

He does my soul good

Fills me with peace

He will not be here long

This world is not his to keep

He knows it

He watches its beauty

With passing eyes

And fades away

Like the summer grass

Hero's Welcome

Gloved hands
Help him from the train
Soldiers stand
Lined at rigid attention
Hand down his gleaming medals
He is an honorable man
But the crowds are silent
Where are the cheers
The flags in tiny hands?
The next generation
Has come to honor him
The last generation,
To mourn.
Hand down the box of broken dreams
Let the tears fall until we drown in them
Bring all the heroes home.

I Thought

I thought you knew

You

Up there in your ivory tower

I was just a child

I thought you had the answers

To all the world's questions.

You were always right

And I was always wrong

If it came down to choosing sides.

I accepted that

Without question

You knew good from bad

Right from wrong

Who had the talent

And who didn't

You were the experts.

So when I spoke up

Eager and excited

Full of ideas

And you gave me that look

I learned

To keep quiet.

What did I know?

Out of the mouths of babes

And unless one has the faith of a child. What did you know

After all?

Children hold the wisdom

Of the world.

Idols

We created idols

From nothing

And worshiped

At their feet of clay

You and I.

Why were we so shocked

When they crumbled?

The shards can still hurt

Cutting into

Our hands and knees

As we crawl to them

Still.

But blood and tears

Cannot glue together

The dream we once thought

We had.

All illusion must die at last.

We grieve

At an empty sepulcher.

Landscape

Everywhere I look
Leaves are withering
Cold winds blow
The earth is dry
And lifeless.
Bare twigs stand starkly upright
Fields are barren
All is suddenly cold and dead
And so very tired.
I rest my back against a rock
Empty as the landscape.
I can't fight anymore
My strength is gone.
I am a waterless well
Waiting to be filled
By a fresh rainfall.
The sky is grey
It holds back life
From the earth and me
We wait together
The earth hopes
I do not.

Learning to Breathe

I've learned to breathe through the pain
Until it passes
Birthing a new me
Is not easy
But it is necessary.
I tell myself
It will be worth it
In the end
New life
From the ashes of the old
Is always painful
New beginnings
Another phase
No longer underwater
Gasping for air
Bursting to the surface
I don't need to hold my breath
Anymore
Creating a new life
I can be
Whatever I want to be
I know how to breathe.

Little Seed

Little seed
Push up
Through the dark earth
Break out into
The light of the sun
Believe the struggle
Is worth it
Stretch out your limbs
And dance

Not Death

This is not Death
In this sterile room
With paid mourners
And lead-lined oaken coffins.
Death is out in the fields
Where the worms do their work
On the battlegrounds
In darkened homes
Where mothers weep
And fathers sit in stony silence.
Don't let them fool you
Death always comes alone
No matter how many cry
Or how many flags fly
Above the grave.
It is always too soon for the young
And too late for the old.
It can't be dressed up
In fine clothes
Or hidden in the finest mausoleum.
It will always be
The unbeatable enemy
Ugly and final
Unbearably painful
Leaving each one of us
Alone.

Psyche in Rags

Psyche in rags
Sits sad and blind
Abandoned
Asa is silent
His great bulk
Pregnant with stories
Yet untold.
I want to see Psyche dance
Hear Asa speak
Joyous and unfettered
Spirits alive again.
What will it take
What must I do
To set them free?
It seems too hard
The road too long
It's so much easier
To keep them in chains
Quiet
Unbidden
Sad dancer
Silent storyteller.

Raw

I am scraping myself raw
Down to hide and bone
Sinew and muscle
To see if I will bleed
If pain lives there too
And what may grow
In place of old wounds
Or if only scars remain

Digging deep
Into old memories
Places dark and primitive
Taboo
Rites of death and destruction
Forbidden caves of tribal drums
And fire, burning bright with menace
Painted faces, ready for war

Scalding myself
Down the layers of skin to marrow
The pain feels right
Relieving pressure
Wanting to see what lies beneath the blood

River Road

So many times
I've taken this road
Wind at my back
Heart singing like the river
Just to see home again
The trees were never greener
Nor the sky as blue
The joyous reunion
Could never be better
Than it was
In those years.
They tell me the river
Will wash away my tears
But every year
That I return
The trees are greener
The ache stronger
The sky so blue
It hurts.
The constant, changing river
Is all that remains the same
Washing the river stones
Making them smooth
Wearing away the etched lines
Making them smaller
But no longer rough
To be a river stone
Unfurrowed

River Stone Lullaby

It is possible that
I may love you
But I need time to think
And time I do not have.
I can see the river from my window
Running its course
To the sea
It ripples like the ocean
Gulls fly above me
Trust and honesty
I never thought I would see
I am confused
I want to stay with you
In your house of river stones
I am almost lulled to sleep
By the winding green river
But I have such a longing
For the sea.

She

She is
Elusive as a thin mist
Sunny as a spring day
Her laughter
Ripples like water over pebbles.
Her frowns
Forbidding storm clouds
over the sun.
She is
The moon
And tides
And freedom.
She smiles her secret smile
And you search
For the hidden meaning.
She runs through the woods
Delighting
In the delicious abandonment
Of cares.
You want to touch her
Hold her
But she slips away.

Sleeping on the Couch

Lately

I've been sleeping on the couch.

I'm not sure

Why

Since the whole place

Is mine now

And I have

A bedroom all my own.

He used to tease me

By saying

We didn't need the rest of the house

Since I spent most of my time

In bed

Reading.

I have so much less now:

Less space

Fewer things

But more of my own:

My own things

In less space

My own bed

And none of him.

So why

Am I sleeping

On the couch?

Small Moments

Now I know

I must go

To those dark places

As we all must

In the end.

There is nothing to be done

No rescue

No triumph

Only living our lives

As best we can

Finding meaning

In the small, everyday things:

A good meal

Laughter

The beauty of a sunset

Leaves changing color

In the autumn

Family and friends

A child

Small moments

Capturing the essence of our lives

In a bead of water

Which magnifies

Everything.

Someone Tells Us

Someone tells us
That a plane has gone down
Everyone aboard died.
We stand shocked and still
Ah, but it wasn't one of us,
Was it?
A child is forced to kill his family
Schoolgirls are sex slaves
Teenagers murdered for drugs
Or their shoes.
But it's not our children.
After an awkward silence
Someone changes the subject
We laugh and drink our wine
And the world's edges
Close seamlessly
Around the chasm.
Halfway round the world
·Mothers cry
And someone tells us
Not to think about it.

Something

Something
Has you by the throat
And will not let go
There is good in you
The light still flickers
But you have turned away
And are lost to me now.

Pilgrims
Move forward
One by one
Candles lit
Brightening the darkness
Brothers and sisters.

The light calls
But you don't hear it
You won't see it
Beloved one
I let go of your hand
And watch you
Slip away.

Springtime

I've got it
I'll wear springtime tonight
Just for you
To see you smile
I'll search high and low
And dig out the rainbow colors
The smell and feel of May
In the midst of winter
And love will grow
Like a sturdy plant.
It has a way
Of pushing through cement
Gently
But firmly
Spring follows winter
Scattering light and life
Onto the dead hopeless earth
Tonight
I'll bring you
Spring

There Will Come
(RSP)

There will come a time

Any day now

When I won't see you

In every stranger's face

I am sure of it

When I will think

Of the mountains

And not of you.

Sometime soon

I will consider what might have been

And be grateful

It wasn't

Any day now

Presently the pain

Will cease its tearing torment

The hurt will heal

I will be whole

In time

Any day now.

This Place

I know this place
I've been here before
The rocks and the trees
I used to call mine.
Always changing
Still so familiar
The hills enfold me
Like a tender mother
Calling to me always.
I had to leave you
But I must always return
The only haven I've been shown
Only love I've ever known
You are all
Gold-bronzed and magenta messengers
Dropping to the earth
Foretelling snow
The greens never die
And I
Homeless wanderer
Am home again at last
Searching through a past life
Hoping to find meaning
Before winter.

Today

Today
I went back to childhood haunts
Places remembered in dreams
Yet different
Changed, like me
There's Julie's house
Sad-eyed Julie, my best friend
Chores and schedules,
Duties and obligations
While I ran wild as the wind
No one looked for me.
What did they do to you?
Some things weren't discussed.

Those two huge stones
Leaning against each other
A perfect cave to hide in
Spying on those walking below
I was an Indian princess
Reporting back on unwelcome settlers
Racing down the trails
Fearless then
Unknowing
Forest-free and alone.

Woman in Black

When you see me
Hold each other tightly
I am pain
Unimaginable to you
The death of love
Loneliness unmeasurable
The face of tragedy
Of tears unshed
Look away and shudder
Grasp hands
Let me be a lesson
Close your eyes
Listen
To the music of love
Pay attention
To the lies you hear there
Look not into
The eyes of Medusa
They will turn your heart to stone.

You Have a Way

You have a way
Of causing pain
That is exquisite
Like an icepick
In and out
Before I know
I've been stabbed
And gone
Before the bleeding begins
I'm dead
Before I know
I've fallen
Sharper than a serpent's tooth
Fanged beloved one

Weaving

I am making myself anew
Weaving the threads
Of a different fabric
Filling in the empty space
Left by you
With me.
Back and forth
In the rhythm
Of warp and weft
Creating something
Where once there was nothing
Waiting for
What might become
Grieving
While slowly turning
Towards the light
Dreaming again
Leaving behind what was
Searching my soul
For a fresh pattern
Different hues
On an unknown loom.

Scars

Suddenly
For the first time
I saw your scar.
I watched it
As you talked and ate
I wanted to reach out
And touch it
To run my finger down it
Explore it tenderly
Lovingly
Your face was beautiful to me.
As I watched
You turned to me
Looked intently at me
Smiling
You slashed my cheek
With your knife

Printed in Great Britain
by Amazon